W9-BXL-290

MAGILL'S
LITERARY ANNUAL
2000

MAGILL'S
LITERARY ANNUAL
2000

Essay-Reviews of 200 Outstanding Books
Published in the United States during 1999

With an Annotated Categories List

Volume Two
M-Z

Edited by
JOHN D. WILSON

SALEM PRESS
Pasadena, California Hackensack, New Jersey

∞ The paper used in these volumes conforms to the American National Standard for Permanence of Paper for Printed Library Materials, Z39.48-1992 (R1997).

LIBRARY OF CONGRESS CATALOG CARD NO. 77-99209

ISBN 0-89356-274-2

FIRST PRINTING

PRINTED IN THE UNITED STATES OF AMERICA

MAGILL'S LITERARY ANNUAL

2000

MAO ZEDONG

Author: Jonathan Spence (1936-   )
Publisher: Lipper/Viking Press (New York). 188 pp. $19.95
Type of work: Biography and history
Time: 1893-1976
Locale: China

A biography of Mao Zedong, communist revolutionary and theorist and ruler of China from 1949 until his death in 1976

Jonathan Spence is the Sterling Professor of History at Yale University and the author of numerous works on Chinese history, including *The Gate of Heavenly Peace: The Chinese and Their Revolution, 1895-1980* (1981), *God's Chinese Son: The Taiping Heavenly Kingdom of Hong Xiuquan* (1996), and *The Chan's Great Continent: China in Western Minds* (1998). He is also the coauthor of a photographic history of twentieth century China, *The Chinese Century* (1996). One of the most respected historians of modern China, Spence is eminently qualified to relate the career of Mao Zedong.

Spence's *Mao Zedong* is a volume in the Penguin Lives series, which encompasses brief biographies of significant historical figures. Mao Zedong obviously belongs in any such list. The leader of the Chinese Communists in their successful civil war against Chiang Kai-Shek's Nationalists, he dominated China as had few emperors during its long imperial history, which ended in 1911. His Marxist theories led to the transformation of China but also to the death of millions, often for ideologically inspired reasons. To many he was the "Great Helmsman"; to others he was one of the bloodiest dictators in a century of bloody dictators. It is a fascinating story, and Spence tells it well.

Mao was born in 1893 during the decades of the waning Qing Dynasty as the West and Japan staked out spheres of influence in the dying imperial China. His father was a moderately prosperous farmer, and the young Mao attended a local primary school until he was thirteen. In a traditional and conservative family (his mother was a devout Buddhist), he learned the rudiments of early Chinese history and studied the works of Confucius and other early Chinese sages. After leaving school he worked on his father's farm, married (it was arranged, as was traditional) at fourteen, and became a widower at seventeen. He left farming and returned to school, where he became exposed to China's more recent history and troubles, but all the while he remained in Hunan province. He briefly joined the New Republican Army but soon returned to his books, reading widely but without any particular purpose. He remained a student until 1918, when he was twenty-four, and traveled little outside Hunan except for a brief sojourn in Beijing.

One of the valuable aspects of Spence's biography is the elucidation of the various influences upon the young Mao, and there were many in that era of intellectual ferment—feminist, socialist, nationalist, and others. He established his own journal and wrote about the need for reform in China; not yet a Marxist, he focused upon the corruption of the local warlord. He was becoming an activist, leading student strikes in Hunan, traveling again to Beijing and elsewhere, and admiring the revolutionary events of the Soviet Union. He opened a bookshop, became a school principal, and agitated for Hunan independence from the rest of China.

Mao was not an immediate revolutionary. Spence describes him as a monarchist until the 1920's, and in 1912, he defended an early authoritarian monarchy as working for the welfare of the population in spite of the stupidity of the Chinese people. In 1920, he discussed Vladimir Ilich Lenin for the first time but doubted the applicability of Lenin's revolution because China lacked a strong party and was too localized. Nevertheless, that same year, under the instigation of Soviet agents, Mao's city of Changsha in Hunan became one of several centers for the study of communism. Mao was one of only fifty invited to the First Congress of the Chinese Communist Party and among the thirteen who actually attended. At that time his knowledge of Marxism was minimal, and Spence suggests Mao's invitation was the result of his considerable energy, courage, and physical charisma. Assigned to build up the communist movement in Hunan, by 1922 he had found his focus as a professional revolutionary.

One issue that divided Chinese Communists was their relation to Sun Yat-sen's Kuomintang, or Nationalist Party. The Soviet Comintern urged an alliance, and although Mao had reservations he joined the Nationalist Party in 1923. The same year he was elected to the Communist Party's Central Executive Committee, and in 1924 he was elected an alternate member of Kuomintang's Executive Committee. In 1925, he dropped out of active involvement in both parties, claiming he was exhausted. Spence accepts that explanation but also suggests that Mao desired direct experience with rural peasant communities, and by 1926 rural activism had become central to his beliefs; it was the peasantry, he believed, who held China's destiny.

The Kuomintang and Communist alliance disintegrated in 1927 as Chiang Kai-Shek's Nationalists turned against the latter. Mao was ordered to use the peasants as insurrectionists but lacked the military means to do so, leading to his famous statement, "Political power is obtained from the barrel of the gun." Fleeing to the mountains, he isolated himself from the Communist leadership but pursued his own radical reforms by seizing land from the wealthy, requiring work from everyone, and using guerrilla tactics against the enemy. By 1929 he had relocated to the Fujian border region where he remained for five years, frequently criticized by Communist Party leaders and under regular attack by the Nationalists, who became so threatening that in late 1934 the party decided upon what would become legendary as "the Long March." During that calamitous year-long affair, Mao's prestige rose again by the time they reached their final destination at Yan'an in the north.

In Yan'an Mao succeeded in holding the party together and strengthening his own power. In the face of Japanese aggression, a reluctant truce developed between Mao's Communists and Chiang Kai-Shek's Nationalists. During the years of war against Japan, Mao also engaged in a struggle for control of the party. Forced for the first time to undertake a systematic study of Marxism and Leninism, with the help of the Soviet-trained Chen Boda, Mao was able to justify himself as a communist theorist.

It was at Yan'an that Mao moved toward dominance and power, becoming less flexible and more demanding, and in particular frequently criticizing his intellectual opponents as being isolated from and illiterate about the proletariat and the peasant masses, which Spence suggests might have been in revenge for slights he had experienced as a peasant child. The correct interpretations were always Mao's, and intellectuals and others were forced to criticize their own inadequacies, sometimes assisted by the use of violence. By 1943 there was a recognizable cult of Mao, and in 1945 the preamble of the Communist Party constitution adopted "Mao Zedong's thought . . . as the guide for all its work."

The war against Japan ended suddenly, and although neither the Nationalists nor the Communists were ready to resume their struggle, Mao, in the north, was at a geographical advantage because of the Soviet presence in Inner Mongolia and Manchuria. Civil war escalated, and Mao entered Beijing in January, 1949, announcing the formation of the People's Republic of China that October. After almost two decades of violent conflict, China was in disastrous straits. Mao met with Joseph Stalin in December, 1949 and January, 1950, and the Soviet leader promised aid. China's reconstruction was an immense task. Land reform was a priority, as was the nationalization of industry and the hunting down of counterrevolutionaries.

Spence argues that given the challenges facing the new regime, Mao could not have desired the Korean War. However, Stalin gave support to North Korea and in March, 1950, Mao learned about the planned invasion. Once North Korea invaded the south, there was a long debate within the Chinese Communist elite about the desirability of joining the war, but with Mao's advocacy Chinese troops entered the fray in October, 1950. Mao lost a son but used the war to mobilize popular support for the regime. After the war he reigned supreme as head of the Communist Party and chairman of the People's Republic, but as the bureaucracy increased he also became more isolated from the lives of most Chinese. Mao, ever the revolutionary, urged the consolidation of peasant cooperatives into larger communes, and in 1957 he launched the Great Leap Forward.

Dividing Chinese society into "the enemy and ourselves," Mao justified depriving the former of their rights and contrasted Western democracy with China's "class freedom" and "democracy with leadership." Claiming that the transformation to socialism could be facilitated by discussion, he said, "Let a hundred flowers bloom, and a hundred schools of thought contend." When criticism resulted, the party crackdown, headed by Deng Xiaoping, destroyed hundreds of thousands of lives. The Great Leap Forward proved disastrous—the agricultural communes and communal kitchens resulted in famine, industry declined, and the backyard iron furnaces were failures. Millions died. Mao was largely isolated from reality. The press was controlled, and Mao's advisers generally told him what he wanted to hear. His angry rages were intimidating, and any dissent led to dismissal or worse. As Spence aptly writes, "The Maoist vision had finally tumbled into nightmare."

During the Great Leap Forward Mao resigned from the position of head of state, giving the office to Liu Shaoqi, and the Great Leap was slowed and abandoned beginning in 1961. A new division, however, was beginning to build over the issue of the "Thought of Mao," with some in the party claiming that, while important, it should not be overused, while Mao's loyalists defended his thought in every area. Fearing a reversal of the revolution, Mao claimed that it was necessary to "set fires" continuously. The result was the appearance of Mao's little red book, first in the military and then throughout all of China. Spence points out that Mao did not institute the Cultural Revolution, which began in 1966, but he established the environment which made it probable. Purging and suicides within the party hierarchy spilled over into the streets of Beijing as posters at the university attacked rightists and "capitalist-roaders." He announced "To rebel is justified" and in August, 1966, at Tiananmen Square Mao received a Red Guard armband before an audience of hundreds of thousands of students. Part of the Cultural Revolution was directed from the center of the bureaucracy, but much of it was spontaneous, carried on by the young against their teachers, parents, and anyone else who appeared to lack revolutionary enthusiasm, and the victims numbered in the millions.

The radicalism of the masses was in time restrained by use of the army and the party, and some of the excesses began to die down by 1969, but under Jiang Qing, Mao's wife and a former actress, it remained pervasive in the cultural arena until the mid-1970's. By the early 1970's Mao's health began to fail. His last major initiative was to invite United States president Richard M. Nixon to China in 1972 as a balance to the Soviets, from whom the People's Republic had been estranged since 1960. Deng Xiaoping, who was purged during the Cultural Revolution, was restored to favor in 1973, perhaps to counter the radicalism of Jiang Qing, and Mao received U.S. president Gerald R. Ford in 1975. By then Mao, though plagued with amyotrophic lateral sclerosis, was alert enough to appoint an unknown, Hua Huofeng, as his successor. After a series of heart attacks, he died on September 9, 1976. Earlier that year he said that his two major accomplishments were defeating Chiang Kai-Shek and forcing the Japanese from China. The revolution he passed on to the future.

Although *Mao Zedong* lacks footnotes, the bibliography is most helpful and illustrates the plethora of recent works, primary and secondary, available on Mao. As a volume in the Penguin Lives Series, it is relatively short, but in less than 108 pages of text Spence gives the reader a well-written and insightful portrait of one of the twentieth century's most influential and controversial figures. One might wish that it had been longer, answering more fully how it was that the child of rural peasants rose to power in the world's most populous country and how he was able to impose his will, often so disastrously, upon his Communist Party peers and the entire nation. The consequences of his life were and continue to be enormous, and not just for the people of China.

Eugene Larson

Sources for Further Study

Los Angeles Times Book Review, October 31, 1999, p. 8.
Publishers Weekly 246 (September 20, 1999): 61.

MARTIN LUTHER
The Christian Between God and Death

Author: Richard Marius (1933-)
Publisher: The Belknap Press of Harvard University Press (Cambridge, Massachusetts). 592 pp. $35.00
Type of work: Biography and religion
Time: 1483-1546
Locale: Western Europe, specifically Germany

A critical biography of Luther that analyzes how his thought and personality drove his work and impacted both his own and succeeding centuries

Richard Marius, professor emeritus of Harvard University, is a distinguished historian, novelist, playwright, and biographer. His numerous works include a well-received biography of Sir Thomas More, and now he has written what may well be the definitive biography of Martin Luther, "a narrative history about both events and ideas" of the sixteenth century. The critical tone of this book and much of its content are not unlike that of Marius's earlier biography of Luther (*Luther*, 1974), but the current biography is a more challenging and scholarly work, broader and deeper in scope than the author's previous attempt to portray the life of the German reformer.

In *Martin Luther: The Christian Between God and Death*, Marius carefully sets the scene for his readers by detailing the historical, social, and cultural context of Luther's time, an age of great change and uncertainty in Western Europe and the Holy Roman Empire of the German nation, Luther's native land. Although the medieval Church was a monolithic unity, presided over by a sovereign pope in Rome and embracing all of Western Europe, there was widespread political and social unrest. The Holy Roman emperor (Frederick III when Luther was born; later, Maximilian I) was ineffectual and had very little real authority. Church leaders, appointed by the pope, vied for political power with princes and nobles in Germany. Flourishing capitalism widened the gap between the rich and the poor, and peasants were by far the majority of the population. There was widespread resentment of the corruption of the medieval Church and the pomp of Rome and the papacy, which drained the coffers of German lands. It was a very superstitious and fearful age. Plague—the Black Death—threatened all of Europe with recurring outbreaks, and sudden death was a fact of life. (In its first outbreak from 1347 to 1350, the plague had killed one-third to one-half of Europe's population. In the sixteenth century, Luther himself survived three outbreaks in Wittenberg.) Finally, the recently invented printing press disseminated knowledge of the discoveries of the New World, other religions, and classical literature (pagan writers and skeptics), causing people to question traditional values and beliefs. This climate of skepticism, unrest, and fear, together with the divisions in Germany, created a propitious setting for Luther's Reformation, according to Marius. He was remarkably fortunate to take a stand against Rome in a land where his prince could protect him and at a time when his beliefs were acceptable to many.

Marius traces the critical events of Luther's early life, his education in Erfurt, his entrance into the monastery, and his work as professor of biblical studies at Wittenberg. Luther was born in Saxony in 1483. In his discussion of Luther's relationship with his father, Marius explores the Freudian perspective of Erik H. Erikson, who believed that Luther's fear of his father Hans contributed to his fear of God and frequent bouts of depression throughout his life. Luther's father wanted him to be a lawyer, and he was enrolled in the faculty of arts at Erfurt in 1501. There, during a violent storm, Luther cried out for help in terror of the lightning and vowed that he would become a monk. He kept this vow, which displeased his father, and entered an Augustinian monastery, where he worked diligently to save his soul from death and judgment. He was a good monk, but he struggled constantly with doubts and feelings of guilt. A year after he was ordained a priest, he was appointed doctor of theology at the new university at Wittenberg in Saxony. There Luther taught, published, and was the official preacher to the Augustinian monks, a job that led him to study Scripture extensively.

When Pope Leo X agreed to the sale of indulgences within German territories in order to finance the completion of St. Peter's Basilica in Rome, Luther was outraged. He believed that this practice was in conflict with biblical teaching, and he opposed any notion that men could win favor with God or earn merit by acts of penance or indulgences. He had become convinced that forgiveness was utterly dependent on God's grace—the sacrifice of Christ on the cross was the only merit a loving God required of believers. (In a lengthy discussion, Marius explains how indulgences were initially a part of penance and depended on the contrition of the sinner.) The Church claimed to have a "treasury of merit," where the accumulated merits of the saints were deposited. The pope could apply the merits of the saints to sinners who needed merit in much the same way as one can write a check on a bank account. Over time, free will offerings for indulgences were replaced by the sale of indulgences, and they could be applied even to those in Purgatory. Luther became notorious in 1517 when he protested the sale of the indulgences in his Ninety-five Theses or propositions for debate, which was the accepted procedure for protest in his time. Although he did not intend a radical break with Catholic tradition, his Theses challenged papal authority and the very nature of the Church. The pope refused to see his power diminished and demanded that Frederick the Wise, Luther's prince, send Luther to stand trial for heresy in Rome or expel him from Saxony. If condemned as a heretic, Luther would face torture and death at the stake, and Frederick, wanting the matter to be settled in German courts, refused to surrender Luther and hid him for a time. In an absorbing narrative, Marius describes the events that followed—Luther's trial and excommunication, his break with Rome, and the tumultuous years of the Reformation. Throughout the book, Marius brings to life the major characters in the unfolding drama of Luther's life. There are convincing descriptions of Pope Leo X, Desiderius Erasmus, Johann Eck, Thomas More, Frederick the Wise, and others, and sixteen pages of illustrations are included.

Even in his discussion of theological issues, Marius writes in an engaging personal style. He clarifies theological concepts such as "penance," "predestination," and "justification by faith" by tracking the historical development of the terms and comparing and contrasting different interpretations. He explores at length Luther's discovery of God's grace and his doctrine of justification by faith. From his study of the Scriptures, especially Paul's epistles, and his own personal experiences, Luther came to believe that salvation came through faith in Jesus Christ alone, not from doing penance. Man could do nothing to please God by his own efforts. This position was contrary to the teaching of the Church. (Marius takes issue with the commonly held view that Luther's great discovery of the meaning of justification by faith came from pondering Romans 1:17, because Luther does not emphasize this understanding in his lectures on Romans.) Influenced by St. Augustine (about whom Marius has nothing good to say), Luther believed in predestination and denied the power of free will. Because predestination is a mystery of God, not subject to human reason or will, however, no one can be sure if he or she is predestined, and Luther waged an ongoing battle against unbelief and anxiety throughout his life. This issue—free will versus predestination—was the subject of a major debate between Luther and Erasmus, the foremost scholar of the day, who believed that people are rational and moral creatures, able to pursue a righteous life by following the example of the Jesus of the Gospels. Luther's vicious attack on Erasmus cost Luther his goodwill.

Marius discusses in detail Luther's doctrines and writings—his translation of the Bible into German, other works written to provide structure and instruction for his followers, and his attacks on Jews, witches, peasants (during the Peasants' Revolt of 1524-1525), and Erasmus, Thomas More, Henry VIII, and others who disagreed with him. He describes Luther's marriage and family life and summarizes Luther's life from 1527 until his death in 1546 in one brief chapter (because "the later Luther is not as interesting as the man who broke away from the pope," and "his ceaseless battles with adversaries descended often into repetitive invective and vituperation that weary the soul"). Marius concludes that Luther's last years were full of frustration and bitterness because the Reformation had not been accepted by all true Christians, and there were no signs of the moral renewal of the Church that he anticipated.

One of the more controversial aspects of the book is Marius's intriguing hypothesis, repeated throughout the book, that Luther's actions, both in his personal life and in the public arena, were the result of his overwhelming anxiety about death—not the fear of Hell, but of everlasting "non-being" or nothingness. (Luther, like the apostle Paul, seldom speaks of Hell.) The only solution Luther found was in Christ and faith in Him, but throughout his life he continued to struggle with doubt and anxiety. According to Marius, his tremendous output (some sixty volumes of devotional and theological works, fourteen volumes of correspondence, and twelve volumes of German translations and prefaces to the Bible) was an ongoing attempt to persuade himself of the truth of his beliefs. It was as if talking and writing about faith became a substitute for the peace that eluded him.

What sets this book apart is Marius's attempt to probe the inner workings of Luther's mind and his personality, character, and temperament. Drawing from Luther's own writings, those of his contemporaries (including the "table talk" recorded by students boarding with Luther and considerable correspondence with friends and enemies), the work of other scholars, and his own impressive knowledge of history, theology, and the Bible, Marius humanizes Luther. He is sympathetic in many respects: He admires Luther's amazing energy and output; he acknowledges that the simplicity that he brought to worship may provide relief to those who need to be free of elaborate rules; he recognizes the debt that democracy owes to Protestantism and its emphasis on the individual. He debunks the myth that Luther left the monastery to get married. He seeks to avoid characterizing Luther as either a furious, demon-possessed, lustful liar and fraud or a bold, enlightened hero who stood against corruption and returned Christianity to its former simplicity and grace.

Marius is a modern liberal, for whom the experience of religion rises above dogma, and although his stated aim is to present an essentially nonreligious, critical, but sympathetic portrayal of Martin Luther, Luther is baffling and full of contradictions, and the overall tone of the book is negative. The great reformer is coarse, obscene, and ruthless to his critics. "Hatreds seemed as common as rocks in a quarry" to him. In the final analysis, Luther is a "catastrophe in the history of Western civilization" because he shattered the medieval church and plunged Western Europe into religious wars and chaos for more than a century. Marius's sympathies lie with Erasmus and other reformers, who recognized the abuses of the Roman Catholic Church but worked for peaceful reform. In Marius's view, the Renaissance popes were immoral, but the Church was probably not more corrupt in the sixteenth century than in earlier times. In any case, Luther's Reformation had no effect on morality. Had Luther been more moderate in his criticisms of the Church and aligned himself with Erasmus and other reformers, Marius suggests, the bloodbath of the next century might have been avoided. Many would argue, however, that such fond optimism discounts the hostility and violence of Luther's time and the political, social, and/or religious self-interests of the major players. Throughout history, individuals, groups, and classes have been reluctant to relinquish their privileges and power without being forced to do so; far from seeing the desirability of a change that threatens their position, they are usually not even interested in considering the merits of the opposing argument. Whatever one's stance, *Martin Luther* is a fascinating, provocative, and scholarly study that is sure to stimulate debate and scholarship.

Edna B. Quinn

Sources for Further Study

Booklist 95 (February 1, 1999): 946.
The Christian Science Monitor, April 8, 1999, p. B20.
Christianity Today 43 (July 12, 1999): 63.
Commonweal, September 10, 1999, p. 27.
Library Journal 124 (January, 1999): 106.
The New Republic 220 (August 16, 1999):40.
Publishers Weekly 246 (January 25, 1999): 87.

THE MERCY

Author: Philip Levine (1928-   )
Publisher: Alfred A. Knopf (New York). 81 pp. $22.00
Type of work: Poetry
Time: The twentieth century
Locale: Detroit, other United States locations, Italy

A collection of poetry from Pulitzer Prize-winning poet Levine that looks at working-class lives

Principal personages:
ESTHER LEVINE, the poet's mother
BERNADETTE STREMPEK, a working-class woman
JOE GOULD, a famed New York City street person
CLIFFORD BROWN, a great jazz trumpeter
FEDERICO GARCÍA LORCA, a Hispanic writer
HELEN GARNER, an Australian novelist
SONNY ROLLINS, a jazz musician

These poems glisten and gleam. It is hard to imagine a working-class consciousness with its sense of injustice and the general hardness of life combined with nostalgia. Levine has produced such a combination. His is the best kind of nostalgia: a wistful examination of lives past or passing, through lenses of love, without a lot of romanticizing. The working-class concern is vintage Levine. The tone of the book is well reflected by the carefully chosen cover, which is Alfred Stieglitz's 1907 photograph "The Steerage." The picture shows the privation and possibility of people of all ages jammed together on the boat, looking oppressed, dingy, exhausted, yet expectant.

The photograph was carefully chosen for its appropriate subject. Esther Levine, the poet's mother who lived from 1904 to 1998, is a dominant presence in the book, and she came to the United States on a ship named *The Mercy* that would have looked much like Stieglitz's photograph. Moreover, the black-and-white tones, the implication of hardship—hard times behind and before these voyagers—and the sense of American myth and history projected by the photograph are very much in tune with the poems in the collection.

Philip Levine was born in 1928 to Russian-Jewish immigrants in Detroit; the lives of the immigrant community and their hardships just scraping together a living are the staples of his work. As a young man, he worked in factories. Although he left Detroit while still young and held many prestigious positions and garnered international honors after his hardscrabble childhood and the industrial jobs of his early youth, the city of Detroit and the problems of the working class there loom large in his poems. His return to Detroit did not show it to have progressed toward fairness and justice. One of his most popular and most widely anthologized poems, "They Feed They Lion," was written after he saw the results of the 1967 riots in Detroit.

Levine first attended the University of Iowa, where he was taught by Robert Lowell, and then Stanford University. Almost from the beginning, his poetry has been widely recognized and honored. Levine won the National Book Award in 1991 for *What Work Is* and the Pulitzer Prize in 1985 for *The Simple Truth*. He taught for many years at California State University at Fresno.

Of *The Simple Truth*, literary critic Harold Bloom said, "I wonder if any American poet since Walt Whitman himself has written elegies this consistently magnificent. The controlled pathos of every poem in the volume is immense. . . . " Other critics as well have commented on Levine's work in the context of Whitman's, because Levine too sings the worker's songs. However, Levine's characteristic voice produces complete, complex narratives, not epic catalogues. From the beginning, Levine created memorable individual working-class portraits that function both as realistic description and at the level of myth. He carried his concern for the common people into other countries and areas, and he wrote about the Spanish Civil War as confidently as about the uprisings in Detroit. Incidents that to most are names and statistics are personalized through his poems.

A poet who has received such great recognition has found a winning formula and may not be likely to branch off in new directions. Indeed, in style and tone *The Mercy* is similar to much of Levine's earlier work. The burnished luminosity of these poems can be found in his earlier collections as well, and his characteristic technique of combining realistic detail with an elegiac distancing—combining instances of experience with a whole life seen in retrospect—is evident throughout his work. Always Levine dares to express feeling directly, and the poems are saved by their emotional and physical precision from any charges of sentimentality. Levine's favored forms in most work are free verse, flexible blank verse, unmetered tercets, and quatrains. These relatively free forms suit the content and allow for exactness of language.

Yet language itself is found wanting in this collection. *The Mercy* places new emphasis on the written language and on questioning its value. Several poems speculate on whether words last, and in what form. "Joe Gould's Pen" examines whether a writer's words are permanent or even real. Gould, a bohemian denizen of Greenwich Village in the 1940's, appealed to other writers as well; e. e. cummings wrote poetry about him, and Joseph Mitchell, a writer for *The New Yorker*, chronicled his life. Gould, a Harvard graduate and a dropout from a wealthy family, was a street person who claimed to be writing "An Oral History of Our Times," a nine-million-word work scrawled in hundreds of school notebooks. When Gould died, however, nothing of this opus was found. (Some of Gould's words and sayings have been published by those he intrigued and inspired, however.)

"Joe Gould's Pen" describes the poet writing with the famous eccentric's pen after Gould's death; it is an elegy for Gould and for language itself. It mourns and celebrates

> . . . Pee Wee Joe,
> who loved to dance, who talked
> to seagulls in their language,
> his pen tried to find him in
> 9,250,000
> words and failed because it had

> no word for what rises in
> your esophagus when night
> starts over at 4 A.M., . . .

The poem catalogs the things at the center of human existence for which the language has no words. Identifying with Gould, who wrote nine million words that vanished into air, the poet wonders about the permanence of any arrangement of words. Describing how Gould always carried his "swollen books" around in a cardboard folder, Levine concludes

> Perhaps he knew that when
> he gave back the last hard breath
> each earned word would disappear
> the way the golden halo
> goes when the dawn shreds the rose
> into dust, the way a voice fades
> in an empty room, the way
> the pomegranate fallen from
> the tree scatters the seeds of
> its resurrection, the way
> these lines are vanishing now.

Yet the one image is positive—the pomegranate, which promises that something fruitful is to come of the vanished words, despite their dissolution. This same kind of query is carried on in "These Words," which describes the assembly of "scraps of odd letters." The poet, assembling fragments of old letters and trying to make them mean something, contrasts the present attempt with the more innocent past, when

> . . . we believed in the comfort words
> could bring, . . .
> though spring was late, the rain beat on the glass,
> beat down on the mounded snow until the streets
> ran with the clear ink of its meaning.

This preoccupation with words and meaning, permanence and poetry, is a major thematic strain in this collection. His elegies for lived lives and lost places are joined by reflections on the dissolving of language itself.

More broadly, the meaning of art and the relationship between artist and work are explored in a number of narrative poems based on the lives and work of musicians, artists, and novelists. Levine is committed to narrative as his genre; as such, his statements about art and artists tend to take the form of stories. He is particularly interested in musicians' struggles to put their world into music. (Useful footnotes are provided to identify some of these people and their lives; unfortunately, the page numbers for the notes are wrong.) "The Unknowable" is musical itself in its tribute to Sonny Rollins, the great jazz saxophonist.

The book and the title poem, "The Mercy," are dedicated to the poet's mother, Esther Levine, who crossed the sea on *The Mercy* in the 1920's at the age of nine. The trip must have been a nightmare—the horror of her particular journey is not reflected in the Stieglitz photograph, for all its vivid representation of the harshness of the crossing. The name of the ship turned ironic when the crew and passengers were held offshore for thirty-one days in a smallpox quarantine. The nine-year-old Esther waited out these long days in fear and incomprehension "while smallpox raged among the passengers/ and crew until the dead were buried at sea/ with strange prayers in a tongue she could not fathom."

The child, who does not know any English, appears to be traveling alone; she prays "in Russian and Yiddish" to find her family in New York. She has never seen a banana before and tries to eat it without peeling it. A young Scot gives her a bite of orange and teaches her the word. Finally the quarantine is over and she can continue on her journey, the long one of her life, with her new knowledge:

> . . . A nine-year-old girl travels
> all night with one suitcase and an orange.
> She learns that mercy is something you can eat
> again and again while the juice spills over
> your chin, you can wipe it away with the back
> of your hands and you can never get enough.

The terror held by this long-ago sea journey is memorably described. The knowledge that the child survived, bore children, and lived into her nineties changes the perspective. The reader is reminded of the many immigrants in the United States' past, the Ellis and Angel Island injustices, and the roles played by these immigrants in the making of the country. The poem is also a paean to simple human persistence. Esther Levine acquires the force of myth, and the reader would like to know more about her. She is also a reproach, in the same way some of the speakers in Edgar Lee Masters's *Spoon River Anthology* (1915) reproach the reader: We have it too soft, we have forgotten what it once took merely to survive. If we take it further, the lesson adds: We should stop complaining about trivial inconveniences, and we should take action against those serious inequities that still exist.

These are poems to come back to, and what brings the reader back is the fascination of the tales they tell. Everyone has a story, Levine believes, and the stories most worth listening to are those of people who cannot or will not tell them, because they are too busy living them. Levine tells these stories in translucent narrative poems that recall the United States' past and remind everyone, as he says in the title of his earlier award-winning book, "what work is."

Janet McCann

Sources for Further Study

The Atlantic Monthly 283 (April, 1999): 108.
Booklist 95 (March 15, 1999): 1278.

Library Journal 124 (March 15, 1999): 83.
The New York Times Book Review 104 (April 18, 1999): 26.
The Progressive 6 (August, 1999): 44.
Publishers Weekly 246 (January 25, 1999): 90.

MORGAN
American Financier

Author: Jean Strouse (1945-)
Publisher: Random House (New York). Illustrated. 796 pp. $34.95
Type of work: Biography
Time: 1837-1913
Locale: The United States

A full-scale portrait of the man who dominated American finance during the Gilded Age, with much new information on his personal and family life drawn from archives opened in the late 1990's

Principal personages:
JOHN PIERPONT MORGAN, American financier during the late nineteenth and early twentieth centuries
JUNIUS SPENCER MORGAN, John Pierpont's father
ANDREW CARNEGIE, founder of Carnegie Steel
JOHN D. ROCKEFELLER, a founder of the Standard Oil Company

Jean Strouse, a freelance journalist, won the Bancroft Prize in American History and Diplomacy in 1981 for *Alice James: A Biography* (1980). Her articles and reviews have appeared in *The New York Review of Books*, *Newsweek*, *The New Yorker*, *The New York Times Book Review*, and *Vogue*. She spent fifteen years researching and writing her biography of John Pierpont Morgan.

The image of Morgan that emerges from the pages of this biography fits neither the laudatory view of his admirers, who considered him a hero of economic progress and defender of competitive free enterprise, nor the derogatory images of his critics, who saw him as an icon of predatory capitalist greed. Strouse's even-handed, nonjudgmental approach provides a detailed—sometimes an excessively detailed—description of Morgan's public and private actions, leaving her readers to judge Morgan for themselves.

Unlike many nineteenth century business leaders who began life in poverty, Morgan was born to wealth and carefully trained by his father for his future career. The son and grandson of successful New England merchants, he attended the public high schools of Hartford, Connecticut, and Boston. His father, Junius Spencer Morgan, who became the leading American banker in England and helped finance much of America's trade with Europe, sent him to a Swiss school to learn French and then to the University of Göttingen for a year to perfect his German. Junius supported Pierpont (John Pierpont Morgan was referred to as Pierpont as opposed to John) during an unpaid two-year apprenticeship to a New York City merchant from 1857 to 1859. During the 1860's and 1870's, Pierpont served as his father's representative in New York.

For Pierpont, the Civil War was just another business opportunity. He never considered serving in the army, paying a substitute $300 to take his place when he was drafted in 1863—Strouse records that this sum was exactly what Pierpont spent on cigars that year. Two of his business schemes would later be subjected to much criticism. In 1861, Pierpont financed the purchase of five thousand obsolete Hall carbines from a government arsenal for $17,000. The carbines were then slightly modified and resold to the army in the West for $110,000. Providing speculators with a loan of $20,000 for less than two months earned Morgan a commission of $5,440—a profit of more than 25 percent. When Congress learned of the deal, it stopped payment of half the money due Morgan's borrowers, who did not get the last $58,000 until 1867, when the Supreme Court ruled the government was bound by its original contract. Strouse accepts the view that Morgan considered the transaction a normal commercial arrangement and saw no moral issue involved in profiteering during wartime. However, Strouse rejects the contention of Morgan's apologists that he did not know he was selling the government its own arms, noting that he went to the arsenal with his clients when they took delivery of the carbines. In 1863, Pierpont was involved in a massive speculation that drove up the price of gold, earning him a profit of $66,000. Junius Morgan was furious when he heard of Pierpont's actions. He was angry not because the scheme negatively affected the value of United States currency, but rather because he believed such risky speculation unbecoming to a banker entrusted with other people's money.

Strouse describes in some detail the Morgans' role in providing British funds to ease the capital shortage in the United States during the last third of the nineteenth century. Cautious British investors showed little interest in American manufacturing, preferring to purchase railroad and government bonds. By financing the creation of a national railroad network, however, these investors spurred an enormous expansion of American industry. Strouse points out that both Morgans saw themselves as morally responsible to the purchasers of their securities and identified with the interests of their clients. Investors desired stability and the steady payment of interest from the railroads, and they wanted the United States to stay on the gold standard so that currency changes would not depreciate the value of their investments. Pursuing the first objective would directly involve Pierpont Morgan in controlling railroads. Achieving the second goal, which conflicted with the desires of farmers and debtors for currency inflation, made Pierpont Morgan the most hated banker of his generation.

As Junius Morgan moved toward retirement in the late 1870's, Pierpont took over leadership of both the American and English bank branches. Most of his time was devoted to railroad finance where, Strouse notes, his activities were designed to reduce or eliminate competition. In 1885, Morgan won investor plaudits for arranging a successful peace conference on his yacht between the presidents of the New York Central and the Pennsylvania—the two warring roads had been cutting prices and building parallel lines that threatened each other's financial stability. During the 1880's, Morgan arranged gentlemen's agreements in which competing roads divided existing traffic among themselves and pledged to maintain stable rates and refrain from building duplicate trackage, but railroad presidents often ignored the agreements when it suited their interests. When reorganizing the bankrupt Philadelphia & Reading, in 1886, Morgan took full control of the road's finances in a pattern that came to be termed "morganization." He cut the road's fixed costs in half by forcing bondholders to accept stock in place of their bonds; the stock was then placed in a voting trust, chaired by Morgan himself, for five years. Unfortunately, this proved only a temporary solution; once the president of the Philadelphia & Reading was free of banker control, he issued so many bonds to finance expansion that, by 1893, the railroad could not pay interest on its bonds and once again went into receivership. During the depression of 1893, the Morgan firm used the pattern of the Reading reorganization to "morganize" the many railroads that went bankrupt. By 1902, Morgan controlled some 5,000 miles of American railroads.

European investors withdrew capital from the United States during the 1890's depression, causing an outflow of gold that drained the U.S. Treasury's gold reserve. Early in 1895, the reserve was so low that it seemed possible that the United States might have to default on its promise to pay interest on the national debt in gold. Strouse describes how Morgan devised a way to sell bonds for gold that brought European gold flowing back into the U.S. Treasury. The successful maneuver kept money tight during the depression, which benefited Morgan and his clients. However, it infuriated inflation-minded farmers and debtors hoping for inflated prices and easier repayment of debts; they mounted vicious personal attacks on Morgan. His critics called it a Wall Street conspiracy to gain from the depression, estimating profits ranging from $5 to $18 million. However, Strouse demonstrates that the total earnings of Morgan's American syndicate were approximately $2 million, of which the Morgan firm's share was less than $300,000.

Morgan once told a colleague that his strengths lay more in consolidating existing projects than in promoting new ones, and Strouse notes that none of Morgan's major industrial combinations originated with him. Between 1890 and 1910, he organized huge mergers of firms when others came to him for help in eliminating or reducing competition. The prime example was steel, where Morgan put together combinations of companies manufacturing tubes, wires, and bridges during the 1890's. When Andrew Carnegie threatened to compete directly with Morgan's companies, Morgan bought Carnegie Steel and, in 1901, united it with his other firms into the U.S. Steel Corporation, capitalized at a previously unheard-of $1.4 billion. The cautious bankers Morgan put in charge of the corporation avoided vigorous competition; the company was profitable but steadily lost market share to more energetic challengers, declining from two-thirds of U.S. steel production in 1901 to one-third by the 1930's.

Morgan's greatest fiasco was his 1902 shipping trust, combining the passenger and freight lines of Great Britain and the United States into the International Mercantile Marine. Strouse records that, in fact, the combination stimulated competition from other nations. Morgan had overpaid for the constituent companies; the line never made a profit and went bankrupt.

The high point of Morgan's financial career was his forceful leadership of the New York banking community, which prevented the Panic of 1907 from destroying the American banking system and setting off a full-fledged depression. Morgan, acting as though he were a one-man central bank, was successful in limiting the panic, which incidentally saved millions of jobs, winning him wide praise from the business community. Such enormous power, in the hands of a single individual who could decide which financial institutions survived and which perished, frightened many people, persuading them that private bankers should not be left in control of the economic welfare of the country. The movement to assert government authority over banking resulted in the creation of the Federal Reserve system.

Two books that supplement Strouse's account of Morgan's public career are Vincent P. Carosso's 888-page *The Morgans: Private International Bankers, 1854-1913* (1987), which provides even more detail on his financial operations, and Ron Chernow's 812-page *The House of Morgan: An American Banking Dynasty and the Rise of Modern Finance* (1990), which covers Pierpont's life in 161 pages but continues the history of the firm to the late 1980's. However, no other work contains the detailed, carefully researched, and thoroughly documented account of Morgan's personal and family life that Strouse provides.

Morgan was passionately in love with his first wife, who died of tuberculosis four months after their marriage. His second marriage produced three daughters and a son but was emotionally unsatisfying. Morgan and his wife were frequently on opposite sides of the Atlantic; he arranged for her to undertake extended tours of Europe, often leaving for Europe as soon as she returned to the United States. Morgan consoled himself in his unhappy marriage with a series of mistresses. Despite a hideously deformed nose—Morgan suffered from rhinophyma, a disease that causes the growth of excess reddish-colored tissue on the nose—he was very attractive to women. Strouse identifies two mistresses by name and suggests there were many others; however, she refutes the rumor that Morgan founded the New York Lying-In Hospital to provide a safe place for his mistresses to bear his children.

Morgan's wealth permitted him to indulge in large-scale philanthropy. He contributed to many religious, cultural, and educational institutions. He was a founding member of, and liberal contributor to, both the American Museum of Natural History and the Metropolitan Museum of Art. The institution that most absorbed Morgan was the Episcopal Church, and he devoted much time and money to church affairs.

In the later part of Morgan's life, the activity that most fascinated him was his collecting. During the 1870's, he had decorated his house with paintings by contemporary artists and also purchased some literary and historical authors' manuscripts. Beginning in the late 1890's, as his income soared, Morgan began to acquire fifteenth century books, illuminated medieval manuscripts, and Renaissance art on a massive scale. Strouse records that Morgan set out to acquire as much art as he could in a short time, often purchasing entire collections en bloc, which he would then upgrade as he came across further outstanding examples. The arrival of Morgan in Europe brought art dealers and booksellers flocking to his hotel; Morgan never bargained over prices, and his purchases drove the art market to new heights. Many of his acquisitions ended up in museums. To house the books, manuscripts, and artifacts he loved best, Morgan built a library next door to his home. Endowed and given to the public by his son in 1924, the Morgan Library continues as a museum and research facility.

When Morgan's estate was settled in 1916, his banking interests, securities, and real estate were valued at approximately $60 million and his art collections at $20 million. Strouse estimates the true value of the art, at 1913 prices, was between $60 to $80 million, which meant that Morgan's collections were more valuable than the rest of his estate. At a time when John D. Rockefeller was already worth nearly $1 billion, the estate of Morgan, the most powerful financier in the United States, seemed surprisingly small. Strouse records that Rockefeller shook his head when he learned of Morgan's net worth and said, "And to think he wasn't even a rich man."

Milton Berman

Sources for Further Study

Booklist 95 (March 1, 1999): 1138.
Business Week, April 19, 1999, p. 18.
Harvard Business Review 77 (September/October, 1999): 166.
Library Journal 124 (March 15, 1999): 87.
The New Republic 220 (October 18, 1999): 29.
New Statesman 128 (July 26, 1999): 49.
The New York Review of Books 46 (May 6, 1999): 4.
The New York Times Book Review 104 (March 28, 1999): 7.
Newsweek 133 (April 5, 1999): 73.
Publishers Weekly 246 (February 15, 1999): 91.
Time 153 (April 19, 1999): 82.
The Washington Post Book World 29 (April 11, 1999): 1.

MORMON AMERICA
The Power and the Promise

Authors: Richard N. Ostling (1940-) and Joan K. Ostling
Publisher: HarperSanFrancisco (San Francisco). 320 pp. $25.00
Type of work: History, current affairs, and religion
Time: 1830-1999
Locale: The United States

A broad and admirably objective survey of the history and beliefs of what may be America's fastest-growing religion

During the late 1820's, Joseph Smith, Jr., an uneducated youth in upstate New York, proclaimed he had found golden plates containing the record of ancient Hebrews who had settled the New World. With the aid of magic stones provided, he translated the plates into English and revealed tales not only about mighty civilizations unknown to the modern world but also about a visitation to the New World by Christ. At a moment when the northeastern part of the United States was alive with Protestant religious fervor, Smith's claims naturally attracted interest. Soon, he and his miraculous book stood at the center of a small, but fervent, new religion.

In 1830 Smith published his golden book as the "Book of Mormon," using the name of its final ancient scribe, and incorporated his new church. Through the 1830's, his church steadily grew and took on form, and Smith revealed more of how he had come by the golden plates. When he was only fourteen, he recalled, he became confused about the conflicting doctrines espoused by different Christian faiths. Turning to his Bible, he found this helpful guidance: "If any of you lack wisdom, let him ask of God, that giveth to all men liberally, and upbraideth not; and it shall be given him" (James 1:5).

In a secluded glade, Smith posed his questions in prayer. To his astonishment, God the Father and his son, Jesus Christ, appeared before him. They told him to join none of the existing churches, as all were corrupt. Three years later, Smith had a second vision. This time he was visited by an angel named Moroni who revealed to him the buried golden plates. Finally, when Smith was twenty-three, he was allowed to dig up the plates and translate them. When his work was done, the plates were removed from the earth, never again to be seen by mortal eyes. Apart from sketchy testimonies of a handful of friends and relatives who acknowledged glimpsing the plates, Smith had nothing except his own word and the content of his book to prove that the plates had even existed.

From this curious beginning arose what eventually became the Church of Jesus Christ of Latter-day Saints—the "Mormon" church to outsiders—a denomination that in the year 2000 would claim more than 10 million members worldwide. The new religion's growth rate has been remarkable; even more remarkable is the fact that the rate is accelerating. Whereas church membership rolls did not reach a million until nearly 1950, they increased sevenfold over the next four decades and rose by 3.5

million members during the 1990's alone. At current rates of growth, the church could have 265 million members by the year 2080. If that happens, Mormonism will rank as a major world religion. For this reason alone, the church commands attention.

The church's importance can be measured in money as well. In dollars per capita, the Mormon church ranks among the world's wealthiest. Its members, to maintain their standing, must pay a 10 percent tithing on their personal incomes, and a remarkable proportion of them (in North America, at least) actually do so. They are also expected to make additional contributions to other funds and special assessments. As Mormons in North America have above-average incomes, the total revenue the church takes in rivals that of denominations of much greater size. Unlike other denominations, however, the Mormon church is secretive about its financial affairs; lay members and outsiders alike can only guess at how the money is used. The money does not, however, go toward clerical salaries, as does much of the money of other churches. Mormons are expected to serve as unpaid volunteers to staff the church's lay clergy and run its many affiliated programs, such as its vast welfare system.

The question of finances is merely one of many mysteries about the church. Winston Churchill once described the Soviet Union as a "riddle wrapped in a mystery inside an enigma." That metaphor might equally be applied to the Mormon church. Few non-Mormons know much about it, how it is run, and or even what its main tenets are. Moreover, there is reason to suspect that the understanding average Mormons have of their church's workings and doctrines is limited. Matters such as how church leaders are selected, how they make decisions, and where official doctrines come from are impenetrable mysteries to outsiders.

In addition to being secretive, the church does not welcome enquiries about its operations. Unlike young Joseph Smith's God, church leaders themselves are not receptive to those lacking wisdom who ask difficult questions. An inescapable consequence of church secrecy is the outside world's curiosity about where the church is headed with its mushrooming membership, financial power, and authoritarian proclivities. In 1999 the president of the church sent letters to all Mormons in California advising them how to vote on a ballot issue. It was an ominous event, one demonstrating that questions about the church's future are more than merely academic.

Aside from the fact that much of what has been published about Mormons is tendentious or one-sided, the church itself has changed so much in recent decades that a great need has arisen for an account that is authoritative, nonpolemical, and up to date. Richard N. and Joan K. Ostling's *Mormon America: The Power and the Promise* is thus a very welcome addition to the literature. Formerly a senior correspondent for *Time* magazine, Richard Ostling specializes in writing about religion and he broadcasts on religion on CBS Radio and PBS television; he has also won awards for objectivity in religious writing. His collaborator on this book is his wife, Joan K. Ostling, a freelance writer and editor.

Although non-Mormon readers will find this book admirably objective, the fact that the Ostlings are not themselves Mormons will doubtless raise objections among the Mormon faithful. However, a book of this nature probably could not be written by a

Mormon—at least not by one in good standing. The problem is simply that the book raises important questions that Mormons are trained not to ask.

The book touches on issues of which even one familiar with Mormonism is unaware. Two issues in particular stand out: the church's penchant for secrecy and the authoritarian nature of its leadership. Democracy is nearly invisible within the church; decisions are made only at the top and are expected to be obeyed without question. Not only is challenging authority considered heretical, even asking for simple explanations of church policies can be cause for censure or excommunication. Lacking forums even for discussion, dissenters either silence themselves or leave. Considering the church's size, it has seen remarkably few significant revolts.

The matter of church finances is an example of a sensitive subject to which the Ostlings give special attention. By their conservative estimates, the church takes in about six billion dollars annually and owns assets worth twenty-five billion to thirty billion dollars. Given the willingness of individual members to reveal their own finances and tithe, it seems natural they might ask where their money goes. However, no lay Mormon would dare raise such a question. To write a study of the church without discussing its finances would be like writing about a government without discussing taxation.

The comparison is apt, as the church itself is much like a government. During the fourteen years that Joseph Smith led the church, his strong and charismatic leadership held the church together. He was a natural autocrat who used his self-defined role as a living prophet to justify all policies and crush opposition wherever it arose. Indeed, his death came at the hands of an anti-Mormon mob after he was jailed for wrecking the press of a newspaper that questioned his leadership. Nevertheless, his authoritarian leadership set a standard for his successors.

Smith's immediate successor, Brigham Young, lacked his charisma and vision but more than made up for it in organizational and administrative ability. Young led most of Smith's followers from the Midwest to Utah, where the church has ever since flourished. As the unchallenged leader of the church and, for a time, federally appointed territorial governor, Young built the church into a true theocracy. He reinforced Smith's authoritarian example while helping to establish long-term stability and prosperity.

Whereas most Christian denominations maintain professional clergy who interpret ancient scriptures for lay members, Mormons have no professional clergy whatever. Instead their church gives them living prophets, along with apostles, who speak directly to God. The messages that the top leaders pass down are subject to neither challenge nor even discussion. When one looks at the makeup of the church's aged First Presidency—as the inner council is called—it is difficult not to think of the old Soviet politburo.

A great appeal of Mormonism is its plain-talking literalism and utter lack of mysticism. For example, Mormons see the Book of Mormon not as a collection of symbolic stories about ancient peoples but as a literal history of the early Americas. Such literalism causes problems, however, when one looks closely at tangible facts, and the facts about the Book of Mormon are that no archaeological, linguistic, or tangible documentary evidence supports its authenticity. In the face of modern scientific research tools, the time for "proving" the Book of Mormon has passed. Now, instead of defending the historicity of the Book of Mormon, the faithful are inclined to dismiss challenges through a curious circular logic asserting that faith alone is what matters. In other words, if one has faith in the truth of the Book of Mormon, that alone suffices; only the unfaithful demand tangible proofs.

Temporal matters aside, the church is of great interest because of its unique doctrines. It presents itself to the world as a mainstream Christian faith with something extra—the Book of Mormon. As the Ostlings show, however, many Mormon beliefs run counter to mainstream Christian theology. Particularly striking are Mormon ideas about the Godhead. Mormons believe that it consists of three distinct and separate beings: God the Father, God the Son, and the Holy Ghost, and that the first two have physical bodies, as do mortal humans. Further, the church holds not only that God himself was once a mortal being but also that all mortals who follow his teachings and go through the correct temple rites can become gods. In other words, God the Father is merely one of many gods.

To other Christians, this belief smacks of polytheism, which is fundamentally contrary to the Judeo-Christian tradition of monotheism. For this reason, many non-Mormons regard Mormonism as non-Christian. (Some would go further and call it anti-Christian.)

The Ostlings pass no judgments on doctrinal matters, but merely examine what such beliefs mean within the church itself. They show how the church plays down its more exotic beliefs, while emphasizing beliefs that Mormons share with mainstream Christians. One might wish the Ostlings had probed further into lay members' beliefs to get a sense of how many ordinary Mormons really understand these doctrines or even give them much thought. One gets the sense that in doctrinal matters, as in questions about the Book of Mormon's authenticity, most Mormons content themselves with vaguely defined faith alone.

One comes away from *Mormon America* with a variety of impressions. While it is difficult to understand why Mormons accept their church's beliefs, it is equally difficult not to admire them as a people. They are fundamentally law-abiding, patriotic, and industrious, and they put into practice the "family values" to which many others merely pay lip service. They are a cheerful, optimistic people who are, for the most part, devoted to their religion. What might they become, however, if their church ever achieves the majoritarian status to which it appears headed?

R. Kent Rasmussen

Sources for Further Study

Library Journal 124 (November 1, 1999): 90.
Publishers Weekly 246 (October 11, 1999): 71.

MOSQUITO AND ANT
Poems

Author: Kimiko Hahn (1955-   )
Publisher: W. W. Norton (New York). 102 pp. $21.00
Type of work: Women's issues
Time: The 1990's
Locale: A city in the eastern United States (similar to New York) and a city in the western United States (similar to San Francisco)

A fictional exchange of letters between two midlife and midcareer Asian American women expressing the angst of gender and ethnic identity formation while dealing with problematic husbands, lovers, children, jobs, and death in the family

Principal characters:
M, an Asian American woman poet living in the eastern United States
L, an Asian American woman poet living in the western United States

In addition to being the author of half a dozen remarkable books of poetry, Kimiko Hahn is a scholar of East Asian languages and literature, and she elucidates the tide of her present collection of poems by noting that "'Mosquito and ant' refers to . . . *nu shu* . . . a now nearly extinct script used by Chinese women to correspond with one another." Beyond this allusion to an Asian feminist practice dating from the tenth century, the title poem of Hahn's book also suggests that the qualities she wants for her writing are the "tenacity not seduction" of ants and the relentless annoyance of mosquitoes. In this purpose Hahn succeeds eminently. The imagery and language of her poems are grim and gripping rather than sweet or dulcet, and their rhetoric tenaciously and bitingly rehearses the woe rather than the weal of being a woman in urban America during the 1980's and the 1990's. Winner of the American Book Award for *The Unbearable Heart* (1995) and the Theodore Roethke Poetry Prize for *Earshot* (1992), Japanese American poet Kimiko Hahn is at the top of her form in *Mosquito and Ant.*

The opening poem of *Mosquito and Ant*, "The Razor," harks back to the death of Hahn's mother in an automobile accident that served as the subject of *The Unbearable Heart.* "The Razor" aptly captures the way ordinary life (which, it is said, must go on) grows calluses over the tenderest and deepest of emotions. The ashes of the mother of the poem's speaker are casually "dropped off" at the Buddhist temple in "some old shopping bag," and "the reverend pull[s] a robe/ over her jeans and blouse" to chant a sutra. Trembling with grief, the speaker ends by recalling that "at times the loss felt like an organ/ one could excise with a razor," an excruciating image that can resonate on many thresholds of association—possibly as a razor that rids unwanted hair, or one that slices away an unsightly mole, or one that circumcises an undesired genital part.

The body of the book is fictionalized as an epistolary exchange of verse and poetic prose letters between two women poets and Asian scholars named "M" and "L." The great majority of the pieces are contributed by M, a thinly veiled persona for Hahn herself (as M's daughters and her Caucasian husband share the same names as Hahn's), while L very much resembles the poet Carolyn Lei-lanilau, who is acknowledged in the front of the book. These letters are grouped into three sections followed by a section of author's notes. A single Chinese ideogram (or kanji) demarcates each section. These ideograms may be romanized (Hahn does not do it for us) as *shuo* (a radical or prefix indicating "speech/speak"), *nu* (female/woman), *xin* (heart), and *yu* (rain). The sensibility that presides over this epistolary exchange, as may be expected, is feminist, Asian American, and aesthetic.

The poems of the *shuo* (speech/speak) section deal mainly with communication—especially the difficulty of communicating between women and men contrasted with the fullness of communication among women. These poems, therefore, introduce the correspondents (the first poem, "Wax," is subtitled "Initial Correspondence to L . . ."), sketch their characters, situate them, and adumbrate themes. M is characterized as a sensual "middle-aged" woman of the baby-boom generation:

> I wanted to f[——] my professor
> (Chaucer 8:30 am M/W)
> . . . .
> . . . Nixon
> was still President.

Even as her youth wanes and her age waxes, she faces a personal crisis of "how to stay a woman," wishing to preserve the "tremulous . . . beauty" she had as a college coed and wanting to feel again her hormones rage and bring her to "pulse at the boiling point."

The next poem, "Morning Light," expresses effectively the doldrums of a career woman resentfully waking to the round of job and family. It also establishes that M's husband is a teacher or college instructor (a later poem reveals that M herself is a creative writing instructor who, like Hahn, translates from the Japanese and Chinese). In this poem, M's marriage is far from ideal. Her husband's affection is more vested in their daughters (aged about ten years old) than in her, and the channels of communication between the couple have dried up as he chides her for interrupting his reading and for asking if he loves her. Indeed, M "feels buried . . . no feeling left in her body only the idea of feelings," and "sometimes she wants to tell him: *why don't you just pack your trashy novel and toothbrush and . . . leave*." After M irritably gets her daughters off to school, she departs for work late, only to realize that she has forgotten her house keys. Through these quick, unsparing details, Hahn captures the grit and grind of the malaise in contemporary middle-class marriage—the partners in mutual disenchantment, harried by jobs and children, their fault lines of communication widening, and locked out from where they most want to be.

L resembles M in many ways. L writes poetry, has been married twice rather numbly ("my second wedding I am three-months pregnant and drink only one glass of champagne which I throw up"), seeks M's advice about dealing with a former lover ("Kafka's Erection"), and teaches in a bilingual program probably in the San Francisco

Bay area where "seals twist and turn." L is a soul sister to M, and they imagine themselves "The Immortal Sisters," alluding to a group of Taoist Chinese women poets.

Communication, then, both good and bad, is a fittingly recurrent theme in this part of the book headed by the ideogram of *shuo* (speech). Communication is bad between M and her husband, L and her former lover. Communication is fiercely passionate between M and her lover "X" who "sends terrifying love letters/ that send so much blood to the chest/ the fingers are cold," and it is intimate and fecund between M and L, resembling that of the community of like-minded women in the Daoist or *nu shu* traditions.

The ideogram *nu* (woman/female) marks off the second section of the book. Most of the poems here are by M, all of them deal with some aspect of women's experience, and many are reactions to reading or translating poems from classic Chinese or Japanese women writers. M is much occupied with Sei Shōnagon and Lady Shikibu Murasaki of the Japanese Heian period (794-1185). "The Downpour" is subtitled "a *zuihitsu* after Sei Shōnagon," who is a very prominent writer, but, as M repeatedly laments, "We do not know her name." (In a similar vein, Virginia Woolf complained that most of the works attributed to Anonymous in the Western canon must have been written by women.) Furthermore, in writing *zuihitsu*, M (and ultimately Hahn) employs a traditional convention of Japanese women's writing, but Hahn infuses it with substance and instances from contemporary American life. In so doing, M/Hahn is making her own connections, finding solidarity, with an Asian feminist tradition. Similarly, in a poem like "The Akashi Woman Speaks Above a Whisper," M/Hahn is writing an absorbing dramatic monologue in the voice and viewpoint of a character from Murasaki's *Genji monogatari* (c. 1004; *The Tale of Genji*, 1925-1933) transposed into twentieth century American language and imagery: "She apologizes when pulling off her jeans/ . . . because she has fine hairs on her ass." Equally effective are her interior monologues, such as this of a sensual Heian court lady passing a faunlike afternoon in masturbatory ennui: "One could lie across the bed fully clothed/ and come once, twice, whatever" ("Annotation in Her Last Court Diary"). L is engaged in a similar enterprise, exploring her Asian female tradition by translating *Immortal Sisters: Secrets of Taoist Women* (1989) back into Chinese. Ruminating on Chinese women's poetry, L comes up with such exquisitely suggestive and sensual images as these by an "anonymous courtesan":

> My hairpins on your fallen jacket—
> My stockings on the tiles—
> My petals on your root—

The final section of Hahn's poetic text is marked off by the ideogram *xin* (heart) at its beginning and *yu* (rain) at its close. It comprises two lengthy pieces, one in verse, the other in poetic prose, both dealing with the subject of mother. These poems bring a sense of closure to the book. M/Hahn seems to move toward a resolution or reconciliation of her resentments through accepting her role as mother, a role that replicates her own much-missed mother as well as one that resonates in her readings of classic Asian women's writings. Resentment at the numbing drudgery of motherhood still abounds:

> She became a sink.
> She became a blind.
> She became a styrofoam coffee cup.
> . . . .
> She became the mother who was at work at work,
> at work at home
> and at work at the shore

There is also a triumph, however, that emerges out of this drudgery:

> She became the mother who taught herself how to read
> and was later tenured at a university
> where she screwed the canon with radiant pleasure.

In addition, there is a mellower approach to her problematic communications with her husband. Rather than merely rage against him, M/Hahn seems more ready to accept some of the responsibility. In fact, she shows a greatly heightened appreciation for his nurturing qualities and blames herself with a rare courage and candor for having locked him out of her mind:

> She had forgotten *how to speak*
> especially to her husband
> who for a dozen years
> had nearly become the mother
> she thought she had . . .
> . . . .
> Th e husband had adored her.
> He had desired her desire.
> . . . .
> Then she forgot. Her tongue
> slept even when her mind sprinted.
> Her teeth locked. . . .

Finally, the piece of poetic prose that closes the book is an elegy on the death of M's/Hahn's mother in the form of a "*zuihitsu* for my sister." Much of the piece is a moving evocation and meditation on the speaker's sense of the loss of the people and things one holds dear. She finds a commonalty between her personal loss and that of the saddest nineteenth century Japanese poet Issa, who lost his mother as a child, his home as a teenager, his father and inheritance as a young man, all his five children, and his wife after ten years of joyless marriage. Besides the loss of her mother, M/Hahn meditates on the loss of her facility in reading Japanese, on how her husband Ted (Hahn's husband is Ted Hannan) explains the loss of their grandmother to their daughters Miyako and Reiko (Hahn's daughters are named Miyako Tess and Reiko Lily), on how her father begins to compensate for his loss by seeking the company of other women, even on how the *zuihitsu* conventions of her own writing are a loss of logical form. Amid this litany of loss, M/Hahn interjects elements of recovery, even of discovery. For instance, M/Hahn remembers and recovers the time when her mother was in Rome and loved to speak in Italian; and she even discovers something new about her mother, her intense jealousy. Gradually, M/Hahn slips into acting toward her own daughters as her mother had acted toward her and her sister. Falling short of reincarnation, it is a recapitulation of one woman by another, of a maternal role repeated and relived undyingly. Fittingly, therefore, the last line of the piece directly addresses the dead mother as if she were there in the flesh before the poem's speaker: "Mother, Rei's feet are narrow and long like Ted's"—which is an apostrophe to her mother, an acceptance of her husband, and an affirmation of her own maternal role. After this, the ideogram of rain (*yu*) is only to be expected—as heralding an end to the spiritual aridity and signaling the thaw of wintry discontent that Hahn has so chillingly realized in her book.

C. L. Chua

Sources for Further Study

The Progressive 63 (December, 1999): 43.
Publishers Weekly 246 (April 26, 1999): 76.

MOTHER NATURE
A History of Mothers, Infants, and Natural Selection

Author: Sarah Blaffer Hrdy (1946-)
Publisher: Pantheon Books (New York). Illustrated. 723 pp. $35.00
Type of work: Anthropology and sociology

Anthropologist Hrdy examines mothers in a broad range of species, exploding many romantic notions of motherhood and concluding that mothers frequently make compromises between infant welfare and their own needs

The long-cherished image of self-sacrificing mothers who go the extra mile for their offspring, who do without so that their children will have what they need, who put the welfare of their children before their own welfare, has never rung entirely true with Sarah Blaffer Hrdy, professor emerita of anthropology at the University of California at Davis. A committed feminist and noted primatologist with three children of her own, Hrdy knows from firsthand experience what it is to balance a demanding career with the even more demanding role of mother. She has been there, done that, struggled with the yin and yang of being pulled in opposite directions by two equally consuming forces.

Early in her lengthy, detailed study of motherhood in many species, she notes the guilt that is the constant companion of working mothers. This guilt is more intense in mothers who choose to work than in those who have to work in order for their families to survive. For a mother like Hrdy, whose physician husband was easily capable of supporting his family, having a professional life becomes a luxury rather than a necessity. Family survival is never in doubt.

Within the bosom of her young family, Hrdy had to shed much of her academic demeanor. Within the bureaucracy of her university department, she had to project the image of a dedicated scholar who put her pursuit of anthropological truth before all else. When she took her oldest daughter, then a toddler, with her to India, where she was doing research, she had to spend grueling, twelve-hour days at her self-directed work, leaving her child with native nannies who did not look, smell, or speak like any people the small child had ever seen before.

The fact that her work was self-directed meant that choices were available to Hrdy. If she opted in favor of her work over her daughter's comfort and welfare, she created guilt for herself. No one forced her to punch a time clock; no one threatened to fire her if she began her working day late. Yet, in the long term, the threats to her working life were substantial: If she did not produce and publish, if she did not conform to the protocols expected of a thoroughly professional academic, she risked being denied tenure and/or not being promoted within the enlightened halls of her institution. Ask any established female professor at a research institution what compromises she made within her family to achieve tenure. The story that unfolds in answer to this question will probably involve guilt, neglect, and compromise in ten out of ten cases.

When Hrdy made a later research trip to India, this time leaving her child and husband at home with a housekeeper, her situation grew even more troubling. She spent time and energy worrying about how her family was faring without her. She lost touch with her daughter at a crucial time in the child's development. She recounts how, when she returned to the United States and called home during a stopover in New York, her daughter cried, "Mama, Mama," in tones that Hrdy calls heartbreaking. She realized that "Personal ambition seemed to be on a collision course with my baby's needs." She also realized that child rearing at its best is an on-call occupation that demands availability twenty-four hours a day, seven days a week.

Added to the pressures that motherhood imposes upon professional women are the pressures that male-dominated academic departments place upon them. For many years, a much smaller percentage of women were granted tenure when they came up for review than of their male counterparts with comparable credentials. The percentage of female full professors per capita is considerably smaller than that of male full professors.

Professional women are faced with another disadvantage: Their biological clocks tick relentlessly just at the time that they are trying to establish themselves in professions. If they plan to have families, they cannot delay motherhood until they have achieved tenure or until they have reached some hoped-for professional pinnacle. The sand keeps running through the hourglass; the best reproductive years slip gradually away even as academic women are completing their graduate educations.

Emotion very much colors conceptions of motherhood among humans. Biblical injunctions urge respect for parents, love of mothers. In order to gain a more objective view of motherhood, Hrdy examines it in various other species. She notes that among primates, the decision to nurse an offspring involves a compromise. The survival of the offspring may be directly linked to the mother's nursing it for an extended period, but doing so may compromise her ability to conceive again in the immediate future. The offspring must be sufficiently attractive to its primate mother to make her commit herself to its nurture over an extended period.

Hrdy contends that among precivilized mothers, abortion and infanticide are equivalent, abortion being the riskier option for the mother because it can compromise her health and even lead to her death. Among civilized mothers, the opposite is the case. Infanticide is construed as murder, which is punishable by drastic penalties, even by death.

Hrdy, attempting to determine what it is that makes humans unique, reminds her readers that human deoxyribonucleic acid (DNA) is 98 percent identical to that of chimpanzees or bonobos. Of all the enormous panoply of genes that humans share with nonhuman primates, only about fifty account for the cognitive differences between apes and humans. Prime among these differences, according to Hrdy, is language, which allows humans to understand what others are expressing but also to understand at an emotional level what others feel. It is at this level that Hrdy differentiates human motherhood from motherhood in other primates. Not all primatologists agree with such a conclusion. Jane Goodall's work with primates attributes more developed emotions to them than Hrdy seems willing to allow.

Especially fascinating are Hrdy's accounts of her own doctoral research regarding infanticide among the langur monkeys she studied extensively. When she gave a paper based on this research at an annual meeting of the American Anthropological Society in 1976, she concluded that infanticide among primates has a long history and that it is, in some cases, an adaptive rather than a pathological behavior. She focused on how unrelated male langurs killed infants sired by competing males.

Her conclusions led one of the nation's most renowned physical anthropologists to conclude and publicly announce in a paper he later delivered before the American Psychological Association that the langur monkeys Hrdy had studied were not normal, indeed that they were deranged. He claimed that langur monkeys elsewhere did not behave in this way. So incensed was this eminent man by Hrdy's claims that he stormed out of the lecture hall even as she was in the midst of responding to his objections about the conclusions she drew from her research.

Probably no issue involved with motherhood is so emotionally charged as that of infanticide. The Medea question, as one might call it, makes pawns of innocent, helpless children and usually results from derangement in the mother, who may also be suicidal. At times, however, and in some cultures particularly, infanticide is condoned or at least overlooked. This is true in societies in which male offspring are valued more highly than female offspring, who might be killed soon after birth. Cases of this sort are documented in such countries as China and India. In the United States in pre-Civil War days, some slave mothers killed their young to protect them from growing up in slavery.

Infanticide has been widely studied, and

> accumulating evidence for beetles, spiders, fish, birds, mice, ground squirrels, prairie dogs, wolves, bears, lions, tigers, hippopotami, and wild dogs led biologists to take for granted that there are a range of conditions under which mothers cull their litters and abandon or cannibalize young, and an even wider range of circumstances in which unrelated males or rival mothers take advantage of the vulnerability of infants.

The repugnance researchers themselves feel toward infanticide has significantly colored scientific views of motherhood, many of which are still based more on sentimentality than on factual evidence that is readily available and that seems incontrovertible.

One can draw interesting analogies between the monkeys and apes that Hrdy has studied so extensively, and humans. She discusses how female monkeys and apes sometimes abandon their offspring, saying that when an infanticidal male enters her group, the mother's worst nightmare is realized. She will usually try to fight off such an intruder, but, as Hrdy indicates, time is on the intruder's side. Sometimes the mother simply gives up, especially if her offspring are nearly weaned, because they might be too old to be of interest to the intruder.

Some mothers react to such exigencies by taking their offspring away, leaving them with their natural fathers or with siblings, but doing so forces premature weaning that may result in the death of the immature offspring. Even if the offspring survives, it may make its way through the forest to find its mother and, upon reuniting with her, will probably be attacked by the infanticidal male that lives with her.

Within the human context, women, often themselves battered by abusive husbands or boyfriends, frequently do not have the emotional stamina to prevent the abuse that such males inflict upon young children in the household. Even in cases where this abuse leads to death, the mothers involved may defend the offending male and attempt to deflect suspicion from him. Hrdy might here have cited the Susan Smith case in South Carolina, in which the mother felt the necessity of murdering her small sons because her boyfriend objected to her children and was on the brink of leaving her.

Perhaps Hrdy's most strident message is that primate infants and youths need a sense of attachment and a commitment from others, primarily mothers, if they are to flourish emotionally. She often cites the work of John Bowlby, a British physician and psychoanalyst. Much affected by the evolutionary theories of naturalist Charles Darwin as articulated in *On the Origin of Species* (1859), Bowlby produced a psychiatric case study entitled *Charles Darwin: A New Life*, published posthumously in 1990, the year in which Bowlby died.

Bowlby's study shows how early childhood experiences directly affect the whole of a person's life. Darwin's mother died when he was a small boy. In his research on Darwin, Bowlby viewed him "as a congenitally sensitive little boy who lost his mother at an early age." He bases much of his assessment of Darwin and his work on this assumption, trying to view the life of this celebrated evolutionist as the maturation of this small, insecure child who had lost the most important attachment in his life, that to his mother.

Throughout life, Darwin was extremely sensitive to criticism. He was remarkably industrious, eschewing idleness as though it were shamefully sinful. He spent his life trying to prove himself but never quite succeeding. Bowlby relates all of these personal traits—which undoubtedly drove Darwin to become the notable scientist that he was, but made his personal life a living hell—to Darwin's early loss of the attachment that infants require if they are to grow up emotionally whole.

In this comprehensive study, Hrdy raises disquieting and thought-provoking questions. She views unsentimentally a topic that has for eons been steeped in the sort of sentimentality that one finds on Hallmark Mother's Day cards. In doing so, she has revealed some disturbing and unembellished realities about motherhood as it exists throughout the animal kingdom.

R. Baird Shuman

Sources for Further Study

Library Journal 124 (October 15, 1999): 77.
Publishers Weekly 246 (September 27, 1999): 83.

MOTHERLESS BROOKLYN

Author: Jonathan Lethem (1964-)
Publisher: Doubleday (New York). 311 pp. $23.95
Type of work: Novel
Time: The 1970's to the 1980's
Locale: Brooklyn and Manhattan

A twist on the hard-boiled detective novel, featuring a murder, the mob, and a sleuth who suffers from Tourette's syndrome

Principal characters:
FRANK MINNA, a small-time criminal and the owner and operator of a shady detective agency
LIONEL ESSROG, an operative for Frank Minna's detective agency

Motherless Brooklyn, Jonathan Lethem's fifth novel, begins with two detectives, Lionel Essrog and Gilbert Coney, on a stakeout, keeping watch over a Zen meditation center in Manhattan. (Essrog is not the typical fictional detective; he suffers from Tourette's syndrome, a psychological condition causing a variety of compulsive behaviors.) Although Essrog and Coney are staking out the Zen center for their boss, Frank Minna, he, typically, has not told them what they are supposed to be watching for or why. Minna's unexpected appearance at the Zen center leads to his abduction and a car chase, albeit an atypical car chase through stop-and-start, bumper-to-bumper traffic, the most thrilling moment occurring when the car Essrog and Coney are pursuing eludes them at a toll gate because the murderous driver carries a frequent-commuter pass. Essrog and Coney finally catch up with Minna, but he is already dying of multiple stab wounds and will not tell them why he was killed or by whom.

Minna's death leads Essrog to trace the history of Minna and his "Minna Men"—four orphaned, outcast boys taken under Minna's wing while still residents of St. Vincent's Home for Boys in Brooklyn. Initially Minna hired Essrog, Coney, Tony Vermonte, and Danny Fantl to perform various tasks for what he insisted was a moving company, but eventually became a father figure to them; the four motherless boys longed to be like Minna, who ruled certain streets of Brooklyn through a series of unspoken agreements and shady connections. He taught the boys everything he wanted them to know; they learned to act as his operatives, never asking questions and never speaking the names of Minna's most frightening clients, menacing godfather types called Matricardi and Rockeforte. Eventually they are all employed by Minna's car company, a front for a detective agency that offers surveillance, wiretapping, collection, and the occasional act of vandalism in the service of Minna's nameless clients.

As Essrog says, "Minna Men follow instructions. Minna Men try to be like Minna, but Minna is dead." With Minna gone, his men are unmoored and become suspicious of each other, even as they try to organize an effort to solve the murder. Essrog determines to find Minna's killer and decides to run his own investigation. The novel follows Essrog over the next two days as he revisits the Zen center and disrupts a Zen meditation session, stakes out the car company/detective agency to spy on the other Minna Men, attempts to negotiate with Matricardi and Rockeforte, and treks to Maine in search of Minna's missing wife.

Essrog is eventually able to piece together the puzzle of Minna's death. The convoluted resolution of Minna's murder is typical of the genre; it needs its own separate narrative and depends on events that occurred years in the past. Also typical of the hard-boiled detective novel are a number of *Motherless Brooklyn*'s stock characters: a Japanese business corporation whose members own the Zen center, the politely menacing mobsters Matricardi and Rockeforte, Essrog's crony Tony Vermonte as Minna's young protégé who wants to move up in the ranks, and Minna's bitter Mafia wife Julia. Critics have cited stereotypical characters as a weakness of the novel, but just as the twists and turns of the plot are simply vehicles for Lethem to use in playing with the conventions of a hard-boiled detective story, the characters serve as effective foils for the central revelation of Essrog's character, his "Tourette's brain," and the essential Essrog that lies underneath.

Tourette's syndrome can be manifested in a wide variety of compulsive behaviors or "tics"; most commonly cited are tendencies to shout obscenities and to make seemingly uncontrolled gestures. Essrog's obscenities are often directed at his personal phantom, Bailey, although Essrog knows no one named Bailey. Essrog frequently breaks forth with a string of variations on words or phrases he has just heard. These verbal tics can serve as an oblique (and often profane) shorthand revealing his unspoken thoughts. Attempting to ask his cronies a simple question, Essrog helplessly riffs on the noun: "Any calls? See that *homosapien, homogenize, genocide, can'tdecide, candyeyes*, homicide cop?" About to be knocked unconscious by a thug, Essrog thinks, "*He's just a big mouse, Daddy, a vigorous louse, big as a house, a couch, a man, a plan, a canal, apocalypse.*" When Minna's brother, a would-be Buddhist, says faith is "spread by what means it finds," Essrog silently chants "*spread by means it finds, fed in springs by mimes, bled by mingy spies.*" Essrog is so constantly engulfed in his Tourette's that it comes as a surprise when he is occasionally able to hold a brief tic-free conversation.

Essrog's Tourette's syndrome takes to an extreme the hard-boiled detective's need to bring order to a world gone wrong; he even admits that one of his compulsions is to count and categorize the tics themselves. Essrog constantly fights the urge to tic, struggling to focus his eyes or his mind elsewhere; often in the throes of some compulsion Essrog will have tears of frustration in his eyes as he simultaneously imposes an artificial order and creates his own chaos. As a boy Essrog felt compelled to kiss those around him and could not stop himself; now he straightens collars or taps shoulders a certain number of times (one day his Tourette's brain might focus on the number 6, another it might be 5). When a thug shoves Essrog, he tries to shove back simply as a compulsive reflex, matching motion to motion. When he takes possession of the killer's gun and tosses it into the ocean, he feels compelled to throw four more objects in for a total of five (the day's magic number), and having no fourth object at hand removes one of his own shoes and hurls it into the surf.

Minna and the three other Minna Men are accustomed to Essrog's compulsive behavior. Minna in his role as father figure was the first to identify Essrog's tics as Tourette's syndrome, although Minna calls Essrog "a free human freak show" and the Minna Men nickname him "Freakshow" thereafter. Minna found Essrog useful as an operative precisely because the latter's Tourette's could be trusted; if asked to listen on a wiretap for certain words or to keep watch on a particular person or location, Essrog would compulsively listen or watch, unable to detach his attention from the task. More important, he could observe Minna's subjects and business associates without being observed; his behavior ensured that others would assume he was mentally defective, someone who could be safely ignored and quickly forgotten.

Essrog is like classic hard-boiled detectives in that he is a loner and an outsider, a man who ultimately works alone; again, however, the typical hard-boiled quality is taken to an extreme as Lethem makes Essrog an outsider several times over, and tweaks Essrog's attempts to conform and create relationships for himself. Orphaned as a child, one of the few Caucasian students in his high school, involved with underworld characters from his teens, Essrog is an outsider even among his peers. Minna's selective tutelage keeps all his Men isolated in a world of Minna's making, but Essrog's incessant verbal and physical tics set him apart even from his fellow Minna Men. Although sexual activity brings Essrog's compulsions briefly under control, his relationships with women are few, far between, and usually fueled by alcohol. Even his attempt to provide himself with the companionship of a pet fails because of his Tourette's; he sadly recounts his effort to keep a cat for company, and how his own compulsive behaviors so affected the cat that he had to find it a new home, although he kept track of the cat's progress and knows it eventually recovered.

Lethem sets *Motherless Brooklyn* largely in the grimy Brooklyn that belongs to Minna, a world of shady deals and scary characters. In Minna's Brooklyn old men are seemingly without occupation but are provided for, no questions asked; Matricardi and Rockeforte hold court in a brownstone now converted to a warehouse for stolen goods; the use of language to define relationships, transact business, and communicate the social norms is a crude art. Essrog has made his home in Brooklyn; he is so much an extension of Minna's business that he lives in an apartment above the detective agency. Essrog perceives Manhattan as a world apart, but learns that the sophistication and spirituality of the Zen center are a thin veneer over the same rough material of which Minna was made. Essrog experiences a small epiphany outside the city when he pursues his clues to Maine; his first sight of the ocean leaves him momentarily speechless, shattering his obsessive dependence on language. Here Essrog realizes that he is part of a world larger than Brooklyn.

Motherless Brooklyn has postmodern elements; Essrog, who spent his childhood in the library of St. Vincent's Home for Boys, is familiar with the hard-boiled detective genre and able to comment on his own story within that context. Preparing to make a philosophical assertion ("As a great man once said, the more things change, the harder they are to change back."), Essrog notes how typical this is of the detective genre and offers an example, quoting Philip Marlowe in Raymond Chandler's *The Big Sleep*

(1939). When Essrog is knocked unconscious in an alley, he ruminates on how the same thing has happened to countless other detectives in countless detective stories. When a minor character is mentioned, then killed before he can appear, Essrog mulls this over as a convention of the genre: "Have you ever felt, in the course of reading a detective novel, a guilty thrill of relief at having a character murdered before he can step onto the page and burden you with his actual existence? Detective stories always have too many characters anyway."

Lethem's earlier novels successfully melded science fiction with various other genres, including hard-boiled detective fiction in *Gun, with Occasional Music* (1994), academic satire in *As She Climbed Across the Table* (1997), and the Western novel and coming-of-age story in *Girl in Landscape* (1998). While the verbal virtuosity and successful melding of genres in Lethem's earlier novels had earned him critical acclaim, *Motherless Brooklyn* was generally considered a more mainstream effort by a serious novelist whose proclivity for science fiction had prevented his widespread acceptance.

Maureen J. Puffer-Rothenberg

Sources for Further Study

Booklist 95 (July, 1999): 1895.
Esquire 132 (September, 1999): 54.
Library Journal 124 (July, 1999): 133.
The New York Times Book Review 104 (October 17, 1999): 7
Publishers Weekly 246 (August 16, 1999): 57.
Time 154 (October 11, 1999): 90.
Village Voice 44 (September 21, 1999): 136.

MOUNTAIN TIME

Author: Ivan Doig (1939-)
Publisher: Charles Scribner's Sons (New York). 316 pp. $25.00
Type of work: Novel
Time: The late 1990's
Locale: Seattle and north central Montana

A dying entrepreneur's last wish causes conflict and anguish for his only son, his son's lover, and the lover's sister

Principal characters:
MITCH ROZIER, a fifty-year-old columnist for an environmentalist newspaper published in Seattle
LYLE ROZIER, his father, who has lived a life filled with grandiose plans he cannot fulfill; now he is dying of leukemia
LEXA MCCASKILL, a caterer in Seattle and Mitch's lover
MARIAH MCCASKILL, a professional photographer, Lexa's sister
JEROME (BING) BINGFORD III, Mitch's employer

This novel, Ivan Doig's sixth, continues the stories of the lives of some of the characters who populated an earlier novel, *Ride with Me, Mariah Montana* (1990), especially Mariah McCaskill and her younger sister, Lexa. The central character, however, is Mitch Rozier, a native of Montana transplanted to Seattle, who earns his living as a columnist for a weekly environmentalist newspaper published by a rich young friend of his. The central action takes place when Mitch is called to his small home town in Montana, ostensibly to hear the details of his father's latest deal and to stop the old man from making another rash decision, in reality to learn that the old man is dying of leukemia and wishes to obtain Mitch's agreement to dispose of his ashes.

This is the central source of conflict in *Mountain Time*, since Mitch's reluctance to acquiesce in the old man's plan ties him to the family home, while taking a leave of absence from the failing newspaper. Mitch's absence, in turn, leads his lover, Lexa McCaskill, to abandon her catering business in Seattle temporarily and drive to Montana with her older sister, Mariah, who happens to be visiting Lexa when the younger woman decides to join her lover. Mariah is a professional photographer who is finishing a year's travel around the world sponsored by Fuji Corporation.

Lyle tells his plan for disposal of his ashes to each of the three younger characters, making each swear not to tell the others. He wants Mitch, accompanied by the two women, to transport his ashes to an abandoned fire tower in the heart of the wilderness and to scatter the ashes there. As a young man, he had been part of a two-man crew which built the tower, but to Mitch, Lyle's plan is a vain gesture, an attempt to impress others with what Lyle wishes them to think is his dedication to the wilderness and its preservation. To Mitch, the crowning irony is that Lyle wants his ashes strewn in the Bob Marshall Wilderness, named for a Forest Service ranger who was a dedicated defender of the wilderness. Lyle's other plan is to sell some property, still a wild area, known as the Rozier Bench, to exploiters who would destroy its wild character, cutting down trees, prospecting for gas, oil, and mineral resources, and in general ruining it. He needs Mitch's agreement to close this deal, but his real aim is to use the threat of selling the land to force Mitch to agree to his plan for his ashes.

This is only the most obvious of the several plot lines in *Mountain Time*; most of the others bear out the concern for the environment which is the underlying theme of the entire novel. For instance, one secondary plot line has to do with the relationship between Mitch and Lexa, which is under some stress. A flashback to one of their early encounters provides an opportunity for a view of the disastrous results of the historic oil spill caused by the wreck of the SS *Exxon Valdez* near the Alaskan shipping port of Valdez. Lexa and her aviator husband are involved in pathetically desperate efforts to rescue wildlife caught in the oil spill in Prince William Sound, while Mitch is sent to cover the story for his paper. Mitch at this point is divorced from his wife and estranged from his two children, and Lexa is bored with her marriage, so the connection they establish is no surprise to either of them, despite the disparity in their ages. The fact that they come from the same area of Montana makes their relationship more plausible, if not more suspenseful. The real bond between them, however, is the revulsion they feel at the destruction of native wildlife caused by the Alaskan pipeline.

A prominent aspect of the hostile relationship between father and son has its origin in an accident that occurred when Mitch was in his teens. For several summers he was one of a crew of young men hired by Lyle to clear rocks from fields full of the detritus left by glaciers at the end of the most recent ice age. Lyle's negligence caused a loaded wagon to be driven over Mitch's leg, breaking it in two places. Unable to work in the fields, Mitch is put to work keeping the books for his father's enterprise. In the course of this employment, Mitch is involved in a dispute over wages when Lyle orders Mitch to pay a worker for days when Mitch knows the man did not work. In the aftermath of Lyle's death, he traces down the laborer involved and gets his story, which implicates Lyle in an adulterous affair with the sexy wife of one of Mitch's best friends. Knowledge of the affair has given the worker the power to get special treatment from Lyle. The facts which Mitch unearths provide no startling evidence of Lyle's character, except to show that Lyle prefers betraying his son to having his infidelity made public knowledge.

Doig's strength is not in his plotting. Mitch's resistance to Lyle's plan for the disposal of his ashes does not become a major element, even to Mitch, until very late in the action, when the three younger people have reached their destination at the lookout tower. Mitch has reluctantly agreed to carry out the old man's wish, but on the way to do so his conscience takes over, much to Lexa's dismay. The climactic action, when Lexa attempts to take the ashes from Mitch to dispose of them and in the ensuing scuffle Mitch falls down the stairs of the tower and breaks his leg, is all too clearly a device preparing for a reconciliation between the lovers. The comic possibilities of the episode are ignored, unfortunately. Another wasted plot line introduces a superfluous flare-up of a sudden attraction between Mitch and Mariah as they wait in the lookout tower for Lexa to complete her hike out of the wilderness to summon assistance. The episode is a brief distraction that is not even consummated. It serves only to prepare the way for a happy ending between Mitch and Lexa.

This is not to say that *Mountain Time* is a failure. Doig's skills as a writer, whether of fiction or of nonfiction, have been demonstrated often enough in his earlier books, several of which are set in the Two Medicine country, on the eastern side of the Montana Rocky Mountains. Prominent among these skills is his ability to present interesting characters, in this novel less the two protagonists, Lexa and Mitch, than Lyle, Mariah, and Bing. These three represent phases in the development of the Northwest. Lyle reflects the rapaciousness with which the area's natural resources have been exploited, as well as the failure of so many enterprises that have brought disaster to the adventurers who have sought easy fortunes at great cost to the magnificent natural setting they exploit. Lyle's business of selling old branding irons is symbolic of the ways in which the Old West is a myth that is peddled to tourists. The branding irons, no longer used, also symbolize the decay of the cattle business and of the economic base provided at one time by ranching. Lyle's willingness to sell the Rozier Bench is even more strongly symbolic of the negligent development of the area's natural resources.

Bing represents a more modern type of northwestern tycoon, having made a fortune in the electronics industry which has burgeoned in the Seattle area, using his money for what he thinks of as good works. In reality the newspaper he runs is not much more than a toy for him, and it is the staff members who will suffer when it inevitably goes out of business. He enjoys the power he wields over the eccentrics who work for him, not recognizing that he does them little good. In fact he puts some of them in harm's way, like the woman correspondent who lies buried beneath the ashes of Mount St. Helens. The new breed of tycoon is not less rapacious than its predecessors; it only pretends to be so.

Mariah McCaskill exists at a different level as a symbolic character, combining technical skill with an interest in the people who are her subjects. At first her request of Lyle that he cooperate in her project of recording on film the final days of his life seems to be callous and even cruel. As the project develops, however, Mariah's skill and her empathy arouse Lyle's interest, and in a way Mariah's project renews his interest in life, even as its end approaches. Mariah and her many cameras form a complex set of symbols: the cameras simply record what they are pointed at; they make no judgments, which are made by the viewer. The photographer does the pointing, but is only rarely more than the operator of a machine. This added element is what Mariah seeks in her photographs of Lyle, but her detachment from personal relationships shows the limitations placed upon her by her profession.

All these characters bear witness to Doig's urgent message in *Mountain Time*, as do his references to figures from real life, especially Aldo Leopold (1887-1948) and Bob Marshall (1901-1939). Leopold was instrumental in the establishment of the first wilderness area, in the Gila area of New Mexico, while Marshall was a ranger with the Forest Service who explored widely in the northern Rockies and urged the preservation of wild areas. The Bob Marshall Wilderness Area in Montana is named for him.

The final chapter of *Mountain Time* depicts a lone hiker stopping at the site of a group of cairns obviously built and left by previous hikers in the wilderness. The hiker builds another cairn and looks upon his work with satisfaction. At first he seems to have followed Mitch, Lexa, and Mariah, who have camped at the same site, but the final sentence identifies him as Bob Marshall. As Marshall is placed firmly in the wilderness he loved, Ivan Doig places himself in the same wilderness and declares his regard for Marshall and for the same wilderness. *Mountain Time* is an eloquent defense of the values Marshall represented.

John M. Muste

Sources for Further Study

Booklist 95 (June 1, 1999): 1741.
Library Journal 124 (August, 1999): 137.
The New York Times Book Review 104 (August 15, 1999): 27.
Publishers Weekly 246 (June 14, 1999): 48.

MY FATHER, DANCING

Author: Bliss Broyard (1966-)
Publisher: Alfred A. Knopf (New York). 224 pp. $22.00
Type of work: Short fiction

A debut collection of short stories about important relationships, most particularly relationships between fathers and daughters, from a rising young American writer

Bliss Broyard, daughter of the late literary critic Anatole Broyard, began her writing career as her father lay dying of cancer. A friend of the elder Broyard repaid an old debt, and the younger Broyard used the money to enroll in a creative writing class at Harvard Extension School. Out of this class came the title story in the collection, *My Father, Dancing*. Her stories have appeared in journals such as *Ploughshares* and *Grand Street*, as well as in *The Pushcart Anthology* and *Best American Short Stories 1998.* Bliss Broyard's reminiscence of her father, published in the anthology *Personals: Dreams and Nightmares From the Lives of Twenty Young Writers* (1998), edited by Thomas Beller, has been consistently noted as the finest piece of writing in the book. Broyard's first book, *My Father, Dancing*, met with high praise from reviewers and from readers. Norah Vincent, for example, writing for *The Baltimore Sun*, called the collection "a startlingly good and enjoyable literary debut from a writer whose ripening talents exist quite apart from, or perhaps even in spite, [sic] of her father's famous name."

Of the eight stories in the book, four focus on father-daughter relationships. In the other four stories, young women approach relationships with lovers, or would-be lovers. Broyard's fathers are larger than life, often overwhelming their quieter, less confident daughters. In this world, fathers and daughters both suffer and enjoy their connections to each other. The daughters all seem to want to please their fathers in some way, and the fathers seem unable or unwilling to be pleased. Nevertheless, the characters in these stories do not degenerate into stereotypical renditions of either fathers or daughters. The young women in the other stories also seem anxious to win approval from the men with whom they interact. It is perhaps troubling that none of the young female protagonists seems able to take charge of her life; rather, each acts in response to the male presence in the story.

The father-daughter stories form the backbone of the collection. The most notable is the title story, "My Father, Dancing." In this story, a young female narrator named Kate reflects on her life with her father as he lies in a hospital room dying of prostate cancer. The story is largely autobiographical; Broyard's father died of prostate cancer. In an essay written for her publisher, entitled "Building Stories," Broyard describes how she came to write the story of her father's illness and death that grew into "My Father, Dancing." She writes,

> I wasn't trying to make sense of the experience of losing my father, because the death of someone you love cannot be understood, only borne. Rather, it was as if I were trying to build a structure to

> house my feelings and memories, with a floor that could hold weight and with walls and a ceiling so that other people might venture inside.

Broyard structures "My Father, Dancing" around Kate's memories of dancing with her father interspersed with scenes of him in the hospital. This structure provides for a heartbreaking, marked contrast between the man smoothly moving across the floor and the man in the hospital bed who wants to go home. Kate describes the feeling of dancing with her father, the way the two of them could communicate with each other without talking. "On those dance floors over the years, we told each other more about ourselves than in any conversation," Kate reveals. Like the other daughters in the collection, she looks to her father for signs of approval. She says that she used her father as "a mirror to understand what I looked like to the world." By so doing, she becomes a reflection of her father's judgments.

When she was young, Kate's father told her that he wanted to be the first man to break her heart "because then he could ensure that at least it would be done gently." The heartbreak that Kate's father gives her, however, is not as he might have imagined. As he lies dying, he does not make a sign that he knows she is there. While she sits with him in the hospital, she holds his hand:

> As I waited for some sign that he was aware of me, I thought it had boiled down to this: all I wanted from him was a simple squeeze of his fingers. As I waited and did not receive any sign, I realized that he was breaking my heart and it wasn't gentle at all.

The story is filled with wrenching scenes. Any adult daughter who has beheld her father's nakedness and fragility in an open hospital gown, had to turn a deaf ear to her father's pleas to get him out of the hospital, sat for long hours stroking her dying father's hand, or returned to her parents' house alone after her father's death will understand the strength of Broyard's writing. The story is powerful and present.

The other fathers in Broyard's book, although they live, fare less well as human beings. "Mr. Sweetly Indecent," the second story in the book, finds a daughter confronting her father's infidelity. What elevates this story from a trite treatment of daughter-disappointed-in-daddy, however, is Broyard's deft juxtaposition of scenes of the daughter's sexual affairs with scenes with her father. When the narrator sees her father kissing a young woman on the street outside an apartment he keeps in the city, she is scandalized by his casual affair. However, interspersed with her dismay is the recollection of the evening she has just spent with a man. The man is never given a name in the story, although he is sometimes referred to as "Mr. Sweetly Indecent." The narrator has slept with the man on their first date, and as the story moves forward, she waits for him to call. Readers also discover that her date with the man has been set up by a coworker, someone with whom the narrator has also slept. Thus, while the narrator is furious with her father, and suddenly uncertain about her parents' marriage, she seems herself to be unable to move from casual sex to a more lasting relationship. Her decision to call the man and ask him to go out suggests that she wants a closeness she is unable to find. His refusal of her offer merely underscores the sterility of the narrator's personal life. In contrast, her parents still exhibit care and love for each other. Although the father in this story is flawed and self-centered, and although his marriage might appear to be a sham, it seems, nonetheless, an existence preferable to the one his daughter leads.

"At the Bottom of the Lake" features another father and daughter. In this story Lucy, engaged to be married to Sam, invites her father and her stepmother to join her at a cabin on an island for a weekend. Her father loved the cabin in his younger years, but had stopped coming there after his divorce and subsequent remarriage. Many reviewers point to the role of the stepmother in the story, saying that she ruins the weekend for everyone. It is possible, however, to examine more closely the relationship between the father and the daughter for clues as to why the weekend goes askew. Lucy, who has taken on all of her father's tasks on the island, struggles for her father's approval. All she wants is for him to nod and say, "Good job!" Instead, when she gives him a tour of the island, he finds fault with her way of doing things. Broyard's talent in portraying this scene is significant; it would be easy to picture a one-dimensional, critical father. However, Broyard deftly reveals that the father's criticism is not aimed so much at Lucy as it is at his own shortcomings. It is hard for him to watch a place he loves become someone else's. Further, Broyard creates a Lucy who is sympathetic in her need for approval, but who does not recognize her own competition with her stepmother for her father's attention. Such deft handling of character builds a satisfying and multileveled story.

Less successful are the stories without fathers in them. In these, the struggle of young women for the approval of the young men in their lives borders on the pitiable. The last two stories have the same protagonist, Lily, a girl of high school age, approaching her first sexual encounter. "Snowed In," the final story in the book, finds Lily and a group of young people spending the day at the house of a friend whose parents have gone away for the weekend. Lily has a crush on Bobby Callahan, who is perhaps the most popular boy at their school. On the other hand, Kyle has a crush on Lily. Amidst the crushes, the young people drink a lot of alcohol. In the final scene, Lily finds herself, drunk, in bed with Bobby, about to have sex. There is no doubt that the story very accurately reflects the situation it proposes. Such accurate reflection, however, does not necessarily result in an engaging story. It is difficult to understand Lily's motivation, or to know very much about her. Further, there is a disconcerting shift in the point of view near the end of the story, made necessary by Lily's passing out. The last scene is clearly separated from the rest of the story by white space, but the effect is jarring nonetheless. The story is now Bobby's for six paragraphs as he undresses the unconscious Lily and himself. Because there has been little development of Bobby before this, it is difficult to garner much sympathy for the young man, particularly since what he is contemplating is rape. In the final paragraph, Lily awakens, and the story returns to her: "But when she opened her eyes, the distance between them was much less than she imagined it would be . . . and she saw that what was about to happen wasn't something that could be turned on or off at whim. And once she saw that, she couldn't look away." These lines, so finely wrought, very nearly salvage the story at the last possible moment, as if the story itself awakens, much closer to the reader than could have been imagined.

In spite of some unevenness of quality among the stories in *My Father, Dancing*, Bliss Broyard demonstrates both her talent and her vision in this, her first book. She is able to mine her own experience in a careful and powerful way to create art that reveals truth. As she writes in "Building Stories," "But I think of Henry James who at seventy-six wrote that the port he had set out from at the beginning of his long creative journey was the essential loneliness of his life . . . and I see my young self digging into that loneliness for the first time, and I think, thank God for the disciplines of art and writing for providing something to do with everything that is unearthed."

Diane Andrews Henningfeld

Sources for Further Study

Booklist 95 (July, 1999): 1921.
Interview 29 (August, 1999): 58.
Library Journal 124 (June 15, 1999): 111.
The New York Times, July 29, 1999, p. B9.
The New York Times Book Review 104 (August 15, 1999): 8.
Publishers Weekly 246 (June 7, 1999): 70.
Time 154 (August 2, 1999): 91.

MY LIFE AS A LIST
207 Things About My (Bronx) Childhood

Author: Linda Rosenkrantz (1934-)
Publisher: Clarkson Potter (New York). 89 pp. $15.00
Type of work: Autobiography
Time: The 1930's and 1940's
Locale: The Bronx, New York

The heartwarming, charming, personal reminiscences of a Jewish girl growing up in the Bronx, New York, during World War II

Principal personages:
LINDA ROSENKRANTZ, the narrator
HER MOTHER
HER FATHER
HER YOUNGER SISTER

Unlike many recent childhood memoirs that capitalize on dysfunction, Linda Rosenkrantz's *My Life as a List: 207 Things About My (Bronx) Childhood* does not deal with tragedy, poverty, drug abuse, satanic cults, pedophilia, harrowing family secrets, or depraved parents. Instead, the author, a native of The Bronx, New York, employs gusto and verve to mix together, within a mere 207 paragraph-sized reminiscence, a hodgepodge of childhood minutiae. Difficult to categorize, and specific to those who grew up in the decades surrounding World War II in the close-knit Jewish communities of The Bronx and Brooklyn, these "paragraphs" comprise an engaging and eclectic inventory of the author's recollections of her first twelve years of childhood. For instance, she recalls her mother opening a bar of (Hershey's? Nestlé's?) milk chocolate to find it crawling with ants, getting scabs on her knees from roller skating, hiding under the bed at the Jewish Community Center of Poughkeepsie summer camp, having her tonsils removed, and, humiliation of humiliations, being put in a crib at age four. These recollections will appeal primarily to those American generations who lived through the Depression, World War II, and Hollywood's golden era of motion pictures.

An assortment of family, friends, and neighbors play the predominant role in forming young Linda's life. Next to the narrator, the mother is the book's most developed, well-rounded "character," one readers could easily visualize on the stage. One of those women who never has a cold, Linda's mother never sits down except to eat or sew. Constantly on the go, she files magazine articles under topics such as animals and birds, famous people, and foreign countries, in preparation for her daughter's school reports. "Nice research work," the teachers always remark. She makes puppets out of peanuts and sews tiny dresses for them. She buys six school dresses at a time at the local department store, has her daughter try them on after school, returns five the next day, and starts the process over again. She sews incessantly, making sure her daughter never has to repeat wearing an outfit all term and explains to her curious youngster that her own breasts are floppy because in her youth she used to bind them so she could be a flat-chested flapper. The young narrator realizes fully that if she waits long enough (stalls), her mother will do anything for her, and that if she cannot find the words she needs, her mother will ultimately find them for her. At one point in the book the author astutely observes the symbiotic relationship she shares with her mother.

Compared with the mother, the narrator's father remains vague, shadowy, but nonetheless interesting because he incites the reader's curiosity. Referred to as "the mayor of 37th Street," he is in the fur-buying business, never learns to swim, does not close the door fully when he uses the bathroom, hands his paycheck over to his wife, smokes unfiltered Chesterfields, reads *The World Telegram* and the *Post*, and enjoys movie stars Joan Blondell and Ann Sothern. A klutzy dancer, he always sneezes precisely ten times and gives his daughter a penny for every word she fills in on the Sunday *New York Times* crossword puzzle.

The author's close-knit extended family also has a major impact on the young narrator: her grandfather (Zada) who, when long ago offered two sisters to marry, said, "I'll take the fat one"; her grandmother, who advises her never to stay in the tub after the water starts draining out (the dirt comes back on). This is the same grandmother (Bubba) who had four sisters and a fifth whose name was never spoken. The author's aunts (all of whom float, but none of whom swim) include Celia, who turned into a bitter woman when her father forced her to marry an older, almost illiterate, cigar-chomping vegetable peddler, and Pauline, who read thick novels like *War and Peace* and related them in great detail. Another stubble-chinned aunt married a wisecracking cabdriver named Milton. The uncles are just as colorful and endearing: Uncle Al, who married three shiksa wives; Uncle Charlie, who bought a farm sight unseen with an eight-hundred-dollar insurance settlement; Uncle Harry, who was afraid to be alone and would not allow his wife to leave him at night; Uncle Eddie, who drove at one hundred miles an hour in the seafoam-green Pontiac he bought after his discharge from the army. Numbered among her friends and acquaintances are a neighbor who punches tiny holes in her husband's condoms in order to conceive a second child and the sad-eyed accordion teacher, paralyzed by polio, who spent his days trying to teach tone-deaf little Jewish girls how to play "Come Back to Sorrento."

School years, of course, comprise many of the author's memories, but there are no beatings, no castigating teachers, no abusive playground bullies. Although there is a fair amount of discipline—walking in the on-time line or in the late line—it is all taken in stride. In her elementary school, teachers have identical handwriting, and many share identical hair color. In this era, being sick meant staying home from school and reading *Modern Screen Photoplay* and *Nancy and Sluggo* comics or listening to *Our Gal Sunday* on the radio.

Rosenkrantz magically re-creates life in America during the earlier part of the twentieth century by engaging the reader's senses of sight, sound, and taste. Weekly trips to neighborhood movie theaters were important events in Rosenkrantz's childhood, and her depth of golden-screen detail prompts the reader to remember life as it used to be. She reminisces over Hedy Lamarr in *Tortilla Flat* (1942), and Peggy Ann Garner in *A Tree Grows in Brooklyn* (1945). Her favorite female stars were, as she says, the impossibly sweet ones: June Allyson, Jeanne Craine, Joan Caulfield, and Joan Leslie. She could not stand Dorothy Lamour, Betty Grable, Bette Davis, Betty Hutton, Jane Withers, Linda Darnell, Ida Lupino, Claudette Colbert (and her stupid bangs), or Sonja Henie (because her skating scenes went on forever). Of the male stars, she remembers Alan Ladd, Gene Kelly, John Garfield, Cornel Wilde, James Mason, Ronald Colman, Joseph Cotten, Robert Walker, Rory Calhoun (solely as a pinup), and Guy Madison. Among those she did not like she numbers Fred MacMurray, Dick Powell, and the Dead End Kids. Her love for motion pictures prompted her to join the Danny Kaye Fan Club and to write letters to Van Johnson and Peter Lawford. Rosenkrantz's recollections of the era's popular children's books also contribute to *My Life as a List*'s nostalgic ambience. These include *Lad: A Dog* (1919), *Lassie Come Home* (1940), and *Here We Are* (1941), an anthology of short stories that includes works by authors Dorothy Parker and Marjorie Kinnan Rawlings.

Music also colored the young writer's life. Like large numbers of little Jewish girls, she played tunes such as "O Sole Mio" on the accordion only because Bronx apartments were not big enough to house pianos. She recollects singers crooning "I'm going to buy a paper doll that I can call my own." Her father contributes to the musical atmosphere, bringing his daughter song sheets, picked up at the subway newsstand, from *Your Hit Parade:* "You'd be so nice to come home to, so nice by the fire"; "You got to ac-cent-chu-ate the positive, el-im-in-ate the negative"; "I'm Always Chasing Rainbows"; and "I'm Forever Blowing Bubbles."

Reading Rosenkrantz's childhood memories, the reader experiences a culinary walk down memory lane: after-school snacks of rye bread piled high with sauerkraut trawled from the big wooden barrel at Olinsky's store; Mel-O-Rolls and pistachio sugar cones; Aunt Pearl's spaghetti that did not come out of a can; licking the inside of Dixie cup covers to reveal the circular movie star portrait of Bing Crosby and Alice Faye underneath, and attempts to camouflage her mother's detestable canned spinach in mashed potatoes. By remembering her mother's concern over what to fix for Daddy every evening, Rosenkrantz reminds us of dinners where meat was paramount, and before lasagna and quesadillas became everyday American fare: lamb chops, breaded veal chops, tenderloin steak, hamburgers, franks and beans, salmon patties accompanied by mashed potatoes, canned vegetables, and fruit cocktail or cling peaches. The author recalls how Francisco Raymundo, a sandal-wearing neighbor, offered her her first taste of forbidden pork, the most delicious thing, she claims, she ever tasted in her life.

Although Rosenkrantz paints a picture of a childhood worth remembering—a splendid, protected childhood in The Bronx, New York—shades of the era's dark side filter through occasionally: recurrent dreams of Adolf Hitler, family recollections of a grandfather who was pelted by stones when he appeared on a neighborhood street wearing a long, white beard and yarmulke, neighbors destined not to return from the war, classmates who die of polio, defense bonds as gifts, V-Mail messages from Uncle

Al or Eddie, her mother's volunteer duty at a day-care center for kids whose Rosie-the-Riveter mothers performed war-related jobs, and her delight in being a girl because she would not have to fight in the army and hide in foxholes between other sweaty, scared young men. From the author's childhood confusion when an older person does not speak English with an accent, the reader realizes that Rosenkrantz, although firmly ensconced in a protective Jewish enclave of The Bronx, is only one generation removed from Europe—a Europe undergoing the Holocaust.

Besides allowing the reader to view the sparkling facets of her life, the author also is personally forthcoming in her autobiographical self-portraiture. Her insight into her contradictory nature actually is quite dauntless and admirable. The numerous family photos, especially of the author in period portrait poses, family memorabilia, and ephemera—report cards, Girl Scout group shots, newspaper clippings, a souvenir ticket from the 1939 New York World's Fair, birth announcements, a one-hundred dollar war bond, and a ten-cent copy of *Photoplay Movie Mirror* magazine—bring the book to life.

The narrative form of *My Life as a List* deserves attention. Its nonlinear, nonchronological structure metaphorically mimics the fluid give-and-take nature of memory. Furthermore, Rosenkrantz invites others to adopt her technique. This advice should indeed be heeded by those who wish to capture what childhood glimmerings remain without committing to the labor, and/or the angst, necessary to complete a full-scale autobiography.

This lively, funny book of magic memories, recalled with such affectionate warmth, provides a wonderful walk down memory lane for those who might have forgotten life before television, when men wore ties and hats even to baseball games, when writing to a pen pal and haunting the mailman for a reply was a daily activity, when children could ask strangers to see them safely across the street, when boys in kindergarten still had names like Bertram and Marvin, and girls were named Arlene and Nadine. It is refreshing to read of genuine (albeit idiosyncratic) relatives without experiencing the heart-wrenching sensational incidents of physical or sexual abuse almost inherent in some memoirs. Although younger readers might be puzzled by some portions of the book, some will find the trivia puzzles—what is an Automat?—intriguing and will seek out older family members and friends, who will delight in providing them answers and in sharing additional memories.

M. Casey Diana

THE MYSTERIOUS FLAME
Conscious Minds in a Material World

Author: Colin McGinn (1950-)
Publisher: Basic Books (New York). 242 pp. $24.00
Type of work: Philosophy

An introduction to the mind-body problem in philosophy, this book argues that understanding the nature of the connection between consciousness and the brain is beyond human capacity

One of the most ancient of human experiences is the perception of a distinction between the world and the mind that perceives the world. The question of how the ideas, images, and feelings that occur in the mind are related to the physical world inspired the work of Plato, giving rise to the Western philosophical tradition. With the rise of the mechanistic, scientific worldview in early modern Europe, the question took on a new form and a new urgency. If the universe consists of a series of causes and effects among objects, how is it possible for human beings to be subjects who are aware of the objects and act on them? Belgian philosopher René Descartes (1596-1650) offered a brilliant solution to this problem by essentially dividing humans into two parts: Humans, Descartes concluded, consist of a material body that participates fully in the causal relationships of other objects and an immaterial soul or mind that perceives and acts upon the body and the physical world.

The dualism of Descartes continues to be one theoretical approach to the nature of consciousness. However, two new areas of development in science have made this kind of mind-body separation increasingly difficult to support. First, advances in neuroscience indicate that events in the mind are directly dependent upon the brain, a physical object. Second, the development of computers that seem to be able to do some of the work of human minds suggests that it may be possible to conceive of physical objects as producing mental processes. Nevertheless, humans still do not understand just how the masses of neuronal connections that make up their brains could give rise to experiences of the world.

The problem of consciousness, with its relevance to both neuroscience and artificial intelligence, has become one of the hottest issues in contemporary philosophy. Colin McGinn, a British philosopher teaching at Rutgers University in New Jersey in the late 1990's, offers a readable introduction to this philosophical problem in *The Mysterious Flame*. McGinn proudly proclaims himself a "mysterian," a label other philosophers have taken from the 1960's pop group Question Mark and the Mysterians and applied to those who claim that consciousness is simply a mystery that cannot be explained.

McGinn's mysterian position is not a form of mysticism. He does not claim that consciousness is a phenomenon that exists outside reason and beyond physical science. Instead, he essentially argues that human consciousness has not evolved in order to explain itself and is therefore incapable of doing so.

McGinn describes and criticizes the two main positions on consciousness: materialism and dualism. The materialist position holds that consciousness can be reduced to material events in the brain, to electrochemical connections among neurons. There is a big gap, McGinn argues, between neuronal processes and experiences. The perception of the color red and the feeling of pain are different from the movement of neurotransmitters across synapses. One could open up a brain and observe the patterns of discharges of someone seeing red, but nowhere would one see the actual experience of someone seeing red.

The classical dualist position is also indefensible. Dualism is haunted by problems McGinn describes as the "zombie problem" and the "ghost problem." If mind and brain are completely separate, then one could, in theory, simply remove consciousness, and the individual without consciousness would go about all the tasks of life as a zombie without any awareness or inner experience. In this case, however, the mind would simply be irrelevant, an observer with no power to bring about action. The "ghost problem" presents an even more serious difficulty with dualism. If the mind exists in the brain only as an immaterial presence without substance, then how can the mind cause the unquestionably physical body to do things? Why, moreover, do parts of consciousness, such as memories or emotions, change in response to brain damage? Alzheimer's disease seems like a convincing demonstration of the dependence of consciousness on the physical state of the brain.

All the explanations one can produce to explain consciousness fail, McGinn argues, because human scientific intelligence is limited. Science and philosophy are results of applying mental faculties developed through evolution to new kinds of problems. Evolution cannot have resulted in infinitely powerful mental faculties, though, so there must be some kinds of problems that humans are unable to solve. When one reaches these kinds of problems, McGinn argues, one has reached a state of cognitive closure.

Aside from the fact that humans have not yet been able to come up with a convincing explanation of consciousness, there are some good reasons to believe that the nature of consciousness may be an area of cognitive closure. The conscious mind implies an unconscious. This is not simply the unconscious of hidden emotions and desires found in modern psychological theories, but also a computational unconscious. The mind does things beneath its own awareness during the process of being conscious. The image of an object in awareness produced by eyesight involves a complicated series of computations, all of which occur prior to the image and outside of it. McGinn uses the example of blindsight to illustrate this idea that consciousness has a hidden understructure. People who suffer from blindsight have suffered brain damage that deprives them of conscious access to their own vision. They will claim to be completely blind and they will sincerely believe themselves to be blind. Still, when asked to guess about an object held up in front of them, they will guess correctly more often than they possibly could if they were really only guessing. The hidden underside of conscious seeing is still present, even though it does not rise into consciousness.

If the mind is a product of the body, then it makes sense to conclude that consciousness has a hidden structure. Other biological products, such as blood, have a hidden structure that renders them different from their outward appearance. It is true that one can uncover the hidden structure of blood in its red and white blood cells, but blood is not explaining itself to itself.

The role of space in consciousness also supports the idea of cognitive closure. Space is basic to our awareness of the world. It may well be impossible to imagine clearly an event that has no spatial aspect. Still, human minds seem to perceive space and not to exist in space. People can think of things that are not immediately present. Minds can project sensation into spaces that do not exist, as happens when someone feels pain or itching in an amputated limb. Some of the products of the mind, such as numbers and mathematical operations, cannot be located clearly in space. McGinn suggests, in an intriguing speculation, that what one calls space is only a limited part of real space. Human brains exist in real space and contain perceived space as an object of awareness.

The concept of the self is fundamental to consciousness. An awareness of things is an awareness of things being in one's own consciousness. Still, the flow of blood and the electrochemical discharges in the brain give no hint of a unified personality. The self, like space, provides a structure for the way in which humans see the world, but it is not known where humans get this perspective on the surrounding world because it is prior to consciousness.

In an intriguing final section, McGinn argues that the difference between philosophy and science is that philosophy exists at the boundaries of cognitive closure. Philosophy asks questions that are difficult because of the nature of the questions, and not simply because humans currently lack the information to answer them. Those questions that people have reformulated so that they can be answered, such as the questions about the physical world that used to be called natural philosophy, move from philosophy to science. Thus, the peculiar value of philosophy may be that it marks out the limits of human abilities to think.

Professional philosophers may fault Colin McGinn for his inclusion of few footnotes and for his informal style. However, this book is not intended primarily for professional philosophers, who may find McGinn's mysterian perspective presented in greater technical detail in his other works. As an introduction to the philosophical problem of consciousness, this is a very appealing volume. McGinn provides clear explanations of the major positions on the mind-brain relationship. His criticisms of these positions do seem to owe a lot to other philosophers. The critique of dualism, for example, is virtually identical to that offered by philosopher Daniel C. Dennett. Much of McGinn's refutation of the computer model of the mind seems to rest on arguments and analogies found in the work of philosopher and linguist John R. Searle. It is unfortunate that McGinn refers to these two influential philosophers only in brief footnotes and does not acknowledge any intellectual debt to them. Still, the book is far from a mere popularization of standard views on the nature of the mind. The discussion of the hidden structure of consciousness provides an inventive response to materialism based on the biological nature of thought. McGinn's suggestion that real space may be quite different from the space that provides a framework for consciousness provides an intriguing defense for the concept of cognitive closure and a reminder of the limitations of human understanding.

There is something unsettling about a book that concludes that one cannot reach a conclusion. The idea of consciousness is so elusive, moreover, that even after reading McGinn's first chapter, in which he attempts to define consciousness, readers have only an impression of the subject rather than a precise description. If consciousness is the awareness that exists in common sense and if common sense can be wrong about something so fundamental as the nature of space, then how can humans know that consciousness is not simply a computational illusion, as Daniel C. Dennett has argued?

Despite his speculations about the true character of space, McGinn's physics often seems curiously old-fashioned. In discussing the relationship between mind and matter, he seems to assume that matter is the kind of solid stuff our senses detect. As matter is investigated in modern physics, though, it disintegrates into smaller and smaller particles arranged in what appears as emptiness. The mind-matter problem, then, may stem from an even more profound cognitive closure than McGinn recognizes. It is not simply our grasp of consciousness that is limited by the functional designs of thought, but our grasp of the nature of our world. The distinction between consciousness and matter could well be seen as a problem that human thought creates, rather than one that human thought perceives.

Colin McGinn has an appealing writing style and a talent for insightful analogies. He is clearly a science fiction fan, with a special fondness for television's several *Star Trek* series, and popular science fiction provides him with a rich source of illustrations for his ideas. There are occasional signs of sloppiness, as when McGinn refers to "David Hume, the seventeenth-century empiricist philosopher." Hume (1711-1776) was a man of the eighteenth century in time and in thought. Still, general readers interested in the mind-body problem will find an excellent starting point in *The Mysterious Flame*, and it will be useful to more specialized readers as a concise summary of Colin McGinn's version of the mysterian position.

Carl L. Bankston III

Sources for Further Study

The Economist 351 (May 1, 1999): 79.
The New York Times Book Review 104 (July 11, 1999): 13.
Publishers Weekly 246 (April 26, 1999): 71.

THE NAZI WAR ON CANCER

Author: Robert N. Proctor (1954-   )
Publisher: Princeton University Press (Princeton, New Jersey). Illustrated. 380 pp. $29.95
Type of work: History and medicine
Time: 1900-1945
Locale: Germany

A detailed history of the various public health campaigns in Nazi Germany, particularly the war against cancer—the attempt to reduce the use of tobacco, limit exposure to X rays, encourage the consumption of healthy foods, and regulate working conditions

Robert N. Proctor is professor of the history of science at Pennsylvania State University. He has written extensively about politics and medicine in his previous works, which include *Cancer Wars: How Politics Shapes What We Know and Don't Know About Cancer* (1995), *Racial Hygiene: Medicine Under the Nazis* (1988), and *Value-Free Science? Purity and Power in Modern Knowledge* (1991).

Proctor's *The Nazi War on Cancer* is an engrossing and relevant study of various aspects of medical research and public health as practiced under one of the world's most despicable regimes. In less than a decade and a half, Adolf Hitler and his Nazi government, in calculated fashion, murdered millions of men, women, and children, among them, Jews, Gypsies, homosexuals, and the disabled. Nazi Germany practiced racial hygiene, euthanasia, sterilization, horrendous medical "experiments," and implemented the "final solution." Germany between 1929 and 1945 was itself a cancer in a century of cancers, and cancer is what Proctor discusses in this controversial work, cancer both as a disease and as a metaphor for the ills—physical, moral, and intellectual—of modern society.

The author's aim is to discuss the positive medical accomplishments that occurred during the era in which Hitler and his party ruled Germany. Secondarily, he explores the connections between what can be considered progressive and enlightened approaches and responses to medical problems with the Nazi regime and its racial philosophy. Were the numerous public health efforts to limit smoking, encourage more healthful diets, and end pollution in the work environment largely divorced from the Nazi program and philosophy, or did its fascist ideology give support to those healthy endeavors? Proctor's study suggests that there were not only sadistic and monstrous Nazis committed to genocide and the final solution but also positive and creative medical and public health elements to be found in the Nazi state, paradoxically sometimes within the same person.

In the late nineteenth and early twentieth centuries, German science ranked among the world's best. Much of the leading medical and scientific research was done in Germany, written in German, and published first in German publications. Significant cancer research began in Germany as early as the 1830's, and cancer was recognized as a major disease in Germany in part because of its early and extensive industrialization. German research led the way; half of the Nobel Prize winners were Germans. World War I and Germany's defeat had an impact upon scientific research, but during the years of the democratic Weimar Germany of the 1920's, German scientific research remained in the vanguard of medical studies, including cancer. Thus the public health concerns of the Nazi government after it came to power in 1932 were not a departure, but instead built upon a long scientific and medicinal tradition. What does give pause and raise issues of the relationship between science and morality is how easily and readily many German doctors and researchers were willing to work within the parameters of the new fascist regime. Proctor points out that 60 percent of all German biologists and 80 percent of all German anthropology professors (most of whom were physicians) joined the Nazi Party.

Given the high rate of cancer in Germany, it was not surprising that prevention played a role in the war against the disease. Of course, prevention antedated the Nazis' accession to power, but under Hitler's regime, the authority of the state was harnessed to the battle. One leading figure was Erwin Liek, often called the "father of Nazi medicine." He never joined the party, but he praised Hitler and was anti-Semitic in his private correspondence. In the 1930's, he argued that cancer was a disease of civilization—the more civilized a society, the greater the incidence of cancer. He believed that cancer was largely the result of environmental factors and could be prevented through a change in lifestyle, particularly diet. Hitler was a vegetarian who neither smoked nor drank, as were a number of other leading Nazi figures, and the führer imposed his beliefs on those around him. Early detection was also a weapon in the anticancer war, and detection likewise had its origins before 1933, but under the Nazis there were increased endeavors encouraging women and others to consult their doctors as an act of prevention, and hundreds of thousands of women were medically examined during those years.

However, the Nazi commitment to prevention and detection was not for the benefit of the individual but for Germany as a whole. The preservation of a healthy and pure German race took priority over the needs of any single individual. Jewish doctors were fired from their research laboratories and university positions. Proctor estimates approximately one hundred Jewish cancer researchers were purged, an obvious loss in the battle against the disease. Racial purity had a higher priority than abstract science, and throughout the Nazi era, scientists and medical doctors joined the politicians in referring to Jews, Bolsheviks, and other undesirables as the tumors or cancers within German society. Some researchers claimed that cancer was a genetic disease and that some races were more subject to cancer than other races, a justification for sterilization of specific undesirable groups, as exemplified by the 1933 Law for the Protection of Hereditary Health, a sterilization law. Inasmuch as cancer was a disease of civilization, it could be dealt with by political means, including the accumulation of statistical information, the institution of mass screening programs, propaganda in newspapers and on the radio, and government coercion. *The Nazi War on Cancer* includes numerous illustrations of the propaganda used during the Nazi era: the antismoking campaign, the push for a better diet, the call for medical examinations, and the emphasis on public health issues generally.

One of the paradoxes of Nazi medicine was that it led to sterilization, inhuman medical experimentation, and the "final solution," but it also encouraged research into the toxic effects of carcinogens in alcohol, in tobacco, and in working conditions. Occupational research was concerned not only with cancer and other diseases in factories and elsewhere in the abstract, or as part of the campaign for racial purity, but also with the consequences disease would have had on its massive rearmament campaign; illnesses would have had a negative impact on the rate of weapons production, worker absenteeism, and productivity. However, much of the research and subsequent legislation, such as that to reduce hours, and protections for children and pregnant women, went into abeyance when World War II began in 1939 and were never applied to foreign workers, slave laborers, or concentration camp inmates. Also, with the coming of the war, protective standards even for racially approved Germans gave way to the war's exigencies, particularly once the course of battle turned against Germany.

As Proctor points out, Nazi medicine was not monolithic. Research and treatment under Nazi rule were often disputed by different scientists. Radium therapy was popular in Germany long before 1933, and the use of radium and radiation treatment was as controversial during Hitler's regime as it was in democratic countries. Studies made during the 1920's documented higher cancer rates among miners, and similar research was continued under the Nazis concerning uranium miners, but the solution in the face of the mounting evidence of radiation damage was to substitute foreign workers for Germans. In spite of the evidence, some Nazi-era doctors still recommended radiation therapy and criticized the research that suggested it was dangerous.

Various kinds of dust were believed to contribute to occupational cancer. In the 1930's, German researchers were aware of the apparent link between lung cancer and exposure to asbestos, long before asbestos was recognized as a health hazard in the United States, even though the findings of German doctors were available. One of the important points that Proctor makes throughout his study is the near-automatic rejection of any Nazi-era medical research, even when valid, an unfortunate if understandable reaction to the well-known record of Nazi atrocities. How could humane and progressive medical knowledge take place in such a depraved system?

The most significant campaign in the war against cancer was the campaign against tobacco. In the United States, the common claim is that nothing was known of the possible connections between tobacco and lung cancer until the 1950's. However, the link between tobacco and lung cancer was established in Nazi Germany. Here, too, the Nazi antitobacco campaign was part of the political climate that stressed racial purity, and valid medical research was put to the political use of supporting the Nazi "master race" philosophy. Antitobacco campaigns were not new in the 1930's; opposition to tobacco use went back centuries, often linked to morality (the use of tobacco and alcohol was often linked to immoral behavior) or the danger of fire. A connection between cancer of the lip or mouth and tobacco was claimed in the nineteenth century, but it was not until late in that century that massive numbers of cigarettes were being consumed. At the same time, incidences of lung cancer were increasing, but until the 1930's, there was little firm evidence linking cigarette use and lung cancer. Germany's leading antismoking advocate, Fritz Lickint, published a 1,100-page study in collaboration with the government's Reich Committee for the Struggle Against Addictive Drugs discussing the many cancers resulting from tobacco use. Franz H. Muller's medical dissertation of 1939 was the world's first controlled study of the connection between lung cancer and tobacco. Both these works remain seminal studies of the subject but again have been largely ignored by American and other researchers.

In 1941, Hitler denounced tobacco as one of humankind's most dangerous poisons, and the Nazis produced considerable antitobacco propaganda. Tobacco use was said to inhibit the physical fitness of soldiers as well as cause automobile accidents. Because Nazi Germany was dedicated to the propagation of a master race of pure Aryans and desired greater fertility among "true" Germans, the antitobacco campaign was particularly waged against women smokers, who, it was said, lost their beauty, had spontaneous abortions, and became sterile as a result of tobacco use. There was an awareness that nicotine was addictive, and there was research into the possibilities of low-nicotine or non-nicotine cigarettes. Laws were passed making smoking a crime in many government offices, workplaces, and elsewhere, and restrictions were placed upon tobacco advertising, similar to what would occur in the United States in the 1980's and 1990's. Jewish capitalists were accused of being supporters of the tobacco industry, thus undermining German racial hygiene. Smoking was also associated with jazz, blacks, Gypsies, and other "decadent" groups and, as Proctor argues, was part of the "fears that inspired the Nazi retreat into a paranoid, xenophobic fortress of purity, cleanliness, and muscular macho health fanaticism."

However, Nazi Germany's antitobacco campaign was largely a failure. Cigarette consumption increased throughout the years, perhaps as passive resistance to the regime's policies. In addition, under the pressure of the war, tobacco allowances were increased for soldiers and workers as an encouragement and perhaps as a consolation to them. Also, the increasingly financially strapped government needed the taxes generated by tobacco sales. Several German tobacco firms used advertising to tie their product to the regime—one briefly sold "Storm Cigarettes," an identification with the storm troopers—and another firm gave millions of reichsmarks to the government in order to do business. Ironically, perhaps as a reaction to the Nazi regime's fervent antitobacco campaign, Germans after the war smoked more than ever.

The Nazi War on Cancer is not only a fascinating story but also a valuable contribution to the history of medical science and public health policy. As Proctor states, "The Nazi war on cancer shows that what many of us would consider 'good' science can be pursued in the name of antidemocratic ideals," and not in spite of Nazism, but because of Nazism. The campaign against cancer was fought in the context of racial and societal purity and in perfecting Hitler's German Volk. Finally, although one would like to believe otherwise, good science is not automatically linked to good politics.

Eugene Larson

Sources for Further Study

Booklist 95 (April 1, 1999): 1371.
Library Journal 124 (April 15, 1999): 138.
National Review 51 (September 13, 1999): 66.
The New England Journal of Medicine 341 (July 29, 1999): 380.
The New Republic 220 (June 14, 1999): 35.
The New York Review of Books 46 (September 23, 1999): 14.
The New York Times Book Review 104 (May 23, 1999): 21.

A NECESSARY EVIL
A History of American Distrust in Government

Author: Garry Wills (1934-)
Publisher: Simon & Schuster (New York). 365 pp. $25.00
Type of work: Philosophy and current affairs
Time: The course of American history up to 1999
Locale: The United States

A Pulitzer Prize-winning author examines antigovernment sentiment throughout American history and exposes the false assumptions of contemporary viewpoints based on radical distrust of government

In *A Necessary Evil*, Garry Wills does his best to debunk popular myths, slogans, and ideologies undermining the public's trust in American government. In doing so, he takes on revered articles of faith held by the Left as well as the Right, contemporary "liberals" as well as "conservatives." He also takes issue with prominent figures in American letters and various political icons, from some of the Founding Fathers down to the late twentieth century. The result is a provocative, well-argued book which adds significantly to themes developed in Wills's twenty-one previous books, particularly *The Inventing of America* (1978), *Explaining America: The Federalist* (1980), and *Lincoln at Gettysburg* (1992), the last of which earned for Wills a Pulitzer Prize.

The structure of *A Necessary Evil* is straightforward. Wills starts by debunking two "revolutionary myths." He points out that the American Revolution was not won by mythical Minutemen or a well-trained militia, but rather by George Washington's success in professionalizing the Continental Army. Wills goes on to discuss the myth of term limits, which played a prominent role in the Republican Party's 1994 Contract with America. While some of the Founders fiddled with the rhetoric of term limits, they did not seriously consider imposing them constitutionally. This leads Wills to conclude that the Founders, on at least some level, appreciated political as well as military professionalism, and that they would not be startled or dismayed by the existence in American politics of so-called career politicians.

Wills then moves on to discuss six "constitutional myths." First, refuting believers in the myth of states' rights, he argues that the Founders specifically rejected any notion of joint sovereignty and clearly established the constitutional supremacy of the federal government. Second, he argues against the myth that the federal government was meant to be inefficient in order to lessen its potential for tyranny. The Founders, according to Wills, wished to establish a federal government that would be capable of pursuing the public good efficiently. Third, he argues against the myth that the Constitution's separation of powers establishes three coequal branches designed to weaken the overall power of the federal government. Wills argues that what was intended was for the legislative branch to be, at the very least, a clear first among equals, and that the object was to impose limited safeguards specifically because what was envisioned was vigorous (rather than weak) legislative government. Fourth, Wills argues against the myth which sees the multiplicity of "factions" of which James Madison writes in *The Federalist No. 10* as an attempt forever to cripple the power of the majority and, therefore, of the federal government. Wills argues that the role of factions was not to substitute for the public good but rather to help the majority to find more ably a lasting consensus through which the public good could be promoted actively. Fifth, Wills offers a brief argument that Madison's real motives in adding a Bill of Rights to the U.S. Constitution had little to do with seriously diminishing federal power and much more, ultimately, to do with limiting the power of states over individuals. Finally, Wills argues that the Constitution clearly allows and even foresees the need for a standing army while, in the Second Amendment, providing only a highly qualified right to bear arms and, correspondingly, a severely limited reliance on militia for national defense and/or the defense of individual liberties.

Wills is not arguing that these mistaken myths have no roots at all in the American founding. Instead, he argues that they represent misunderstandings of the principles of government which triumphed at the time of the founding and which are necessary for the country's political system to fulfill properly the needs of the American people. Throughout American history, various critics and gurus have rejected the actual principles and assumptions of American government, instead promoting antigovernment myths as a somehow truer Americanism. For most of the remainder of the book, Wills categorizes and illustrates the forms in which these antigovernment myths have been forwarded during the founding and throughout American history down to the present. More specifically, he discusses "nullifiers," "seceders," "insurrectionists," "vigilantes," "withdrawers," and "disobeyers." By nullifiers, Wills means those theorists such as John Calhoun who thought that national laws could be vetoed by the states (Madison and Thomas Jefferson, on rare occasions, also sounded the cry of nullification). Seceders refers mostly (but not exclusively) to the southern states during the events which led to the Civil War. Among the insurrectionists are figures as disparate as Daniel Shays, John Brown, the "Weathermen," and Oklahoma City bomber Timothy McVeigh. Numbered among the vigilantes are the Ku Klux Klan, some "Red baiters," and abortion clinic bombers. Withdrawers include Henry David Thoreau, Henry Adams, H. L. Mencken, hippies, and David Koresh's Branch Davidians. Disobeyers include Students for a Democratic Society and Martin Luther King, Jr., though Wills indicates that King's disobedience was indeed civil and therefore partly affirmative of law and government.

Wills closes the book with two brief chapters. The first argues that government, when properly constituted and kept within the narrow bounds of its special competencies, is a useful tool and should be understood as "a necessary good." The closing chapter admits, on the other hand, that government power may also be abused, so that the wrong kind of government should, in fact, be feared.

Though he wades through history displaying broad knowledge of events and ideas, Wills's critique is anything but academic. It is aimed squarely at such contemporary right-wing targets as the National Rifle Association, the militia movement, and even the Contract with America. On the other hand, the angry street movements which emerged from the Left during the late 1960's, as well as the phenomenon of "dropping out" ("yippyism" as well as "hippyism") are also subjected to thoroughgoing criticism in the light of what American politics and government are supposed to be about.

Yet, *A Necessary Evil* presents much more than a critique. In tandem with Wills's previous work, it presents a well-developed political philosophy of its own, one that confronts not only the foibles of contemporary left-wing and right-wing ideologues but also the political apathy and cynicism that these ideologues have wrought. According to Wills's political philosophy, it is a mistake to have blind faith in government, but it is also a mistake to lose faith entirely in this useful and indeed indispensable mechanism. If Americans understand government and politics as necessary goods, they will be more attuned to the things that go right in their political system, though such achievements may not make it onto the nightly news. On the other hand, they may also demand more from politicians, holding them to higher professional standards. In the past, Wills has referred to himself as a "conservative." This designation for his political philosophy is as accurate as any other label one might apply, as long as Wills is not thoughtlessly tossed in with any of the dozen varieties of conservatism so often bandied about in American political campaigns or by right-wing think tanks. In the end, Wills's thought is simply too fresh and original to fit easily into the usual categories.

A Necessary Evil is not without its flaws. Wills covers a very broad range of thinkers, ideas, and movements. While he is an extraordinarily well informed generalist, he is not a trained specialist in many of the areas he is covering. As such, it is likely that scholars will find any number of points on which they might quibble or even offer more serious criticism. For example, Wills twice quotes Thoreau to the effect that, since the government that governs least governs best, the best government of which one can conceive governs not at all. It is important to note, however, lest one think of Thoreau as an anarchist, that Thoreau immediately follows by saying that, when people are ready for it, they shall indeed have government that governs not at all. This qualifier makes it clear that there is more to Thoreau's idea than a mere repudiation of government. Rather, he has a sense of history and human development which informs and tempers his antigovernment sentiments.

The example of Thoreau brings up another shortcoming in Wills's book: its failure to provide in-depth treatment of a theme seen in political philosophy since its early formulation among the ancient Greeks. For Plato as well as his student Aristotle, there is inherent tension between universal and conventional values (or, correspondingly, philosophical and citizenly, "higher" and human values). It is this tension which partly informs Thoreau's thought and which later becomes the basis for the law-affirming civil disobedience of King. Indeed, this tension is central to the enterprise of democracy in a nation of self-proclaimed individualists such as in the United States. Most Americans believe (to some degree, at least) that they must devise their own values rather than merely conform to secular authority, even if it be the authority of the majority. At the same time, Americans can be highly conformist in deciding what is "un-American" or simply "uncool." In short, Americans seem to want to be both philosophers and citizens. The problem is that, all too often, they fail to be either, settling instead into the more comfortable (though sometimes frenzied) role of consumer. This theme in political philosophy (as well as its application to the United States), seems to be closely related to Wills's inquiry. It deserves his explicit attention.

Finally, Wills lumps together so many kinds of antigovernment sentiment and movements that his categorization sometimes seems strained. After all, 1960's hippies and 1990's survivalists may both be dropping out of mainstream politics, but the essential values (and political philosophies) of these groups are so different as to make their inclusion in the same broad phenomenon perhaps more misleading than it is enlightening.

None of these criticisms, however, mars the overall effect, or the importance, of *A Necessary Evil.* Wills has identified a meaningful stream of thought and action in American history, one which is alive and well as he writes and which has subversive effects on American politics and government. The implication is quite straightforward: If Americans expect their politics to be corrupt and even go so far as to fear the effects of efficient government, then American government will, in fact, be corrupt and inefficient. Moreover, Americans will be satisfied with cloying, mealy-mouthed politicians and be unwilling to take the measures necessary to cut their way through image politics. In the end, seeing government as a necessary evil becomes a self-fulfilling prophecy, and American politics, if not quite evil, will not even aspire to provide the "necessary good" that citizens, as what Aristotle called "political animals," require from it. As such, Wills's book is aimed at changing not only people's thoughts but also their deeds. It seeks to make dominant in the United States a consciousness of government that will persuade Americans to use the tool of politics proactively and more wisely so that the country's experiment in self-government might ultimately be called a success.

Ira Smolensky

Sources for Further Study

Booklist 95 (August, 1999): 1984.
Commonweal 126 (October 22, 1999): 14.
Library Journal 124 (September 1, 1999): 218.
The New Republic 220 (November 1, 1999): 37.
The New York Times Book Review 104 (October 31, 1999): 14.
Publishers Weekly 246 (August 2, 1999): 59.
The Wall Street Journal, October 26, 1999, p. A24.
Washington Monthly 31 (October, 1999): 50.

THE NEW NEW THING
A Silicon Valley Story

Author: Michael Lewis (1960-)
Publisher: W. W. Norton (New York). 269 pp. $25.95
Type of work: Biography, economics, and technology
Time: The 1990's
Locale: California's Silicon Valley; Plainview, Texas; Amsterdam; and London

In his portrait of entrepreneur Jim Clark, Lewis exceeds the scope of most biographers, providing essentially a pocket history of how the world has moved from an industrial to a technologically based information economy

Principal personages:
JAMES "JIM" CLARK, the founder of Silicon Graphics, Netscape, and Healtheon
MICHAEL LEWIS, his biographer
WOLTER HUISMAN, the builder of Clark's schooner, the *Hyperion*
ALLAN PRIOR, the captain of the *Hyperion*
GLENN MUELLER, a venture capitalist
ED MCCRACKEN, the president and CEO of Silicon Graphics
D'ANNE SCHJERNING, Clark's secretary
HAZEL MCCLURE, Clark's mother

Some reviewers have criticized Michael Lewis for focusing his biography of Jim Clark, founder of Silicon Graphics (SGI) and Netscape, on Clark's building of the world's largest schooner, the *Hyperion*, and on its transatlantic crossing virtually without human intervention. Lewis, toward the middle of this exciting and informative book, justifies his focus by quoting Clark, who said, "There is nothing more satisfying to me than to create a complete self-contained world when a computer is controlling it." Doing this has been the focus of much of Clark's work.

The conception and construction of the *Hyperion* in the Amsterdam shipyard of Wolter Huisman have had far-reaching implications for the direction Clark's creative life has taken. His conception of Healtheon, his most recent major project, views the entire health delivery industry as a self-contained world that can be computer controlled. He also conceives of constructing houses—smaller, self-contained worlds—that will be computer controlled, houses in which routine functions are programmed and executed by smart machines.

Clark's career provides the kind of heterodox adventure story that makes for exciting reading. Because Clark lives barely in the present, always reaching impatiently toward a future that darts about furtively in his highly charged imagination, Lewis's job in writing about him was both challenging and complicated. Lewis says of his subject, "As a practical matter, Clark had no past, only a future." When Lewis tried to talk with him about his past, Clark's attention wandered. When he got him into a conversation about the future, about what was to happen next, however, Clark surged with vitality, sprang to life with ideas.

Clark's most salient personal characteristic is impatience. A visionary who dreams up huge schemes, he has little interest in the details of carrying them out. He is resolutely uninterested in looking back upon the past and is totally bored with talking about it. His chief motive in life is to create, but once he has formulated the idea of something, the logistics of keeping it going bore him to the point that he begins to withdraw from it.

In the case of SGI, he believed sincerely that the corporation, to remain healthy, had to cannibalize itself. He argued that for a technology company to remain successful, it had continually to destroy itself, thereby making room for new ideas and applications, much as a forest that is leveled by a huge fire is reborn stronger in the years that follow the conflagration. He is convinced that if a corporation does not find the means of destroying itself and emerging from its ashes, its competitors will do the job for it.

In this context, Clark points out the need for technology to become increasingly democratized. This means providing cheaper and less intimidating technological implements that the public at large will be drawn to purchase and use on a daily basis. The early computers of the 1960's were not conceived of as implements that people would use in their homes, and at that time, few people could envision any practical advantages to having a personal computer. Lewis's book is particularly strong in chronicling the dizzying growth of the computer industry, especially the personal computer segment, during the late 1980's and the 1990's.

Clark, while he was striving to make computers simple and more accessible to ordinary people, was also creating incredibly complicated computer programs involved with SGI's entry into the interactive television (ITV) experiment on which it was collaborating with Time Warner Cable, which sought to bring ITV into thousands of homes in Orlando, Florida. The lines of computer code required to complete this experiment exceeded the lines of computer code that it took to put a human on the moon at the end of the 1960's.

Lewis's decision to make the *Hyperion* a major focus of this biography is significant because the *Hyperion*, with its main sail of 5,600 square feet, is like a schooner of old, but it is the largest schooner built up to the time of its launching. It sails resolutely into a new world in which computers prove themselves capable of conveying such a ship across the Atlantic without human intervention. People reading about this voyage might think that they are reading a work of science fiction. Lewis, however, is not speculating on something that exists only in some Orwellian imagination but is reporting, rather, on an actual voyage during which he was a passenger and participant.

In essence, Lewis suggests the progression of the United States economy from an agricultural economy to an industrial one, and now, finally, to an information economy based upon complex technologies that can be fueled only by the work of well-trained engineers. He cites Thorstein Veblen (1857-1929), a Stanford economist until he was dismissed for bedding too many of his colleagues' wives, who coined such phrases as "the leisure class" and "conspicuous consumption."

In 1921, Veblen quite presciently predicted that in time engineers would rule the economy of the United States, arguing that the American economy is based upon technology and that engineers are the only people who understand technology sufficiently to advance it and use it productively. In Veblen's scheme of things, out of which grew the New Growth Theory of economics, financiers and titans of industry, who scaled the heights during the Industrial Revolution, would finally serve the real masters, engineers.

Although Clark cooperated with Lewis as he gathered information for this biography, he was not forthcoming with much information about his early life, not because he wished to obscure anything but because looking back does not interest him. He reminds one of Henry Ford, who proclaimed that all history is bunk.

The information Lewis unearthed about Clark comes largely from interviews with people who had known him through the years, but, more significantly, from his discovery in a closet in the guest bedroom in Clark's Atherton, California, home, of a stash of boxes containing thousands of documents—newspaper clippings, magazine articles, correspondence—that provide insights into Clark's past.

D'Anne Schjerning, Clark's secretary through his ascent into the pantheon of Silicon Valley computer billionaires, collected these documents through the years and kept them in the offices of SGI until the company needed the space in which she had stored them. Clark took them home and, fortunately, kept them safe in the closet where Lewis stumbled upon them and, with Clark's consent, opened the boxes and reviewed the enormous collection of documents they contained.

Clark is a contemporary Horatio Alger. Born in Plainview, Texas, into a desperately poor family whose alcoholic father abused the mother, Hazel McClure, and finally abandoned the family, Clark had a difficult childhood. He is not remembered as having shown any great potential. Were he currently a secondary school student, he would probably be diagnosed as suffering from Attention Deficit Disorder (ADD). An indifferent high school student who caused many discipline problems, he was expelled in his junior year.

He joined the United States Navy at seventeen and was soon put into a class of recruits who were high school dropouts. The Navy was training them in a program that would prepare them to earn high school equivalency certificates. When Clark was forced to take objective multiple-choice tests, to which he had never before been subjected, he found justification for selecting more than one of the four or five choices given for each item as correct. In some cases, he circled all of the choices, which thwarted the computer that graded the tests and led his Navy superiors to accuse him of dishonesty and to drop him from the program. Assigned to sea duty for the next nine months, he was given the most onerous shipboard jobs.

Finally, he began to study again and showed such a remarkable aptitude for mathematics that he was soon assigned to instructing new recruits in algebra. In time he entered Tulane University and continued to Louisiana State University, where he received a master's degree in physics, after which he entered the University of Utah for graduate work. Twelve years after his expulsion from high school, he received a doctorate in computer science from the University of Utah.

After receiving that degree, he taught at the University of California at Santa Cruz for four years before moving to Stanford University, which hired him to teach in its computer science program. Stanford's most promising graduate students gravitated to him. Within three years, he left Stanford to establish his own company, which grew into Silicon Graphics. He took with him the most brilliant and creative of his graduate students, thereby forming the most formidable pool of computer talent yet assembled in the United States.

Lewis is particularly effective in showing how Clark, the idea man, scorned the day-to-day details of running a multimillion dollar corporation. When SGI needed venture capital to support its operation, Glenn Mueller, a venture capitalist associated with the Mayfield Fund, was brought in to raise the required $800,000. When more money was needed, Mueller found it, but each time increasing quantities of SGI's stock and options fell into the hands of Mueller and the financiers he represented.

Mueller forced Vern Anderson, SGI's Chief Executive Officer (CEO), to resign as CEO, bringing in Ed McCracken, a successful vice president of Hewlett Packard, to replace him. Clark became chairman of the board of SGI, but as such had little power. As he and McCracken, a typical organization man whose eye was strictly on the bottom line, clashed, usually quite openly, Clark became virtually powerless within the corporation. McCracken increased the sales staff, and SGI's profits soared, but unlike Clark, McCracken was not looking ahead to the future in a rapidly developing industry that was creating its unique paradigms.

The public at large did not realize the hollowness of Clark's lofty title as chairman of the board, and Clark exploited his position by making speeches and expounding ideas quite counter to McCracken's to influential computer groups throughout the country, much to McCracken's displeasure. In essence, Clark was in a life-and-death struggle with McCracken, but seen in the light of what Lewis has revealed about Thorstein Veblen's view of the American economy, the struggle is not merely one between two men; rather it is the struggle of two opposing universes, one—McCracken's—clinging to the past and trying to preserve an outdated paradigm, the other—Clark's—embracing the future and seeking to promote a brave new world in which smart machines wield control.

Clark had already foregone a large part of his financial stake in SGI by the time McCracken took over, but in time McCracken managed to keep Clark, the motive force behind the entire organization, from receiving the stock options that every other officer in the company received. By this time, Clark was a millionaire, but it was not until after he left SGI to form a new company, which grew into Netscape, that he achieved billionaire status. In making his break with SGI, Lewis shows, Clark demonstrated one of the most salient aspects of his personal philosophy: The best way to get revenge is to succeed extravagantly.

R. Baird Shuman

Sources for Further Study

Booklist 96 (October 1, 1999): 307.
Business Week, November 8, 1999, p. 15.
The New York Times Book Review 104 (October 31, 1999): 10.
Newsweek 132 (October 25, 1999): 94.
Publishers Weekly 246 (September 27, 1999): 81.
Time 154 (October 25, 1999): 132.
The Wall Street Journal, October 22, 1999, p. W8.

NO OTHER BOOK

Selected Essays

Author: Randall Jarrell (1914-1965)
Edited, with an introduction, by Brad Leithauser
Publisher: HarperCollins (New York). 376 pp. $27.50
Type of work: Essays

These twenty-five essays, selected by poet-critic Brad Leithauser from Jarrell's four previous collections (1940-1969), demonstrate anew that in the sixty years since the earliest entry and the thirty-five since the most recent, none has aged in its freshness and luminosity

Elizabeth Bishop (1911-1979) once said of Randall Jarrell: "He always seemed more alive than other people, as if constantly tuned up to the concert pitch that most people, including [other] poets, can maintain only for short and fortunate stretches." These words, as quoted by Brad Leithauser in his necessary introduction to *No Other Book*, perfectly describe most of the essays in this volume. Within the scope of the critical essay, it is difficult to imagine anything produced since its original appearance that is more compelling on Walt Whitman (1819-1892), Robert Frost (1864-1973), Wallace Stevens (1879-1955), or Rudyard Kipling (1865-1936). *No Other Book* contains nine single-poet studies, those on W. H. Auden (1907-1973), William Carlos Williams (1883-1963), Marianne Moore (1887-1972), A. E. Housman (1859-1936), and Robert Graves (1895-1985) being the others. The longest essay that Jarrell ever wrote—in its original setting, a forty-eight-page paean to Christina Stead's (1902-1983) *The Man Who Loved Children*, published in 1965, the year of Jarrell's death—anchors the collection. Eleven commentaries on the state of American culture, generally, and that of poetry and poetry criticism, specifically, dazzle still. "A Jarrell Gallery" is the editor's compromise, a gathering of favorite excerpts from essays that could not be—or did not need to be—included wholly. Leithauser's roundup includes Emily Dickinson (1830-1886), André Malraux (1901-1976), John Crowe Ransom (1888-1974), Franz Kafka (1883-1924), Walter de la Mare (1873-1956), E. E. Cummings (1894-1962), Allen Tate (1899-1979), Jose Garcia Villa (b. 1914), Stephen Spender (1909-1995), Ezra Pound (1885-1972), and Bishop.

In "Contemporary Poetry Criticism," Jarrell rates his competition—figures such as R. P. Blackmur (1904-1965), Cleanth Brooks (b. 1906), William Empson (1906-1984), and Robert Penn Warren (1905-1989)—as "about as good as we can find—and better than we deserve." All wrote in the time's dominant mode of judgmental scrutiny which, following the lead of T. S. Eliot (1888-1965), would not allow a poem to be analyzed in the light of either biography or psychology.

Jarrell could practice *explication du texte* with the best of the new critics, as he does in analyzing galvanically every word of just eight lines of a Housman poem, but can also illumine as complex an aesthetic theory as Robert Graves's White Goddess by convincingly demonstrating that the theory was inevitable, given the poet's life. After more than a half century, the editor deems Jarrell the only critic among his contemporaries who still connects with the reader immediately, emotionally.

Jarrell can be said to have confronted most of the problems serious students of modern poetry encounter in its major practitioners and, by working his way, poem by poem, through everything, has tried to reconcile their preeminence in his own day and beyond.

What is there to reconcile about the icons assembled here? In chronological order, these are Jarrell's disclaimers. On Whitman: " . . . just as few poets have ever written better, few have ever written worse. . . . only a man with the most extraordinary feel for language, or none whatsoever, could have cooked up Whitman's worst messes." On Kipling: "Not so much his poems, whose sheer resonance speaks to inner domains that poets rarely address seriously, as his tales," in Jarrell's view, exhibit, "a lack of dispassionate moral understanding . . . [and are the writings] of someone who has to prove that God is not responsible for part of the world, and that the Devil is." On Frost: There is what Jarrell calls a "Yankee Editorialist side . . . [that] gets in the way of *everything*—of us, of the real Frost, of the real poems and their real subject matter." On Stevens: "He has the habit, unfortunate for a poet, of philosophizing. He thinks of images as emblems of truisms or as abstractions merely to be contemplated. [T]he last demand that we should make of philosophy (that it be interesting) is the first we make of a poem. . . . Stevens has every gift but the dramatic." On Auden: A poet in whom stunning originality of language turned into predictable rhetorical strategies, "Auden has been successful in making his poetry more accessible, but the success has been entirely too expensive," writes Jarrell about the only one of his heroes born, like himself, in the twentieth century.

Shortly after he abandoned the editorial chair of *The New Yorker* book section in 1943—a post taken over for the next thirty years by Edmund Wilson—Clifton Fadiman observed ruefully that, while he had produced tons of literary journalism and reviews, he had never written a line of literary criticism. Reading and rereading a scholar-critic like Jarrell affirms the distinction. Reviewers damn with faint praise or praise with faint damning or apply a combination; they do anything to appear to be fair in disapproval, objective in approval. Jarrell never does an overt balancing act. As Leithauser notes, "he brought sincerity to the compliments he injected into an otherwise negative review . . . and [could] reconcile, in contiguous paragraphs, a pair of [opposed] judgments." Jarrell's extraordinary capability is to show why one great poem almost worked or why another almost did not. When he reaches the end of an assessment on a positive note, the reader knows that Jarrell has played every note on his scale.

Thus, for him, Whitman's faults "*do not matter*. . . . one responds to him, willingly or unwillingly, almost as one does to the world, that world which makes the hairs of one's flesh stand up, which seems both evil beyond any rejection and wonderful beyond any acceptance." Thus Kipling, "neither a Chekhov nor a Shakespeare . . . is far closer to both than to the clothing-store-dummy-with-the-solar-topee we have agreed to call Kipling." Thus, "When you know Frost's poems you know surprisingly well how the world seemed to one man, and what it was to seem that way [and know] . . . that a man can still include, connect, and make humanly understandable or humanly ununderstandable *so much*." Thus, "when you have finished reading Stevens's best poems you remember once more that man is not only the jest and riddle of the world, but the glory."

Robert Lowell, writing a tribute to his friend after his mysterious death, identified eulogy as "the glory of Randall's criticism" but also called attention to Jarrell's ability, rare in a critic, to "chip away at his own misconceptions." Having written of Robert Graves, "he is not a good poet," and "even his best poems just miss," Jarrell can subsequently call Graves "a fine poet . . . an extraordinary one." Leithauser attributes such about-faces not to "some shift in the poet's development but to a shift in his own judgment; he'd learned to read Graves better."

There are two dangers in his unpredictability—one for the poets he critiques, an uncertainty of alliance, and one for Jarrell himself, a defect of his virtues, a sort of casuistry and oversubtlety that could be a disguise for evasion. Leithauser exemplifies the first in Jarrell's ambivalence about Moore's poetry. He was her champion until he found in her antiwar poem "In Distrust of Merits" a woeful "lack of facts, or imagination, or *something*." Cummings's best poems are a joy to the reader of modern poetry, especially the unwilling reader, "but all that is heartbreaking in the world, the pity and helplessness and love that were called once, . . . the heart of heartlessness—these hardly exist for him."

Occasionally in the essays in the back of the book, which are not heavily devoted to poets and poems—the seven pieces that Leithauser calls "The Rest of It"—Jarrell writes dismissively of the "common reader." He regrets that these readers differ from Virginia Woolf's vision, which is of an audience that is receptive to ideas, sensitive to beauty of expression, capable of the concentration good books require. In contrast, America's common readers are uncultivated, addicts of popular culture, who draw their reading preferences from best-seller lists. "It is perpetually tempting to the critic to make his style and method so imposing to everyone that nobody will notice or care when he is wrong," Jarrell writes in "The Age of Criticism" (1952), one of his most famous essays. These critics, Jarrell goes on to say, are impostors who hide behind not only inhospitable styles and methods but "institutional magnificence" that veils from the reader the naked human beings who do the judging. To be of any use, the critic must stick his neck out, take a chance of making a fool of himself.

There is another risk that Randall Jarrell, perhaps the best critic of poetry of his day, takes. By the very asperity of his criticism, he can decline into a loose noblesse-oblige and lose both his way and his readers. At one point, he mercilessly flails Stephen Spender's poem beginning "I think continually of those who were truly great," the kind of poem many readers commit to memory. In the three sentences excerpted for "A Jarrell Gallery," only cruel overkill ("That a poem beginning . . . should ever have been greeted with anything but helpless embarrassment makes me ashamed of the planet upon which I dwell.") makes print. This sort of badinage can numb the disinterested reader, who does not care to mix partisanship with literature. Randall

Jarrell should never risk losing this browser in the back stalls, the literate uncommon "common reader."

Richard Hauer Costa

Sources for Further Study

Booklist 95 (June 1, 1999): 1771.
The New York Times Book Review 104 (August 1, 1999): 4.
Publishers Weekly 246 (May 31, 1999): 75.
Time 154 (August 9, 1999): 73.

NOT FOR OURSELVES ALONE
The Story of Elizabeth Cady Stanton and Susan B. Anthony

Authors: Geoffrey C. Ward (1940-) and Ken Burns (1953-)
Publisher: Alfred A. Knopf (New York). 240 pp. Illustrated. $35.00
Type of work: History, biography, and women's issues
Time: 1815-1920
Locale: Mainly New York and the eastern United States, but also Kansas and the West

The companion volume to the recent television documentary on the half-century friendship and partnership of the two women who founded and organized the United States' women's movement

Principal personages:
ELIZABETH CADY STANTON (1815-1902), founder and theorist of the women's movement
SUSAN B. ANTHONY (1820-1906), fifty-year organizer of and activist in women's rights

Not for Ourselves Alone: The Story of Elizabeth Cady Stanton and Susan B. Anthony is a lavishly illustrated accompaniment to the film by the United States' premiere documentary filmmaker Ken Burns. Geoffrey Ward, author and screenwriter, has worked previously with Burns and the team at Florentine Films on the miniseries *The Civil War* and *Baseball*. It has been said that more Americans get their history from Ken Burns than from any other source, and that forty million Americans have watched *The Civil War*. If that is so, then readers should be glad about the latest collaboration on Elizabeth Cady Stanton and Susan B. Anthony, the most important (and, say the filmmakers, least-known) women of the nineteenth century. The project was affectionately known to the production team as "The Babes" because of an editorial cartoon picturing "Ken Burns' TO DO list." The first thing on the list was "WAR," which was checked off. The second thing on the list was "SPORTS," and it was checked off. The third thing on the list was "BABES," which was not checked off. Saying that Stanton and Anthony are unknown, however, denigrates the restoration work of women's studies scholars over the past quarter century. Burns and company are admitting that they were not familiar with Stanton and Anthony, whereas most colleges and universities now include women's studies and women's history in the curriculum.

As the guest historians make clear in both book and film, the process of making the United States a more democratic institution—"the largest social transformation in American history"—really began with Stanton and Anthony's strategies in the nineteenth century. Jeffersonian democracy was only for white males while the vaunted Jacksonian period of the 1830's did nothing for women or African American slaves. All the twentieth century movements for expanding the electorate (the Civil Rights movement, the gay rights and Native American movements) use the techniques and arguments first pioneered by Stanton and Anthony: petition drives, grassroots organizing, lecture tours, national conventions, direct action, and arguments based on the common humanity of all citizens.

These two women formed a partnership and intense friendship based on their mutual belief in women's rights, but they were dissimilar in many ways. Their childhoods could not have been more different. Stanton's wealthy lawyer-father, after the death of his sole surviving son, kept saying to Elizabeth throughout her childhood and brilliant school days, "I wish you had been a boy." Stanton soon learned what she could not do as a female of middle-class status: She could not get a college education, become a lawyer, vote, control her own money, sue for divorce, have custody of her children; if married she could not earn her own living, sue or be sued, and she was not to speak in public.

Anthony, on the other hand, grew up in a rural Quaker family where the Quaker meeting was so strict that when her father married "out of Meeting" (her mother was a Baptist), he had to appear before the elders for chastisement and sentencing. Still, Daniel Anthony was adamant about equality for daughters and sons, so when the elementary teacher refused to teach Susan long division because she was a girl, he began his own home school for his children and the young women who worked in the textile mills.

Stanton's awakening to the necessity of a women's movement came at the 1840 London World's Anti-Slavery Convention where she accompanied her new husband Henry, an abolitionist organizer, on their wedding trip. The female American delegates, duly elected by their antislavery societies in the United States (some female-only groups and some mixed groups), were denied credentials on the grounds of their sex: It was not ladylike for women to participate in such public groups. The debate on whether to seat the women took up several days at the beginning of the convention, and although well-known male abolitionists like William Lloyd Garrison supported the women, they were forced to sit upstairs behind a curtain and were not allowed to speak. Stanton met Lucretia Mott, a well-known Quaker preacher, at the convention, and together they vowed to have a meeting about women's rights on their return.

Holding that meeting took eight years, during which Stanton was busy as a housewife and mother. In 1848, Mott traveled to upstate New York from Philadelphia, and Stanton was invited to tea in Waterloo with five other women. There they determined to hold a meeting on women's rights five days hence at the Wesleyan Chapel in Seneca Falls, Stanton's hometown. Stanton wrote most of the document presented at the meeting, the "Declaration of Sentiments," modeled on the Declaration of Independence but beginning, "We hold these truths to be self-evident, that all men *and women* are created equal." The grievances listed are laid not at the feet of King George, but at the feet of man, all men. The resolutions, which called for equal access to the professions, no sexual double-standard, equal education, consciousness-raising, and, finally, the vote, were far-reaching and radical—in keeping with the 1848 revolutions being played out all over Europe that summer. The demand for female suffrage was the only resolution that failed to pass unanimously by the more than three hundred women and men in attendance; it passed with a majority after abolitionist Frederick Douglass spoke in favor. Of course, no slave and many men could not vote in 1848, so the call by women was indeed radical. It is not true that no women anywhere had the vote as both the book and film claim: women of the six nations of the Iroquois confederacy (Haudenosaunee) living in that area of New York had been participating in governance since long before contact with Europeans in the seventeenth century.

Anthony's transformation to feminism took a different path. She began teaching school and soon learned that she was paid about half of what male teachers made. Her reform efforts first turned to the temperance movement but that movement also discriminated against women organizers. As soon as she met Stanton three years after the historic Seneca Falls convention, they began their partnership to work on women's rights. Anthony was a born organizer and politician; Stanton was a philosopher and a wonder with words. So Stanton wrote the speeches and Anthony gave them—everywhere. Anthony traveled to every county in New York as they worked on changing the laws which discriminated against married women.

After the passage of the Fourteenth and Fifteenth Amendments giving rights to the freed male slaves (and putting the word "male" into the Constitution for the first time), Stanton and Anthony were disillusioned that women, who had helped so much during the Civil War, were not also to be enfranchised. Anthony proposed a brilliant strategy: Women were citizens and therefore should already have the right to vote. So in 1872, Anthony and women in several states registered and voted; startled registrars did not know what to do. Only later was Anthony arrested for illegally voting. Preparing for her trial, she spoke in every town in that region of New York, but the trial was fixed, the judge having written his opinion before witnesses were called. Anthony refused to pay her fine of one hundred dollars, saying, "Resistance to tyranny is obedience to God." Virginia Minor from St. Louis took her case (*Minor v. Happersett*) all the way to the Supreme Court, which found that women were indeed citizens, but that did not give them the right to vote. The women's movement knew then that they must work for an amendment to the Constitution.

In the 1880's Stanton and Anthony, working with compatriot Matilda Joslyn Gage, wrote and published the three-volume *History of Woman Suffrage*. These huge volumes are compendiums of all the speeches, newspaper articles, reports of conventions, and state campaigns for women's rights over a period of fifty years: a wonderful source of information. Again, Stanton wrote the bulk of the copy while Anthony did more of the practical work of finding a publisher and getting subscriptions. As always, Stanton hated the practical side of politics and convention-going, doing her best work on the lecture circuit while Anthony was a great negotiator and politician. The movement had split after the Civil War over the issue of suffrage for "the Negro [man]," and Anthony was instrumental in bringing the two groups back together, united in their single-minded emphasis on the vote.

Stanton, always the more radical of the two, was not ready to cast aside all the other issues for women. In particular, she wanted to focus on the Judeo-Christian religion as the premiere cause of women's oppression. Her last great project was a rewriting of key passages in the Bible using Biblical exegesis to give a feminist reinterpretation. *The Woman's Bible*, published when Stanton was over eighty years old, caused a huge furor in the movement and around the country. In 1896, the National American

Woman's Suffrage Association voted, over Susan B. Anthony's objections, to censure Stanton and disassociate themselves from her work. Stanton was hurt, but in truth the movement had become more conservative, and Anthony made allies wherever she could, even southern whites who refused to let African American women be equal members of the movement.

Stanton died first, and Anthony carried on for four more years; both knew that they would not live to see the fruits of their efforts. Eighteen and fourteen years, respectively, passed after their deaths before women would be able to vote; great numbers of women worked in the World War I effort, likely as important as the whole suffrage movement in the final approval of votes for women. Even after the Nineteenth Amendment passed in Congress, women had to persuade thirty-six state legislatures to ratify. Finally, on August 26, 1920, Harry Burn, the youngest man in the Tennessee legislature, changed his vote on the third reading of the bill (to satisfy his mother), and women were granted suffrage in the United States, seventy-two years after the first call for the vote at Seneca Falls.

The book includes articles by well-known female historians on women's legal and economic status in the nineteenth century, on the mature women's suffrage movement of the last third of the century, and on how Stanton and Anthony have been portrayed since their death. These add scholarly clout to an otherwise popularized narrative. Additionally, the book reprints in their entirety three key documents: "The Declaration of Sentiments" that Stanton wrote in 1848 for the Seneca Falls Convention; "Homes of Single Women," a speech that Anthony first gave in Denver in 1887; and "The Solitude of Self," Stanton's farewell speech to the National American Woman Suffrage Association in 1892. These three primary sources add a wonderful flavor to the book on each woman's thought and language.

Various public events have surrounded the premiere of the film and the book, including the unveiling of a new statue in Seneca Falls, New York, which commemorates the 1851 meeting of Stanton and Anthony introduced by mutual friend Amelia Bloomer. Other events have been held at the National Women's Rights Park in Seneca Falls, owned and operated by the National Park Service, with a special exhibit on Stanton and public visits by the descendants of both Stanton and Anthony.

The strength of the book is in its illustrations, not only photographs but prints of documents, buttons, ribbons, and newspaper clippings. Most of these were, of course, black and white originally, but the book uses sepia tones very effectively and even reprints hand-colored photographs from the nineteenth century.

The weakness of the scholarship of the book lies in its single-minded focus on the American situation. Both women, but especially Stanton, were very involved in the transatlantic women's movement, often traveled in Europe, and were much known there, influencing women from countries as far away as Finland. Stanton and Anthony were greatly influenced by European events, especially by the revolutions of 1848. Stanton herself was a transatlantic mother and grandmother in the last third of her life, as her daughter Harriot studied in France and then married an Englishman, while son Theodore married and settled in France. The United States' nationalistic blinders were much more transparent in the nineteenth century, and European events and ideas were very much a part of the American psyche. Still, the book is a triumphant picture of these two women and of the situation for all women in the nineteenth century, giving readers much more detail than even specialists know and retelling the story with grace and excitement for those to whom it is entirely new.

Margaret McFadden

Sources for Further Study

Booklist 96 (September 1, 1999): 6.
Library Journal 124 (October 15, 1999): 84.
Publishers Weekly 246 (September 6, 1999): 91.

THE NOTHING THAT IS
A Natural History of Zero

Author: Robert Kaplan (1933-)
Publisher: Oxford University Press (New York). 225 pp. $22.00
Type of work: Mathematics, science, philosophy, and history
Time: 5000 B.C.E. to the present

A bedside book with surprising depths, using the history of the concept of zero as a pretext for all manner of reflections on "nothing"

Book publishing, like culture more generally, is subject to "trends" that suddenly appear, flare into prominence, and, after a short burst or a surprisingly long run, fade away. One trick for publishers, writers, investors, and trend spotters of all kinds is to estimate the probable life span of a given trend, while others—columnists, media gurus, and so on—discourse on the trend's meaning.

Why, for instance, has there been a proliferation of popular books about mathematics? Such books have been around for a very long time, but still the average book browser would have been startled to find on the local superstore's "New Arrivals" table not only one but two books devoted to a itinerant Hungarian mathematician. Yet, in 1998, two books about Paul Erdös were neatly stacked there, cheek by jowl with the latest John Grisham novel.

With the same odd synchronicity, readers were offered not one but two books devoted to zero: Robert Kaplan's *The Nothing That Is: A Natural History of Zero*, published in the fall of 1999, and Charles Seife's *Zero: The Biography of a Dangerous Idea*, published early in 2000. Seife's mode is standard science journalism with a few extras deemed to be audience-pleasing. Kaplan tries something trickier, in the vein of David Berlinski's quirky masterpiece *A Tour of the Calculus* (1995).

The dust-jacket photograph of Kaplan, a smiling older man with a walrus mustache, and the brief biography below it give a hint of his approach:

> Robert Kaplan has taught mathematics to people from six to sixty, most recently at Harvard University. In 1994, with his wife Ellen, he founded The Math Circle, a program, open to the public, for the enjoyment of pure mathematics. He has also taught Philosophy, Greek, German, Sanskrit, and Inspired Guessing. Robert Kaplan lives in Cambridge, MA.

Translated, this is very informative. It says (as the glint in his eye already has suggested) that Kaplan is a free spirit, not a Typical Academic, not a pedant, heaven forbid. (Lest the reader may be inclined to dismiss Kaplan as a lightweight, there is that reference to Harvard.) He is a populist. He is in love with mathematics—and his wife is, too. (She provided the whimsical illustrations.) He likes children. He is a polymath, not a narrow specialist, but despite all that learning he does not take himself too seriously.

All this is winsome, and Kaplan is a winsome writer. Where the typical science writer seems unable to resist the nearest piece of prefabricated prose, Kaplan writes sentences that force the reader to do a double take, often followed by a smile. True, he seems at times too eager to entertain, like a preacher afraid the congregation may be dozing off. Taken in small doses, however, as it is meant to be taken, *The Nothing That Is* is absorbing, communicating Kaplan's sheer sense of wonder at the manifold strangeness of the Real.

Calling on the "sense of wonder" is the stock in trade of the typical science journalist, who seems to think this sense can be evoked by pushing the right button (lots of galaxies—that does it every time). Kaplan, by contrast, leads the reader to experience wonder. So as he begins to relate the history of zero, tracing its origins to the clay tablets of the Sumerians, he highlights the gaps in the historical record. Instead of textbook history, with all the troublesome parts blandly smoothed over, he offers the pleasingly rough texture of imagination and informed conjecture.

One fertile subject for conjecture is how the two wedges that signified something like zero in Babylonian recordkeeping were transmuted, around the third century B.C.E., into a Greek symbol very much like the familiar zero, but with a bar above it. Some scholars say this symbol simply represented the Greek omicron, the first letter of the Greek word for "nothing" (and the word for "not"); others say it was an arbitrary symbol. From Greece the symbol migrated to India, where it was called *sunya* ("void"), and from there it was translated into Arabic as *al-sifr*, from whence the Italian *zero* is derived (as well as the word "cipher").

All the while, not only the word but also the meaning was changing. Why did English get the word "zero" from Italian? Because it was in the thriving merchant culture of Italy that double-entry bookkeeping was invented, "some time before 1340." This, Kaplan explains, transformed the meanng of zero: Zero became "a balance-point between negative and positive amounts," making "negative numbers as real as their positive counterparts." From there it is not too far—though several centuries in the passage—from the "utter abstractions" of twentieth century mathematics. ("The uncomfortable gap between numbers, which stood for things, and zero, which didn't, would narrow as the focus shifted from what they were to how they behaved.")

All this Kaplan relates with great brio and the skills of a master teacher. Yet he wants to do even more. He wants not only to give readers a "natural history" of zero (that is, a richly discursive account, meandering, alert to the odd fact, indulgent of the tangential anecdote) but also a dose of philosophy. He wants to ring the changes on "nothing" in every imaginable sense.

Clearly this was in Kaplan's mind from the start. The book's opening sentence says, "If you look at zero you see nothing; but look through it and you will see the whole world." The very end of the book quotes the line from the poet Wallace Stevens from which Kaplan's title is taken. Kaplan reminds the reader of Stevens's snowman, who listens and beholds, "Nothing that is not there and the nothing that is." Between the flourish of his opening sentence and that poetic conclusion, Kaplan seeks to show how the history of zero illumines what he calls a "shift in the Great Paradigm."

This shift, Kaplan says, began around the fifth century B.C.E. and became "firmly established some thousand years later." According to the new paradigm, found in Plato, in "the Buddhist theory of sunyata, from about the first century A.D.," and, "most familiarly for us," in "the revelation embraced by Christianity and Mohammedanism, but resisted by Judaism, the more ancient religion," everyday reality is "an imitation or intimation of the Real" that lies "beyond, below, behind." This is so also, Kaplan says, in the mathematical history he is tracing:

> The change in mathematics we've been following, where names for numbers narrow down to signs of them, and the numbers themselves are subordinated to the laws they obey, began when someone first counted, and evolved through the on-going project of deriving those laws from as thrifty a set of axioms as mathematicians could manage. In keeping with the shift of the background paradigm, the interplay of numbers came to be understood as manifesting those axioms, which from afar hold taut the fabric of our understanding, like a trampoline's frame.

Those sentences, impressive enough when first taken in, are even more potent in their delayed impact. Some while later—twenty or thirty or forty pages—the reader will stop and thumb back until he or she has found pages 77 and 78, and the audacity of Kaplan's argument will hit like a sledgehammer. For without explicitly rehearsing the Received Account of the rise of modern science, Kaplan has slyly insinuated that it is a lot of hot air. How radically different his account is from the notorious aphorism of the Nobel Prize-winning physicist Steven Weinberg: "The more the universe seems comprehensible, the more it also seems pointless."

Science, so the story goes, has "disenchanted" the world. No, says, Kaplan, that is backward. *The Nothing That Is*, like Berlinski's *Tour of the Calculus* and Mark Steiner's *The Applicability of Mathematics as a Philosophical Problem* (1998), finds in the evolution of mathematics—the lingua franca of modern science—compelling arguments against the naturalism that modern science is widely believed to have established beyond doubt.

As Steiner points out, "many great physicists have expressed amazement that mathematics should be applicable to physics." Why should mere constructions of the human mind turn out to map the underlying structure of the cosmos? The answer, Steiner suggests, is "that ours is (or appears to be) an intellectually 'user-friendly' universe, a universe which allows our species to discover things about it." Human beings are not imposing arbitrary constructions willy-nilly on an indifferent universe; rather, the language of mathematics expresses deep and mysterious intuitions into what Kaplan calls the Real that lies beyond, below, behind.

Unlike Steiner, however, Kaplan works by indirection, by a sort of intellectual jujitsu. He feints and dances, so that it is easy to lose track of what is at issue in this paragraph or that. He is not careless; he means to enforce a slow reading—not the dreary slowless of a tedious text but a slow savoring of the Real, wildly unpredictable and delightfully full of meaning.

John Wilson

Sources for Further Study

Booklist 96 (September 15, 1999): 206.
Library Journal 124 (October 1, 1999): 131.
Publishers Weekly 246 (August 16, 1999): 67.
The Wall Street Journal, November 10, 1999, p. A20.

NOVEMBER 1916
The Red Wheel: Knot II

Author: Aleksandr Solzhenitsyn (1918-   )
Publisher: Farrar, Straus and Giroux (New York). 1,014 pp. $35.00
Type of work: Novel
Time: The early twentieth century
Locale: Russia and Eastern Europe

In the second part of his trilogy exploring the causes of the Russian Revolution, which led to the creation of the Soviet Union, Solzhenitsyn captures the intrigue among party politicians and military officials during World War I

Principal characters:
ALEKSANDR "SANYA" LAZHENITSYN, a lieutenant serving with the Russian army in Romania
ARSENI BLAGODAREV, a peasant serving an enlistment in Lazhenitsyn's unit
GEORGI VOROTNYTSEV, a colonel in the Russian Army
ALINA VOROTNYTSEV, his wife
ANDREI SHINGAREV, a political activist and member of the Russian Duma
OLDA ANDOZERSKAYA, a professor in St. Petersburg
V. I. LENIN, a Russian revolutionary and eventual leader of the Soviet Union
ALEKSANDR GUCHKOV, head of the War Industry Committee in Russia

Fans of Aleksandr Solzhenitsyn waited long for the appearance of the second installment of what he promised would be a trilogy explaining the causes of the revolution that paved the way for Vladimir Ilich Lenin and his henchmen to impose Communist rule on Russia and its neighbors. *Avgust chetyrnadtsatogo* (1971, rev. 1983; *August 1914*, 1972), the first volume, which detailed the defeat of the Russian Army at the Battle of the Tannenberg Forest, had been acclaimed by Western audiences when it appeared in translation in 1972. The second "knot," as Solzhenitsyn calls each novel in his trilogy, was begun in 1971 and occupied the author for more than a decade. Although he secured copyright to the novel, *Oktiabr' shestnadtsatogo*, in 1984, it would be fifteen years before an English translation appeared, giving Solzhenitsyn the wide readership outside the Soviet Union that he so desperately wanted for all his works.

Unfortunately for him, in the decades between inception and publication of *November 1916*, one of the most significant events of the twentieth century took place: the fall of Communism and the dismantlement of the Soviet Union. Hence, a work intended to explain the causes of a destructive yet still vigorous ideology to an oppressed people in Russia and a sympathetic audience in the West lost much of its political impetus. What had begun as a novel using history to rationalize politics had become merely another historical novel.

What is even more curious is that Solzhenitsyn had chosen to write about the causes of the Russian Revolution by focusing not simply on events involving open warfare, terrorism, or *coups d'état*. He had done so to a certain extent in *August 1914*. By contrast, in *November 1916* Solzhenitsyn chooses to concentrate on a period significantly less tumultuous. "The interval between 27 October and 17 November 1916 contains relatively few events of historical importance," he tells readers in the author's note preceding his story. He focused on this rather uneventful month, he continues, because "it encapsulates the stagnant and oppressive atmosphere of the months immediately preceding the Revolution." Like many writers of historical fiction, Solzhenitsyn is less concerned with momentous action (in this case, considerably less so) than he is with helping to capture the intellectual, social, political, and military milieu of the time. Because, as he acknowledges, historical records of prerevolutionary Russia are sparse, he resorts to fiction to give himself wider latitude not only to tell his story but also to re-create the atmosphere of the age.

Were he not so serious about his work, Solzhenitsyn might have adapted Mark Twain's famous adage about looking for a moral in *Adventures of Huckleberry Finn* (1884) to describe the story line of *November 1916:* "Persons looking for a plot will be shot." There is no single narrative thread that binds together the disparate parts of Solzhenitsyn's story. Instead, Solzhenitsyn weaves together more than a dozen major vignettes of individuals whose lives are touched by the war, interspersing fictional accounts with pages of history taken from records he found within Russia and in archives throughout the West. The effect is decidedly disjointed, and readers may find it difficult to recall details from the various real-life and fictional episodes that make up this thousand-page saga.

If there is one dominant character, it is the fictional Colonel Georgi Vorotyntsev. Assigned to the front after years serving in staff positions, he has become resigned to completing his career in obscurity, carrying out his duty as a soldier. His wife Alina is even more disappointed than he that he has been sent to the front, because she has dreams of mingling within the best circles in Moscow. When her husband returns by way of Moscow on a visit to General Headquarters in St. Petersburg, she is initially elated, but her joy turns to bitter disappointment when she learns he can stay only a day. Though he promises to return quickly on his way back to his unit, Vorotyntsev spends more than a week in St. Petersburg. There he meets Olda Andozerskaya, a professor and political activist, at the home of Aleksandr Shingarev, a member of the Russian Duma and leader of the Kadet Party, which was influential in Russian politics during the first decades of the twentieth century. Vorotyntsev finds that Olda possesses qualities of intellectualism and feminine charm sadly lacking in his wife, and he risks marriage and career to be with her for most of the time he was to have been briefing members of the General Staff. Upon his return to Moscow, however, he confesses his affair to Alina, and the deterioration of their marriage is related with agonizing psychological detail.

To Vorotyntsev's story Solzhenitsyn grafts those of Sanya Lazhenitsyn, a young lieutenant whose concern for his men and for traditional values gives the author an opportunity to discuss matters of religion and morals. Through the adventures of

Arseni Blagodev, a private in Lazhenitsyn's unit, Solzhenitsyn explores the reaction of the peasants to the war and the effect the continued fighting has on their villages. Vorotyntsev's conversations with real-life political and military figures such as Shingarev and Aleksandr Guchkov, head of the War Industries Committee, provide Solzhenitsyn the opportunity to comment on the state of politics and the economy during the war years. Dozens of other historical figures make appearances in the work, and an equal number of fictional men and women are created to give readers an idea of how the war and attendant political unrest affected citizens at all levels in a country ill prepared for its role in the conflict and unable to mobilize its resources to carry out its military commitments efficiently.

Solzhenitsyn is at his best when delineating characters, whether they be made from whole cloth or constructed from the historical record. For example, he introduces readers to Fyodor D. Kovynev, a self-styled writer whose indiscriminate ramblings about his native countryside and his inability to provide any substantial insights through his work are strongly reminiscent of the Soviet writer Mikhail Sholokhov, whose novels of peasant life were so pleasing to Joseph Stalin and other Communist Party leaders. Solzhenitsyn includes a chapter in which the events of the period are viewed through the consciousness of the czarina Aleksandra. She is worried to distraction about the long separations from her husband Nikolai II, who had rashly decided to assume field command of the Russian army. Through her internal monologue and her chaotic attempts to control the government in her husband's absence, she reveals her perceptions of the revered spiritual counselor on whose advice she relies for deciding the fate of ministers and generals. Her portrait of Grigori Yefimovich Rasputin stands in sharp contrast to the commentary of many others, both historical and fictional, who can see with great clarity the damage this madman and lecher is doing to the prestige of the royal couple and, by extension, to all of Russia. By moving his perspective from the small circle around Nikolai and Aleksandra to the politicians and military leaders trying valiantly to carry out their tasks in government and warfare, Solzhenitsyn displays the degree to which the royal family had been cut off from the people they were ostensibly ordained to rule.

Perhaps the most intriguing portrait is that of Lenin. In 1916 Lenin was merely one of a number of revolutionaries who had been forced to flee Russia when his efforts to bring about political reform were unsuccessful. Situated in Zurich, Switzerland, Lenin is shown manipulating subordinates and honest reformers so that, when the time is ripe, he will be able to orchestrate sweeping changes inspired by his reading of the radical political philosopher Karl Marx. Though not dominating the landscape of the novel, Lenin emerges as a man with exceptional intellect, clear vision, and little concern for those who might stand in the way of his new workers' state.

It is easy to get caught up in the history that underpins *November 1916* and to miss the fact that it is principally a work of fiction. The novel is carefully structured to balance documented events with imagined accounts of the impact of events on fictional characters. Not bound slavishly to the historical record, Solzhenitsyn is free to speculate about feelings and motivations, not only for fictional characters but for historical personages as well.

A number of other literary qualities enrich the text. The panoramic vista of a country at war is clearly meant to remind readers of that other great fictional account of the Russians' struggle for survival, Leo Tolstoy's *Voyna i mir* (1865-1869; *War and Peace*, 1886). The apparent collective madness that sweeps through segments of the populace suggests eerie parallels to Fyodor Dostoevski's *Besy* (1871-1872; *The Possessed*, 1913). Throughout, too, Solzhenitsyn provides lengthy, detailed descriptions of a seemingly unchanging natural landscape; apart from the little strip in the west where fighting takes place, it lies largely unscarred while the men and women who inhabit it find themselves undergoing radical changes.

The novel is filled with narration, description, and dialogue that bring to life this chaotic period in Russia's history. Perhaps there is no more poignant section in the novel than the final one, in which a mother comes to church to mourn her dead son and seek forgiveness for her trangressions, which she somehow realizes have led to her tragedy. It would be hard not to see the scene as metaphor for what is going on in the country at large. Even if the need for justification on political terms is no longer necessary, Solzhenitsyn's novel provides insight into the continuing human problems of any individual's struggle with sin and the need for redemption, or any community's or nation's need for sanity and compromise in the conduct of society's business. For these reasons, *November 1916* may live long after the Soviet Union is but a dim memory.

Laurence W. Mazzeno

Sources for Further Study

Booklist 95 (September 1, 1998): 7.
Library Journal 123 (September 1, 1998): 217.
The Nation 268 (May 3, 1999): 32.
The New York Times, February 12, 1999, p. E49.
The New York Times Book Review 104 (February 7, 1999): 4.

ORIGINAL BLISS

Author: A. L. Kennedy (1965-   )
First published: 1997, in Great Britain
Publisher: Alfred A. Knopf (New York). 214 pp. $21.00
Type of work: Novel
Time: The 1990's
Locale: Glasgow, London, and Stuttgart

The story of a Glasgow housewife's search for love and personal fulfillment from one of Scotland's finest fiction writers

Principal characters:
HELEN BRINDLE, a repressed as well as depressed Glasgow housewife
MR. BRINDLE, her taciturn, abusive husband
EDWARD E. GLUCK, a self-help specialist

There is, for want of a better word, an almost Jamesian quality to the young but already highly and justly acclaimed Scottish writer A. L. Kennedy's work. Unlike Henry James, however, whose fiction grew increasingly difficult as his career progressed and his readership dwindled, Kennedy, although equally intent on depicting states of mind and feeling, writes in a way that seems transparent and effortless on one hand, finely wrought and slyly calculating on the other, with a bit of understated, offbeat humor thrown in for good measure. The opening of *Original Bliss*—Kennedy's third novel (she has also published three collections of short stories)—lulls the reader into a sense of unearned security and superiority that the rest of the novel will complicate if not entirely dispel:

> Mrs. Brindle lay on her living-room floor, watching her ceiling billow and blink with the cold, cold colours of British Broadcasting light. A presumably educative conversation washed across her and she was much too tired to sleep or listen, but that was okay, that was really quite all right.

Writing such as this rewards attentiveness on the reader's part and quietly undermines the smug complacency that the language encourages. Small doubts arise, barely breaking the surface of the reader's consciousness—questions concerning point of view, perhaps a bit less detached and ironically distant than one would like, the slightly jarring use of "washed," "billow," and "blink," and the dialogical implications of repeated words and sentiments ("the cold, cold colours," "but that was okay, that was really all right"). These nuances are all but drowned out by the raucous low comedy of the very next line issuing from the BBC program to which the unfortunately, even comically named Mrs. Brindle has been only half-listening, "'What about the etiquette of masturbation?'" The comic disparity between "etiquette" and "masturbation," as well as between "masturbation" and "Mrs. Brindle," seems to confirm a feeling of superiority on the reader's part that comes, of course, at the hapless Mrs. Brindle's expense. In this, however, it is the reader who has been deceived, for *Original Bliss* is a novel that is as remarkably and deeply compassionate as it is carefully and subtly written. It is gauging accurately the degree and angle of ironic detachment that most tests the reader's mettle in dealing with a novel about a character far less self-deluded and far more intelligent than the deeply depressed as well as repressed Mrs. Brindle first appears. By page 18, even the dullest reader can see how it is not, or not solely, the anonymous narrator who is using irony at Mrs. Brindle's expense, but Mrs. Brindle herself in a way that is at once self-mocking and self-abasing.

> On the third Friday of June Mrs. Brindle found what she needed at only her second high-street shop. A belligerently cheerful magazine winked out at her, shamelessly covered with posing and pouting fruit flans: almond paste, cherries, apricots, vanilla cream and appropriate liqueurs; each of their impossible elements boded well. She could explore a good dessert theme for weeks. This would be today's encouraging victory of the positive.

The full horror of this self-effacing woman's severely constrained life only slowly comes into focus, and as it does, the humor seems less comical, more cutting, which is to say more self-lacerating: "Radio Two, Mrs. Brindle's favourite; it didn't pretend to be better than it was." It is not just her lack of self-confidence and fear of revealing herself that make the reader wince, but the emptiness of her carefully controlled life, her living without what she vaguely but accurately calls "Something Else." Mrs. Brindle is not mad, though the reader may well begin to wonder first whether she is, then why she is not. Her doling out her daily life in small pieces is her way of making do, of appearing normal, and is duplicated in Kennedy's careful doling out of that life piece by piece (there are no chapters, only small narrative bits separated by nothing more than two blank lines). Only gradually does the reader learn that Mrs. Brindle has a name—Helen—if not a room of her own and a husband as well as a God in whom she has lost faith, a loss of far greater importance to her than to her author. Keenly aware of that loss, she has begun looking for guidance in all the usual modern places: television, radio, magazines, bookstores, where she finds no "sections assigned to FEAR OF DYING, or ABSOLUTE LOSS" but does seek out and buy a book written by the self-help guru Edward E. Gluck. Gluck is the man whose voice she heard on the television speaking of masturbation and subsequently on the radio as he becomes a "persistent presence" in her otherwise dreary existence. In the book, "He personally assured her that she was the miracle that makes itself." Suddenly, before the reader has time to think about either his sincerity or her gullibility, Gluck himself is there, or, rather, Mrs. Brindle is in Stuttgart, where she has heard he is to speak.

Gluck, whom the reader has earlier dismissed as nothing more than a bit of humorous background noise, now becomes shockingly real and pretty much everything that Mrs. Brindle is not: confident, assertive, articulate, well known, well traveled, and, at 6 foot, 3 ¾ inches, physically imposing. She hunkers down and makes do (her impulsively flying to Stuttgart notwithstanding); he, on the other hand, is the man with a plan, the Process, that will make it possible for everyone to live psychologically if not geographically in the Bailey Park that the James Stewart character in the film *It's a Wonderful Life* (1947) dreams about building, the edenic suburb where people can live in bliss. A few hours in Gluck's company does Mrs. Brindle a world of good. Helen, as she is now known, is clearly younger and more attractive than the formerly condescending reader first thought, even if any thoughts of original bliss seem offset by her puritanical obsession with original sin. Any idea of the two living happily ever after are put on hold when Gluck exposes his own dark side: an obsession with pornography, in which he finds a clarity that makes his own work-driven existence seem unreal by comparison.

As the novel teeters between neogothic horror and low comedy, Mrs. Brindle returns to the safety and confinement of her home a changed woman, forced to lie about her trip. Unlike Gluck (the voice made flesh about whom the reader comes to learn a great deal), Mr. Brindle is left deliberately and frighteningly unrealized. His existence unconfirmed for more than forty pages, he remains a dark, brooding presence in Mrs. Brindle's life, the object of her fear and loathing: always exacting, usually silent, at times taunting, occasionally violent. Kennedy's depiction of that violence is so harrowing because it is so understated, in keeping with Mrs. Brindle's own reticent, deeply repressed character. Part of the horror derives from her feeble attempt to use humor to defend herself after the fact, as much against her own feelings of responsibility and guilt as from his violence. Thinking back to one particularly violent episode that occurred two years earlier, she recalls realizing that "she'd picked the wrong night" to try to deal with her husband's anger according to an advice column in one of her women's magazines.

Edward begins writing to Helen, seeking both her love and her help, understanding that he "he can work the process for anyone but myself." She meets him secretly, dressed not for a lover but for the depressed sister she tells her husband she is visiting. Unsure how to proceed, she tries to take refuge in her cooking, only to fail. "Opened cans and the good knives she had bought a long time ago—as an investment and as things to make her glad slashed at her palms and fingers." Complaining about the food, Mr. Brindle begins the slow buildup to the violence that will explode when he finds one of Edward's postcards.

This time, though, Helen flees Glasgow for Edward's flat in London. Although Edward is appalled by her injuries, Helen quickly points out that had the beating taken place on video, Edward would have enjoyed watching it. She also realizes that that is the kind of remark "scared and angry people make," and when Edward tries to escape from his "massively embarrassing" self into a more comfortable James Stewart persona, Helen, with surprising firmness and considerable compassion, says, "'No, leave Jimmy out of it, I'm talking to you.'" For a second time, the narrative swerves away from the happy ending it seems to have reached. Partly out of fear, partly out of guilt, she returns home to a surprisingly contrite husband, and they resume their brittle life together until nothing more than her dropping a cup full of coffee is enough to trigger one last violent attack. This time, believing he has killed her, the ever remorseful but chronically violent Mr. Brindle will take an overdose of paracetamol tablets, in this way ensuring the poetic, rather than divine, justice of a suitably painful, lingering death. Edward is, of course, devastated; he feels responsible for her having left London and for having failed to protect her. However, freed of the shadowy Mr. Brindle, Helen and Edward can now begin to "live happily ever after," not in the fairy-tale sense exactly, but, as their fumbling, comically tender lovemaking at novel's end suggests, in a way that moves ahead much the way Kennedy's narrative does, by small, decidedly human increments rather than startling leaps of faith.

Adding to the pleasure that the reader takes in Helen and Edward getting what they do in fact deserve (something denied the narrator of Kennedy's best-known work, the chilling, slowly revealing story "Night Geometry and the Garscadden Trains") is the pleasure derived from Kennedy's masterful yet also mischievous prose, which both embodies and parodies "the sternly grey perspectives" of Glasgow's Calvinist architecture. Kennedy's language, which is just as interesting as her story, seems at once ingenuous and ingenious, clinically precise and ominously vague, even dreamlike, transparently offhand yet at times wondrously, even hilariously (though occasionally horrifically) off-kilter, which is to say as much in Helen's character as the more broadly farcical similes found in Robert Coover's *Spanking the Maid* (1981). For Coover's maid, sunshine appears "as if flung from a bucket"; for Helen, more sedately, "Something bloomed at the back of her thinking like an unpredictable pilot light." Often, though, the language jars in a very different way, the intensely inward Mrs. Brindle rendered in more feverish Plath-like tones as Calvinist grays suddenly erupt into gothic grotesquerie: the sky "raking between the flimsy curtain . . . screaming heat"; a door "muttering close"; a man in a dream "sinking and slurring away"; fingers "unmuzzling buttons."

Although in many ways a version of that most English of films, *Brief Encounter* (1946), which it seems both to parallel and to parody, *Original Bliss* is deeply rooted in Kennedy's native land. Mrs. Brindle and Edward Gluck are themselves variations on familiar themes from Scottish literature: the one all God-obsessed and sexually repressed, the other a latter-day Dr. Jekyll and Mr. Hyde. Kennedy, whom *Granta* magazine has judged one of the twenty "Best of Young British Novelists," represents the other, less well known pole of contemporary Scottish writing that has been enjoying such a renaissance in the 1990's: not the shock-prose of Irvine Welsh, Alan Warner, Iain Banks, James Kelman, Duncan McLean, and others, but the no-less-interesting and culturally attuned but more finely crafted and carefully nuanced writing of Jane Galloway and Candia McWilliam. The latter will never have its *Trainspotting* (1993), but it already has a new novel, Kennedy's longest, *Everything You Need*, published July, 1999, in Britain.

Robert A. Morace

Sources for Further Study

Booklist 95 (November 1, 1998): 475.
Library Journal 123 (November 15, 1998): 91.
New Statesman 128 (May 24, 1999): 49.
The New York Times Book Review 104 (February 14, 1999): 18.
The New Yorker 74 (January 18, 1999): 79.
Publishers Weekly 245 (October 19, 1998): 52.

OUT OF PLACE
A Memoir

Author: Edward W. Said (1935-)
Publisher: Alfred A. Knopf (New York). Illustrated. 295 pp. $26.95
Type of work: Memoirs
Time: Mostly 1935 to 1962, with flashforwards
Locale: Palestine, Egypt, Lebanon, England, and the United States

Said writes, Proust-like, this recollection of his first twenty-seven years—from his birth in 1935 in Jerusalem to well-off Palestinian-Lebanese Christian parents, through an anguished childhood, caught among political, religious, and social crosscurrents in three Arabic cultures, up to 1962, when he had nearly completed a Harvard doctorate but not yet become a world spokesperson for the Palestinians

Principal personages:
EDWARD W. SAID, the memoirist, Palestine-born literary scholar and Arabist
WILLIAM A. SAID , formerly Wadie Ibrahim, the late father of the memoirist
HILDA MUSA SAID, the Lebanese, intensely beloved mother of the memoirist
ROSY,
JEAN,
JOYCE, and
GRACE, four siblings of Edward
AUNT NABIHA, Edward's aunt, who is passionately devoted to cause of Palestine relief
CHARLES MALIK, an eminent Lebanese statesman, a mentor to Edward
JACK BALDWIN, an English teacher at Mount Herman, whose writing assignments opened new vistas for Edward
JEFF BRIEGER, one of the few other foreign-born students at Mount Herman; with Edward, the lone dissenter against teachings of Mount Herman founder Dwight Moody
KEITH GATLEY, Edward's first English teacher at Cairo's Victoria College
GRIFFITH and
LOWE, acting headmaster and English teacher, respectively, at new campus of Victoria College, tormentors of—and tormented by—Edward
IGNACE TIEGERMAN, a Polish piano virtuoso, Edward's most vital musical mentor

Two-thirds of the way into this engrossing memoir, Edward W. Said describes his temporary expulsion at fifteen from Cairo's Victoria College, the school he disdainfully calls, with a nod to the bitter satires of George Orwell (1903-1950) and others, "the British Eton in Egypt." A Christian native of Palestinian Jerusalem and born to privilege, the boy finds himself losing his sense of self as an unchallenged student on a new campus where family and class count for nothing—dress code and colorless British teachers and textbooks everything.

Said recalls a prank involving Lowe, his "blustering, weak, and incompetent" English teacher. Young Said locks Lowe inside a windowed cubicle in full view of the class. Assuming the role of circus barker, he points to the hapless Englishman in captivity: "Take a look [at Lowe] in his natural state." Later the same Lowe calls for the boys to take out their Shakespeare readings. They set up a chorus of protest and demand Sir Walter Scott (1771-1832) instead. Lowe goes on the attack and picks out his chief tormentor for special punishment. Classmates come to Said's rescue, but their teacher's anger frightens them off. Lowe bodily ejects his most gifted student.

Griffiths, the acting headmaster, tells Said's parents that were it not for their son's superior intelligence he would have been sacked long ago. Looking back fifty years, Said finds it "ironic that a teacher should feel that a bright student was an impediment to his authority." Irony aside, might Griffiths not have tolerated his tormentor out of respect for him as the brightest of the boys, one worth salvaging?

For Said, misadventures such as the ones just described and an even earlier instance of caning are evils of the empire, "colonial" experiences. Yet, as writer Tan Buruma points out, the treatment given to Edward was no more or less than what most British private-school students of his age underwent.

Born in Jerusalem because his mother did not trust Egyptian hospitals, Said dates his endless suffering from the family's having been uprooted to move to Cairo, where his dominating father Wadie set up a prospering business a decade before his son's birth in 1935. It was there that Edward began to feel—perhaps even to cultivate—the persona of the misfit that would give his memoir its inevitable title.

Deep down, although an Arab, he believed he would always be a foreigner to the Egyptians. In passages like the following, Said reverses Blanche Dubois's play-ending words, being always ungrateful for the [feigned] kindness of strangers: The Saids became

> *khawagat*, the designated and respectful title for foreigners which, as used by Muslim Egyptians, has always carried a tinge of hostility. Despite the fact that I spoke—and I thought I looked—like a native Egyptian, something seemed to give me away.

What, in a sense, will give Edward W. Said away for some readers is the inherent nature of this genre. As long as memoirs remain anecdotal—items of personal biography of the great by the ungreat (although sometimes "ingrate" might not be amiss), self-aggrandizing can be held in check. A memoir that mounts its author as hero, however, can be self-serving. The memoirist claims to set the record straight while actually attempting to mitigate guilt or get back at his enemies. The self-chronicler usually cannot be monitored. "As-I-remember" should be "as-I-*want*-to-remember."

In the relentless selectivity of memory as decoder of experience, only Edward Said's mother, Hilda, remains inviolate, her caretaking inseparable from love for the only son among four daughters. He was easily her favorite. They shared a love of music; they read Shakespeare's *Hamlet* together. From their first distant separation, when Edward entered Mount Herman in Connecticut, to her last months of confining illness in

Washington, D.C., while he taught in New York, Hilda Musa Said defined her son's lifelong sense of estrangement. Exile, Said writes, is the sense of being somewhere one does not wish to be. Where he wanted to be was with his mother.

Everywhere he goes in the Islamic world, he complains that he is either the wrong kind of Arab or, if in an Arabic city such as Cairo, where the dominant culture was British, an Arab of any sort. Although Said's parents are members of an exclusive club, he is *persona non grata* there: "Arabs aren't allowed here, and you're an Arab!" he is told. He reports the incident to his father, who is only "mildly disquieted."

About his father, Wadie Ibrahim Said, the son is much more than mildly disquieted. Even after a half-century, he is unable to resolve the Janus-faced force that his father represented. Always a "demanding and hectoring presence"—a formidable figure who lectured Said for not having semen stains on his pajamas, a sure sign that instead of having wet dreams, he was masturbating—the elder Said accords only formal acknowledgement to the boy's talents. Yet when the father suffers a decade's physical decline, the son fears he will be left unprotected and vulnerable.

Melanoma, his father's doctor warns, is "very treacherous, the worst of the cancers." Although "escaping" the Arab world for the United States and beginning the American education that will lead to Princeton and a distinguished career as a literary and Middle-East scholar at Columbia University, he lives in a haunted house where he envisions his father's body "being taken over by a dreadful, creeping invasion of malignant cells, his organs slowly devoured, his brain, eyes, ears, and throat torn asunder by this dreadful, almost miasmic, affliction."

Perhaps most of all, Said blames his father for the "fatalistic compact" cosigned by parent and son to accept "a necessarily inferior status." He was saved the shame of accommodation by the emergence of "the polarizing, charismatic figure" of Charles Malik, who became Lebanon's leading player on the world scene in the 1970's. Malik, husband of Said's mother's first cousin Eva, was not only a regular visitor to the Saids' Lebanese Christian circle at their vacation refuge in idyllic Dhour but the first person of intellect to spur the young man's literary and political passions. Although later disenchanted by his mentor's uncompromising espousal of a Christian Lebanon, Said credits Malik with being the major liberating influence of his life:

> [At Dhour], Malik represented our first symbol of resistance, the refusal of Christian Lebanon to go along with Arab nationalism, the decision to join the Cold War on the United States's side, to fight and turn intransigent rather than to enthuse about . . . [Gamal Abdel] Nasser's rousing exhortations.

Out of Place will reward the determined reader many times over. Said writes out of near total recall in a belle-lettristic idiom that links the inventive and the necessarily self-referential, and affirms at all points a keen awareness of the frequent complicity between culture and state power. In those instances, mostly in the last two chapters, where he is obliged to flash forward forty years and more, Said never leaves the reader adrift. The early nineties not only bring him to America (1991), but to the crushing knowledge, in 1993, that he suffers from chronic lymphatic leukemia (CLL). He still writes letters to his mother—herself dead of cancer eighteen months before his diagnosis—and he finds himself "thinking regressively about hiding a place to die in." Instead, Said clings to the "second self he had discovered during an abortive love affair—a long-buried response to the world traveler's secret fear of not returning." Especially since receiving his sentence of death, Said has exorcised fear of not returning in favor of a chronic zest for setting out: "I say to myself: if you don't take this trip, don't prove your mobility and indulge your fear of being lost, don't override the normal rhythms of domestic life now, you certainly will not be able to do it in the near future."

In 1992, with his second wife Mariam and two children, he revisits his birthplace in Jerusalem after forty-five years. A year later he goes on his own to Cairo, all this time being monitored, without treatment, by his oncologist, Dr. Kanti Rai, to whom, along with Mariam, this book is dedicated.

Christopher Lehmann-Haupt wisely concludes in *The New York Times* that, although Edward W. Said claims to dissociate American attitudes from those of Israel more than other Palestinians, he cannot help seeing his adopted country as "less of a haven for the dispossessed and more of a refinement of the colonialist outlook toward third-world people." Yet what an extraordinary mind has enabled Edward Said to transcend his Palestinian-Arab-Christian-American out-of-placeness—at least for the purposes of writing his remarkable story.

Richard Hauer Costa

Sources for Further Study

Booklist 96 (September 1, 1999): 66.
The Economist 352 (September 25, 1999): 102.
Library Journal 124 (September 15, 1999): 84.
The New York Times Book Review 104 (October 3, 1999): 10.
Publishers Weekly 246 (July 12, 1999): 84.

OUT OF THE WOODS
Stories

Author: Chris Offutt (1958-)
Publisher: Simon & Schuster (New York). 172 pp. $21.00
Type of work: Short fiction
Time: 1950-1999
Locale: Kentucky, Oregon, Idaho, Colorado, and Wyoming

Eight new stories about men who leave, but can never escape, the mountains of eastern Kentucky

Principal characters:
GERALD, a man driving to a hospital in Nebraska to pick up his wife's brother, who has been shot
HAZE GIBSON, the last of the old Gibsons, who have been feuding with the Mullins clan for sixty years
EPHRAIM GOINS, a deputy who allows him to stay in jail for his own protection
BEULAH MULLINS, Haze's nemesis, who shoots him in his jail cell and takes his place
TILDEN, a former convict who has taken a job moving graves
BAKER, a fellow former convict
RAY, a man who left Kentucky for the assembly lines of Detroit and has returned

The stories in Chris Offutt's first book, the well-received 1992 *Kentucky Straight*, were so firmly situated in the mountains of eastern Kentucky that, in the tradition of William Faulkner, he included a map, with story locations labeled. In this, his second collection, he has moved most of his characters out of the mountains, mainly to the wide-open spaces of the West. However, the eastern Kentucky hill country remains a central force in these stories, for no matter where Offutt's mountain men go, the hills haunt them.

This is a thin but not an anemic book—less than a two-hour read—richly flavored with Appalachia, but not by local color descriptions, sentimental nostalgia, corny dialect, or trendy marginalized social context, rather by characters who think and sound genuine. The stories in which talk dominates, rather than place or plot, are the most powerful ones in this collection.

Out of the Woods is wisely structured, beginning strongly with the best stories and, once having hooked readers, compelling them to finish even the weakest. The collection's title story about a thirty-year-old man who has never been out of the county is the best. To secure his position with his new wife and her family, Gerald agrees to drive an old pickup for two days to pick up his wife's brother, Ory, who has been shot and is in a hospital in Wahoo, Nebraska. While this may seem like a simple task, for a mountain man it is fraught with unease; the land in Indiana and Illinois is as flat as a playing card with no place to hide, and at night the sky seems to press down on Gerald in a threatening way. When he arrives to find his brother-in-law has died, Gerald meets the woman who shot him—marveling at her purple hair, the gold ring in her nose, and the fact that it all happened over a dispute about a blond wig.

Gerald makes some commonsense arrangements and a few man-to-man deals with the authorities and heads back to Kentucky with his brother-in-law's body in the back of the pickup, stopping once to mound a pile of rich Illinois topsoil for his garden onto the body. This homey traveling grave becomes comically grotesque when Gerald stops at a gas station and a dog starts to dig in the dirt; the smell is so bad, a man thinks Gerald is taking a dead hog to the renderers. In this carefully controlled account of a simple man's heroic management of an extraordinarily ordinary situation, Gerald's final gesture is to tell a public lie—that Ory was accidentally shot—for the sake of his in-laws.

"Melungeons," which appeared in the 1994 *Best American Short Stories* collection, is another mountain story, told in the same understated way with a similar stoically heroic character. Not as powerful as "Out of the Woods" but more popular because of its exotic multicultural context, "Melungeons" is, on one hand, a variation of the oldest subtype of the Kentucky mountain story—the family feud, à la the Hatfields and McCoys. On the other hand, because it deals with the Melungeons, a small mixed-race (American Indian, African American, white) tribe that live in the Appalachian Mountains of Kentucky, Virginia, and Tennessee, it has a faddish appeal to the current literary craze for all things culturally marginal.

The focus of the story is on Deputy Ephraim Goins, who puts seventy-six-year-old Melungeon Haze Gibson in jail at his own request for his own protection. Gibson has left the mountains because of a family feud but now has returned because he has missed every wedding and funeral his family has ever had. Goins, also a Melungeon, has suffered racial prejudice and recalls being assigned to an all-black company when he was in the army after a dentist noticed his gums were tinged with blue. Scorned both by whites and by blacks, Melungeons are thus doubly exiled and marginalized.

Haze Gibson is one of the last of the older members of his family still alive, while his nemesis, Beulah Mullins, is one of the last old members of her clan and has heard he has returned. Beulah, who has never voted or paid taxes, who has not been off the mountain in fifty years, and for whom there is no birth record, makes the trip into town in answer to a bone-deep demand; more than thirty people from the Mullins and the Gibson clans have died over the years in the feud that started sixty years before over disputed bear meat. She goes to the jail with a sawed-off shotgun hidden in her skirt, implacable in her duty, kills the last of the old Gibsons, and takes his place in the jail cell. Deputy Goins walks out of the jail and heads toward the nearest slope, having been called by this primitive ritual back to the hills. The story is told in the restrained classical tones of mythic inevitability.

"Moscow, Idaho" and "Two-Eleven All Around" focus on displaced eastern Kentucky men, the first, a former convict who has taken a job moving graves in Moscow, Idaho, and the second, an out-of-work drunk with an alcoholic girlfriend in Casper, Wyoming. What makes "Moscow, Idaho" so strong is the dialogue, for most of the story records the conversation of Tilden, the central character, and Baker, a fellow former convict, who are unearthing coffins to make way for a new highway through the cemetery. The men talk about prison life, which Baker misses because of the comfort of its routine and the camaraderie he felt there. However, Tilden, the Kentucky man, likes the quiet and the empty space of Idaho. When Baker steals a car and takes off, Tilden remains, unwilling to be on the run or to risk prison again. He lies on his back in a wheat field, wondering if he will ever find a woman he likes or a town he wants to stay in, happy that there is not a fence or a wall in sight.

If dialogue and anecdote characterize "Moscow, Idaho," basic character concept is the foundation for "Two-Eleven All Around." The central character is another displaced mountain man, thirty-five years old, out of work, homeless, with a girlfriend who is obsessed with listening to a police scanner when she is detoxing from alcohol with Prozac. The only thing he has going for him is a "two-eleven all around," police language for someone who has no warrants against him in the city or county, and thus is free to go. Jealous of the time his girlfriend spends with the scanner, he loiters on a street corner, knowing the police will ask for his identification and that she will hear the whole thing on the scanner; he hopes that at least she will be happy that he is two-eleven all around. The story ends with an abrupt insight; the protagonist has a sudden vision that one night he will be awakened by his son banging at the door looking for a place to flop. While a part of him wants to tell his son to take a look at the empty beer cans, the beat-up furniture, and the dirty sheets, realizing that if he does not change his ways, he will be doomed to such squalor, instead he opens the door wide and lets him in.

For various reasons, the last four stories in the collection are not as strong as these first four. In "High Water Everywhere," an Appalachian truck driver must abandon his load in Oregon because of flooding. When plot complications take over—not Offutt's forte—the story becomes muddied and mired. First the man is accused of blowing up a dike and is arrested; then he is bailed out by a woman he has met in a bar, who, he discovers, for reasons never made clear, is the one who blew up the dike. All this is complicated further by the fact that the sheriff who arrested him is the woman's brother. There is some sex out in the rain, some guilt over a man killed in the resultant flooding, and some talk about moving around as opposed to being a stayer. These plot complications never really come together convincingly, and the man's final decision to sell the truck, apply for work, and get a wife is not really motivated or compelling.

In "Barred Owl," it is not plot, but clichéd character that weakens the story. The protagonist, a former Kentuckian, who, after a divorce settled in Greeley, Colorado, because that is where his car threw a rod, becomes acquainted with another displaced mountain man who asks him to skin a dead owl for him. Although the story takes place in Colorado, there are more mountain traditions and rituals here than in any other story in the book as the men share ritual greetings with tobacco and stylized formal talk. The story is about the lonely protagonist, lost in meaningless activities, coming face to face with his displaced double; he realizes he must do something about his life when the depressed double takes his life by rigging a bow and arrow so he can shoot himself in the chest.

"Target Practice" is ineffective because Offutt's habit of using unmotivated epiphanies at the ends of his stories finally fails here. The story focuses on Ray, a man who left Kentucky for the assembly lines of Detroit and has returned, only to be unsure that he has made the right decision. He is living in poverty and his wife has left him, but he is too embarrassed to tell anyone. The story's single event centers on Ray's buying a used rifle from a man and inviting his father to test it. As usual, Offutt expertly conveys just the right intonations of the tight-lipped father and son as they talk and shoot and spit.

The story turns ominous when the father puts the barrel of the gun in his mouth, but returns to the ordinary when Ray sees he is only blowing out the dirt. However, it abruptly turns ominous again when, just as Ray is about to tell his father of his wife leaving, the older man suddenly points his gun at Ray, who, without thinking, fires twice, the second shot making a hole in the father's chest. It is a shocking event, for nothing has prepared the reader for it; although Ray and his father have never been close, Offutt has shown no overt animosity between them. Both the father and the son take the shooting relatively calmly, Ray thinking that there is not enough blood to have hit an artery. The Offutt epiphany ending comes when, putting his father in the car, Ray realizes that he has never touched him before. Looking at him without being afraid for the first time in his life, Ray realizes that he loves his father. However, how Ray's shooting his father causes this new realization is not made clear.

Chris Offutt is the first fiction writer since James Still to capture the life of the people of the mountains of eastern Kentucky. Like Still, he understands and respects his characters. He does not exploit them as trendy exotics, nor does he revel in local-color quaintness. Offutt knows how to use language to reflect the essential humanness of his characters. He is not a sociologist playing back a tape recording or illustrating abstractions, but an artist, transforming mere external reality into poetic meaning.

Charles E. May

Sources for Further Study

Booklist 95 (December 15, 1998): 727.
Boston Globe, January 17, 1999, p. E2.
Library Journal 123 (December, 1998): 160.
Los Angeles Times, February 26, 1999, p. E3.
Milwaukee Journal Sentinel, February 14, 1999, p. 13.
The New York Times Book Review 104 (March 7, 1999): 16.
St. Louis Post-Dispatch, January 31, 1999, p. G5.

PERSONAL INJURIES

Author: Scott Turow (1949-)
Publisher: Farrar, Straus and Giroux (New York). 403 pp. $27.00
Type of work: Novel
Time: 1992-1993
Locale: Kindle County, a fictionalized version of Turow's Chicago

When a flamboyant trial lawyer is discovered to be bribing powerful judges—some of whom are reputed to have mob ties—he agrees, in a desperate bid to avoid prison time and attend to his terminally ill wife, to participate in an elaborate sting operation that will implicate the guilty

Principal characters:
ROBBIE FEAVER, a personal injury attorney
LORRAINE FEAVER, his wife
GEORGE MASON, an attorney representing Robbie
MORTON DINNERSTEIN, Robbie's law partner
STAN SENNETT, a prosecutor
EVON MILLER, an undercover agent with the Federal Bureau of Investigation (FBI)
JUDGE BRENDAN TUOHEY, a chief target of the case

Of the tremendous spate of legal thrillers published in the wake of John Grisham's blockbuster novel *The Firm* (1991), few can match—and perhaps none surpass—the writings of attorney Scott Turow for emotional depth and sheer literary quality. When Turow's 1987 novel *Presumed Innocent* came on the scene, followed by *The Burden of Proof* in 1990, reviewers praising the two international best-sellers recognized that the author's page-turning suspense format was in the service of a larger goal: writing about what William Faulkner once called "the problems of the human heart in conflict with itself, which alone can make good writing . . . love and honor and pity and pride and compassion and sacrifice."

Nowhere is this more true than in *Personal Injuries*. On its first page, readers meet attorney Robbie Feaver (pronounced "favor"): He is flashy, egotistical, manipulative, crass, and an inveterate womanizer. He is also scared to death. Government agents have turned up a secret bank account Feaver maintains, apparently unbeknownst to his straight-arrow law partner and childhood best friend Morton Dinnerstein, for the sole purpose of bribing judges and other court officers to assure positive outcomes for many of the firm's clients.

Feaver seeks out defense attorney George Mason, narrator of the book, who initially describes his client this way:

> I did not know Robbie Feaver well. When he'd called this morning, he'd reminded me that we'd met several times in the lobby of the LeSueur Building where we each had our law offices, and of the committee work he'd done for the Kindle County Bar Association a couple of years ago during my term as president. My memories of him were vague and not necessarily pleasant. Measured according to the remaining reflexes of a proper Southern upbringing, he was the kind of fellow who'd be described simply as "too much." Too good-looking in the sense that he was too well aware of it. Too much stiff, dark hair that reflected too much fussing. He was tanned in every season and spent

> too much money on his clothes—high-styled Italian suits and snazzy foulards—accompanied by too much jewelry. He spoke too loudly, and too eagerly to strangers in the elevator. In fact, in any setting, he talked too much—one of those people who went one up on Descartes: I speak, therefore I am. But I now saw one apparent virtue: he could have told you all of that. Diminished by fear, he maintained an air of candor, at least about himself. As clients went, therefore, he seemed, on first impression, better than average.

Feaver is a major-league paradox, by turns charismatic and obnoxious, greedy and softheartedly altruistic. He dotes on his wife and mother, both of whom are seriously ill: His wife Lorraine is in the final stages of amyotrophic lateral sclerosis (ALS, or Lou Gehrig's disease), and his mother Estelle has been confined to a nursing home after a stroke. As the story unfolds, Feaver becomes what is possibly Turow's most enigmatic and memorable character yet.

The deal that Feaver strikes with the devil (in the person of prosecutor Stan Sennett) is to pretend business-as-usual, continuing to make his illegal payoffs—though now with a body wire and surveillance cameras to nail down evidence against the accused. Feaver, whose true passion has always been amateur theater, finds himself giving the most important performance of his life.

The pressure cooker is turned up several more notches when a full-scale FBI surveillance team hits town, including undercover agent Evon Miller, the second most intriguing character in *Personal Injuries*. Miller is a former Olympic athlete, now a loner who has made her career her life. She has the unenviable task of posing as Feaver's new paralegal and incidental girlfriend, while keeping round-the-clock tabs on him to ensure that he plays by the rules.

The ongoing verbal and psychological sparring between the two, remarkable for its lack of cliché or stereotype, is electric in its intensity, particularly when Evon begins to form an unlikely emotional bond with Robbie's dying wife.

After elaborate coaching and preparation, the FBI's grand scheme goes into action. Almost immediately, their best-laid plans start going badly astray in ways no one reasonably could have predicted. The plot turns and personal revelations pick up speed throughout the second half of the book.

It is to Turow's artistic credit that there are no white hats or black hats here, just regular people with strengths and flaws and irrevocable personal histories, trying—rightly or wrongly—to make the best of the hands that have been dealt them. The author affords them the opportunity to plead their cases eloquently, if sometimes indirectly, in the course of the narrative.

At one point, Evon angrily confronts Robbie after seeing him cry, apparently on cue, while comforting potentially lucrative clients at their dead daughter's hospital bedside. She demands to know whether he really cares about the people he represents, or if he does it for the money:

> "Look, I love the spotlight. I dig the bucks. I adore getting the chance to strut around on my victory lap down Marshall Avenue whenever I win a case. But hell," he said, "you actually think I drop to these judges *just* for myself? Get real. I can't bear to come back to these people and say, I lost, you lost, f— hope, it's only pain, and it's only going to get worse. I can't do that. That's why it's a play.

> They need it, and *I* need it." Carried away, he had briefly taken hold of her hands . . . He touched his bright muffler and softly said one more thing before he again put the Mercedes in gear.
> "It's a *play*."

Ambivalence and its shifting prism of "truths" form a constant thread throughout the drama, and at the climax, none of the principal players is quite what they seemed at the outset. Even attorney Mason, the objective narrator, admits that he "swam, as defense lawyers do, in the brackish waters of compromise."

The compromises on all sides begin to mount drastically as word of the sting hits the streets, and Sennett and the highest-level decision makers of the FBI have to keep playing double-or-nothing—eventually with Feaver's life in the balance—to keep the whole investigation from unraveling before their eyes.

Personal Injuries is not without its comic relief, much of it at the expense of the judges themselves. Feaver is a master of improvisation under pressure. When he tries desperately to get a crucial private conversation with one of the judges in chambers and is rebuffed—he never meets with lawyers alone, the jurist tells him, only when his secretary is present—Robbie announces that a young woman has just filed a paternity suit against the judge. After some sputtering, a private audience is immediately granted.

Another judge, bumblingly lovable in his sheer ineptitude, is said to have passed his long-ago bar exam and been elevated to the bench through the courtesy of his mobster brother. "The guy can't zip his fly without an instruction book," Robbie tells Mason. "He just sort of sits there with this sweet, terrified expression: 'Gosh, I like you all. Please don't ask me any hard questions.' . . . This schmo's been on the bench twenty-six years, and he couldn't guess what hearsay is if you gave him multiple choice . . . "

As a reviewer for *The Chicago Tribune* observed of *Personal Injuries*, "Turow knows the weight of institutions and is interested in what happens when the good set out to reckon with the bad and the ugly. His characters are very much of this moment—rogues in the know, dragged by greed and self-promotion into moral swamps, matched up against moralists who also have their price. His sense of the human comedy is laced with tragedy. Not a pretty picture, but a true one."

In this novel, Turow breaks new stylistic ground as well. The language seems a bit more abrupt and telegrammatic, occasional echoes of hard-boiled masters such as Raymond Chandler and Dashiell Hammett, but without sacrificing the graceful delivery that is one of Turow's trademarks. He also bites off a lot structurally, with the unusual device of a viewpoint narrator who is not present throughout much of the action. Yet with a strong storytelling instinct and some technical sleight of hand, he pulls it off with narrative authority—and with style.

In some writers' hands, authorial asides can be annoying because they tend to stall the action. Turow's brief addresses to the reader (through the character of George Mason) give the benefit of an enriching perspective—as when Mason, while watching a surveillance monitor which shows a judge about to accept a payoff, reflects:

> The bribery of judges is eternal. At common law, before there were statutes and codes, the word "bribe" meant only this: a benefit conferred to influence a judge. It began as soon as King John signed Magna Carta and set up the courts. Probably before. Probably when Adam tried to reason with God about Eve, the first man offered Him something on the side. What we were there to see held the fierce primal attraction of any elemental wrong.

The resolution of *Personal Injuries*, while not a traditionally happy one, is nonetheless apt, wise, moving, and in many ways, redemptive—an impressive creation from a contemporary writer working at the top of his form.

Carroll Dale Short

Sources for Further Study

Library Journal 124 (August, 1999): 143.
The New York Times Book Review 104 (October 24, 1999): 7.
Newsweek 133 (September 27, 1999): 66.
Publishers Weekly 246 (August 2, 1999): 69.
Time 154 (October 18, 1999): 114.

THE PITY OF WAR
Explaining World War I

Author: Niall Ferguson (1964-)
Publisher: Basic Books (New York). Illustrated. 520 pp. $30.00
Type of work: History
Time: 1914-1918
Locale: Europe

A stimulating revisionist analysis of the Great War, this book argues that the conflict was a tragedy that could have been avoided

World War I was the defining event of the twentieth century. The period 1914-1918 stands as one of the watersheds of history; it reshaped the world made by the French Revolution and brought to an end one hundred years of unparalleled peace, prosperity, and political progress in Europe. The Great War's immediate impact was profound—ten million lives lost and an economic cost almost incalculable. Its effects were far-reaching. Four empires—the Russian, German, Austro-Hungarian, and Ottoman Turkish—were defeated and destroyed. The victorious British and French empires survived, but in an enfeebled state. The Great War gave birth to the Soviet Union and laid the foundation for German National Socialism; World War II was its bastard offspring.

Niall Ferguson's *The Pity of War: Explaining World War I* is a stimulating work of revisionist scholarship. This young historian, hitherto the author of studies of German business and the House of Rothschild, dares to challenge much of the conventional wisdom that has grown up around our understanding of World War I. His aims being analytical rather than narrative, he has not written a chronological account of the Great War. Instead, he organizes his book as a series of questions, exploring aspects of the conflict's origins, conduct, and conclusion.

Ferguson attacks his subject with a passion. Though a product of the era of television and rock and roll, Ferguson grew up in a world that reverberated with echoes of World War I. The school he attended as a boy was dedicated as a war memorial. Every day he passed a granite slab which bore the names of former pupils who had died in the conflict. Official commemorations were reinforced by more direct connections at home. Ferguson's grandfather had fought in the war, serving in a Scottish regiment. Ferguson is careful to point out that during the war, the Scots suffered disproportionately high casualties. The old man was a living link to an epochal experience. As he grew up, Ferguson was exposed in school to the writings of Great War poets and memorialists like Wilfred Owen and Siegfried Sassoon. This reading made a lasting impression upon Ferguson. Indeed, the title of his book comes from a line of Wilfred Owen's poetry. These writers told a tale of waste, describing the self-sacrificial heroism of a generation, expended in pointless offensives which achieved nothing but devastating casualty lists. The best, the brightest, disappeared, and with them the hope of the future. Victory, in such books, brought only debilitation, and the inevitable, ironic sequel of World War II. By Ferguson's youth, the vision adumbrated by these writers, of a war in which helpless, trapped men were driven to slaughter by the authority of old men and meretricious notions of honor, had hardened into an orthodoxy. The Great War was seen as a searing tragedy, which tore down a comfortable edifice of traditional verities and ushered in the complexities, confusions, and horrors of modernity. The continuing preoccupation of novelists, playwrights, and filmmakers with the divide separating the world of 1914 from the present is testimony to the continuing power of the myth of the "lost generation."

Ferguson casts the cool eye of a skeptic over the traditional narratives of the Great War. He accepts that the war was a disaster; his dismay over the havoc it wrought fuels the fury of his analysis. What he emphatically rejects is the implicit fatalism and passivity he sees in customary accounts of the war. The war is usually regarded as an inevitability, both in the works of historians who detail the pernicious effects of a European arms race, divisive alliance systems, and nationalist tensions, and in the writings of novelists and memoirists, who see it as the price of human folly, or perhaps as the act of an angry God. Ferguson argues that the war was none of these things. For Ferguson, the Great War was something worse than a tragedy; it was a mistake.

Ferguson takes aim at a number of shibboleths about World War I. He questions the common assumption, often found in textbooks, that the war was precipitated by a combination of militarism, imperialism, and secret diplomacy. He points out that, in the years leading up to 1914, militarism was in retreat rather than flourishing. The international peace movement was increasingly vocal and influential. Big business, even arms manufacturers, the so-called merchants of death, opposed war as a threat to commerce. Germany, purportedly the most militaristic of the European states, was actually spending a smaller percentage of its gross national product on its armed forces than were its rivals France and Russia. At the same time, imperial disputes between the great powers were being resolved, not exacerbated, by diplomacy. Relations between Great Britain and Germany were thought to be improving in 1914. The British government did not conclude a formal accord with Germany, as it had with other powers, because Germany was not believed to pose a serious threat to the interests of Britain's empire.

Ferguson also challenges the folk memory that the people of Europe greeted the war with enthusiasm. Cheering crowds did send the troops off, but these were largely middle class and soon dissipated. Ferguson finds expressions of gloom more persuasive as indicators of the general mood. The businessmen controlling Europe's financial resources certainly showed no confidence in the future. The war set off an economic crisis. Many men in Britain volunteered for service in the army, but Ferguson points out that this influx of recruits was stimulated by economic uncertainty; large numbers of workers found themselves suddenly unemployed in the late summer and fall of 1914. Apocalyptic imagery colored much of the early rhetoric of the war. Many sermons and other early commentaries on the war predicted various forms of catastrophe. Speculative novels about imaginary wars between the great powers had been popular for years; these gave people some sense of the bloodshed and disruption that lay in store. Ferguson believes that the dominant response to the war was resignation. The people of Europe were first stunned, and then transfixed, by the enormity of what had come to pass. The soldiers who marched off to the front in the first month of the war, with flowers in the barrels of their rifles and bands in the lead, were heading into Armageddon, and people knew it.

Ferguson offers refreshing new insights on other topics as well. He acknowledges that the Great War was a "media" war, but he notes that wartime propaganda was less the product of governmental agencies than the spontaneous expression of influential groups of national opinion leaders. Journalists, academics, writers, and filmmakers vied with each other to release works extolling the war effort and vilifying the enemy. The resulting flood of propaganda had little impact on the soldiers, few of whom trusted the news from home. The main effect of this effort was to debase and vulgarize cultural and intellectual life and to lay the foundation for the troubling mass culture which would flourish later in the century.

Though the Allies ultimately won the war, Ferguson argues that they waged war much less efficiently than Germany. Scholars have long charged the Germans with mismanaging their wartime economy. Ferguson dismisses this as a myth. He believes that the Germans did an effective job of harnessing their shrinking economy. The Allies enjoyed a substantial material edge over Germany. Their advantages included a 60 percent greater combined national income, 4.5 times as many people, and 28 percent more men mobilized. Despite this, it took the Allies more than four years of combat to wear Germany down. For virtually the whole of that period, the Germans consistently killed or captured roughly 30 percent more men than they lost. Ferguson notes that this figure makes a mockery of the Allied battlefield strategy of attrition. Similarly, German economic resilience foiled the Allied attempt to starve their enemies into surrender. By combining military and financial figures, Ferguson calculates that it cost the Allies more than three times as much as it did the Germans to kill an opposing soldier. In the end, German military resistance collapsed because of its high command's strategic mistakes, most important the enormously costly spring and summer offensives of 1918, which failed to bring a promised victory.

Conditions at the front during World War I were terrible. Major battles were infrequent, but when they took place, the carnage was appalling. Machine guns, snipers, and shells exacted a toll of men's lives even on "quiet" days. The odds that an ordinary British soldier would become a casualty in France were an even 50:50. Some sanguine historians have asserted that the army provided working-class soldiers with an improvement in their standard of living. Ferguson refutes this by pointing out that no slum, no matter how squalid, could equal the trenches' filth, discomfort, and danger. The surprising steadiness and loyalty of the soldiers who endured these conditions has long puzzled historians. What kept the soldiers from turning on their officers and governments, and refusing to fight? Ferguson acknowledges that his answer to this question offers no comfort. He does not believe that the troops' obedience was coerced. The ferocious disciplinary measures taken by the Germans and Russians during World War II were not necessarily taken during World War I. Nor does he credit propaganda, which generally rang hollow at the front. Instead, he makes a persuasive case that most men were not profoundly bothered by the fighting and killing. The postwar literature which emphasized the anguish and rebelliousness of the soldiers misrepresented reality. Ferguson observes that, contrary to popular memory, most war books published during and after the conflict did not question the morality or necessity of the fighting. Ferguson reinforces his argument by noting that one reason the war went on as long as it did was that soldiers on both sides were reluctant to surrender. This reluctance, he says, resulted from a propensity of some officers to discourage their men from taking prisoners. The willingness of private soldiers to acquiesce in this bloody-mindedness further undermines the traditional image of Great War soldiers as reluctant killers. In fact, some men could not escape the habit of war and enlisted to fight in the various conflicts which erupted in the wake of the Armistice.

The most striking and controversial judgment in Ferguson's book is his assertion that British intervention in the war was an unnecessary blunder. Britain's involvement in the conflict was by no means inevitable. British generals and diplomats had engaged in military planning with the French, but the government had no formal commitments obligating it to engage in a continental war. Many ministers were opposed to the prospect, and little had been done to prepare the country or the military for war with Germany. Yet, when the crisis came, Britain entered the war. Officially Britain fought to vindicate the neutrality of Belgium, which had been violated by a German invasion. Ferguson claims that the real reason was the ministry's fear of being turned out of office. This decision, he believes, led to tragic consequences. With Britain standing aside, Germany probably would have won a shorter, limited war. Ferguson believes that German war aims at this point were modest. The kaiser's government would have created a Central European Customs Union and taken some French colonies. Something like the European Union would have emerged eighty years early. None of this, in Ferguson's opinion, would have posed a threat to the British Empire. Instead of being bled white in Flanders, the Empire would have continued to thrive. In this scenario, the Bolshevik Revolution never takes place, and Adolf Hitler never emerges from obscurity. There would have been no Gulag, no World War II, no Holocaust, no Cold War. It is a tantalizing counterfactual picture that Ferguson draws, of a world which escapes most of the disasters of the twentieth century. Unfortunately, it is hard to imagine that any British government could have realistically stood by passively as Germany united the continent under its domination—to have done so would have repudiated a long-standing policy of opposing any power seeking European hegemony, a tradition that stretched back to the days of Louis XIV and Napoleon I. Nevertheless, Ferguson's argument demands attention, if only for reminding us of the perennial poignance of what might have been. It is the strength of *The Pity of War* that it compels us to examine once again the catastrophe which gave birth to the modern world.

Daniel P. Murphy

Sources for Further Study

The Atlantic Monthly 283 (May, 1999): 118.
Commentary 108 (October, 1999): 48.
The Economist 349 (November 14, 1998): 5.
Foreign Affairs 78 (May, 1999): 139.
Library Journal 124 (March 15, 1999): 92.
National Review 51 (July 12, 1999): 50.
The New Republic 220 (June 28, 1999): 51.
The New York Review of Books 46 (August 12, 1999): 36.
The New York Times Book Review 104 (May 9, 1999): 12.
Publishers Weekly 246 (March 8, 1999): 56.
The Times Literary Supplement, November 13, 1998, p. 3.
The Wall Street Journal, April 14, 1999, p. A24.

PLAINSONG

Author: Kent Haruf (1943-)
Publisher: Alfred A. Knopf (New York). 301 pp. $24.00
Type of work: Novel
Time: The late 1990's
Locale: Colorado

How several characters in a small town cope with change

Principal characters:
TOM GUTHRIE, a high school teacher
IKE and
BOBBY, his young sons
VICTORIA ROUBIDEAUX, a high school student
RAYMOND AND HAROLD MCPHERON, old ranchers, brothers

Like Kent Haruf's previous novels, *Where You Once Belonged* (1990) and *The Tie That Binds* (1984), the latter the winner of a Whiting Writers' Award, *Plainsong*, as the title suggests, uses simple characters to dramatize basic events. In support of this, the author gives his plot a rural setting, and makes its main characters speak as little as possible. Also, *Plainsong* is democratic in that it has several protagonists, and it is moralistic in that it condemns its antagonists to the roles of minor characters, in line, perhaps, with how mean-spirited they are.

Except for one chapter a third of the way through, entitled "Ella" after the wife of Tom Guthrie, one of the main characters, and the chapter at the end entitled "Holt" after the town in the story, each chapter is named for the protagonist it features; this stresses these players' equality, avoids the confusion of switching points of view without warning, and keeps the plot lines clear.

The earlier chapters of *Plainsong* show the problems of its main characters, and its later chapters show how these problems play out. Though this mechanism gives the impression that the plot is as slow to work itself up as its chief characters are to express themselves, it is faithful to the simple world in which they live and to the unadorned way in which they do so.

Beginning with Tom Guthrie, the cast of main characters presents itself. Guthrie is an American history teacher in the high school in Holt, Colorado. He has two problems to deal with: his wife Ella and one of his students, Russel Beckman. Ella and Guthrie have grown apart, with Ella becoming neurotically vague and remote. She stays in bed, then rents her own house, then moves in with her sister in Denver. At the same time, Guthrie has a fight with Beckman, who is failing the course; one day, Beckman makes a comment that drives Victoria Roubideaux, another student, from the room. When Guthrie tries to make him explain himself, Beckman hits him and runs away. This conflict worsens in a meeting with the principal, Lloyd Crowder, when Beckman's parents, against all logic, viciously take their son's side.

Guthrie's sons, Ike and Bobby, also have a problem: How are they going to get their mother back? This puzzle seems to drive less their curiosity about Sharlene, a high school student they see through the window of an abandoned house naked and having sex with Russel Beckman and, after him, his friend Murphy, than their need for Iva Stearns, an old woman on their paper route whom they help bake cookies and who shows them a photo of herself with her son Albert, who was in the Navy and died in World War II.

Victoria Roubideaux (Vicky), another main character, has problems which stem from her pregnancy. First of all, she is seventeen and a student, and her baby's father, Dwayne, is out of school and lives in Denver. Her effort to pretend she is not pregnant fails, and her mother disowns her. Maggie Jones, a teacher at the high school, takes her in, but Maggie's father, who lives with her because he lost his mind to old age, becomes violent toward Vicky, so she must leave. Maggie convinces Raymond and Harold McPheron, old bachelors with a ranch outside town, to let Vicky stay with them, an awkward arrangement at first.

The McPheron brothers, the last of *Plainsong*'s major characters, have no problems before Vicky appears. It is one thing for them to vaccinate their pregnant heifers (which they do, with Guthrie's help, in an early scene) and see them through their birthing, for they are adept at treating their livestock; it is quite another for them to deal with Vicky's pregnancy, especially since their parents were killed when they were boys, and since all they have ever done is run the ranch.

Guthrie, realizing that he and his wife Ella are through with each other, does his best to soften this for his sons by encouraging their access to her. He solves his need for a woman by first sleeping with Judy, the high school secretary, then becoming the lover of Maggie Jones, whose generosity and strength Ella lacks and Guthrie needs. As for Russel Beckman, Guthrie's battle with him and his parents comes to a head after the boy abducts and humiliates Ike and Bobby; Guthrie comes to blows with Russel and his father on the front porch of the Beckman house. Though he takes a worse beating than he gives, Guthrie proves to them that he will not retreat from any threat they pose to him and his sons.

Ike and Bobby Guthrie try to stay close to their mother. When she first moves out, they buy perfume for her, and even sleep in her bed with her. When she moves to Denver, they stay with her during the Christmas holidays. Eventually, they have to accept that she will not return, and this becomes one of the lessons they begin to learn about life. The sex they see in the abandoned house is another of these lessons, and if they are too young for it to do more than fascinate them, they come to see that loss is not limited to their mother, but may extend to anything they treasure, such as their horse Elko, which dies of a misaligned intestine, and which they watch the vet and their father autopsy and leave in their field to decompose. They also lose Iva Stearns, whom they have substituted for their mother, for they find her dead in her apartment one day.

They learn as well, that finding what they need complements losing what they want. For one thing, they need to survive, which they manage to do when Russel Beckman and his friend Murphy abduct them in Beckman's car one night in early spring. Sharlene urges Beckman and Murphy not to, but they leave the boys all but naked on the side of the road five miles outside town. Later, the Guthrie boys ride their horse Easter all the way to the McPheron ranch, and though they cannot explain why, what readers know of them implies that they want to become part of the family the McPheron brothers and Vicky have formed with each other.

Vicky's goal is to have her baby and care for it, and to this end she learns to accept Raymond and Harold McPheron as stand-in fathers. This is a drawn-out process, and the moment its obstacles are smoothed out, Dwayne, the baby's father, convinces Vicky to go with him to Denver, where they become lovers again. Vicky's need to protect her baby, however, outdoes both Dwayne's need for sex and hers to have the baby's real father at hand. The parties to which Dwayne takes Vicky threaten the baby, for Vicky drinks and dances and is the object of some kind of violence—probably sexual—which she cannot remember the next morning, and she packs up and sneaks out. Dwayne fails to stop her at the bus station in Denver, and she returns to Holt. Later, when Dwayne comes to Holt to take her and the girl to whom she has given birth away with him, she will not let him, and the McPherons drive him off.

Raymond and Harold McPheron progress from letting Vicky live with them to committing themselves to her care. Maggie Jones, all through the novel a maternal figure exemplifying the energy that Ella Guthrie lacks and the hope that old age has leeched from Iva Stearns, advises the McPheron brothers to close the distance between them and Vicky by talking with her. Once they do this, the brothers take on the concerns of proper fathers. One of the most endearing scenes in the story happens when, with Vicky between them in their pickup, they drive to Phillips, a town with a department store, where they buy the best crib for the baby, then assemble it in her bedroom, which used to be their parents'. For her part, Vicky cooks for them and takes on the housework. When she disappears with Dwayne, and while Maggie Jones tracks her down, the McPherons are too worried about her to sleep, and when she returns like the Prodigal Daughter, Raymond says, awkwardly trying to comfort her as she weeps, "If you come back here we're glad." Vicky finally tells them what happened to her, and they become even more protective of her. Taking her to old Dr. Martin in town, they bully him to tell them in detail about her condition, and during her labor and the birth itself, they stay with her; though Harold is forced to return to the ranch to see to the cattle, Raymond will not budge from the hospital. At Vicky's bidding, they learn how to hold the baby. Indeed, thanks to Vicky, their lives acquire a meaning they lacked before, until, at the end, they and Vicky have become part of a kind of extended family which includes Tom Guthrie and Maggie Jones, and Guthrie's sons, whose only differences from the McPheron brothers are their ages.

Haruf uses images to highlight his concerns in *Plainsong*. The imagery of the seasons gives the story a time-line that matches the events in it, beginning with early fall signaling the main characters' troubles, and early summer signaling their triumph.

Along the way, animals are important images. The maverick heifer on the McPherons' ranch foreshadows Vicky Roubideaux's arrival there, as the heifer the brothers later help through a difficult birth foreshadows their standing by Vicky—fiercely, in fact—during the birth of her daughter. The lone coyote they and Vicky see as they drive her to get the crib seems to stand for Dwayne, a scavenger who tries to steal Vicky and stay clear of her needs at the same time. The death of Ike and Bobby's horse foreshadows the death of their friend Iva Stearns, both of which saturate them with repulsive details. Further, leaving the dead horse out in the field points to death as a source of nourishment in nature, as Guthrie and the vet washing themselves off after the autopsy points to the need for renewal that comes with death. Finally, on the last page of the novel, the old dog on the McPheron ranch, sniffing and looking at everyone gathered there on Memorial Day, seems to be a comment on the author himself, examining his characters without forcing himself upon them.

The windows from which Ike and Bobby, more than other characters in the story, stare (perhaps in lieu of talking) are an image for looking at the world itself, with its possibilities and puzzles, from a safe distance, and the color red seems to be a metaphor for discord—for example, Russel Beckman's red hair, Vicky Roubideaux's red purse, the sweater in the wrong size that Ike and Bobby give their mother for Christmas, the red maverick heifer on the McPheron ranch, and the red cow there giving birth to an incorrectly positioned calf.

The characters and settings in *Plainsong* feel authentic, as if they were based on the kind of people and milieu the author knows. Though Maggie Jones and Russel Beckman's parents speak their minds easily—the one to help and renew, the others to destroy—the main characters' silence, a feature of their simplicity, is equated with virtue in *Plainsong*, and if this is hard to believe, and if the laconic style—which evokes that of Ernest Hemingway's (1889-1961) and Raymond Carver's (1938-1988) fiction—holds the plot hostage for the first half of the story, the ties the characters have with each other, particularly the tie between the McPheron brothers and Vicky Roubideaux, secure the reader's interest in their fate.

Mark McCloskey

Sources for Further Study

Booklist 95 (August, 1999): 1986.
Library Journal 124 (September 1, 1999): 232.
The New York Review of Books 46 (October 21, 1999): 30.
The New York Times, October 8, 1999, p. B45.
The New York Times Book Review 104 (October 3, 1999): 7.
Newsweek 133 (October 4, 1999): 67.
Publishers Weekly 246 (August 2, 1999): 70.
Time 154 (October 25, 1999): 130.

PLAYING FOR KEEPS
Michael Jordan and the World He Made

Author: David Halberstam (1934-)
Publisher: Random House (New York). Illustrated. 426 pp. $24.95
Type of work: Biography and history
Time: 1979-1998
Locale: Chicago and other National Basketball Association (NBA) cities; North Carolina; and Europe

An exciting play-by-play account of professional basketball, which also uncovers the cultural and economic forces that turned the game and its superstar, by the end of the 1990's, into international icons

Principal personages:
MICHAEL JORDAN, perhaps history's greatest basketball player and, in 1998, one of the most famous Americans in the world
PHIL JACKSON, his coach on the Chicago Bulls for their championship years in the 1990's
DEAN SMITH, his college coach at the University of North Carolina
DAVID STERN, the commissioner of the NBA
JERRY REINSDORF, the owner of the Chicago Bulls
JERRY KRAUSE, the general manager of the Chicago Bulls
DAVID FALK, Jordan's agent
SCOTTIE PIPPEN and
DENNIS RODMAN, two of Jordan's teammates on the Bulls

David Halberstam has been retelling recent history as best-sellers for some years—from *The Best and the Brightest* (1973) to *The Fifties* (1994)—and *Playing for Keeps* is another clear demonstration of his exceptional talents. Using his keen historian's eye, and the broadest possible canvas, Halberstam portrays one of the most phenomenal athletes of modern times, and the sport he has helped raise to international popularity, and reveals the interconnected powers that color both. Halberstam goes behind the television game-of-the-week to show the complex economic and cultural forces which came together in the 1980's and 1990's to elevate Michael Jordan to superstardom and professional basketball to one of the most profitable businesses in the world. Halberstam's history is not always pretty, but it is consistently exciting and well told.

The thirty-plus chapters of *Playing for Keeps* move back and forth from the 1997-1998 professional basketball season—with its climactic championship series between the Chicago Bulls and the Utah Jazz—to the years leading up to that pivotal moment: from Jordan playing at Laney High in Wilmington, North Carolina (1979-1981), through his years under coach Dean Smith at North Carolina (1981-1984), his early years with the struggling Bulls, to the final and triumphant seasons in the 1990's when Jordan and the Bulls were the dominating forces in basketball.

Part of the attraction is Jordan himself, not only a consummate athlete, but a competitive man with a very strong work ethic. Halberstam shows readers Jordan's childhood and the values his parents instilled in him and his brother Larry; "you were not to waste your talent and you were always to work hard." Jordan turned out to be an attractive, talented, and personable man who, in the end, became the new marketing symbol of his age, and gave Americans "nothing less than a new definition of beauty for a new age."

Jordan, great as he was, however, is only the tall figure in the foreground of a much more complex picture Halberstam paints for readers. Part of the story is the rise of the NBA itself which, under the canny and inspired leadership of David Stern, grew from the poor stepchild of professional sports to become the economic power it was by the 1990's. In the early 1980's, college basketball was still perceived as an extension of mainstream America; the professional game was something closer to professional wrestling. Halberstam dates the modern NBA from the all-star game of January, 1984, when the slam-dunk contest was introduced. Suddenly television networks like the National Broadcasting Company (NBC) and other corporations saw the economic potential of this sport, and were competing to sign up its stars as their spokespersons.

Another part of the story is the colorful history of different franchises, like the Boston Celtics and the Los Angeles Lakers, and particularly the saga of Jerry Reinsdorf, the astute owner of the Bulls, his abrasive general manager, Jerry Krause, and the incredibly profitable franchise they built around Jordan, beginning in the 1980's. Halberstam digs deeply into the economics of this history, escalating player salaries (like Kevin Garnett's incredible $126 million contract for seven years in 1997), and the lockout in the fall of 1998 when negotiations between greedy players and their agents, and greedier owners—a strike, one newspaper pundit called it, between tall millionaires and short millionaires—threatened to undo all the progress, and profit, the sport had made in the previous fifteen years.

Luck plays no small part in this drama, Halberstam shows—for example, the fortuitous beginnings of ESPN, when Bill Rasmussen, in Bristol, Connecticut, started a small cable company which would eventually take professional basketball, and any other sport, into people's homes across the country twenty-four hours a day. Luck plays no small part, either, in the story of how Jim Riswold, a copywriter for the small Portland, Oregon, ad agency of Wieden and Kennedy, got the Nike account and then hired a little known filmmaker named Spike Lee to shoot the commercials—a serendipitous conjunction of stars which would produce ads which meant millions in the sale of Air Jordans, and elevated Jordan himself into the celebrity stratosphere.

Halberstam's story, in short, is social history at its best, for he not only gives readers exciting accounts of the crucial college and professional games in this twenty-year span, and inside looks at basketball's stars, but uncovers the complex web of economic and cultural forces which propelled Jordan and his game into the world's spotlight. As in all good social history, many of the most fascinating stories take place just off the arena floor. Halberstam is particularly good on the coaches who guided Jordan's meteoric career, like Smith at Chapel Hill, who demanded sacrifice and patience of his players, and who taught them that the team was more important than the individual and other lessons that had as much to do with life as with basketball. Behind Smith's program at North Carolina, Halberstam writes, "was a series of old-fashioned, almost Calvinist values more and more at risk in the increasingly material culture of American sports." If Jordan's loving family had instilled the right values in the young man growing up in Wilmington, Dean Smith nurtured them for a number of years after that in his own North Carolina basketball family. Smith, Halberstam marvels, seemed to pay even more attention to his players once they left his program.

Part of the tension in Halberstam's book (and there is plenty) comes from the conflict between younger and older players in the league, between stars like Jordan, Larry Bird, Earvin "Magic" Johnson, and Patrick Ewing, who learned the ethic of hard work early in their lives, and the coddled younger players who came into the league in the 1990's expecting millions, but with a questionable work ethic. Their attitude from the moment they arrived seemed to be: "What are you going to do for us?" After the 1994 World Games in Canada, Dick Ebersol, the head of NBC sports, Halberstam reports, sent Sony television sets to every player on the American team; he did not get a single word of thanks.

Perhaps the most fascinating coach in Halberstam's book, however, is Phil Jackson, who breaks most of the stereotypes of what it takes to win in the NBA. Born into a fundamentalist religious family in North Dakota, Jackson came of age in hippie New York City in the late 1960's and early 1970's as a player with the New York Knicks, and learned values most coaches cannot share. Before the playoffs at the end of the 1998 season, for example, Jackson called Bulls players, coaches, and trainers into a special team meeting and asked each of them to write down anything, even a poem, "about their time together and what the season had meant to them." Jackson knew that, even more than the eventual championship, "the journey itself, the friendship and human connection they shared together in good days and bad days" was important. The exercise ended in some intimate moments shared together. Then there is another championship.

Playing for Keeps is full of moments like this, when Halberstam drops readers into the huddle, to participate with the players in the excitement of the game. Chicago assistant coach Tex Winter at one point tells Jordan, "There's no *I* in the word *team*." "There is in the word *win*," Jordan answers him. In Salt Lake City before a preseason game, Denver coach Bill Hanzlik drags his rookies into a gym at 7:00 A.M.; "there, sweat pouring off him, deeply engaged in a brutal workout, was the NBA's most valuable player, Karl Malone. 'Gentlemen,' Hanzlik said, 'that's what the NBA is all about.'" Often, younger players seem to be ignorant of the history of their own sport; Shaquille O'Neal is the only living player who did not show up at the League's fiftieth anniversary celebration, Halberstam reminds readers. Other players seem to forget the sacrifices earlier athletes made; discussing Jordan's apolitical career, Halberstam cites Arthur Ashe, who remarked that being black in America when he was playing professional tennis was like having a second full-time job.

Finally, Halberstam reveals American culture in all its splendor and vulgarity: the $78 million Jordan would earn a year in salary and endorsements; "no American salesman of any color had ever entered more homes, here or abroad, or successfully sold more products." By the 1980's, Halberstam concludes, "America exported not its machine products or its cars but its culture." Kids on playgrounds everywhere dreamed of playing professional basketball; American diplomats and journalists on assignment to the most isolated parts of Asia and Africa were often surprised when they visited villages to find young children wearing worn replicas of Jordan's Bulls jerseys. *Playing for Keeps* begins in Paris in 1997, where the Bulls (by this date the "Beatles of basketball") are playing in a McDonald's tournament against teams from Europe. What has brought them this far from home? "Stern understood, as not everyone in the world of sports did yet, that image was more important than reality in their business."

The book is filled with brilliant athletic scenes, like Jordan's performance in game five of the finals against Utah, when he battled the flu to score 49 points. There is nothing more poignant, however, than a scene before the game in Paris, when Michael Ray Richardson, then playing for an obscure European team, came up to David Stern to thank him for the NBA's tough three-and-out drug policy, which had sobered Richardson up, and probably saved his life. On the societal level, Halberstam opines that Jordan's career reflected "the willingness of corporate America, however reluctantly, to understand that a stunningly gifted and attractive black athlete could be a compelling salesman of a vast variety of rather mundane products." Halberstam records a sport with a potential for so much good, and yet representative of so much that is repellent in American life.

David Peck

Sources for Further Study

Booklist 95 (February 15, 1999): 1096.
Boston Globe, January 31, 1999, p. F1.
Commentary 107 (June, 1999): 46.
Kirkus Reviews 68 (January 1, 1999): 42.
Library Journal 124 (February 1, 1999): 100.
The New York Review of Books 46 (July 15, 1999): 11.
The New York Times Book Review 104 (January 31, 1999): 11.
Publishers Weekly 246 (January 18, 1999): 317.
The Seattle Times, January 31, 1999, p. M8.

A PRAYER FOR THE DYING

Author: Stewart O'Nan (1961-)
Publisher: Henry Holt (New York). 195 pp. $22.00
Type of work: Novel
Time: The late 1860's
Locale: Friendship, Wisconsin

A town full of ordinary people living out their ordered lives becomes the setting of a tale of intense horror, as an epidemic ravages the bodies of the townspeople and ultimately the very soul of the novel's protagonist

Principal characters:
JACOB HANSEN, Friendship's sheriff, undertaker, and sometime pastor
DOC GUSTAFSON, the town physician
MARTA HANSEN, Jacob's wife and mother of his infant daughter, Amelia

A gifted young author, Stewart O'Nan has already produced a number of books, including a collection of stories and four novels. The Pittsburgh native and former aerospace engineer has received recognition for his work, having won the Drue Heinz Literature Prize for *In the Walled City* (1993) and having been named by the literary magazine *Granta* in 1996 as one of the nation's best young novelists. *A Prayer for the Dying* propels him to what may be the top of his craft. It is not that the themes he uses are new: Albert Camus long ago inoculated readers against the horror of contagion; Bret Harte painted the varied hues of bucolic life; many have captured on paper the fortitude and fault of complex protagonists. What is new is that O'Nan has taken the genre of horror directly to the interior of the human person, forcing not only the main character but also the reader to confront the cauldron of the potential for evil that boils within.

The novel opens, innocently enough, with a wide-angle view of a rural American town shortly after the Civil War (1861-1865). The author serves up the scene slowly, allowing the reader to steep gently in the steamy cup of summer. One notices workers in the field, small children and tiny streams giggling their way through a heavy summer day, insects annoying the requisite cows, people moving through their everyday lives. They love, laugh, and argue, kill their kin and tend their tomatoes, perform the pedestrian and not so pedestrian tasks of living and of dying.

Jacob Hansen, Civil War veteran, functions in the tiny community not only as constable and preacher but also as undertaker. He is a person of honor and humility. He is family man, gentle man, model citizen—almost too good to be true. He is devoted to his talented and lovely wife, Marta, and to his young daughter. His life is ordered and controlled, as he takes time for both the pleasures of the flesh and the prayers of faith. He accepts the townsfolk and himself as they are, fully appreciating their good qualities and overlooking their faults. "They'll all come to you someday," he remarks to himself, "and they know you'll do right by them." Jacob certainly does right for the town. He is the sturdy warp upon which the town weaves its successes and troubles. Its fabric is strong because he is strong; it is orderly and good because he is orderly and good; it keeps the patterns of family and social life intact because he does; it is able to absorb and cope with its problems because in his own psyche he sets the design for how to behave. Friendships are closely woven and richly ornamented; lapses are dealt with in orderly fashion. While readers may not be drawn to like him—a bit too Milquetoast perhaps—they cannot help but admire him.

O'Nan's plan is to capture interest not so much in the living of the town, but in its dying. The sunny reality of Friendship becomes overcast when a local farmer discovers an itinerant soldier dead beside his campfire, presumably the victim of murder and robbery. As Jacob arrives to claim the body, he marks the physical resemblance of the dead soldier to himself: There is the same battle-worn and dirty uniform, the same tin drinking cup. A shadow from Jacob's dark history as a soldier in the Civil War passes briefly, but its meaning is made clear to the reader only later in the novel. Jacob's congruence to the corpse is deeper than physical likeness. The soldier functions as a kind of metaphor for the main character. The corruption of disease in the dead man foreshadows what the author will reveal later about the constable himself. Questions of why Jacob travels by bicycle and not by horse and what really happened in the war linger among the gathering clouds in the reader's mind.

As constable and undertaker, Jacob has a duty to solve the mystery of the soldier's death as well as to prepare his corpse for burial. Both tasks are undertaken with equanimity and seriousness. The reader sees the undertaker's meticulous care, his gentleness, and his almost too-good-to-be-true character. He speaks to the deceased and says a respectful prayer. It is both office and obsession for him to bathe the body, carefully drain the blood and clothe the rigid form, and arrange it in a coffin for burial. Jacob demonstrates the same care here as he had with the bodies of his fallen comrades in battle. Throughout the novel he is portrayed as a man who takes seriously his appointed task and is not to be distracted, even at jeopardy to himself when it becomes clear that there is a contagious disease present.

O'Nan is accurate in his description of the telltale physical signs of contagion. The awful truth is exposed: The soldier has met his demise not through foul play but from diphtheria, which threatens to ravage the entire town. Jacob faces decisions of quarantine and the keeping of the peace, what to do with his own family, and a mounting number of dead to bury. Tragedy heaps upon tragedy, metaphored in the bodies of the deceased. His friend and confidant, the town doctor, succumbs to the disease as do his wife and daughter. To complicate matters, an out-of-control fire is poised to destroy what is left of Friendship. With all the senseless tragedy to cope with, Jacob's carefully controlled emotional life and the relationships which hold it in place begin to unravel. As he disintegrates personally, the wider human depravity and desperation gripping the town begin to show through the frayed fabric of fear and the breakdown of normal civilized life. The more the breach widens, the more a picture of horror emerges. People are poisoned, shot, and burned alive. Corpses rot, and mayhem grows. Jacob cannot cope. The whole of what supports his stability disintegrates. He stands by helplessly, finally unable to keep up with the multiplication of chaotic events. To preserve a patina of sanity at least in his own home, Jacob digs up his buried daughter, embalms his dead wife, and postures them as if they were still alive. This attempt underlines his mental instability. In the second-person voice, which O'Nan uses throughout the novel, he describes Jacob's horrific denial: "You give [the baby] a kiss and return her to Marta, get up and check on your cornbread, but at the doorway you turn back to look at them, to admire them sitting there, the ones you love, and count yourself lucky, yes, even blessed, having almost lost them." It takes a while for the reader to realize the full impact of what has happened. Denial is not the exclusive arena of the protagonist. Flashbacks to the experience of war are interspersed with the unbearable reality that confronts him. The man of equanimity dissolves into a man overcome by evil and despair. In his own words, he is "a murderer. A lover of the dead."

The full impact of what Jacob's self-indictment means becomes clear only in the last few pages of the novel, as the puzzling questions which the author has embedded in the story finally are resolved. Readers almost cannot believe what they have read but hasten to retrace their literary steps to see if there is not something that has been missed along the way. No, the horror is exactly as the author has written it. He has led the victim reader into his grisly trap, and it has snapped shut. No escape is possible. In the end, a lingering stench remains of the awful. The full story of the epidemic that has the potential to destroy the town and the horror of the dormant disease that now rages within Jacob himself are revealed.

In a certain sense, O'Nan out-Kings Stephen King. His prose is restrained and compelling, yet at the same time he employs a richness of description that paints a vivid picture. It is perhaps this quality that moves the reader from being a mere bystander to living inside the skin of the main character. As Jacob speaks to himself in the second person, readers sense that they have become the addressees in the macabre monologue. As the main character disintegrates into confusion, the reader does so right along with him. The result is an unsettling feeling that lingers after the book is finally closed.

O'Nan's work will not go unnoticed. He has taken Michael Lesy's historical montage, *Wisconsin Death Trip* (1973), which documents a diphtheria epidemic that occurred in the late 1800's, and has woven it into a tale of horror not only medical but also psychological. Can a mature person who has life in perspective, who accepts himself and his neighbors as they are and treats them with respect and care, maintain this attitude of faith and stability in the face of disaster? Disaster stories are not new: William Golding visited them in *Lord of the Flies* (1954). The story of the *Titanic* has been told in film a number of times. O'Nan's twist is to insert the question and the horror into the very soul of his protagonist.

The late twentieth century saw its share of senseless violence in the form of massive bombings and shootings, heinous crimes of war on almost every continent, notorious sprees of sequential murder characterized by depravity and unbalanced personalities. Thanks to modern media, the horror of such events is made immediate, and yet the audience is able to turn back from them to the shelter of comfortable lives. These nations, these depraved people are not personally known. These stories may prompt readers to be more protective of their children and more careful with security, but the horror remains at bay. O'Nan will not let that stand. He thrusts the horror right into the midst of every man in Everytown, USA. What is more comforting than "Friendship?" What enhances security more than the warmth of rural America in the idyllic peace that followed the Civil War? What is more unsettling than the ideal man who loses not only those he loves but also hope and faith? This novel addresses the fears within society's repression and denial, and it will have its effect in bringing them into the light of day.

Dolores L. Christie

Sources for Further Study

Booklist 95 (January 1, 1999): 793.
Library Journal 124 (February 15, 1999): 184.
National Catholic Reporter 35 (May 7, 1999): 32.
The New York Times Book Review 104 (May 2, 1999): 8.
The New Yorker 75 (May 31, 1999): 112.
Publishers Weekly 246 (January 11, 1999): 52.

PROPERTY AND FREEDOM

Author: Richard Pipes (1923-)
Publisher: Alfred A. Knopf (New York). 328 pp. $30.00
Type of work: History

A veteran scholar of Russian history develops at length his long-held theory that ownership of property is indispensable to personal freedom

Richard Pipes has written almost exclusively on various aspects of Russian history over a period of thirty-five years, and *Property and Freedom* is not altogether a change of pace. In composing it, this longtime Harvard University professor has drawn on the insights gained in his area of specialization. Furthermore, the thesis of the book has been prefigured in several of his earlier works. It is a paradoxical thesis: While individual ownership of property can occur without personal liberty, freedom cannot exist without property. This is true, the author insists, whether the concept of property is understood as consisting simply of things (land, capital, and items of personal use such as housing, clothing, and the like) or, more broadly, as encompassing even a person's life and liberty.

The author contends that although the ideas of liberty, property, and their interconnections have long been studied, they have not been examined by historians. Thus, although Pipes's subject matter is philosophical, his approach is historical. Realizing that anything like a comprehensive study of the relationship between property and political systems over several thousand years of recorded history would prove an impossibly large study, he has chosen to survey property briefly as idea and institution in the Western world, then to devote substantial chapters to critical eras in the history of England and Russia, and finally to focus on salient developments in the twentieth century with emphasis on the United States. He acknowledges his inability to extend his study to areas of the world other than Europe and the United States.

In his preliminary pages on the idea of property in classical antiquity, Pipes finds Plato and Aristotle setting forth the grounds of a disagreement about property that has resonated through the years into the twentieth century. The guardians of Plato's *Politeia* (388-386 B.C.; *Republic*, 1701), significantly, own no property lest it promote disputes, while in the less utopian *Nomoi* (360-347 B.C.; *Laws*, 1804) private property, while allowed, still must be carefully regulated by the state. Aristotle, on the other hand, in his *Politica* (335-323 B.C.E.; *Politics*, 1598) objects to common ownership not only for theoretical reasons but also for the practical reason that people do not take care of things that are not their own.

As Pipes works his way through thinkers about property in subsequent centuries, he finds the benefits of private ownership gradually winning out over utopian idealism: "Aristotle has triumphed over Plato." The author's treatments of landmark works along the way, for example Sir Thomas More's *De Optimo Reipublicae Statu, deque Nova Insula Utopia* (1516; *Utopia*, 1551), Jean-Jacques Rousseau's *Discours sur l'œconomie politique* (1755; *Discourse on Political Economy*, 1797), and *Manifest der*

Kommunistischen Partei (1848; *The Communist Manifesto*, 1850) of Karl Marx and Friedrich Engels, are necessarily briefer than the secondary sources he cites. In the process, Pipes falls into the error of discussing a work like More's as though it were a treatise. This weakness, common among political historians and political polemicists when dealing with literary texts, results in his taking too literally such a complex and ironic work as the *Utopia*. It simply cannot be assumed, as Pipes does, that More the author (as distinct from More the character, who takes part in a conversation with Raphael Hythloday, the mythical returnee from the island republic of Utopia in the less well known first part of the *Utopia*) is unequivocally endorsing the social and political principles of the imaginary Utopians. To write that More, a man with extensive legal and political experience, "believed that the abolition of money would cause all evils afflicting mankind to vanish" fails to take into account the sophistication of this shrewd and ironic Renaissance man.

Pipes notes that acquisitiveness has persisted throughout human history, from the time of hunters and food gatherers through that of farmers and on into that of urbanized and industrialized masses. There have always been possessions, whether simple weapons and tools, land, or traded commodities. Possessions become property when states formulate laws to secure this property. Monarchs might rule but over the centuries have understood they could not expect to own, that is, regard as their personal property, all that they rule. Furthermore, they have recognized that they could not appropriate the belongings of their subjects. Although Pipes stops short of claiming that the necessity of guaranteeing property rights is the sole reason for the emergence of national states, it is for him a paramount reason. He sees the right to property as the most "elementary" right, more basic even than the other rights which the Western world came to regard as inalienable in the seventeenth and eighteenth centuries.

Pipes rejects the argument that the notion of freedom arose from the consciousness of the difference between slave and non-slave in the ancient world. Slavery was universal in the ancient world, but Greece and Rome were conspicuous for developing the concept of freedom: *eleuthereia* for the Greeks, *libertas* for the Romans. The Greeks and Romans, Pipes says, set themselves apart from other peoples by developing self-sufficiency, which in turn was a product of ownership, of people working for themselves. In such a society as Athens, therefore, democracy could flourish; in Near and Middle Eastern lands, where private ownership existed only sporadically, it could not.

An eventual consequence of this dichotomy between West and East was the early development of institutions to safeguard property and freedom by England at one end of the European continent and the relative inability of Russia to protect its people from despotism at the other end. Paying considerable attention to that much-studied phenomenon, the development of the English parliament over the centuries, Pipes is particularly struck by the significance of the trial of a well-to-do Puritan landlord, John Hamden, late in the reign of the last would-be absolutist ruler of England, Charles I. Charles, like other ambitious monarchs, needed money, but he found ways to raise it without calling upon the agency whose main reason for being at the time was to approve taxation: Parliament. Hamden had the effrontery to refuse the king's demand to comply with one of his favorite expedients, the so-called ship money, a levy on the inhabitants of coastal towns and counties in times of national emergency. It appeared to Hamden, on whom the levy was incidentally quite small, that no such emergency existed, for no foreign invasion threatened. Tried before an ordinary court in 1637, Hamden lost the case and had to pay. Significantly, five of the twelve judges, all appointed by Charles and all removable at his pleasure, upheld Hamden. Pipes asserts that in the entire history of Russia "not a single instance can be found of a subject defying his sovereign and being given his day in court." Thereafter, defying the king's acquisitiveness became a national habit. By 1689, England had a Bill of Rights, and the House of Commons controlled all the crown's expenditures.

As might be expected, the story in Russia is quite different. Private property there, according to Pipes, did not facilitate the emergence of the state, as in Athens or Rome, or develop concurrently, as was later common in Europe, but was conferred by an already existing state. The Russian word for property from medieval times, when Mongols ruled Russia, *votchina*, is a synonym of the Latin term *patrimonium*, or "inheritance from one's father." Property, whether from a private or public source, was *votchina*. The northern Russian principality of Novgorod, which was settled by Swedish Vikings and managed to escape Mongol rule, developed self-rule and was led by princes with no patrimonial claims. Pipes thinks that Novgorod might have proceeded along lines analogous to those of Western European political entities, but late in the fifteenth century it was taken over by the principality of Moscow, whose ruler, Ivan III, regarded political sovereignty as implying property title. Subsequently a system of conditional land tenure arose in which land that the sovereign dispensed to his civil and military functionaries reverted to him when their services terminated. Peter the Great, the eighteenth century ruler commonly regarded as a relatively liberal, westernizing monarch, not only retained but extended czarist control over property, including the factories which were then arising. The czars did not commit themselves to the idea of private property and civil rights until shortly before the 1917 revolution swept away all liberalizing tendencies in the political and economic realm.

Despite the fact that Pipes announces in his introduction his intention of criticizing the modern welfare state, the tone of his chapter on property in the twentieth century comes as something of a jolt. After a section on Soviet Communism and another on fascist Italy and Nazi Germany, he devotes most of his final chapter to a long litany of perils to American freedom. Here Pipes abandons his objective historian's manner in favor of an impassioned argument against what he views as runaway social welfare legislation restricting property rights in the name of social justice. Obviously, Pipes aims his criticisms not at the concept of social justice itself but at what he sees as an unwarranted enlargement of the concept. He singles out especially the "four freedoms" of President Franklin D. Roosevelt's 1941 State of the Union address. Roosevelt's "freedom from want," Pipes argues, was a euphemism for what the president considered a right: "the right to the necessities of life at public expense, i.e., the right to something that was not one's own." Pipes fiercely opposes expansion of the concept of rights to include anything gained at the expense of someone else. Taxation deals a double blow to Pipes's tandem of property-and-freedom: It takes property away from people and establishes in the receiver of the redistributed largesse a dependency that endangers liberty.

Spiraling entitlements particularly distress him. He finds the poorest one-fifth of the population almost totally dependent on government outlays, while the next poorest one-fifth receive more than a third of their income in the same way. Thus, the more productive 60 percent of the population completely or significantly supports the other 40 percent. Minimum wages, rent control, regulations imposed upon banks, affirmative action—these and other familiar governmental initiatives come in for a lambasting. All too easily Americans accept progressive assaults on the concept of property, "transforming it from absolute dominion into something akin to conditional possession." Because Americans elect their legislative and executive officials, they are not tyrannized as were the citizens of the former Soviet Union or Nazi Germany; rather, they are doing it to themselves.

It is of course possible to quarrel with the author's interpretation of the social and economic changes during and since the Roosevelt administration. Many will be inclined to question the extraordinarily high value that he places on property rights, but it will be difficult for anyone to read the epilogue, which he titles "Portents," without discomfort, for he raises troublesome questions. For instance, considering the large numbers of potential voters who fail to exercise the franchise, are Americans today in danger of tyranny at the hands of politically passionate minorities? Do Americans care more about the security provided by federal largesse than about freedom? Whether or not the right to property is, as Pipes claims, the "most fundamental" right, have prosperous citizens today forgotten the extent to which they owe the liberties they enjoy to "a long struggle for rights"?

Property and Freedom begins as exposition and ends as argument. Pipes has challenged the complacency of the citizenry in clear and forceful prose buttressed by nearly one thousand references to sources representing a wide range of disciplines. *Property and Freedom*, with its thesis that property is a *sine qua non* of personal freedom, is hardly unassailable, but neither can it be dismissed out of hand.

Robert P. Ellis

Sources for Further Study

Booklist 95 (April 15, 1999): 1492.
Insight on the News 15 (August 23, 1999): 26.
National Review 51 (May 31, 1999): 63.
The New York Review of Books 46 (September 23, 1999): 68.
The New York Times Book Review 104 (May 9, 1999): 38.
Publishers Weekly 246 (April 26, 1999): 62.

PROXIMITY TO DEATH

Author: William S. McFeely (1930-)
Publisher: W. W. Norton (New York). 206 pp. $23.95
Type of work: Current affairs and ethics
Time: The 1990's
Locale: The Deep South

McFeely takes a generous slice of local color, criminal justice, and prejudice and spices it with sufficient description to render what could have been a trite and tired book into a good imitation of a first-rate novel on capital punishment

Principal personages:
WILLIAM S. MCFEELY, a historian
STEPHEN BRIGHT, lawyer and advocate against the death penalty
KENNY,
WILLIAM,
CARZELL, and
TONY, murderers

What could be a better substitute for sheep-counting than a book of nonfiction on the death penalty? Add a pinch of historian and presidential biographer and a sprinkle of statistics, and the result promises a reliable recipe for a soporific evening. The formula is not a new one. One anticipates an inedible if generous repast: ponderous page upon page slathered with tiresome facts, graphic descriptions of the methods of death, and predictable cruel-and-unusual-punishment arguments. The reader is pleasantly surprised, therefore, to encounter a book which could well pass as a novel, and which keeps him or her turning pages until the end. William McFeely's *Proximity to Death* is well crafted and intriguing.

As one might expect, the author's purpose is not merely to entertain. His appeal is to those who, like himself, oppose the death penalty and to the innate humanity that drives those who favor it out of concern for the families of the victims. McFeely holds little illusion that the book will occasion a metanoia in those who staunchly support killing those who kill. He does feel compelled to tell the story nonetheless.

His own opposition to capital punishment precedes the event that provoked his writing this book. In 1995 he was called to testify as an expert witness at a pretrial hearing for a Georgia murder case. He expected little more than to drive into town, do his stint on the stand, and return to his research. The experience so moved him, however, that as he drove away from the courthouse, McFeely was prompted to dig deeper into the subject of capital punishment. His experience of facing it graphically for the first time in his own life, literally in the faces and lives of those accused and potentially sentenced to be killed for their crimes, motivated and shaped the project. The particularity of the people involved—certainly the lawyers and prosecutors but most especially the accused—drew him into writing a book that would re-create this experience for the reader. "Murderer" has become for him no longer an anonymous collective of those convicted of killing others but a fleshy litany of persons with significant histories, pain, and the possibility of an empty future. The author invites the reader to join him in his journey into the scrapbook lives of accused murderers and those who try to keep them from being killed.

An interesting device is used to frame his story and his passionate argument and to draw the reader into the plot. The proscenium that serves as the introductory matter in several of the chapters is a description of the physical setting in which the events he plans to describe take place. The reader walks with McFeely into "the law's palace," taking in the elegance of the county courthouse that dominates the landscape of Sparta, Georgia. It is difficult to miss the embodiment of what passes as Southern justice in the Victorian gingerbread and massive blocks of brick. Politeness of space slip-covers over the violence that is meted out within its walls, hiding its tears and its blemishes. Violence to human persons, as McFeely perceives capital punishment to be, is gentrified by the prescribed procedures of the justice system. Lawyers and prosecutors, judges, and jury—each speaks appointed lines and acts out the plot until the inevitable final curtain falls heavily on the accused.

Later the reader accompanies McFeely into the shabby digs of those who try to keep death for the accused at bay. Here the set is dressed in sharp contrast to the expected affluence of the paradigmatic law office. The decor is good intentions and stark walls rather than ponderous thoughts and corporate paneling. No expensive art hangs to signal the fee schedule. Rather, posters espousing antideath themes compete loudly with the white paint. The energetic idealism that hangs on the walls in the random portraits of lawyers who have interned here announces the cost of engaging those who work here. There is no photo gallery of the corporate partners but rather a crazy quilt wall of snapshots of the criminally accused. The metaphor of hope in the face of incredible odds is stark.

Finally, scenes are set in a Southern prison, sanitary behind sharp wire. It holds the lifeless life of a man who will never be able to use his summa cum laude education outside its walls; it is the backdrop for the action which the author wishes to portray. The solitary cell of the accused killer, tiny, dank, and dark, seems apt in the face of his circumscribed possibilities. Knee to knee in the visitors' room, McFeely interviews a man who will never leave confinement nor wear clothes other than prison garb.

Enter the players. McFeely gives face and voice to the actors in this drama for life, a drama not without pathos and violence and certainly not without guilt. It is clear who wear the white hats and who the black hats in the play. As in most good theater the "good guys" are not without faults; in fact they are the perpetrators of violent and often sadistic acts. Most of the men profiled in this book are frankly responsible for the crimes for which they have been brought to judgment. The acts they have committed are not pretty. The author does not spare the details of each crime, providing the reader the "evidence" to make up his or her own mind about the fate of each man in the graphic face of what he has done. Cast as heroes are the lawyers and their support personnel, people who work tirelessly under the most difficult odds to win their clients' lives, even if those lives will always be contained in prison. The people who work with attorney Stephen Bright are comprehensively described as well, the author detailing their physical characteristics, their medical conditions, their life stories, their loves.

One of the strengths of the book is McFeely's ability to tell graphically the stories of each of the accused he selects. They are men of great mental ability or very little comprehension, rehabilitated after their crimes or not. Each has a poignant history that contextualizes his crime and renders the logic of why the men have come to be where they are. The author does not try to argue for them or defend their goodness or innocence. Rather, he lets each story speak. The dry boxes of trial accounts and evidence in the basement of the Bright law offices become animated with the author's prose. Not unlike the technique of John Grisham, the author follows one trial in depth, including the profiles and sentiments of members of the jury who eventually vote not to send the accused to death. The reader is treated to courtroom drama at its best, but in this case the play is an authentic slice of real life.

Never heavy handed, McFeely allows each reader to make a personal judgment on the issue of capital punishment. It is abundantly clear where he stands, but the reader is left to form his or her own conclusions. McFeely's critique of what he terms "odd racial patterns" of Southern justice is telling, however. While there is no sentiment in his frank accusation of racial prejudice in the application of the death penalty, he documents with statistics its overwhelming levy on those defendants who are of color and whose victims are not. The South, in his view, is still not a good place to be dark-skinned and accused of murder.

Overall this is a marvelous book. McFeely pulls no punches as he speaks about "the ultimate expression of violence, the state killing its own people." His narrative uncovers the unequal balance of the pain of justice in the South and its effects on persons of color without rancor but with clarity. His prose is passionate, if restrained, that of someone who is convinced that this form of punishment does not make the world a more civilized place but rather contributes to the coarsening of American society. Echoing the position of Sister Helen Prejean in her book *Dead Man Walking: An Eyewitness Account of the Death Penalty in the United States* (1993), he affirms the intrinsic dignity of all human beings, even those who have taken the lives of others of their kind. There is a fragile poignancy in his expression. There is a caring in his account.

After nearly two hundred pages of stories that seem without hope, the author's final message is, by contrast, hope-filled. The last picture, the final scene presented to the reader as he or she prepares to leave the drama proximate to death, is of the same Georgia courthouse described in the opening lines of the first chapter. In this idealized time the courthouse drama records only one death, that of the person murdered. Justice elects a happier ending as it affirms the dignity and sanctity of life, even a perpetual life behind bars for those who kill. It is unlikely that there will be a film version of this book, but the reader will have been left with a new perspective.

As the millennium drew to a close and the American polity celebrated and rang in the new century with peaceful and optimistic thoughts, the shadow of the death penalty continued to cloud the landscape. A citizenry of advancement and plenty, Americans remain a people unwilling to give up a form of punishment that most civilized countries have abandoned. As McFeely documents, there have been attempts in the past to move beyond the sanguine killing of citizens who kill. The contemporary tenor of the land, however, is one of "getting tough" on crime. More jails are being built, and the tools of death are again in use on death row. Perhaps this well fleshed-out series of stories, bringing the reader face to face with killers in their poverty both material and spiritual, their history, and indeed their crimes, will cause a "retrial" of attitudes toward the death penalty. Narrative often has the power to do what logic and persuasive rhetoric have been unable to accomplish. The significance of this book is its power to put flesh on the logic of argument and to allow the reader to see the horror and injustice that follow the path of "dead men" walking to execution. It should contribute to the public debate on the topic and perhaps change the ending of the ongoing drama of race and rancor that embodies the issue of capital punishment in contemporary American society.

Already noted as a biographer of Ulysses S. Grant, McFeely has opened up a new arena of civil war in this book, one which has been brewing for a long, long time. Will the United States, almost the last civilized nation to hold on to its love affair with vengeance in the form of lethal injection or electric chair, follow his gaze into the eyes of the real people who bear its brunt? McFeely calls his book "a simple story of a few people . . . who carry a large responsibility." He hopes that it will provoke some caring for those about whom few had cared. It is good enough that it might.

Dolores L. Christie

Sources for Further Study

Booklist 96 (October 1, 1999): 312.
Boston Globe, December 2, 1999, p. D5.
The New York Times Book Review 104 (November 21, 1999): 77.
Publishers Weekly 246 (October 18, 1999): 59.

PUSHKIN
A Biography

Author: Elaine Feinstein (1930-)
Publisher: Ecco Press (Hopewell, New Jersey). 309 pp. $29.95.
Type of work: Literary biography
Time: 1799-1837
Locale: Russia

Drawing on recently discovered documents, Feinstein explores the life of one of nineteenth century Russia's greatest writers

Principal personages:
ALEXANDER SERGEYEVICH PUSHKIN, a Russian writer
NATALYA NIKOLAEVNA PUSHKINA, his wife
VASILY ANDREEVICH ZHUKOVSKY, his friend, a poet
TSAR NICHOLAS I, the ruler of Russia
BARON JACOB DERK ANNE BORCHARD VAN HEECKEREN-BEVERWEERD, the Dutch ambassador to Russia
GEORGES CHARLES D'ANTHÈS, an officer in the Horse Guards, the slayer of Pushkin

On January 29, 1837, Maximilian von Lerchenfeld-Köfering, Bavarian ambassador to Russia, wrote,

> Russia has just lost its greatest man of literature, Mr. Alexander Pouschkin, the most famous Poet it ever had. He died at the age of thirty-seven, at the apex of his career, after being gravely wounded in a duel. The details of the catastrophe, unfortunately provoked by the dead man himself with a blindness and a kind of frenetic hatred well worthy of his Moorish origins, have for days been the sole talk of the town here in the capital.

In her biography, coinciding with the two hundredth anniversary of Pushkin's birth, Elaine Feinstein traces the forces that drove Russia's greatest poet to his great literary achievements and to his untimely death.

As the Lerchenfeld-Köfering letter indicates, Pushkin's maternal great-grandfather, Abram Petrovich Hannibal, had been born in Abyssinia and had become a favorite of Peter the Great. Pushkin owed to Hannibal his swarthy complexion, frizzy hair, and an interest in Peter the Great. In 1827 Pushkin began a novel about his African ancestor, and he refers to his African heritage in his masterpiece, *Evgeny Onegin* (1825-1832; *Eugene Onegin*, 1833).

Pushkin's father, Sergey L'vovich Pushkin, traced his lineage to the beginnings of Russia itself. Though Sergey L'vovich owned an estate in Nizhny Novgorod with twelve hundred serfs, he spent more than he earned. One of future poet's classmates noted that in the Pushkin household there was "never enough of anything, from money to the last glass." One thing not lacking in the Pushkin household was books. Sergey was especially fond of French literature, which he enjoyed reading aloud to his family. He gave Alexander free rein in the family library, where the young lad devoured Jean Racine (1639-1699) and Molière (1622-1673), Voltaire (1694-1778), ninth century B.C.E. Greek poet Homer (in

French), and the Latin classics. By the age of eight, Alexander was composing competent imitations of his favorite French authors. Sergey also enjoyed entertaining and numbered among his guests some of the leading literary figures of the day, including Vasily Andreevich Zhukovsky. Little known outside Russia, Zhukovsky was the father of Russian romanticism. The conversations and readings of these literati must have delighted Alexander.

As was typical among Russian aristocrats, Sergey and his family spoke French at home. Pushkin's grandmother taught him Russian, and his nanny, Arina Radionovna, told him folk tales. These women's lessons would prove more influential than those of Pushkin's early tutors, from whom he claimed to have learned nothing. In 1811 Tsar Alexander I established a school at Tsarskoe Selo near Petersburg; Pushkin was part of the first class. He looked back on his six years there with affection.

Pushkin did not shine as a student, and a report at the end of his first year described him as having a fiery temper. The young man did, however, distinguish himself as a writer. At the age of fifteen, he had a poem accepted by the prestigious *Messenger of Europe*. In January, 1815, Gavril Romanovich Derzhavin, Russia's leading poet of the late eighteenth century, came to Pushkin's school to hear the pupils recite their verses. Derzhavin nodded off during the recitation but snapped to attention when Pushkin began to read "Recollections in Tsarskoe Selo." When the young man concluded his poem, Derzhavin proclaimed Pushkin his successor. While still a student, Pushkin was elected to the Arzamas Society, created in 1815 to promote new literature.

Feinstein demonstrates that the child proved father to the man in two other ways. In a poem written at the age of fifteen, Pushkin imagines himself a piece of snuff lucky enough to fall inside a lady's dress. He claimed to be in love with all the pretty women he met, and, judging from a Don Juan-like notebook that he kept, his feelings often were reciprocated. Pushkin carried on various affairs throughout his life and fathered at least one illegitimate son.

While still in school Pushkin met the reform-minded Colonel Pyotr Yakovlevich Chaadaev. Pushkin shared Chaadaev's liberal sentiments, as is evident in Pushkin's revolutionary verses, which circulated in manuscript. In 1820 these led to his being sent to southern Russia. He knew many of the officers involved in the ill-fated 1825 Decembrist uprising, and under interrogation several claimed that Pushkin's "Ode to Freedom" had given rise to their liberal ideas. Had he not been deterred by bad omens, Pushkin himself would have stood with the conspirators in Petersburg in December, 1825, and might then have been executed or sent to Siberia.

A little over a month before leaving Petersburg, Pushkin finished *Ruslan i Lyudmila* (1820; *Ruslan and Liudmila*, 1936). He sent a copy to Zhukovsky, who replied with a portrait inscribed, "To the victorious pupil from the defeated master." Feinstein notes that both the irony and the colloquial idiom in Pushkin's poem were new to Russian poetry. Pushkin's verses show great technical virtuosity and a wide readership; his subjects and language appealed to the common man even more than to the aristocracy.

Away from Petersburg, Pushkin longed for the capital's literary society. Nonetheless, his development as a writer proceeded. He began reading George Gordon, Lord

Byron (1788-1824) and fell in love with *Childe Harold's Pilgrimage* (1812-1818). Though Byron later yielded to William Shakespeare (1564-1616), Johann Wolfgang von Goethe (1749-1832), Friedrich Schiller (1759-1805), and Sir Walter Scott (1771-1832) in Pushkin's pantheon of poets, the English romantic remained an important influence. Feinstein observes that *Kavkazskiy plennik* (1822; *The Prisoner of the Caucasus*, 1895) is modeled on Byron's eastern tales. *Domik v Kolomne* (1833; *The Little House at Kolomna*, 1977) uses the stanza form of Byron's *Beppo: A Venetian Story* (1818), and *Eugene Onegin* in various ways recalls Byron's *Don Juan* (1819-1824). The places in southern Russia that Pushkin visited also informed his verses. *Bakhchisaraiskiy fontan* (1827; *The Fountain of Bakhchisarai*, 1849) recalls a site he toured with General Nikolai Nikolaevich Raevsky; the poem is dedicated to the general's son. The gypsy camps Pushkin saw in the Bessarabian steppes prompted *Tsygany* (1827; *The Gypsies*, 1957), begun in 1822. Then there were the women whom he met in the region and who inspired his love poetry, including Amalia Riznich and Elizaveta Vorontsova.

Under Tsar Nicholas I, Pushkin's life improved in some ways. On September 3, 1826, the new tsar ordered the poet to Moscow, where the two met privately. Nicholas declared that he would serve as Pushkin's censor, ostensibly freeing the writer from interference from the Third Section of the government bureaucracy, and Pushkin was free to live anywhere he chose within Russia.

The promise of greater literary freedom proved false; a private reading of *Boris Godunov* (1831) led to an official inquiry. Pushkin used his newfound mobility to visit Petersburg and Moscow, where he carried on various affairs. His writing, however, flourished not in the literary salons of the capital but in the isolation of the family estate of Boldino in Nizhny Novgorod. Here in the fall of 1830, for example, he finished *Eugene Onegin*, *Malen'kie tragedii* (1832-1839; *Little Tragedies*, 1946), the prose work *Povesti Belkina* (1831; *Tales of Belkin*, 1947), the narrative poem *The Little House at Kolomna*, and some thirty other poems. Three years later at Boldino he composed his brilliant short story *Pikovaia dama* (1834; *The Queen of Spades*, 1858), began his novel *Kapitanskaya dochka* (1836; *The Captain's Daughter*, 1846), finished his *Istoriya Pugacheva* (1834; *The Pugachev Rebellion*, 1966), about an eighteenth century Russian revolutionary, and drafted *Medniy vsadnik* (1837; *The Bronze Horseman*, 1899), about the statue of Peter the Great erected by Catherine the Great in Petersburg.

By 1833 Pushkin was married to the beautiful Natalya Nikolaevna Goncharova. Tsar Nicholas I appointed Pushkin a Junior Gentleman of the Bedchamber at a salary of five thousand rubles a year, perhaps less to pay tribute to Pushkin's literary abilities than to keep Natalya in Petersburg. Though Nicholas almost certainly did not carry on an affair with Natalya, his fondness for her was evident, and he proved more generous to her after Pushkin's death than he ever was to the living poet.

That death resulted from Natalya's flirtations with a Franco-German officer in the Queen's Horse Guards, Georges d'Anthès. Tall, blond, and genial as well as an excellent dancer, he fell in love with Natalya, and she found his attention flattering.

On February 5, 1836, the maid of honor Marya Karlovna Mörder wrote in her diary that she had seen d'Anthès and Natalya together. "They are madly in love," Marya noted. Nine days later d'Anthès wrote to his adoptive father, Baron Jacob Derk Anne Borchard van Heeckeren-Beverweerd, that Natalya had confessed her love to him but had said she never would give him more than her heart.

D'Anthès wanted more. On November 2, 1836, he lured Natalya into an indiscreet private meeting. The tête-à-tête was soon interrupted, but two days later Pushkin and his friends received anonymous notes welcoming the poet into the Serene Order of Cuckolds. Long angry at d'Anthès for the officer's attentions to his wife, Pushkin that night challenged d'Anthès to a duel. Pushkin's friends succeeded in delaying the meeting, and when d'Anthès asked for the hand of Natalya's sister Ekaterina in marriage, the duel seemed to have been averted.

Pushkin's anger remained unslaked, though, and in public d'Anthès showed more interest in his sister-in-law Natalya than in his wife. When Pushkin became convinced that Heeckeren was the author of the anonymous offensive letter of November 4, 1836, he sent an offensive letter to the baron (January 23, 1837). D'Anthès replied with an insulting message of his own. At 5:00 P.M. on January 27, d'Anthès and Pushkin met outside Petersburg. Both were wounded, but Pushkin's injury proved fatal. He died some thirty-six hours later.

Feinstein tells the story of Pushkin's life and death clearly and concisely. Though the emphasis is on the life rather than the writings, her account helps the reader appreciate Pushkin's literary achievement. The biography would have been helped by careful copy editing: Dates often are wrong; and one wishes that somewhere Feinstein had given full names. Still, these are minor flaws in what serves as an excellent introduction to the father of modern Russian literature.

Joseph Rosenblum

Sources for Further Study

The Economist 349 (November 14, 1998): 13.
Library Journal 124 (May 1, 1999): 76.
New Statesman 128 (January 8, 1999): 57.
Publishers Weekly 246 (April 19, 1999): 54.
Russian Life 42 (June/July, 1999): 53.
The Spectator 281 (November 14, 1998): 44.
The Times Literary Supplement, January 29, 1999, p. 29.

QUANTUM PHILOSOPHY
Understanding and Interpreting Contemporary Science

Author: Roland Omnès (1931-)
First published: Philosophie de la science contemporaine, 1994
Translated from the French by Arturo Sangalli
Publisher: Princeton University Press (Princeton, New Jersey). 296 pp. $29.95
Type of work: History of science, science, and philosophy
Time: 582 B.C.E. to 1999

A profound essay outlining a path that links the formal mathematical expressions of fundamental scientific principles that operate in the atomic world to a commonsense reconstruction of the real macroscopic world

Roland Omnès is a specialist in quantum mechanics and a professor of physics at the University of Paris XI. Omnès thinks deeply and writes clearly about the conceptual framework of physical science. He has received high recognition for his books: *The Interpretation of Quantum Mechanics* (1994), a book for specialists, and *Understanding Quantum Mechanics* (1999), a text for beginning science students, experienced physicists, mathematicians, and philosophers. Omnès also wrote *Introduction to Particle Physics* (1971) and coauthored *Mandelstam Theory and Regge Poles: An Introduction for Experimentalists* (1963) with Marcel Froissart.

Omnès separates the contents of *Quantum Philosophy* into four major parts. Part 1 reviews key individuals and ideas in the historical development of classical logic, physics, mathematics, and the philosophy of knowledge. By retracing the establishment of past foundations, an appreciation can be developed for the evolution of scientific knowledge. Furthermore, with this approach, Omnès hopes to clear up the difficulties in understanding and interpreting contemporary science. In part 2, Omnès documents the historical break between classical, commonsense physics and formal, mathematically based physics. This fracture continues to haunt science to this day and contributes to an unfortunate cleavage of our culture in a time when many of the possible applications of science require the enlightened judgment of the public. Therefore, in part 3, starting from the fundamental principles of quantum physics, Omnès builds a bridge from the formal mathematical formulation to the real, visible world. Part 4 then briefly explores some possible directions that may be taken to bring logic and reality closer together and to open up new domains of knowledge. Although the amount of redundancy in this book may be viewed as a weakness, it is also a strength for the general reader, providing the repetition necessary to understand some unfamiliar, formal, and quite difficult scientific points.

Omnès points out that the first individuals to use logic and mathematics to infer a representation of the world were the Pythagoreans. In particular, Pythagoras observed that there is a harmony in nature that is commanded by numbers. He became convinced that the basic objects in nature, including the sun, the moon, and the stars, are controlled by basic harmonies that can be described mathematically. By using numbers and geometric shapes to analyze the world, Pythagoras and his followers hoped to understand its nature and interrelationships. Math was born. Proof by reasoning became established.

During the 1500's, classical physics was rapidly developing. Aristotle's concept of an earth-centered universe started to crumble when Nicolaus Copernicus suggested a new system that placed the earth and the planets in orbits around the sun. Johannes Kepler's description of planetary motion, deduced from Tycho Brahe's data, demonstrated that empirical rules could be cast into mathematical form. Subsequently, with the aid of the telescope, Galileo helped usher in the modern scientific method: Pose hypotheses, design experiments, build the apparatus, make observations, and expose conclusions to peer review by publishing the results. Omnès reviews the continuing evolution of classical physics by recounting how Galileo used experiments with balls and inclined planes to represent reality visually in a way fully understood by intuition. He also relates the introduction of the inductive method by Francis Bacon, in which observations of many specific examples are generalized into the laws of nature.

According to Omnès, the pinnacle of science was reached by Sir Isaac Newton. Newton's greatest contribution was the ability to see the world in a new way. Falling bodies, planetary motions, and collisions were all described using universal principles that were expressed in terms of logical mathematics. His laws could predict the future of each body in a decisive, deterministic way.

However, Newton's extensive use of mathematics began the unfortunate removal of the ideas of science from the reach of the layperson, who was almost always unversed in that esoteric language. For example, Newton's universal law of gravitation required a mathematical device in order to calculate the gravitational force. The idea of an instantaneous force acting at a distance, a purely mathematical construct, was introduced. Omnès calls this construct the first step in moving from a conceptual to a formal description of science.

The next major step in the development of science was introduced in an attempt to understand and describe light. According to the experiments and analysis of Thomas Young and Augustin-Jean Fresnel, light behaves as a wave. In order to describe the propagation of light through a vacuum, an immaterial, all-pervasive medium known as the ether was fabricated. Omnès states that this disturbing ether, which was later discounted, further increased the gap between scientific interpretation and reality.

The gap between classical and formal physics widened further in the 1860's when James Clerk Maxwell formulated a mathematical theory for the laws governing the interconnectedness of electricity and magnetism. These four physical laws, Maxwell's laws of electromagnetism, were consistent with all the existing empirical data and rules, but they were purely mathematical equations that described the dynamics of a system of electrical and magnetic fields. The concept of an electromagnetic field could be described only by mathematical language. With formal mathematical concepts being used more frequently by scientists, Omnès suggests that intuition was gradually going blind. However, welcome or not, the mathematical description was unavoidable. Toward the end of the 1800's, mathematics was quickly becoming the universal language of science. The relationships between things had become more important than the nature of things.

At this juncture, Omnès poses some profound, far-reaching questions: What is the meaning of understanding? Philosophers represented the world with mental images constructed by reasoning and ordinary language. Is the mind limited to exploiting the observed facts, as suggested by philosopher David Hume, or can knowledge be expanded by further investigation into the origins of the laws of nature? Omnès then asks how understanding is even possible. In contrast with Immanuel Kant, Omnès concludes that a new philosophy is imperative and that reason must be complemented by logic and reality. Omnès points out that the world is really quite different from the way it is generally perceived. Nature is governed by laws whose form is mathematical. However, mathematics has no meaning by itself. Although mathematics is an integral part of an all-encompassing philosophy of knowledge, its meaning must be found in the science itself.

By the end of the nineteenth century, a major problem existed: The mathematical formulation of the laws of science seemed incomprehensible to the classical philosopher. The more scientists proclaimed to know, the less seemed to be understood. Mathematics appeared to be only a game of relations that tried to accommodate everything. This eventually led to the complete fracture between classical and formal science in the early 1900's, when the mathematical formalisms developed by Albert Einstein to explain the theory of special relativity and the relativistic theory of gravitation developed by Werner Heisenberg and Erwin Schrödinger to explain the phenomenon of the microscopic world in terms of quantum mechanics was introduced. Omnès looks for a way to build a bridge to reality and formulates the last half of his book on the premise that physical reality is governed by the laws of quantum physics. Although quantum mechanics is a formal, unfamiliar language to most, all of physics and chemistry depend on it. Quantum mechanics most deeply penetrates the whole set of scientific laws.

Omnès describes quantum theory as a set of rules that interrelate the facts of nature. With quantum mechanics, the atoms of an object are replaced by a wave function, a blurry cloud of probabilities. Matter can behave as a wave or a particle but not both at the same time. Quantum physics is a set of propositions that can be expressed in ordinary language, but due to the underlying formalism, the meaning is very obscure. Heisenberg's uncertainty principle is a direct consequence of the basic principles of quantum theory. Omnès suggests that Niels Bohr made a mistake in concluding that there are two distinct categories of laws, the classical and the quantum. Omnès then chooses to recover the classical, visual representation of the world from the formal quantum representation.

Because physical science had become mired in the formalism of unfamiliar mathematics, Omnès looks to regain a real image of the world by following a reverse path to the historical development of physical science. His course starts with the quantum world and proceeds to an understanding of the classical world. Deduce common sense from quantum premises, he urges. In other words, instead of explaining reality in terms of a mental representation of it, explain it in terms that account for both the mental and the intuitive. Reason must be deduced from the underlying scientific principles of the world as opposed to determining those principles through the ordinary language of reason.

Omnès proceeds from the foundation of quantum physics by recounting the concept of "consistent histories" that was introduced by Robert Griffiths in 1984 and expounded upon by Omnès, Murray Gell-Mann, and James Hartle in the late 1980's. A history is a sequence of various properties that take place at different times. After specifying the time of each event, the history can be rewritten by using appropriate mathematical operators called "projectors." Wave function probabilities are just numbers assigned to events that predict the probability of a given history. Only histories that can be assigned a probability are consistent and meaningful.

Omnès explains that by using the concept and language of consistent histories, the quantum world can be described. By defining an object as a collection of wave functions, consistent histories translate quantum words into classical terms. The description of a physical system is constructed from the propositions belonging to a unique, consistent quantum logic which is supported by implications that can be demonstrated. The fracture between the classical and formal descriptions of science closes, and a commonsense, intuitive representation of the world emerges. Schrödinger's formulation of quantum mechanics that describes the microscopic world becomes Newton's classical mechanics in the macroscopic world. As Omnès points out, the laws of reality are ultimately quantum and formal, but the logic of consistent quantum histories reconstructs a commonsense representation of the classical world.

In direct contrast with traditional epistemology, Omnès suggests that common sense is merely the result of the basic laws of nature. Although Bohr wanted to use classical physics as the unique reference point, Omnès demonstrates that the correct starting point is the deeper quantum principles that govern the world. Omnès clarifies some of the possible contradictions of the consistent histories approach by explaining the concept of decoherence. For example, the old legend of Schrödinger's mythical cat, that a cat might be both dead and alive at the same time, results from the assumption that wave functions typically interfere on the macroscopic level. However, decoherence is a physical effect that quickly suppresses quantum interference at the macroscopic level. Quantum paradoxes, such as Schrödinger's cat, are resolved without any mysterious action-at-a-distance, and the conclusion makes good sense out of quantum measurements. From the concept of consistent quantum histories governed by decoherence and the principle of inertia, the quantum world disguised by wave function probabilities emerges into ordinary reality, the three-dimensional world envisioned by the Greeks.

According to Omnès, the reconstruction of the macroscopic world from the theoretical model of quantum mechanics exhibits every characteristic of reality except for uniqueness of the facts. Omnès refers to this problem as the chasm between quantum and classical descriptions of the world. The problem arises because the probabilistic nature of a wave function is still manifest even at the macroscopic level. However, the present interpretation of quantum mechanics through the use of consistent histories is perfectly compatible with the uniqueness of reality. Uniqueness is not predicted, but it is not contradicted. Consistent histories may not succeed totally in reaching realism, but their primary goal is only to provide a method of interpretation. The uniqueness of reality must come from philosophy or metaphysics and not from science.

In the last part of the book, Omnès superficially explores future directions that science might take to find the source of the order of all things or even a new philosophy of knowledge. A fully consistent form of quantum theory still needs to be developed, one that includes its relativistic counterparts. Can science organize reality from the smallest to the largest scale? Can science give rise to its own philosophy? These questions are profound and difficult to address, but Omnès is optimistic about a positive outcome.

Alvin K. Benson

Sources for Further Study

Booklist 95 (April 15, 1999): 1495.
Library Journal 124 (August, 1999): 133.

REASON FOR HOPE
A Spiritual Journey

Author: Jane Goodall (1934-   ), with Phillip Berman
Publisher: Warner Books (New York). 282 pp. $26.95
Type of work: Religion, science, and autobiography
Time: 1934-1999
Locale: England and Tanzania

Goodall chronicles her extraordinary life as the world's leading primatologist, highlighting those events that challenged and strengthened her faith in God

Dr. Jane Goodall's groundbreaking studies of the chimpanzees living in Tanzania's Gombe preserve revolutionized the understanding of what it means to be human. Her startling observations of chimps making and using tools prompted the now famous comment by her mentor, Dr. Louis Leakey, "Ah! We must now redefine man, redefine tool, or accept chimpanzees as human!" Her discoveries are documented in her many books, including *In the Shadow of Man* (1971), the seminal *Chimpanzees of Gombe: Patterns of Behavior* (1986), and *Through a Window: My Thirty Years with the Chimpanzees of Gombe* (1990). Goodall is also known for her active role as a conservationist and humanitarian. In 1986, she began traveling to raise funds on behalf of reforestation, improved conditions for captive chimps, and Roots & Shoots, a program for youngsters designed to foster environmental awareness. She is often asked how she can be so peaceful and optimistic in the face of environmental destruction and human and animal suffering. She attempts to answer this question in *Reason for Hope* as she retraces the personal, professional, and spiritual paths that have given her life direction, meaning, and purpose.

Born in pre-World War II England, Goodall was raised on her family's estate by a group of strong, independent women that included her grandmother, mother, sister, and two aunts. Recollections of her childhood are bathed in warmth, innocence, and simplicity. The memories she chooses to share offer a glimpse of a time when children had to find ways to amuse themselves without the aid of television, computers, and video games. An avid reader, she spent her days in the family's garden doing homework or reading Edgar Rice Burroughs's *Tarzan* novels. She also roamed the cliffs near her house with her dog, Rusty, and closely observed the nature around her. Her precise descriptions of what she remembers seeing on her childhood explorations reveal her exacting nature and passion for detail—traits that she would put to good use in the forests of Gombe.

In addition to encouraging her interest in animals, her family's Christian beliefs molded Goodall's spiritual views, and she attributes her strong faith in God to her secure childhood. She notes, "Like most children who grow up in happy homes, I never had cause to question the religious beliefs of my family." Her grandfather had been a Congregational minister and her grandmother, Danny, and mother, Vanne, quoted Scripture often. During the difficult times of her life, Goodall has often drawn strength from the verses she heard as a child. Although her childhood was "gently permeated by the ethics of Christianity," Goodall began to move away from orthodox belief when, as a teenager, she read the Bible "extensively and carefully." She questioned dogmatic beliefs such as the Virgin birth and the real presence in the Eucharist. She also wrestled with the problem of evil. She was shocked by the horrors of the Holocaust and began to wonder about the nature of God, asking herself, "If God was good and all powerful as I had been led to believe, how could He allow so many innocent people to suffer and die?" Her doubt launched her on a search for an alternative spirituality that made more sense to her, although she did not jettison Christianity completely. For example, influenced by theosophy in her late teens, she embraced belief in reincarnation and rejected the Christian doctrine that an individual has only one life to live on earth and then, after death, faces final judgment.

"Death," one of the most emotionally wrenching chapters in the book, recounts the final illness and passing of Goodall's second husband, Derek Bryceson, and more explicitly reveals Goodall's religious views. When Bryceson died of cancer, his passing left Goodall in deep mourning. However, a series of paranormal events after his death brought Goodall comfort and healing. She tells of one particularly vivid episode where she believes that she saw and talked with Bryceson while she was having an out-of-body experience. Many scientists would undoubtedly scoff at such a revelation, especially when it comes from one of their own colleagues. Goodall is all too aware of the scientific emphasis on logic and objectivity, but is resolute in her belief:

> I do not feel the need to prove this to anyone; there are many who feel the same but we are ill-equipped by Western education for the task of convincing unbelievers of the reality of the spirit. Science demands objective factual evidence—proof; spiritual experience is subjective and leads to faith. It is enough, for me, that my faith gives me an inner peace and brings meaning to my own life.

For Goodall, there is no conflict between science and religion. She belongs to an emerging group within the scientific community that believes science and faith are not mutually exclusive but are two equally valid ways of reaching the truth.

Goodall returns to the issue of good and evil when she recounts her experiences in the forests of Gombe. She first offers an idyllic description of her initial years at the preserve in spite of the risks that living in the wild presented. Although she suffered from malaria and had to deal with the intrusive threat of wild animals, Goodall's close relationship with the chimps overshadowed any discomforts she experienced. Her life in the forest bordered on the Edenic. She dared to name the subjects she was sent to study, a practice shunned in scientific circles because it was thought to compromise objectivity. Because Goodall was not initially university-trained, she brought to her study a naïveté concerning scientific convention that helped rather than hindered her. Her gentle nature and respectful attitude toward the chimpanzees elicited their trust, and they accepted her into their world. One of the most moving and lyrical passages in the book is Goodall's description of an extraordinary encounter with David Greybeard, a leader of the chimpanzee band:

> When David Greybeard moved off along the well-marked trail, I followed. When he left the trail and moved through some dense undergrowth near a stream, I was sure I would lose him, for I became hopelessly entangled in the vines. But I found him sitting by the water, almost as if he were waiting for me. . . . As David and I sat there, I noticed a ripe red fruit from an oil nut palm lying on the ground. I held it toward him on the palm of my hand. David glanced at me and reached to take the nut. He dropped it, but gently held my hand. I needed no words to understand his message of reassurance. . . . To this day I remember the soft pressure of his fingers. We had communicated in a language far more ancient than words.

For one brief moment, the touch of David's fingers dissolves the barrier between observer and subject. The passage evokes a mythic image of Eden, a restoration of the harmony that existed between humans and other animals before the fall. This and other encounters caused Goodall to believe that "chimpanzees, though very like us in behavior, were rather *nicer*."

In 1971, ten years into the study, Goodall discovered that the Gombe "paradise" was no more than an illusion. The research staff observed a series of brutal attacks between chimpanzee communities, some of which resulted in infant killings and cannibalism. Stunned by the unexpected observations, Goodall and her colleagues nevertheless impartially reported their findings to the scientific community. Goodall's account of those dark days leads her to further reflect on the origins of good and evil. In chapters entitled "The Roots of Evil" and "Precursors to War," she explores the parallels between chimpanzee aggression and human violence. She concludes that while chimps act according to their nature, humans have the ability to curb their violent behavior by virtue of reason and acts of will.

Although she sadly accepts the fact that humans are prone to evil, Goodall's optimistic nature reasserts itself in the subsequent chapters "Compassion and Love" and "Moral Evolution." She offers examples of the compassion she has observed in chimpanzee society as well as instances of heroic self-sacrifice in human culture. Central to her feelings of optimism are the teachings of French physician and philosopher LeCompte DuNuoy, who believed that humanity was "in the process of acquiring the moral attributes that would enable us to become increasingly less aggressive and warlike and more caring and compassionate." Goodall enthusiastically endorses DuNuoy's ideas as she envisions the possibility that culture could be transformed if the majority of people committed themselves to building a moral and just society. Many readers may find her solution to the world's social and political problems somewhat idealistic, especially when she suggests that to accomplish such a feat, "We will have to evolve, all of us, from ordinary, everyday human beings—into saints! Ordinary people, like you and me, will have to become saints, or at least mini-saints." Although Goodall's vision may seem unrealistic, she makes it clear that she is taking the long view. The moral evolution of the human race would take years to develop. Understood in this way, her contention that flawed human beings must become saints in order to build a truly moral society does not seem so impossible considering that some visible progress in social reform has been made. Yet time may not be on humanity's side because of the urgency of many environmental and social problems to be faced, in which case her noble vision may never come to fruition.

In the closing chapters, Goodall clearly states her reasons for hope, among them her faith in the human spirit and intellect, the resilience of nature, and her confidence that young people will continue to work toward making the world a better place. She is a tireless crusader on behalf of environmental causes. Her activism is inseparable from her deep religious and moral convictions; in this way she is much like Mahatma Gandhi and Martin Luther King, Jr., before her. Unlike the campaigns of these and other social reformers, Goodall's causes do not have the high visibility or appeal to the grassroots that can transform a cause into a full-fledged movement. Her call to action is heartfelt and passionate, yet it lacks the sharp focus necessary to mobilize large groups of people. Does she accomplish what she set out to do by writing a book about hope—namely, to inspire the reader to see the future in a more optimistic way? The answer is yes. Her compassion, commitment, and gentle spirituality illuminate every page and lend a mystical quality to the narrative. Her optimism encourages readers to look beyond themselves and the trying situations they face and to be open to the wonderful possibilities of a hope-filled vision of the future.

Pegge Bochynski

Sources for Further Study

Animals 132 (September, 1999): 37.
Booklist 96 (September 15, 1999): 195.
Library Journal 124 (September 15, 1999): 91.
The New York Times Book Review 104 (October 24, 1999): 21.
Publishers Weekly 246 (August 2, 1999): 61.

THE RETURN OF LITTLE BIG MAN

Author: Thomas Berger (1924-)
Publisher: Little, Brown (Boston). 432 pp. $25.00
Type of work: Novel
Time: 1876-1893
Locale: Deadwood and Standing Rock, Dakota Territory; Dodge City, Kansas; North Platte, Nebraska; Tombstone, Arizona Territory; Chicago; New York City; London; Paris; and other locations in the United States and Europe

Jack Crabb, the hero of Little Big Man *and the only white survivor of the Battle of the Little Bighorn, continues his adventures, including encounters with several famous historical figures*

Principal characters:
JACK CRABB, an observer of legendary events in the history of the American West
AMANDA TEASDALE, a social reformer
WILLIAM F. "BUFFALO BILL" CODY, a frontier scout turned entertainer
SITTING BULL, a Sioux chief
JAMES BUTLER "WILD BILL" HICKOK,
W. B. "BAT" MASTERSON,
WYATT EARP,
VIRGIL EARP, and
JOHN "DOC" HOLLIDAY, famous lawmen and gunfighters
ALLIE EARP, Virgil's wife
ANNIE OAKLEY, a sharpshooter
FRANK BUTLER, her husband
ELIZABETH "LIBBIE" BACON CUSTER, the widow of the general
PARD, Jack's dog

Thomas Berger's *Little Big Man* (1964) is both an entertaining comic novel and a moving exploration of divisions within the American character. Jack Crabb, a 111-year-old resident of a nursing home, recounts his life, from an Indian attack on his family, resulting in his being raised by the Cheyenne, to his being the only white survivor of the Battle of the Little Bighorn. In between, Jack moves between the two cultures, never truly feeling at home in either. *The Return of Little Big Man* continues Jack's story for another seventeen years, during which he encounters numerous famous Americans and Europeans and watches helplessly as the Indians are gradually robbed of much of their dignity.

In *Little Big Man*, Jack recounts his early life to historian Ralph Fielding Snell and expires. *The Return of Little Big Man* reveals that he has faked his death to rid himself of Snell so that he, now 112, can tell his own story. After witnessing General George Armstrong Custer's demise, Jack makes his way to Deadwood in the Dakota Territory, where he discovers his old friend Wild Bill Hickok. After being hired as the aging gunfighter's bodyguard, Jack sees Hickok murdered by Jack McCall. Moving on to Dodge City, he becomes friends with yet another legendary lawman, Bat Masterson, who hires Jack as a bartender.

His sojourn in Dodge is most notable as the occasion for meeting Amanda Teasdale, who enlists Jack as an interpreter at an Indian school. Jack does not approve of trying to convert Indians to white ways, but he is fascinated by Amanda, the most beautiful woman he has ever seen. Like most of Jack's experiences, this one ends ignominiously, and he soon finds himself following Masterson to Tombstone. Jack develops unfriendly relations with Wyatt Earp and Doc Holliday and witnesses the famous shootout quite near the O.K. Corral, his account of this event varying considerably from the legend.

Jack next joins Buffalo Bill's Wild West, initially as his boss's personal bartender, and spends several years traveling with Cody's show throughout the eastern United States and Western Europe, becoming friends with Annie Oakley and meeting such celebrities as Queen Victoria and the Prince of Wales. When Sitting Bull joins the show, Jack is his translator and confidant. The famous Sioux warrior's commonsense wisdom is comparable to that of Old Lodge Skins, Jack's mentor in the earlier novel.

In *Little Big Man*, Jack and Old Lodge Skins constantly encounter each other. Here, he finds himself crossing paths with Amanda, falling more deeply in love with her. Both are present at the Standing Rock reservation when Sitting Bull is murdered. The embarrassing display of the chief's cabin at the 1893 World's Fair in Chicago brings Jack and Amanda together again, and he joins her in working at Jane Addams's Hull House. *The Return of Little Big Man* ends with the promise of more adventures to follow.

The critical reputation of *Little Big Man* has increased considerably since its publication for several reasons. One is Berger's realistic, unsentimental portrait of the American Indian, and he continues this concern in the sequel. In the earlier book, the Indians fight to protect their way of life. In *The Return of Little Big Man*, even warriors like Sitting Bull recognize that change is inevitable. Going to school, learning English, wearing strange clothing, adopting currency, and becoming farmers is not giving in, from their perspective, but simply a necessary means of survival: "They kept thinking they could stay completely Indian despite all the evidence to the contrary. That was what was both great and hopeless about them."

As in the first Jack Crabb novel, Berger not only tries to explain Indian ways but also attempts to show how the dominant culture appears to the original Americans. The Indians accompanying Cody's show to Europe "had gotten tired of looking at the wonders of civilization that the whites had come up with before they went across the ocean to a land that didn't have none of them and started from scratch, which didn't make sense." Such displays of logic are balanced with observations about the Indians' lack of imagination and stubbornness, qualities that make them merely spectators in New York, London, and Paris, incapable of absorbing any ideas of improving themselves from the white perspective. The prevailing prejudices on both sides preclude any hope of serious communication. Reformers like Teasdale see Indians almost as innocent children. When she wonders how his own kind could kill Sitting Bull, Jack explains, "They're human."

The Indians with Buffalo Bill's Wild West enjoy staging battles in which they whoop and shoot more than any Indians ever did in reality. Having to lose each battle fails to bother them because they are well compensated and care little about distorting the reality of their wars with whites, knowing the truth themselves. As in *Little Big Man*, Berger is concerned with correcting misconceptions about the West while examining the American habit of romanticizing the past. "You don't know what the truth was," says Jack, "unless you was there—like me, on so many well-known occasions, and I never claim anything I can't vouch for." Buffalo Bill is thus central to *The Return of Little Big Man* for his propensity to take facts and embellish them in the name of show business, the major source of misinformation about the West. Jack describes Cody as "one of the greatest masters of the art of throwing buffalo chips who ever lived, in a time when there was a lot of competition."

Jack throws some chips himself. When he meets a dandy, not knowing the stranger is Bat Masterson, Jack takes credit for teaching Wyatt Earp how to shoot when, in his only meeting with the surly lawman to that point, Earp had knocked him out with the barrel of his pistol. For the most part, Jack corrects errors such as the infrequency of showdown gunfights. In fact, during Masterson's time as sheriff of Ford County, Kansas, only seven homicides occur. Jack especially suspects eyewitness accounts, noting that all the supposed witnesses of the famous Tombstone shootout give conflicting accounts. He cannot tell Buffalo Bill and Sitting Bull about how Custer died because he knows they will not believe him. Jack trusts only what he sees himself, prefacing one account with "everything from here on is hearsay."

Even artifacts are untrustworthy, such as Sitting Bull's autograph on the postcards sold at Buffalo Bill's Wild West. The chief first traces a signature written by Jack; then Annie Oakley modifies it to make it easier to read; finally, her husband, Frank Butler, decides it should be more masculine and improves it further. Berger presents the signature as a metaphor for the untrustworthiness of history in general. Jack observes that Indians do not talk about the past because "time belongs to everybody and everything, and nobody and nothing can lay claim to any part of it exclusively, so if you talk about the past as though there was just one version of it that everybody agrees on, you might be seen as stealing the spirit of others."

For all Jack's suspicions about others' flawed interpretations of reality, however, he gradually develops an acceptance of such distortions, eventually preferring the make-believe world of Buffalo Bill's Wild West to the harsher world outside its tents. Berger's novels are often subtle commentaries not only about how people perceive the world but also about how they use the arts to convey these perceptions. Jack's fond feelings for show business illustrate Berger's view of the power of the imagination in molding the chaos of experience into art—or at least something approximating art.

The young Jack Crabb of *Little Big Man* is a benignly unreliable narrator in the tradition of Mark Twain's *Adventures of Huckleberry Finn* (1884). He slightly misinterprets some events and the motives of some characters out of naïveté, but his view of things is always more good-hearted than those of the people he encounters. In Arthur Penn's 1970 film version of the novel, Dustin Hoffman presents Jack as a straight-faced slapstick figure reminiscent of Buster Keaton. The aging Jack of *The Return of Little Big Man* mellows considerably, is much more sentimental. He progresses from the Keatonesque to being a more pathetic, almost Chaplinesque figure, especially in his relations with Pard, a bedraggled stray dog who takes up with him and seems a canine version of Jack himself.

As American free enterprise flourishes in the decades following the Civil War, Jack longs desperately for economic success, envisioning himself as the prosperous owner of a Dodge City saloon or as the innovative proprietor of his own wild West show. Jack is an observer, not an actor, and nothing comes of all his dreams. Like his picaresque predecessors, every time he builds up a nest egg, something happens to it. The successful American entrepreneur, Berger suggests, possesses a ruthlessness of which Jack is incapable.

Jack sees himself as an almost hopeless case who can be saved only by the love of a good woman. He always idealizes women. In *Little Big Man*, he has a crush on Mrs. Pendrake, his foster mother, only to see her become a prostitute. A mere glimpse of Custer's wife inspires him to see her as the personification of female perfection. He finally meets her in New York in *The Return of Little Big Man*, only to find her encased in a morbidly defensive obsession with her hugely flawed husband's memory. Jack can be friends with women only if they are happily married, like Allie Earp, wife of Wyatt's brother Virgil, and Annie Oakley, and pose no romantic threat. Jack adores Amanda but resists placing her on a pedestal, seeing her do-good tendencies as spunky but slightly misguided. Once they realize how they feel about each other, after years of miscommunications, and accept each other's flaws, Jack becomes willing to make sacrifices, such as reading newspapers, to be worthy of her.

The young Jack Crabb is more of an existential outsider than his middle-aged self, and the earlier novel, one of the greatest portraits of the contradictions within the American character, has a poetic resonance lacking in the sequel. If its themes seem more subdued than in the earlier book, *The Return of Little Big Man* is also the creation of a writer who has changed his approach to fiction in the intervening thirty-five years. Proclaiming himself uninterested in plot, character, and theme, repulsed by journalism and sociology masquerading as fiction, Berger is more interested in storytelling as an end in itself. Berger's account of the middle-aged Jack's experiences is admirable.

Michael Adams

Sources for Further Study

Booklist 95 (February 1, 1999): 940.
Library Journal 124 (February 15, 1999): 181.
Los Angeles Times Book Review, May 16, 1999, p. 10.
The New York Times Book Review 104 (May 9, 1999): 14.
Publishers Weekly 246 (January 4, 1999): 73.
The Washington Post Book World 29 (February 28, 1999): 15.

ROBERT FROST
A Life

Author: Jay Parini (1948-   )
Publisher: Henry Holt (New York). 514 pp. $35.00
Type of work: Literary biography
Time: 1874-1963
Locale: San Francisco, New England, Britain

Taking issue with Frost's previous biographers, Middlebury College professor Parini offers a major reassessment of Frost, America's "national poet"

Principal personages:
ROBERT FROST, distinguished American poet
ELINOR MIRIAM WHITE FROST, the poet's wife
BELLE MOODY FROST, the poet's mother
WILLIAM PRESCOTT FROST, the poet's father
JEANIE FROST, the poet's younger sister
LESLEY FROST, the poet's eldest daughter
CAROL FROST, the poet's son
IRMA FROST, the poet's second daughter
MARJORIE FROST, the poet's youngest daughter
EDWARD THOMAS, Welsh poet, friend of Frost
KAY MORRISON, Frost's personal secretary
LAWRANCE THOMPSON, Frost's "official" biographer

Some famous writers, like Samuel Johnson, were fortunate in their choice of a sympathetic biographer, notably James Boswell, while others, such as Edgar Allan Poe, have had their reputations suffer as the result of a hostile biographer, in Poe's case, Rufus Griswold. Frost's choice of Lawrance Thompson, then a young Princeton English professor, as his "official biographer" had unfortunate repercussions after Frost's death when Thompson produced a massive, three-volume biography that was suffused with clear malice and dislike. Thompson set out to demolish Frost's public persona as a kindly, white-haired New England poet and offered instead a monster of selfishness and egotism who used friends and family to his own ends. More recently, Jeffrey Meyers presented an equally unflattering view of Frost's later life in his 1996 biography. Unfortunately, these biographies debunking Frost have all too often been uncritically accepted as fact rather than as a version of a life much too complicated to be captured in any single biography.

In *Robert Frost: A Life*, Middlebury College professor Jay Parini offers a fairer and more balanced version of the poet's life. Parini does not scant or ignore the unpleasant facts of Frost's life, but he tries to place them in a broader context, recognizing that all biographies are versions or interpretations of a life and cannot possibly be definitive, no matter how exhaustive the research. His thesis is that Frost was "a major poet who struggled throughout his life with depression, anxiety, self-doubt, and confusion." He depicts Frost as a poet of contradictions, deeply influenced both by his dreamy, visionary Scottish mother and by his impetuous, strong-willed New

England father, who died of tuberculosis when Frost was only eleven. Often seen as the quintessential New England poet, Frost was actually born and raised in San Francisco, where his father had taken his bride to seek his political and journalistic fortunes.

Part of the complication of the Frost persona is that many of his poetic qualities that seem most innate were consciously chosen and cultivated. Though often considered a nature poet, Frost was a city boy who discovered the pleasures of country life, a westerner who assimilated New England mores as an adopted son. After her husband's death in 1884, Belle Frost brought her two children back east to live with their grandparents in Lawrence, Massachusetts, a textile mill town north of Boston. Always short of money and uncomfortable with her in-laws, Belle earned a meager living as a grade school teacher, living in a series of shabby apartments and boardinghouses. Frost's younger sister Jeanie showed early signs of mental instability, and Belle came increasingly to depend upon Rob for emotional and financial support from part-time and summer jobs. Yet Frost was also a talented and able student at Lawrence High School, where he and his future wife Elinor White were co-valedictorians.

To an extraordinary degree, Frost shaped and directed his career through what he called his "inflexible ambition" or will to become a poet. Yet Parini demonstrates that he was not, as Thompson charged, selfish or neglectful of his wife or children. On the contrary, Frost was quite dedicated to Elinor and his family. Not only did Frost hold himself together during his difficult adolescent years, but he discovered in writing poetry a means of self-affirmation, of holding the forces of depression, self-doubt, and mental chaos at bay. Dissatisfied with college, which he tried briefly at Dartmouth (1892) and later at Harvard (1897-1899), Frost found his essential creative resources in marriage, family, and the Derry farm.

The Derry years (1900-1911) were central to Frost's gradual development as a poet. Through the assistance of his grandfather, Frost was able to purchase the Magoon place, an attractive thirty-acre farm in Derry, New Hampshire, about eleven miles north of Lawrence. The farm became a "strategic retreat," where, supported by his grandfather's generous five-hundred-dollar yearly annuity and his modest efforts at poultry and fruit farming, Frost had the time and leisure to write. All of his children were born on the Derry farm, and Frost and his family later recalled this decade as the happiest period in their lives. Frost's notebooks were filled with the rough drafts of poems written during the time and later revised or expanded for publication. Frost was able to draw upon the memories and experiences of this period for the rest of his career.

By the rural standards of their time, the Frosts lived a somewhat unconventional or even bohemian life, with no fixed mealtimes or domestic schedule. Yet Robert and Elinor were devoted parents who home-schooled their children using progressive methods of education. The direct experience of nature was an essential part of the Frost children's education, with long walks, picnics, gardening, and pets. Frost himself kept irregular hours, writing late at night after the children were asleep. As Lesley Frost recalls in her memoir of these years, the Frosts were close-knit and resourceful, making the best of their limited means.

In 1906, Frost found a teaching position at Pinkerton Academy in Derry, which supplemented the family's meager income and gave Frost an opportunity to apply his progressive methods of education. Invitations to read his poetry and occasional magazine publications built Frost's confidence in his poetic abilities. Had it not been for the death of their infant daughter Elinor in 1907, the Frosts might have remained at the Derry farm longer, but the ache of grief was too much for them, and they moved into town that fall to be closer to Pinkerton. However, the crucial decade of Frost's poetic development, from his mid-twenties to mid-thirties, was spent at Derry, and by the time they left he had accumulated a stock of poems and experiences that would last a lifetime. His crucial values and attitudes as a poet—his pastoralism, his interest in farming and country life, his aesthetic concern for colloquial speech and the "sound of sense"—were all shaped by the Derry years. His poetic development away from academe gave him a distinctiveness and originality of voice unique among modern American poets.

Beginning in 1907, Frost returned to teaching, first at Pinkerton and later at the New Hampshire State Normal School (a teachers' college) in Plymouth, New Hampshire, and entered into an uneasy alliance with academe that would last for the rest of his life. In 1912, after his grandfather's death and the sale of the Derry farm, the Frosts made another daring move, to England, in the hope of finding a British publisher for his poems. The Frosts debated briefly over whether to choose England or Vancouver, but Frost acquiesced to Elinor's desire to "live under thatch," and they chose England. It is difficult to overestimate the risks of this move by a thirty-eight-year-old, relatively unknown poet with a wife and four children to support on limited means. Yet these three years, from 1912 to 1915, paid off in the publication of his first two poetry volumes, *A Boy's Will* (1913) and *North of Boston* (1914), two of his most significant works. Frost had a gift for friendship, and his new circle of English literary friends and acquaintances wrote favorable reviews that helped to expand his growing literary reputation. Frost met the young American expatriate poet Ezra Pound in London and for a while accepted Pound's patronizing advice and encouragement, though he recognized how different his poetics were from Pound's or T. S. Eliot's literary high modernism. Frost was always a poet of the ear rather than the eye, and he did not choose to make his poems deliberately inaccessible to the ordinary reader. His complexity was subtle and syntactical, not created by ponderous textual notes and references or quotations. Though Frost later distanced himself from Pound and Eliot, he benefited from Pound's favorable reviews and encouragement. By the time the family returned to America in early 1917, Frost was recognized as a major American poet.

For the rest of his career, Frost felt torn between teaching and farming as a means of earning a living. He was drawn to farming but realized that it would not provide a sufficient income or leisure for writing. Through a fortuitous invitation from President Alexander Meiklejohn of Amherst in 1917, he loosely affiliated himself within the academe as virtually the first American poet-in-residence, gradually shaping the position to his own purposes. Frost was an iconoclastic and unconventional teacher who never fit well into a formal academic setting, but teaching did provide a guaranteed income and some free time (though never enough) for poetry writing. He cultivated a reputation as a "progressive" teacher, with unstructured classes and a conversational approach to instruction. Frost would often adopt a tone of self-deprecating irony in describing his "laziness," but in fact he was merely protecting the privacy and energy needed for creative work.

Frost increasingly became a public lecturer and performer, much in demand for poetry readings, or "barding about," which took him throughout the country and increased his celebrity status. During the next thirty years, he would move back and forth between Amherst and the University of Michigan, and he would buy a series of farms in New Hampshire and Vermont, perhaps seeking but never quite recapturing the idyllic years at the Derry farm. These restless moves, motivated in part by academic feuds and by Frost's dissatisfaction with academe, grew increasingly difficult for Elinor and the children, who longed for the stability of a permanent home. It is ironic how thoroughly Frost, the academic rebel, became a part of the academic establishment, with appointments at Amherst, Michigan, Harvard, and Dartmouth. It was not until after Elinor's death in 1938 that Frost settled into a semi-permanent arrangement, with an apartment in Boston and a summer cottage at Bread Loaf, Vermont, near Ted and Kay Morrison, a young Harvard couple who looked after him.

There has been much speculation about the exact nature of Frost's relationship with Kay Morrison after Elinor's death, which plunged him into deep grief and depression. Jeffrey Meyers claimed, on the basis of interviews with Kay's daughter, that she became his mistress. Parini, while acknowledging Frost's deep dependence upon Kay and some fantasizing on his part, believes that Kay was attracted to him primarily as a father figure and managed to avoid any intimacies that would have damaged her marriage. Some of Frost's most compelling love poems, such as "The Silken Tent," were written after Elinor's death, and critics disagree over the source of Frost's inspiration—the memory of Elinor or infatuation with Kay Morrison.

One of the most interesting sections of Parini's biography is his "Afterword," in which he evaluates and compares the various Frost biographies, indicating their critical strengths and weaknesses. He cautions against reading Frost's life too closely into his work and committing the biographical fallacy. Parini identifies what he calls "three waves" of Frost biography: the early appreciative or hagiographic works; the biographies debunking Frost, most notably Thompson's three-volume biography and Meyers's 1996 life of Frost; and the revisionist biographies, starting with William Pritchard's *Frost: A Literary Life Reconsidered* (1984), John Walsh's *Into My Own: The English Years of Robert Frost, 1912-1915* (1988), and including Parini's new biography of Frost. The continued biographic interest in Frost testifies to his continuing prominence as a major American poet.

Andrew J. Angyal

Sources for Further Study

Booklist 95 (January 1, 1999): 790.
Insight on the News 15 (May 24, 1999): 36.
Library Journal 124 (February 15, 1999): 150.
National Review 51 (May 3, 1999): 52.
The New York Review of Books 46 (October 21, 1999): 17.
The New York Times Book Review 104 (April 25, 1999): 13.
Publishers Weekly 246 (February 15, 1999): 93.
Time 153 (April 5, 1999): 69.
The Times Literary Supplement, January 23, 1999, p. 29.
The Yale Review 87 (October, 1999): 118.

ROCKS OF AGES

Science and Religion in the Fullness of Life

Author: Stephen Jay Gould (1941-)
Publisher: Ballantine (New York). 241 pp. $18.95
Type of work: Science, religion, and history of science

Gould argues that science and religion should be considered as distinct intellectual spheres that focus on different aspects of human life and do not conflict with each other

Warfare between science and religion has been a fundamental tenet of the history of science in the United States since 1869. During the last third of the nineteenth century, scholars began documenting the numerous clashes between the worlds of scientific investigation and religion. Focusing initially upon the Roman Catholic Church, the studies soon expanded to include Protestants as well. This effort culminated in Andrew Dickson White's two-volume *History of the Warfare of Science with Theology in Christendom* (1896), which quickly became a classic. Thereafter, history texts and science texts alike provided portraits of narrow-minded theologians preventing, or at least attempting to prevent, enlightened scientists from searching for the truth.

Various disciplines were alleged to have felt the heavy hand of theologians. The conclusions of geologists regarding the age of the earth clashed with the biblical chronology. In biology and anthropology, Charles Darwin's theory of organic evolution as presented in *On the Origin of Species by Means of Natural Selection* (1859) and *The Descent of Man, and Selection in Relation to Sex* (1871) generated fierce opposition, but it was in astronomy that the issue first arose. Galileo's being forced by the Inquisition to renounce the implications of his own discoveries—the heliocentric solar system—is an event well known to science students.

For many Americans, a more recent event—both chronologically and geographically—recapitulated the conflict. The Scopes trial in Dayton, Tennessee, in 1925, over the issue of teaching evolution in the public schools, was familiar to them through the mass media, especially thanks to the fictionalized account of the trial—*Inherit the Wind* (pb. 1955)—which was originally a play and later a film and a television production. Science, truth, and the right of humans to think about the world they live in were contrasted with religion and narrow-mindedness.

Post-World War II scholarship has begun to question the accuracy of this inherited picture of warfare between religion and science. White, if read carefully, ultimately identified dogmatic theology, not religion, as the great opponent of science. Without denying that there has been friction between theologians and scientists, historians have found that numerous scientists during the last four centuries have seen no conflict between their search for scientific truth and their religious beliefs. For such scientists, the study of nature and the study of the Bible were two paths to truths which did not necessarily conflict. Numerous theologians have accepted, even embraced science.

The motivations of the participants in the Scopes trial turn out to be much more complex than *Inherit the Wind* would lead its audience to believe.

However, there is no question that since the 1960's there has been some bitter warfare. The rise of creationist science and the efforts by fundamentalist Christians and others to exclude evolution from the public school curriculum have renewed the conflict in the United States at a level of intensity not seen in years.

Stephen Jay Gould, paleontologist, evolutionist, popular essayist, historian, self-proclaimed agnostic whose Jewish parents did not provide him with formal religious training, and worrier about the moral decline he sees about him, has offered a solution. He does not believe that science and religion can be successfully unified or synthesized into a single truth system, as happened in earlier centuries. Instead, he suggests that scientists, theologians, and the public accept the principle of Non-Overlapping Magisteria (or NOMA). A magisterium "is a domain where one form of teaching holds the appropriate tools for meaningful discourse and resolution." Science is a magisterium for the empirical world. It answers questions concerning "what is the universe made of (fact) and why does it work this way (theory)." In contrast, religion deals with "questions of ultimate meaning and moral value." According to Gould, science provides no guidelines for defining human ethical behavior, while religion is useless for describing the nature, history, and future of the universe.

Gould makes and defends two claims about NOMA. The first is that the two magisteria have equal status. The second is that the two magisteria are independent. In making the latter claim, Gould does not deny that historically there has been overlap. However, logically there should not be any.

Greatly influencing Gould's thinking about NOMA were the responses of Darwin and Thomas Henry Huxley, Darwin's supporter and so-called bulldog, when each man was faced with coming to terms with the death of a young and beloved child. Gould found in each man's reaction evidence of their acceptance of the principle of NOMA.

The death of ten-year-old Annie Darwin ended her father's belief in a caring God and the possibility of religion proving solace in times of need. He concluded that there was too much misery in life for this to have been the result of the plan of a beneficent God. Instead, there were the laws of nature and chance. In Gould's interpretation of Darwin, the latter, having removed God from nature, then concluded that nature could tell nothing about the existence of God, the foundation of morality, or other questions within the magisterium of religion.

Huxley had to confront the sudden death of his three-year-old son. Already known to be skeptical about religion, Huxley rejected the suggestion of a friend that he reexamine his position and seek solace in the hope of the eternal life of the soul and a future meeting in heaven. Instead, Huxley found peace by staying true to his intellectual convictions. In the spirit of NOMA, Huxley identified the three sources for his intellectual and philosophical outlook on life. Religion, absent theology, provided morality. Science gave him a way to judge truth free of the influences of tradition and authority. Finally, love made him realize the sanctity of human nature.

Gould admits that there have been and continue to be strong historical and psychological reasons for conflict. The first reason is that humans are often reluctant to give up authority voluntarily. For centuries, religion held both immense secular power and domination over most intellectual activities. (Gould tells his readers that history has taught that when religion and secular power are linked, great evil can and often will occur.) Some theologians have been reluctant to yield authority over the study of nature to anyone else. Second, clashes between institutions sometimes take on the guise of a conflict between science and religion—at least on the level of the specific incident, when the general issues are really quite different. Although Gould does not develop his argument completely, he appears to be arguing that science has often been identified with liberalism, modern society, and tolerance, while religion and religious leaders have taken the more conservative side. Third, in general, clashes between science and religion have occurred when the subject has been the nature of humans. The psychological crutch that religion provides by claiming a special status for humans is very important for people. When science threatens that status, it strikes fear in many. Finally, although science and religion may be distinct magisteria, they, in Gould's words, "belly right up to each other and interdigitate in the most intimate and complex manner." In these circumstances, conflict is not surprising.

Gould identifies two contemporary major threats to NOMA: creationism and the justification of human misbehavior by the misapplication of scientific ideas. In earlier publications, Gould has related the history of the efforts of creationists to modify the content of public school science through legislative fiat. He was, after all, an expert witness against the Arkansas law requiring equal time for creationist science in the trial sometimes designated as "Scopes II." Here, he argues two particular points in his brief discussion of creationist science. First, he claims that these efforts by creationists to use the law to overrule the scientific community on an issue of science do not represent a legitimate example of warfare between science and religion. He believes that the creationists represent only a small minority of the American religious community, while most religious leaders and theologians oppose the imposition of religious views upon the public school curriculum. Instead, this is a clash between supporters and opponents of NOMA, between those who want to separate church and state and those who want to integrate their theological positions into state policy. Second, he believes that this is a peculiarly American problem. Western European countries have not had to face this issue. (Unfortunately, Gould does not actually address the question of whether state-supported education in Europe, let alone the rest of the world, is legally as divorced from religious values as it is in the United States.)

Equally threatening to NOMA as the imposition of religious values upon public science education is the use of scientific theories to justify foreign policy, oppressive or restrictive legislation, or exploitation of segments of society by other segments. Gould explores the opposition of William Jennings Bryan to evolution. Bryan, who had been a secretary of state and a three-time candidate for president, represented the state of Tennessee at the Scopes trial. He has been stereotyped in *Inherit the Wind* as ignorant and narrow-minded. The truth is much more complex and disturbs Gould. Opposed to American entry into World War I, a spokesman for the poor farmer and laborer, Bryan believed that evolutionary theory had been used to justify that war, as well as American legislation (or lack of legislation) which allowed the exploitation of the politically and economically weak.

Gould does not fully endorse Bryan's analysis. He rejects Bryan's solution. However, he agrees with Bryan that there has been a problem. Evolution was being used to justify the status quo, and hence prevent social reform. More serious from Gould's perspective, scientists have presented their personal social preferences as objective facts through the misuse of data. Textbooks have presented subjective social doctrines as undeniable scientific facts. Racism, sexism, bias against the disabled and poor, and other social policies have all been endorsed and supported by "scientific data." Gould accuses scientists of overstepping the proper boundaries of science, opening science to attack by individuals like Bryan.

How successful is Gould in convincing the reader of the viability of NOMA? The logic of his argument is overwhelming, if one accepts as a first premise that the magisterium of religion is only human ethics and not the entire universe. What of those who do believe in a religion that does make that claim? Nothing Gould writes represents a convincing argument. What Gould is asking everyone to do is agree to disagree in a civil and respectful manner and to respect expertise. However, faith, as history has taught, frequently leaves little room for respect for the beliefs of others. Gould presents an argument grounded in logic, but humans are more often swayed by their passions.

What many will interpret as evidence of the strength of passion to overwhelm logic appeared, coincidentally, shortly after this book was published. On August 11, 1999, the Kansas Board of Education appeared to have explicitly rejected NOMA, voting to establish a science curriculum which removed evolution as the foundation for the teaching of biology and cosmology in that state's public schools over the objections of the teachers of science. Thanks to his very successful efforts at popularizing science, often by utilizing the history of science, Gould is one of the best-known American scientists of the last quarter of the twentieth century. He has been a vocal leader of the scientific opposition to creationist science. He has a loyal following, and any book he writes would in the normal course of events attract attention. However, the events in Kansas make *Rocks of Ages* relevant to current events. It should be of interest to a wide audience. This book could serve as a rallying point for those who are outraged by the actions of the Kansas Board of Education.

Marc Rothenberg

Sources for Further Study

The Christian Century 116 (June 2, 1999): 624.
Commentary 107 (May, 1999): 67.
The Washington Post Book World 29 (April 11, 1999): 9.

ROSS MACDONALD
A Biography

Author: Tom Nolan (1948-)
Publisher: Charles Scribner's Sons (New York). Illustrated. 496 pp. $32.00
Type of work: Literary biography
Time: 1915-1983
Locale: The United States and Canada

The first full-length biography of one of the most important crime fiction writers of the twentieth century, this is an admiring portrait of Kenneth Millar, whose life experiences and fictional creations—mainly as Ross Macdonald—are inextricably entwined

Principal personages:
KENNETH MILLAR, an American crime fiction writer (mainly as Ross Macdonald)
MARGARET STURM MILLAR, the wife of Kenneth Millar, also a crime fiction writer

Though Edgar Allan Poe is credited with having originated the detective story in the 1840's, the genre was popularized primarily by British authors, and not until the 1920's and 1930's did distinctly American crime fiction emerge, with the stories and novels of Dashiell Hammett and Raymond Chandler. At mid-century, when Kenneth Millar began publishing novels (and some short stories) in the Hammett-Chandler tradition, the American crime genre started to come of age. He soon developed a hard-boiled style of his own, took on the pseudonym Ross Macdonald, and eschewing his whodunit predecessors, turned to the ancient Greeks, using such Sophoclean and Homeric motifs as the search for one's father, the past impinging upon the present, and the self-identity quest. He created multilayered plots more complex than those of Chandler and Hammett, and he wrote a richer prose, replete with metaphor. By the time his career ended three decades and twenty-four novels later, he had become the country's most highly regarded writer of crime fiction and had elevated its status to a place in the literary mainstream and acceptance by the academy. In addition, Millar is a distinguished American regionalist because of his memorable evocation of the Southern California milieu.

Books have been written about Millar's fiction, and he has been the subject of doctoral dissertations, but Tom Nolan's *Ross Macdonald* is the first full-length biography of Millar, who was born in Los Gatos, California, in 1915, raised in Canada, and spent most of his adult life in Southern California. Millar was determinedly secretive about his past and most family matters, particularly regarding his only child, Linda, who had a history of emotional problems, ran afoul of the law when she was in college, and died at thirty-seven. Nolan, a mystery fiction reviewer for *The Wall Street Journal*, had access to thousands of letters (Millar was a prodigious correspondent), documents, and notebooks in the Kenneth and Margaret Millar collection at the University of California, Irvine, and at other libraries. He also interviewed Margaret Millar as well as dozens of relatives, friends, and literary agents. Because of these conversations and quotations from letters, Millar is a living presence throughout the book, revealed in all his complexities by his own words and the detailed (almost always laudatory) recollections of those who knew him. Nolan's occasional pauses for discussions of the works, when his chronology calls upon him to do so, are brief and focus mainly on biographical connections, but to have done more would have distracted from his purpose. What he has produced is a definitive life of an American novelist who not only wrote some of the best crime fictions of the century but also significantly influenced the course of a genre he somewhat reluctantly pursued.

Though Kenneth Millar was born in California, his parents were from Canada and soon returned there, living briefly in Vancouver. They separated when Millar was four, and he went with his mother to live in Kitchener, Ontario, but she became destitute and sent him to a cousin in northern Ontario. Then he was sent to live in Alberta, but soon returned to Ontario and attended Waterloo College for a time before transferring to the University of Western Ontario, where his brilliance intimidated some of the faculty. Rejected by Harvard University for graduate studies, he went to the University of Michigan, where he eventually received his Ph.D. in English literature. In 1938, he wed Margaret Sturm, a high school friend, with whom he had a difficult though enduring marriage. She was high-strung, emotional, hypersensitive, and asocial, whereas he was eerily self-possessed, gregarious, and socially active. Both needed their own space, so from the beginning they lived almost separate lives under the same roof, but a strong interdependence developed between them. She became a published author first, though her early success was achieved with his assistance as plotter and editor. He was pleased when her career blossomed, but once he outpaced her in books published and in critical and public recognition, a pronounced rivalry developed.

Even after the Millars finally settled in Santa Barbara, California, and he became involved in community matters, he continued to consider himself an outsider. How his bipolar and peripatetic background shaped his personality and is reflected in his characters and plots is one of Nolan's theses. "The Split Man," a potential book title with which Millar toyed but which he never used, is an accurate self-description, according to Nolan. "Millar himself," he says, "was a man split along national, cultural, intellectual, professional, and even sexual fault lines."

A turning point in Millar's life and career was a course he took at Michigan from W. H. Auden, the English poet and a visiting lecturer, for whom Millar wrote a paper on imagery in Dante's *La divina comedia* (c. 1320; *The Divine Comedy*, 1802). An avid reader of detective fiction, Auden was impressed with young Millar and encouraged him to become an author. According to Nolan, "*The Divine Comedy* would be a frame of reference for Ross Macdonald's southern California, whose many-leveled populace evaded or were exposed by or struggled toward a harshly clarifying light." Another influence was John Buchan, whose classic *The Thirty-nine Steps* (1915) is reflected in *The Dark Tunnel* (1944), Millar's first published mystery, which combines Buchan spy story elements with a standard whodunit puzzle. This debut novel received favorable critical response, but Millar's nascent career was interrupted by a stint in the U.S. Navy in the Pacific during World War II. While aboard ship, however, he finished a spy novel, *Trouble Follows Me* (1946), and back in civilian life, he quickly turned out two more novels: *Blue City* (1947), in the Hammett hard-boiled tradition, and *The Three Roads* (1948), which he dubbed "a psychothriller" and is his first book with a Sophoclean motif.

Pleased with the progress of his career, Millar decided to write "serious fiction," as he phrased it. His attempt at a real novel was an unashamedly autobiographical piece "about an adolescent boy being shoved into delinquency by social and economic pressure," he reported in a letter to detective fiction critic Anthony Boucher, who already had become a Millar's patron and promoter. Though he worked on "Winter Solstice" for years, it remained unfinished and became emblematic of his unfulfilled yearning to break out of the crime fiction genre, or at least to write, in the manner of Graham Greene, both serious novels and what Greene labeled "entertainments."

When Millar submitted his first Lew Archer novel to Knopf, which had published *Blue City* and would be his publisher throughout his career, the firm initially rejected it but relented after he did suggested rewriting. What Millar had called "The Snatch" became *The Moving Target* (1949), and its author became John Macdonald (his father's first two names). Though the critics liked it, many noted an obvious indebtedness to Hammett and Chandler. The latter did not think much of the book, and his remark about the "rather repellant [sic] . . . pretentiousness" of the style and subsequent reference to Millar as a "literary eunuch" led the younger writer to hold a grudge against Chandler for years. The second Archer book marked an advance: *The Drowning Pool* (1950) is a full-fledged Southern California novel filled with the fakery that Millar thought pervaded the region. *The Way Some People Die* (1951) turned out to be not only an adventure story in the hard-boiled tradition but also, Nolan says, "a vivid tableau of postwar southern California and a stylish retelling of certain Greek myths." The immediacy and timelessness of this book also are common to those that followed with almost annual regularity, Millar carefully honing his plotting, enriching his themes, and more fully delineating his hero. With his twelfth novel, *The Barbarous Coast* (1956), he became Ross Macdonald, once and for all ending the confusion with fellow mystery writer John D. MacDonald, "whose writing fails to improve with time, I'm afraid," Millar commented. On the other hand, Millar thought his latest "a more human book than either of the others, more original, not so slick, and a truer picture of our very messed-up society." Highly praised by the reviewers, it was his first novel without strong echoes of other writers, so it appropriately bore the pseudonym that would carry Millar through the rest of his ascendant career.

The Doomsters (1958), his "diary of psychic progress," he wrote in the wake of traumatic problems with his daughter—among the many extremes of good and bad fortune that were juxtaposed throughout his life. Filled with "damaged people" of the sort that increasingly would populate Archer novels, it demonstrates Millar's artful transformation of reality into fiction. He hoped the book would mark his success at writing a mystery that also was a mainstream serious novel, but reviewers' reactions were mixed. More favorably received was *The Galton Case* (1959), his contemporary version of Sophocles' ancient story of Oedipus. Nolan calls it "the first of Macdonald's mature works: a dozen or so books that belong with the best American mystery fiction." Millar followed it with *The Ferguson Affair* (1960), a non-Archer mystery that was "another autobiographical fantasy," says Nolan, about the identity question. In his next book, *The Wycherly Woman* (1961), Millar again drew upon recent experiences and utilized Archer as a "protective disguise in which to approach autobiographical ore." *The Chill* (1964), which Nolan says was "brilliantly conceived and beautifully written" and shows Millar at "the height of his mature style and near the peak of his vision," incorporates Coleridgean and pre-Socratic philosophy into a California fable. He continued to grow in subsequent books. One reviewer described *The Far Side of the Dollar* (1965) as having the power and dimension of a Greek tragedy, and of *The Goodbye Look* (1969), Millar himself said, "I seem to be moving further in the direction of the 'mainstream novel,' a development which is deeply satisfying to me." In fact, Nolan tells how critics, such as Macdonald fans John Leonard and Raymond Sokolov, set the stage for his major career breakthrough. Thanks to the former, *The New York Times Book Review* printed a long, favorable review of *The Goodbye Look* on its front page and devoted the second page to a Leonard interview with Millar; Sokolov orchestrated a *Newsweek* cover story. For the first time in his career, Millar/Macdonald had a commercial success and made *The New York Times* best-seller list. Two years later, *The New York Times* again gave a Macdonald book first-page treatment, with an unprecedented thirty-two-hundred-word review of *The Underground Man* (1971) by Eudora Welty. This book—a complex narrative of conflicting psychic and natural forces, of guilt and suffering in bold relief—Welty called a "stunning achievement."

For *Sleeping Beauty* (1973), the next Archer novel, Millar used a seventeenth century fairy tale by Charles Perrault as his inspiration and introduced into the narrative his environmental concerns (specifically, the polluting danger of oil slicks), as well as reverting to past themes and motifs. Further, Millar uncharacteristically spills some family secrets in a book that is notable for its complementary tension and tenderness. Though it received mixed reactions from reviewers, it made the major best-seller lists. Three years passed before the twenty-fourth novel and the eighteenth Lew Archer, *The Blue Hammer* (1976), appeared to nearly unanimous praise. Robert Kirsch in the *Los Angeles Times* saw it as perhaps a precursor, a "bridge between the older Archer novels and some new shoreline of fiction," and called Macdonald "a master in his own right who's ready to explore new terrain." The longest book in his canon, it also was Millar's last, for his strength and memory waned, and in 1981 he was diagnosed with premature senility, now known as Alzheimer's disease. He died two years later.

In a 1953 lecture at the University of Michigan, Millar said:

> I wanted to write as well as I possibly could, to deal with life-and-death problems in contemporary society. And the form of Wilkie Collins and Graham Greene, of Hammett and Chandler, seemed to offer me all the rope I would ever need.

Nolan's *Ross Macdonald* demonstrates that Millar succeeded in his personal quest, producing a body of work that not only enriched the genre and brought it to new heights but also influenced its course. Many later writers in the genre "owe him," as one such, Robert B. Parker, says. Among the others are James Ellroy (who called Macdonald "the great teacher"), Sue Grafton, Joseph Hansen, Jonathan Kellerman, and Marcia Muller, and in Spain, Catalan writer Jaume Fuster (who named his detective Lluis Arquer). Millar is the rare genre writer who warrants serious critical attention, and Nolan's comprehensive and illuminating biography increases both understanding and appreciation of the Millar/Macdonald canon.

Gerald H. Strauss

Sources for Further Study

Booklist 95 (February 15, 1999): 1027.
Los Angeles Times Book Review, April 4, 1999, p. 10.
The New York Times Book Review 104 (March 14, 1999): 19.
Publishers Weekly 246 (February 1, 1999): 66.

SAINT AUGUSTINE

Author: Garry Wills (1937-   )
Publisher: Lipper/Viking Press (New York). 152 pp. $19.95
Type of work: Biography
Time: 354-430, the years of Saint Augustine's life
Locale: Numidia Proconsularis (Roman North Africa); Rome, Milan

An introduction to Augustine and a basic examination of his essential works

Principal personages:
AUGUSTINE (AURELIUS AUGUSTINUS AMBROSIANUS), rhetorician, bishop of Hippo, Father of the Church
MONNICA, his mother, a Christian and later saint of the Roman Catholic Church
PATRICK (PATRICIUS), his non-Christian father
UNA, the author's name for the mistress to whom Augustine remained exclusively faithful
GODSEND (ADEODATUS), the author's name for their son
AMBROSE, the bishop of Milan, whose teachings inspired Augustine's conversion

Saint Augustine is one of the most important early Christian writers, yet serious general readers read him less frequently than his influence justifies. In his own lifetime, Augustine almost single-handedly codified the standards for the priesthood and consecration of bishops. His aggressive attacks against Donatism thwarted a serious challenge to the rights of the Catholic hierarchy to ordain. The early Christian Church included Augustine among its Fathers, a distinction reserved for those whose writings it considered essential in the formulation of Christian doctrine.

In the Middle Ages, Augustine's *Confessiones* (397-400; *Confessions*, 1620) became not only the literary model for conversion but for conversion literature, an influence felt in Dante's *La divina commedia* (c. 1320; *The Divine Comedy*, 1802). The Renaissance ranked Augustine as at least of equal importance to Saint Thomas Aquinas as a Christian philosopher. This period's manuscript iconography thoroughly Europeanized the African saint. American Puritans such as William Bradford, following John Calvin's theory of cyclical history, considered Augustine's conversion voyage to Italy a model of Israelite release from Egypt and, in turn, a parallel to the journey to the Promised Land of America. The twentieth century deconstructed Augustine's writings to posit what Kenneth Burke calls a "rhetoric of religion" based on Plotinan hierarchies of language that move from the word to The Word.

Readers of Garry Wills's *Saint Augustine* will find none of this literary history in his volume. Following the format of the Penguin Life series, Wills sets to one side most of what history has made of his subject and presents instead only what selected secondary sources and some important passages from essential primary material can tell him about Augustine.

For those readers wanting a quick lesson on the saint, this method has its advantages.

The biography opens to a broad audience challenging but rewarding works, such as *De ordine* (386; *On Order*, 1942), *De Trinitate* (c. 419; *On the Trinity*, 1873), and Augustine's exegesis of Genesis, the Psalms, and the Gospel of Saint John, not to mention the *Confessions*. Wills has successfully tackled the clearly formidable task of limiting the life and thoughts of any person as complex as Augustine to slightly more than 150 pages, given the restrictions of the series format.

There is nothing utterly wrong in Wills's treatment, as long as readers keep several things in mind. First, the book is essentially a primer and only that. The biography lacks the subtlety of Peter Brown's classic study *Augustine of Hippo* (1967), from which it quotes frequently. Brown's work is as much an introduction to Augustine as Wills's, and it is just as accessible to general readers, with the real advantages of detail and unobtrusive documentation. W. H. C. Frend's *The Donatist Church* (1952), another study to which Wills often refers, is a fascinating account not only of Donatism but also of daily life in early Christian North Africa. This book also is wonderfully readable and in no way abstruse.

The second caveat is that Wills aims to popularize, running the serious risk of distorting his subject. This objective may have been less a problem in Wills's Pulitzer Prize-winning *Lincoln at Gettysburg* (1992), if only because of its greater proximity to the culture and era of most of its readers. Here, though, are several examples of the kind of popularizing that occurs often in Wills's book. Readers of this essay can judge whether they distort or otherwise interfere with the work.

In discussing Augustine on the nature of memory, a central topic in the *Confessions*, Wills writes as follows:

> Vladimir Nabokov had obviously been reading Augustine when he made Humbert Humbert describe his own self-awareness as "a continual spanning (*distentio*) of two points, the storable future and the stored past" (*Lolita*, Section 26).

Nabokov's *Speak, Memory* (1966) is a confessional autobiography and, on that account, might be compared to Augustine's *Confessions*. Nabokov's *Lolita* (1955) is, on the other hand, a satirical novel. Humbert Humbert, in describing the "spanning of two points," is thinking of German author Immanuel Kant on the nature of time, *die Spanne*, not Augustinian *distentio*. For Augustine, time moves in gyres, coming back upon itself in variation. For Kant, time is a linear series of present events, without past or future. Just as bothersome as this error is Wills's citation of *Lolita*, a novel of sexual obsession, to illuminate Augustine's *Confessions*. He writes in his introduction:

> People feel, for instance, that they understand intuitively Augustine's testimony to his own sexual sins. In fact, they are convinced that Augustine was a libertine before his conversion, and was so obsessed with sex after his conversion that they place many unnamed sins to his account—though his actual sexual activity was not shocking by any standards but those of a saint.

Having implied that a fault of previous critical analysis on Augustine has been its excessive reliance on psychoanalysis and sensationalism, Wills proceeds to inaccurately cite Nabokov, not his autobiography but his controversial popular novel *Lolita*.

This seems very close to the approach he implies at the outset that he is not going to follow.

Then, there is the less problematic question of names. In the final analysis, it is of no special consequence if one refers to Augustine's son by the name he actually bore, Adeodatus ("Gift of God") or uses Wills's breezy alternate "Godsend." It may not matter to most readers if the mysterious, intentionally anonymous consort to whom Augustine was exclusively faithful suddenly has a name, "Una," to symbolize this exclusivity. It may not matter that Wills has renamed Augustine's *Confessions* as *The Testimony*, supposedly to circumvent the implications true confessions have for modern readers. Even so, the conventional title, derived from the Latin *confessiones*, conveys a dual meaning: bearing witness and explaining. Wills's altered title eliminates possible sensational implications but signifies only a theological or legal process.

Typology and symbol are important for Augustine. For example, Augustine devotes more than half of *Confessions* 2 to an evocative recollection of the nighttime raid he and some of his teenage friends staged on a pear orchard. Having stolen pears much less tasty than those he could have had without stealing, he throws the uneaten fruit to swine. Wills avoids discussing the awakening sexuality often assigned to the episode, though he does note its Edenic imagery.

The pear theft is just one of several garden episodes in the *Confessions*. Others include Augustine's conversion in the garden at Milan, Italy, his last conversation on the nature of eternity with his mother Monnica at Ostia, the port of Rome, and his exegesis on the Tree of Knowledge and rebirth in the Lord with which the *Confessions* concludes. Each of these episodes resets the garden motif of the pear theft episode to highlight some greater degree of self-knowledge. Augustine places them so carefully into various contexts of *Confessions* that they assume the value of incremental metaphor tracing a heightened awareness of linguistic signification that corresponds to increasing spirituality. It is this textual complexity, largely overlooked in Wills's study, that makes Augustine such a fascinating writer. His texts make free use of the symbolism already familiar to early Christians and foreshadow the systematic use of typology that becomes medieval allegory.

Wills provides a good overview of Augustine's early schooling, a model based on the old Roman system that was even then degenerating. It is likely that Augustine received an even more conservative education in provincial Numidia than he would have obtained in Rome itself at the time. His education was strongly grounded in rhetoric, memorization, and grammatical analysis of texts. The *Confessions* reports the acclaim that Augustine received for his declamation of Juno's speech from Vergil's *Aeneid* (c. 29-19 B.C.E.). This training predisposed Augustine to his career as rhetorician, just as it led him to privilege the value of language and memory as avenues for understanding one's relationship to creation and to creation's source. Wills makes a good connection in this regard with Augustine's *De ordine*, for Augustine consistently explains the spiritual in aesthetic terms. It is, Augustine argues, as if one perceived only one tile of a mosaic, beautiful in itself but of itself conveying nothing of the whole.

Developing an aesthetic sense leads Augustine to the spiritual, just as one tile leads the eye to a larger mosaic. This aesthetic sense parallels Augustine's deepening sensuality, a negative aspect of his life that Augustine believes is his greatest obstacle to spirituality. The *Confessions* depicts this conflict vividly in its Carthage episodes. Augustine plays on the words *Carthago* and *sartago* ("cauldron," which Wills translates as "frying pan"). The point of the wordplay is that Carthage brought the young Augustine's sensuality to its boiling point. Theater spectacles, with their bawdy comedy and lewd mimes, led Augustine to misdirect his aesthetic as much as his moral sense. Here again is an episode that parallels the spiritual and the aesthetic.

Augustine was a Manichean initiate, both while a teenager at Thagaste and later when a student at Carthage. As *Confessions* 4.17 notes, he found the Manicheans attracted intellectual young people much like himself and considered this a compelling reason to join their number. The Manicheans, who took their name from the mid-third century Persian sage Mani, held a dualistic cosmology in which good and evil are roughly equal forces always in contention. The doctrine of self-control and personal discipline that they preached had definite appeal for the young Augustine. He no doubt considered personal discipline his own greatest challenge, and his long association with the Manicheans, coupled with the fact that he never rose above the level of initiate, is one indication of how great the challenge was for him. To rise above initiate required a vow of celibacy, which would have been awkward considering Augustine's long association with the unnamed woman of the *Confessions*.

A telling moment of the *Confessions* concerns Augustine's disillusionment with Faustus, the Manichean teacher he had anticipated meeting. Not long after determining that Faustus's learning was neither broad nor deep, Augustine decides to take the voyage that brings him, like his boyhood hero Aeneas, to Italy. Here again is a small inaccuracy. Aeneas was not, as Wills writes, "steering for Rome," nor could Augustine view "the Rome he had come to love in Virgil," since the city that Romulus would found in 753 B.C.E. exists only as its Etruscan antecedent Pallanteum in *Aeneid* 8. The events of the *Aeneid* take place after 1184 B.C.E. The more important affinity, which Wills misses, is that fate drives Aeneas to Italy so that four hundred years afterward, Romulus can found the fledgling city of Rome upon an amalgam of Etruscan, native Italic, and Trojan blood. Fate impels Augustine to Italy so that he may hear the preaching of Ambrose, bishop of Milan, experience conversion to Christianity, and complete the circular journey of life that allows him to become bishop of Hippo. In both the *Aeneid* and the *Confessions*, personal duty elevates the life of the community. For Augustine, this spiritual and temporal community of Christians will be his City of God.

Robert J. Forman

Sources for Further Study

Booklist 95 (June 1, 1999): 1748.
Christianity Today 43 (October 4, 1999): 91.

The Economist 353 (November 13, 1999): 10.
Library Journal 124 (May 1, 1999): 85.
The New York Review of Books 46 (June 24, 1999): 45.
The New York Times Book Review 104 (July 25, 1999): 9.
Publishers Weekly 246 (May 17, 1999): 70.

SCARS OF SWEET PARADISE
The Life and Times of Janis Joplin

Author: Alice Echols (1949-)
Publisher: Henry Holt (New York). 408 pp. $26.00
Type of work: Biography
Time: 1943-1970
Locale: The United States

An intimate, well-researched, readable account of America's preeminent white blues singer, from her roots in Port Arthur, Texas, to her death from a drug overdose in Los Angeles while recording tracks for her album Pearl

Principal personages:
JANIS JOPLIN, the lead singer of Big Brother and the Holding Company
PETER ALBIN,
SAM ANDREW,
DAVE GETZ, and
JAMES GURLEY, band members in Big Brother
CHET HELMS, the acid rock impresario who was the first manager for Big Brother
PEGGY CASERTA, the owner of a boutique and Janis's lover
MYRA FRIEDMAN, a publicist for Albert Grossman, Janis's agent

Scars of Sweet Paradise, the title of Alice Echols's biography of Janis Joplin, comes from the Bob Dylan song "Where Are You Tonight?" (1978): "If you don't believe there's a price/ For this sweet paradise/ Just remind me to show you the scars."

Bad girl rock superstar Janis Joplin was never more in character than on *The Dick Cavett Show* in June, 1970, four months before her death, chortling about the stir she would cause at her upcoming ten-year high school reunion. "They laughed me out of class, out of town, and out of the state, so I'm going *home*," she cackled. Daring and resilient, she put on a brave face to win over audiences with tomboy charm and charisma. Few knew how thin was her veneer of bravado, how fragile her ego. To "Sixtophiles," those baby boomers to whom the decade was a golden Age of Aquarius, the mythic Janis was an avatar helping an uptight society shed its inhibitions. In human affairs, Echols reminds her readers, nothing is as simple as it seems. Joplin overcame stifling family pressures and suffocating adolescent humiliations but could not escape the relentless grip of alcohol and drug addiction.

In 1973, Myra Friedman's *Buried Alive* portrayed Joplin as victim of a narcissistic society without moral boundaries. That same year, Peggy Caserta's *Going Down with Janis* presented her as a lusty hedonist who preferred defying death to compromising her full-tilt lifestyle; typical of that book's tell-all flavor was an anecdote describing Janis and Peggy shooting up inside a portable toilet at the 1969 Woodstock Festival, in the midst of excrement "piled up so high you couldn't sit down." Literary bottom-feeding (Echols's phrase) continued with David Dalton's *Piece of My Heart: A Portrait of Janis Joplin* (1991) and Ellis Amburn's *Pearl: The Obsessions and Passions of Janis*

Joplin (1992). Biographers blamed Joplin's unseemly demise on such disparate sources as her oppressive upbringing in a sterile setting, the excesses of her pleasure-seeking generation, uncaring friends and business acquaintances, and her own self-destructive tendencies.

Echols avoids excessive finger-pointing, although she offers caustic comments about the sexist orthodoxies of postwar America, in particular the music business. A sophisticated historian of American popular culture, she demonstrates her understanding of the complexity of personality development and the subtlety of Joplin's environmental influences. Joplin's weak-willed father Seth, in all likelihood a closet alcoholic, compared life to "The Great Saturday Night Swindle," where things never live up to expectations. Pretty and precocious until she started high school, Janis suddenly found herself stereotyped as an acne-scarred, frizzy-haired loser. Alienated from her hometown, which she considered "The Great Nowhere," she discovered the honky-tonk bars of nearby Vinton, Louisiana, where she was exposed to Cajun and black music far richer than the Top 40 fare consumed by most teenagers. Like musical contemporaries Dylan, Lou Reed, Jim Morrison, and Patti Smith, she found validation and inspiration in the Beat writings of Jack Kerouac and Allen Ginsberg. Attending the University of Texas in 1962, she fell into a small but growing folk music scene, playing jams with the Waller Creek Boys at the student union and Kenneth Threadgill's beer joint, a converted gas station.

Thumbing her nose at the still-dominant university pecking order headed by crew-cutted frat rats and bouffanted sorority bubbleheads, Joplin was featured in a *Daily Texan* article entitled "She Dares to Be Different." According to legend the first University of Texas coed to go braless, she acted like one of the boys, living in an enclave nicknamed the Ghetto, eschewing makeup and female clothes, and looking to get laid. Pranksters at the university entered her name in an ugly man contest, but Joplin refused to accept the indignities traditionally heaped on outsiders like herself by the collegiate "in" crowd. At a time before the feminist movement provided a support system for nonconformists, she was struggling against the tyranny of societal standards of beauty and codes of etiquette, such as a Cult of Domesticity that pressured coeds into feeling guilty if they were not preparing to become compliant homemakers. While virtually nonpolitical in the traditional sense, Joplin was a vocal critic of double standards such as the segregationist practices in place in Austin during that time and other institutional intrusions on personal freedom.

Setting out for California in 1966 with her friend Chet Helms in pursuit of a singing career, Joplin ultimately joined a band with the satirical, antiestablishment moniker of Big Brother and the Holding Company. Along with the Jefferson Airplane and the Grateful Dead, Big Brother became identified with a burgeoning hippie scene centered in San Francisco's Haight-Ashbury neighborhood. This milieu was far from idyllic but held a fascination for many dropouts who viewed the "straight" world as a "rat race."

Old verities evaporated in the wake of war, riots, and assassinations; the central question of the 1960's became "Why not?" Janis was doggedly determined to live her life on an uncharted path free of strictures or taboos. Once, at a Hell's Angels bash, she ended up in a pile of brawling bikers after refusing to give one of them a swig from her whiskey bottle. She nearly died on a joy ride with speed freaks Freewheelin' Frank and Neal Cassady. She pored over books on how to develop a healthy libido and pursued sex zestfully, flirting with others' boyfriends, coupling with strangers, faking orgasms, or cutting off intercourse in mid-act if she was not satisfied with her partner's prowess. She did not flaunt her female affairs like she did her heterosexual conquests—Joplin made sure that her one-night stand with New York Jets quarterback Joe Namath was mentioned in *Rolling Stone* magazine—but neither did she try very hard to cover them up. As Echols explains in *Daring to Be Bad: Radical Feminism in America, 1967-1975* (1989), prior to the advent of the gay liberation movement, bisexuality was somewhat in vogue among some swingers later considered to be lesbians.

For Joplin, life was sweetest when lived on the outer limits. She sought out drugs not to heighten feelings—she hated LSD—but to obliterate them. A slave to her ambitions, she believed it natural for blues artists to suffer and experiment. Like Judy Garland and Marilyn Monroe, two others who died too young, she became trapped into playing a dangerous real-life role. On the night that she died, Joplin was anticipating a *ménage à trois* with Peggy Caserta and boyfriend Seth Morgan. (Three-way sex especially titillated her, although she frequently complained that guys were more interested in her girlfriends.) When neither lover showed up, she turned to the needle, and her body was, as Echols puts it, blasted into unconsciousness and not discovered until eighteen hours later, wedged between her motel room bed and a table. "She burned her candle at both ends and it did not last the night," was the way historian William L. O'Neill put it in *Coming Apart: An Informal History of America in the 1960's* (1971).

Echols claims that Joplin was not suicidal, though there had been previous close calls from overdosing; nor does *Scars of Sweet Paradise* devote much space speculating about might-have-beens had Joplin survived her demons. The Grateful Dead's Jerry Garcia, an addict most of his adult life, called her a "skyrocket chick" who went out at the best time possible, on top. Years later, former deejay Milan Melvin could not shake his guilt at once forgetting to pick her up after a performance because he was high on mescaline. Joplin reacted "like I drove a stake in her heart," he recalled. Joplin is destined to be forever linked to guitarist Jimi Hendrix and Doors lead singer Jim Morrison, who also traded their tomorrows to let it all hang out. Joplin bragged that she slept with both of them, although Echols is not so sure; Fillmore West promoter Bill Graham would have loved booking Joplin and Morrison on the same bill, but they despised each other after Joplin cracked a whiskey bottle over Morrison's head in retaliation for pulling her hair. Like former junkies Joe Cocker and Ray Charles, fellow "screamers" whom critics scoffed would quickly fade once they lost their voices, Joplin had the potential to have aged gracefully. Her image might have played well during the 1990's, when contemporaries Tina Turner and Cher made surprisingly successful comebacks. A flamboyant persona worked well for diva Bette Midler, whom Joplin regarded as her chief rival when she was performing torch songs for gay men at New York City's Continental Baths (Midler played a character based on Joplin in the 1979 film *The Rose*). The openly lesbian rock singer Melissa Etheridge, who initially distanced herself from Joplin's compositions because of their frightening explorations into the nuances of pain, eulogized her in 1995 at the Rock and Roll Hall of Fame induction ceremonies when she expressed the wish that Janis was still around being ballsy, fighting bigots, and singing the blues.

In the end, Janis Joplin's place in history rests primarily on her musical achievements during a period of tremendous interracial cross-fertilization. Trying to emulate the soulful sound of African Americans, Joplin considered Bessie Smith, Billie Holiday, and Odetta to be her mentors. She had a genius for taking other performers' songs, such as Nina Simone's "Little Girl Blue," and making them her own. Worried that she was a derivative charlatan, in truth she was sui generis, pioneering an "outlaw" blues sound that was part Texan, part Californian, and pure American. Her discography includes just three albums and one hit song, "Me and Bobby McGee," which reached number one after Joplin died. The prevailing wisdom, echoed by Echols, is that she was better in concert than on vinyl (her 1967 breakthrough Monterey Pop Festival set is described as incandescent). She was frequently too drunk, however, to sustain her best numbers in concert and so bent on audiences dancing in the aisles that she was actually banned from performing in the entire state of Texas. Critics were unfairly harsh to her Big Brother bandmates on their 1967 album *Cheap Thrills* (remixed in 1968), which is more groundbreaking than the technically superior *I Got Dem Ol' Kozmik Blues Again Mama!* (1969) or *Pearl* (1971). Her lineal descendants in the 1990's were not so much alternative rockers such as Courtney Love, Alanis Morissette, and Sheryl Crow but male soloists for heavy metal bands such as Metallica's James Hetfield.

A persistent oral historian, Echols interviewed more than one hundred fifty people, including many initially reluctant to cooperate in an endeavor that they feared might trash Joplin's memory. At times carrying empathy too far, Echols is relentlessly nonjudgmental and even rationalizes away the behavior of Caserta, who opened *Going Down with Janis* with the line, "I was stark naked, stoned out of my mind on heroin, and the girl lying between my legs giving me head was Janis Joplin." Recounting an exchange of insults between Joplin and Jerry Lee Lewis which culminated in the 1950's rocker punching her, Echols characterized the assault as "a charged encounter," inspiring *Village Voice* reviewer Evelyn McDonnell to write, "Just once, I wish Echols would let her nipple poke through." Like an upwardly mobile, nineteenth century San Francisco prostitute or the bawdy Mae West, who asked handsome strangers to come up and see her sometime, Joplin seemed a throwback to a pioneer age of "red hot mamas" rather than a "new age" hippie love child. She was constantly fighting conflicting impulses to please and to shock. When her parents visited her apartment, for instance, they came face to face with photographs of her dressed only in beads and with her erect left nipple in full view. Janis argued that the photographs were in good taste, but leaving them on the wall was tantamount to giving her distressed mother the finger.

A thorough researcher, Echols does not rely solely on the memories of people who lived during an era when, as the saying goes, "If you can remember it, you were not really a part of the action." She gleaned insights from such sagacious 1960's social critics as Joan Didion, Lillian Roxon, Hunter S. Thompson, and Tom Wolfe and made good use of scholarly interpretations contained in Todd Gitlin's *The Sixties: Years of Hope, Days of Rage* (1987), Joel Selvin's *Summer of Love: The Inside Story of LSD, Rock and Roll, Free Love, and High Times in the Wild West* (1994), and Gillian Gaar's *She's a Rebel: A History of Women in Rock and Roll* (1992). In addition to useful indexes and endnotes, *Scars of Sweet Paradise* contains a where-are-they-now section chronicling the casualties and survivors of those tumultuous times.

James B. Lane

Sources for Further Study

Booklist 95 (January 1, 1999): 790.
Library Journal 124 (March 1, 1999): 86.
Mother Jones 24 (March, 1999): 73.
The New York Times Book Review 104 (May 2, 1999): 13.
People Weekly 51 (March 29, 1999): 51.
Publishers Weekly 246 (February 8, 1999): 203.

THE SEA CAME IN AT MIDNIGHT

Author: Steve Erickson (1950-)
Publisher: Avon Books (New York). 259 pp. $23.00
Type of work: Novel
Time: The 1960's through the 2010's
Locale: Tokyo, San Francisco, Los Angeles, New York, Paris, and Brittany

In this postapocalyptic novel, characters who have lost even the capacity to dream seek a remedy for their despair

Principal characters:
KRISTIN, a seventeen-year-old girl from Davenhall, California
THE OCCUPANT, a reclusive "apocalyptologist"
ANGIE "SAKI" KAI, the Occupant's Asian American wife
NADINE "MAXXI MARASCHINO" SIENKIEWICZ, a singer and stripper
LOUISE PAGEL "LULU BLU" BLUMENTHAL, Kristin's mother
BILLY PAGEL, Louise's brother, a Davenhall bartender
CARL, a cartographer

In such earlier novels as *Days Between Stations: A Novel* (1985), *Arc d'X* (1993), and *Amnesiascope: A Novel* (1996), Steve Erickson presented his pessimistic vision of the future. *The Sea Came in at Midnight* again shows human society declining into a postmillennial dystopia, which the author emphasizes is a logical extrapolation given the course of history and especially the events of the twentieth century. The central character in *The Sea Came in at Midnight* is a seventeen-year-old girl, Kristin. Unhappy with her life in the small Northern California town of Davenhall, Kristin runs way from home, leaving the uncle with whom she has lived as long as she can remember, and joins a group encamped near the sea. What she does not at first realize is that they are pleased to see her because they need her for their millennial observance. At midnight on New Year's Eve, two thousand females are expected to jump off a cliff into the sea, and the male priests who organize this venture have just discovered that they are one person short. Once she finds out what is going on, Kristin resolves to escape. Of all the women who are being driven to their deaths by the armed cult leaders, who obviously do not intend to join their flock in death, only Kristin has the will and the wit to escape. Afterward, she likes to look at the newspaper clipping that says two thousand women perished, for she knows that by fleeing, she threw off the count and invalidated the project. Kristin's clear-sightedness and her practical common sense, so clearly revealed in this episode, later enable her to survive a series of bizarre adventures, including one episode as a sex slave and another as one of the girls who work at Tokyo "memory hotels," where men pay to recite their memories and to listen to those of their hostesses.

Though Kristin's resolute rationality may preserve her, it also keeps her from being fully human. Ever since the day when, as a small girl, she was taken to meet her birth mother, only to see her hesitate and then walk away, Kristin has not allowed herself to become emotionally involved with anyone. For this reason, she is ideal for the purposes of the man known only as the Occupant. The Occupant, too, has retreated from emotion and indeed from the outside world because of his experiences with loss. He, too, has been abandoned. As an eleven-year-old boy, living in a Paris flat with his mother and his father, who was a famous American poet, the Occupant had no premonition of tragedy. Then one night he heard a shot, ran to his parents' bedroom, and caught a glimpse of a dead girl lying on the bed. He never did find out just what happened. There was a riot in the streets outside the apartment building, and it was easy for his mother to disappear into the crowd. When his father was sent to prison for murder, the Occupant was taken in by various friends. He never saw either of his parents again. However, he was still willing to chance caring for someone. During a return trip to Paris fourteen years later, the Occupant met Angie Kai, a nineteen-year-old Asian European. Though she insisted she did not love him, she was willing to live with him. Eventually they were married and settled down in a house in the Hollywood hills. Angie became pregnant. Then the Occupant awoke one morning to find her gone—he did not know where; he did not know why. Eventually he became convinced that Angie and her baby daughter were among the cult members who died.

By the time he places the advertisement that is quoted at the beginning of the novel, the Occupant has willed himself into detachment. He seldom emerges from his home in the Hollywood hills, where he is creating a great calendar of events he sees as apocalyptic. However, though he intends to live without love, he needs a convenient sexual outlet. In veiled terms, he advertises for an employee to serve his purposes, and because Kristin is hungry and homeless, she takes the job. Although initially she is understandably quite apprehensive, she soon settles in and for some months is actually quite contented. Even though the Occupant keeps her a prisoner in his house, in most respects he is quite considerate. Even having her clothes taken away does not particularly bother Kristen. Indeed, she finds that nakedness makes her feel free. Moreover, for the most part her time is her own. Except when he claims her as a sex partner, the Occupant lets her wander about the house and make use of his extensive library. Kristin might have been willing to stay permanently had the Occupant not decided to write a date on her body, thus involving her in his mind games. Kristin is willing to be the focal point of the Occupant's passion, for sex with him is merely a mechanical process, but she does not want to become the focal point of the chaos that occupies his mind. Therefore she makes what is undoubtedly a wise decision, to escape while she can. With her usual resourcefulness, she finds someone to help her get away. However, despite himself, the Occupant has become fond of Kristin. When she, too, disappears without an explanation, the Occupant has still another reason to live apart from the rest of the human race.

Alienation is not just presented as a possibility in *The Sea Came in at Midnight*; it seems to be almost inevitable. Like the Occupant, Angie's onetime lover Carl avoids real life by devoting himself to a project, in his case, the making of maps. However, Carl, too, discovers that even the most mechanical tasks lead eventually to troubling questions about the meaning of life. It is one thing to map the streets and sewers of

Manhattan, as he once did; being hired by the city of Los Angeles to map the dreams of its residents is a very different matter.

Ironically, often what begins as love ends in alienation. There is no doubt that Angie Kai's father doted on his little "Saki" or that his evaluations of her conduct were meant only to help her fulfill her potentialities. However, even after leaving home, Angie continues to apply her father's rigid standards to everything she does. As a result, she becomes an emotional cripple, so preoccupied with herself and her own defects that she cannot love anyone, not her husband, not even her own child. By the time that Angie leaps off the cliff with her baby in her arms, she has obviously decided that love is not worth the price one must pay for it. Her act is the ultimate expression of alienation.

However, *The Sea Came in at Midnight* does much more than merely explain why so many human beings feel alienated from one another and even from life itself. It also shows that an isolated existence is both unhealthy and ultimately impossible. Though the author focuses on one character at a time, utilizing either first-person narration, as with the Occupant, or a very limited third-person perspective, the fact that he lets his characters wander so readily in and out of one another's lives suggests that he believes one cannot live apart from others. Even the most self-obsessed of Erickson's characters are sometimes driven to help people they do not know. Hearing someone pounding on a door, Angie unlocks it, thus enabling the Occupant to escape from Nadine "Maxxi Maraschino" Sienkiewicz, who has held him captive for seven months. On another occasion, Maxxi warns a girl away from some pornographers making "snuff" films, in which an actor is killed on camera, thus saving Angie's life.

Similarly, after she finds a woman outside the Hollywood hills house in a car that has broken down, Kristin invites her in, and the two spend some hours together. However, though they converse, the women do not reveal themselves to each other. If they had opened up at all, if there had been any mention of Davenhall or of the name Pagel, Louise Pagel Blumenthal would have realized that Kristin is the daughter she had sought for so long. Their detachment costs them dearly.

Even though Louise's quest for her daughter and the Occupant's search for his baby girl fail and even though no one in the novel ever fully comprehends the meaning of life, *The Sea Came in at Midnight* is not a pessimistic book. Erickson's characters do discover some important truths. When he finds himself regarding Kristin as a human being, the Occupant sees that it is almost impossible to stifle one's need for other people. When Louise learns that because she featured fake murders in her pornographic films, actors are now being killed, she realizes that the world is built on an ethical system and that she must find her way to redemption.

The Sea Came in at Midnight also shows evidence of the influence of the Magical Realists, in that the reader is constantly reminded that the spiritual is very much a part of the real. As the characters move through their everyday lives, they are accompanied by their memories and visited by dreams. The lack of a clear chronological structure, along with the frequent shifts in point of view, does make the novel difficult to follow. However, by patterning his book in this way, Erickson means to show that one cannot live detached from the things of the spirit any more than one can exist in isolation. Thus Kristin cannot dream until that point near the end of the novel when she rejoins humanity. Similarly, the Occupant finally discovers that even if his baby is dead, he can reach her in dreams, and, moreover, that by reaching out toward others, he can in some sense keep her alive. It is the spirit, not the mind, that can keep chaos at bay.

If at times *The Sea Came in at Midnight* seems to be primarily a catalog of twentieth century wrongdoing, the author suggests that in the postapocalyptic world, we may do better. Erickson foresees a time when humanity will realize the importance of the spirit. Thus the city of Los Angeles hires Carl to trace the presence of dreams, while in Tokyo, men employ women to listen to their memories, thus affirming their reality and perpetuating their existence. By showing his characters as living simultaneously in the past and in the present, as finding truth in memories and dreams and worth in the people around them, Erickson has produced a book which, for all its recognition of the evils of contemporary life, offers some hope for the new millennium.

Rosemary M. Canfield Reisman

Sources for Further Study

Booklist 95 (April 1, 1999): 1384.
Library Journal 124 (March 15, 1999): 108.
The New York Times Book Review 104 (April 18, 1999): 13.
Publishers Weekly 246 (February 22, 1999): 65.

SECRETS OF THE FLESH
A Life of Colette

Author: Judith Thurman (1946-)
Publisher: Alfred A. Knopf (New York). 592 pp. $30.00
Type of work: Literary biography
Time: The late nineteenth century and the first half of the twentieth century
Locale: France

An admiring but candid account of the life and times of one of modern France's most celebrated writers

Principal personages:
SIDONIE-GABRIELLE COLETTE, famous French writer and literary figure
ADÈLE-EUGÉNIE-SIDONIE COLETTE ("SIDO"), Colette's mother
JULES COLETTE, Colette's father
HENRY GAUTHIER-VILLARS ("WILLY"), a prominent literary figure who became Colette's first husband
MATHILDE DE MORNY, Colette's lover after her divorce from Willy
HENRY DE JOUVENEL, Colette's second husband
BERTRAND DE JOUVENEL, Colette's stepson and lover
MAURICE GOUDEKET, Colette's third husband

Among the most successful series of books in French publishing history are the Claudine novels, five mildly salacious volumes from the turn of the century, recounting the sentimental education of a young girl from the provinces who makes the fabled journey to the big city—in this case, Paris. The first four novels bore the name "Willy," pen name of Henry Gauthier-Villars, a tireless self-promoter and man-about-town, but had been written almost entirely by his attractive young wife, Sidonie-Gabrielle Colette. She was but the latest in his stable of lovers and ghost-writers, categories that frequently overlapped.

Willy's wife was, of course, the famous French writer now known simply as Colette. As Judith Thurman makes clear in this new biography, the Claudine novels are a record of Colette's early years, true in many respects to the actual facts of her life and in most respects to her sexual and emotional development. Even the novels' titles—*Claudine à l'école* (1900; *Claudine at School*, 1956), *Claudine à Paris* (1901; *Claudine in Paris*, 1958), *Claudine en ménage* (1902; *Claudine Married*, 1935), *Claudine s'en va* (1903; *Claudine and Annie*, 1934), and *La retraite sentimentale* (1907; *Retreat from Love*, 1974)—suggest the archetypal progression of events that went into making Colette the forthright, self-reliant figure familiar to countless readers. Although Colette's subsequent novels and stories might be less obviously autobiographical, her life and works continued to be inextricably entwined.

Colette grew up in a village not far in objective distance from Paris, yet distant in social terms. Her mother ("Sido"), whom she would subsequently revere but seldom visit, offered her lessons in a kind of tough-minded love, while her father ("the Captain") treated her with genial neglect. The Captain composed verse on subjects of popular interest in his tiny community, and was discovered after his death to have prepared notebook after notebook for an account of his eventful life. Yet he never got any further in this autobiographical project than a handful of titles and a series of heartfelt dedications to his wife; otherwise the volumes remained blank. Although she seems to have cherished few illusions about provincial life, Colette idealized nature, and retained an empathy for plants and animals unmatched in French literature.

One of Thurman's theses in *Secrets of the Flesh* is that the first two men in Colette's life failed her: "Willy's obsessive philandering and Jules Colette's single-minded fidelity were two sides of the same coin, which left her, in both cases, feeling abandoned and desexed." (In his own way, each man was a failed writer as well.) Yet Colette's life and works would turn out to be so varied and expansive that no single theory can actually explain them, and Thurman allows her subject that freedom.

Retreat from Love was the first Claudine novel to bear Colette's name, and appropriately enough, at the time of its publication she and Willy were separating preparatory to a divorce. Yet the two remained linked—and not just platonically—for several years after their divorce became final. It is one of Thurman's accomplishments to restore to Willy a measure of dignity, if not of respectability. In the many biographies of Colette that have appeared in English, Willy has come across as a stock character, a womanizer far older than Colette who seized upon her young body and her burgeoning talent for his own ends. As Thurman makes clear, Willy and Colette seem to have loved each other deeply, even if the former lacked the emotional wherewithal to sustain the match and the latter finally tired of that lack.

One of the methods Willy chose to distance his wife from himself was to introduce her pointedly to his many mistresses and to yet other women who had no interest in men whatsoever. It was to the resulting relationships that Colette turned after her divorce, to the world that Thurman calls "Lesbos." In one of several miniessays Thurman inserts at key points of her narrative, she explores the thriving underground of Parisian homosexuality and lesbianism, describing it as a natural result of the debilitating strictures of contemporary French social life. Colette would identify increasingly with this world, and for several years was the lover of Mathilde de Morny, a prominent and wealthy marquise who cropped her hair and dressed as a man.

Thurman also discusses the importance of the theatrical world in Parisian society, and it was to this world that Colette now turned for a living. Having appeared in several nonspeaking roles, she progressed to speaking parts, aided more perhaps by her gamine-like good looks than her native acting talent. In what would otherwise have been an eminently forgettable melodrama, she bared a breast. The resulting publicity did nothing to deter her career. As she would later write, the theatrical world " made me . . . a tough and honest little businesswoman. It's a profession which the least gifted of women learns quickly, when her freedom and her life depend on it."

One of Colette's rapt spectators was Henry de Jouvenel, a handsome journalistic colleague who would prove to be her match in spirit if not in talent. Neglecting her dying mother for her new lover, who was already betraying her, Colette conceived a child, a daughter destined to be born exactly nine months after Sido's death. Yet later

Colette would write, "But I'm tormented by the stupid thought that I can't write to Mother anymore, the way I used to so often do." Like many daughters, Colette had for years worshipped her mother, but from afar. Again, like many mothers, she would prove to be a less than ideal parent herself.

During this period, Colette had begun to produce the novels that would assure her fame. *La vagabonde* (1911; *The Vagabond*), based on her years as a mime and actress, had appeared in English in 1954. Its suggestively titled sequel, *L'entrave* (1913; *The Shackle*, 1932), written for the most part while she was pregnant, records the journey of a woman much like Colette from wariness of love to total surrender. Perhaps not coincidentally, Colette married, gave birth and finished *The Shackle* (in its original French) all at about the same time, near the end of 1912.

Distracted by her new marriage—that is, initially by its pleasure and subsequently by its disintegration as Jouvenel continued his philandering—Colette produced nothing remarkable for several years. When she did, however, it was one of her finest works, the short novel *Chéri* (1920; English translation, 1929). An account of the affair between the aging courtesan Léa and her young lover, *Chéri* was criticized in some quarters for the "immorality" of its characters, but was greeted by most critics as a masterpiece of French prose, distinguished by what Thurman calls Colette's "lucid irony." According to Thurman, Léa is a transitional figure in her creator's oeuvre, allowing Colette to come to terms with her mother (who had, at least in Colette's imagination, favored Colette's brother Achille) as well as with her own aging body. The memoirs *La maison de Claudine* (1922; *My Mother's House*, 1953) and *Sido* (1929; English translation, 1953) continued the process in equally memorable if more conventionally acceptable terms, and proved to be among her best-loved works.

In Colette's world, life imitated fiction as frequently as fiction imitated life, and it is here that Thurman's readers may find her subject's pursuit of pleasure distinctly less than admirable. Soon after she began writing *Chéri*, Colette began a passionate and unabashedly carnal affair with Henry's teenaged son Bertrand. The author herself was then approaching fifty. Colette's marriage to Henry de Jouvenel was legally dissolved in 1925, and her affair with Bertrand would end about the same time.

In the meantime Colette continued the story begun in *Chéri* with *La fin de Chéri* (1926; *The Last of Chéri*, 1932), a shorter but perhaps even stronger work. It concludes with Chéri's suicide as he finds himself unequal to the task of living, a task that the aging but still vital Léa takes in her stride. In one sense Chéri is merely the latest in the long string of attractive but ineffectual males inhabiting Colette's world, and it may scarcely matter to the reader that some of these flashy figures are fictional and others "real."

Yet waiting in the wings was the man Colette would eventually call "my best friend," a pearl merchant named Maurice Goudeket who would become her third and final husband. The two were married in 1935, and the partnership survived at least one further instance of Colette's infidelity as well as Goudeket's imprisonment during World War II as a Jew. Over the years Colette had become famous, if not rich. After the publication of *Chéri* she had been made a Chevalier of the French Legion of Honor, and in 1935 she was elected to the Belgian Royal Academy of French Language and Literature. In addition to her many novels, stories, and memoirs, she had produced a prodigious amount of journalism and other occasional writing.

Colette died in 1954. She received a state funeral (the first given a woman in the history of France) that attracted some six thousand mourners, but was nevertheless forbidden a religious ceremony by the archbishop of Paris—a snub she presumably would not have minded. Having once been asked on French radio whether she thought life had "any higher direction," the renowned author had replied, "It only goes in one direction, as far as I know, which is toward the exit."

The first biography of Colette was published in 1927, and since then the literature on this fascinating writer, most of it biographical in tone if not substance, has grown substantially. Judith Thurman's entry in the field is gracefully written, and each of its chapters is developed and shaped as carefully as a story. In addition, Thurman's scholarly apparatus is impressive: *Secrets of the Flesh* concludes with over sixty pages of notes, an extensive bibliography, and an index. There are twenty-four pages of photos. Yet the wealth of detail that Thurman assembles is often daunting, making it hard to determine the exact year in which particular events are occurring—a situation that a chronology would have alleviated.

A competing work in two volumes, *Creating Colette* (1998-1999), by Claude Francis and Fernande Gontier, was published in English immediately before Thurman's work appeared. Thurman has profited from Francis and Gontier's research, particularly their investigation into Colette's Afro-Caribbean ancestry, yet *Creating Colette* is a pedestrian work in English translation, scarcely worthy of its elegant subject. By contrast, *Secrets of the Flesh* is the most satisfying biography in English to date. Given the fascination Colette is bound to exercise for future generations, Thurman's biography will not be the last, but it is likely to be the benchmark for years to come.

Grove Koger

Sources for Further Study

Booklist 96 (October 15, 1999): 411.
Library Journal 124 (October 1, 1999): 92.
Los Angeles Times Book Review, October 31, 1999, p. 9.
The New York Times, November 3, 1999, p. B8.
The New York Times Book Review 104 (October 17, 1999): 12.
The New Yorker 75 (November 29, 1999): 122.
Publishers Weekly 246 (September 6, 1999): 89.
Time 154 (November 1, 1999): 104.

SELECTED NON-FICTIONS

Author: Jorge Luis Borges (1899-1986)
Translated from the Spanish by Esther Allen, Suzanne Jill Levine, and Eliot Weinberger
Edited by Eliot Weinberger
Publisher: Viking Press (New York). 559 pp. $40.00
Type of work: Essays, literary criticism, literary history, and philosophy
Time: 1922-1986

A broad selection of essays, prologues, reviews, lectures, and notes by one of the greatest South American writers of the twentieth century

This unusual selection is actually the first comprehensive selection of Borges's nonfiction in any language. More than a hundred of these writings have never before appeared in English. Readers who know the earlier anthology in English, *Borges: A Reader* (1981), will recognize Borges on authors Herman Melville and Walt Whitman, but they may be surprised to read his thoughts on Ray Bradbury, Lady Murasaki, and Bret Harte, or, for that matter, *King Kong* (1933) and *Citizen Kane* (1941).

Part 1, "Early Writings," contains material from the 1920's taken from his earliest books, which he later disowned. The master was unnecessarily severe on himself, and, in retrospect, these early metaphysical meditations on infinity, the illusions of subjectivity, and the mysteries of language all represent a fascination with subjects that would ultimately define his fiction. From the beginning Borges wanted "to tear down the exceptional preeminence now generally awarded to the self. . . . [P]ersonality [was] a mirage maintained by conceit and custom, without metaphysical foundation or visceral reality."

This war on the self was motivated largely by Borges's hostility to what he felt was the psychologizing of experience in the aesthetics of the nineteenth century. The typical Romantic or realist protagonist of the modern novel in search of a self struck Borges as an illusion. Readers of his fiction will remember his famous story, "The Aleph," in which a highly intellectual narrator is forced to confront the shattering truth that the universe is "unimaginable" and that the self cannot attain unity in a world that is totally seamless and where everything impinges on everything else. The same insight, in a much less cerebral tale, is struck in "The Life of Tadeo Isidoro Cruz (1829-1874)." Here, a brutish and illiterate gaucho rediscovers his lost identity in the person of a fleeing murderer and sheds one subjectivity for another.

These stories, both written in the 1940's, show how Borges's distrust of self never left him. He fled to language as an alternative to self. This observation is made clear in the selected essays from the 1920's, when he seems to find in the intricacy of language an apology for the chaos of experience. Literature can use language to celebrate the very chaos that maddens the mind and reduces self to an illusion. From an essay on "The Nothingness of Personality," he moves to a self-conscious account of James Joyce's *Ulysses* (1922), in which he comments, "I am the first traveler from the Hispanic world to set foot upon the shores of *Ulysses*." He admires Joyce's appreciation of the kaleidoscope of "a day in modern life" and attributes his powers as a literary artist to the observation, "He is a millionaire of words and styles." Indeed, the rich style and fascination with words that Borges praises in Joyce seems to be evolving in these early essays in Borges himself.

Part 2, "1929-1936," draws on what was to become, as the editor tells the reader, the "canonical" Borges. In these years Borges is trying to hold on to his faith in language and style at the same time that his studies in gnosticism and medieval theology feed a growing skepticism. He is intrigued by the gnostic belief that the world can be imagined "as an essentially futile process, like a sideways, lost glimpse of ancient celestial episodes. Creation as a chance act."

In "The Duration of Hell," he reflects on the endless fascination that hell holds for the Western mind well into its modern phase. Here, he stumbles into the importance of dreams: "This desolate awakening is in Hell, this eternal vigil will be my destiny. Then I really woke up, trembling." This oneiric element comes to play an important role in Borges's lifelong need to reach the reality beyond the illusion of self, a reality that filtered through language far more readily than it did through the fragmented memory of the individual consciousness. Perhaps this is why, in these relatively early pieces, he is riveted on the problems of translation. Literary critics John Henry Newman and Matthew Arnold, who debate the subtleties of Homeric translation, seem to push the envelope of the verbal imagination and force language into giving up more of its secret understanding of reality. In a brilliant essay entitled "The Homeric Versions," Borges compares the translations of a passage from Homer by George Chapman, Alexander Pope, and William Cowper. After reviewing the gradations of literalness and interpretation in these various passages, Borges asks, "Which of these many translations is faithful? my reader will want to know. I repeat: none or all of them."

The translator dreams the task of translation, and the reader is witness to a recalled dream. All of his life, Borges was drawn to the Kabbala, the teachings of Jewish mysticism. In the Kabbala's conception of Scripture as a palimpsest for the word of God, Borges found both a metaphor and a principle for his own trust in language and bookishness as the only reliable lenses for peering into the infinite:

> [The Kabbalists] turns the Scriptures into an absolute text, where the collaboration of chance is calculated at zero. The conception alone of such a document is a greater wonder than those recorded in its pages. A book impervious to contingencies, a mechanism of infinite purposes, of infallible variations, of revelations lying in wait, of superimpositions of light. . . . How could one not study it to absurdity, to numerical excess, as did the Kabbalah?

What the Kabbala made of Scripture, Borges made of reality, and he had to change reality into dreamlike codes to do it. The cinema is fraught with oneiric elements, and Borges is reputed to have been a great film buff all of his life. Nevertheless, he moves through his film reviews with the detachment of someone who knows exactly where he is but is not very much impressed with the situation. He carps constantly at the unconvincing sets in Hollywood films, such as Josef Von Sternberg's *Morocco* (1930) and shows disdain for Hollywood's clumsy illusionism and lack of verisimilitude. Here, he addresses what he perceives as inept filmmaking in *King Kong:*

> His only virtue, his height, did not impress the cinematographer, who persisted in photographing him from above rather than from below—the wrong angle, as it neutralizes and even diminishes the ape's overpraised stature.

If film reviewing in the 1930's did not allow Borges to use his aesthetic system to good effect, the capsule biographies and book reviews he wrote for *El Hogar* (home) magazine, the Argentine equivalent of the *Ladies Home Journal*, were another story. He was dealing mostly with significant writers and works and was able to indulge his affection for mystery and detective stories by reviewing Ellery Queen. It is typical of him to use the opportunity to make comparative judgments with archetypal plotmakers, such as Edgar Allan Poe and Israel Zangwill. It is technique that interests him most because technique is almost always a question of rhetoric and language or style. He cannot ignore the continuing interest of modern writers in "self" and "subjectivity," but he will never pass the opportunity to encourage the importance of language, as he demonstrates in this review of *Absalom! Absalom!* in 1937:

> I know of two kinds of writers: those whose central preoccupation is verbal technique, and those for whom it is human acts and passions. . . . Among the great novelists, Joseph Conrad was perhaps the last who was interested both in the techniques of the novel and in the fates and personalities of his characters. The last, that is, until the tremendous appearance of Faulkner.

Borges's love of labyrinths as plot devices and symbols may very well have been inspired by William Faulkner's manipulations of time, "deliberately shuffling chronological order, deliberately complicating the labyrinths and ambiguities," as he notes in a review of *The Unvanquished* in 1938.

In part 4, which covers the period of World War II, the editor introduces us to the politically engaged Borges, the opponent of Argentine president Juan Perón and the enemy of fascism in Europe and Argentina. Not only did this take great courage under Perón's regime, but the sagacity of Borges's political analysis is surprising. He makes shrewd observations of Germany in several essays, in which he is among the first to see that Adolf Hitler's policies of racial hatred are as harmful to the victimizer as the victim. German culture has been sacrificed to political fanaticism. It seems clear that Borges saw Hitler's Germany as a dark allegory for what could happen to the liberal world and for what was happening in the Argentina of his day. To read the world as if it were a book is central to Borges's metaphysics and becomes more of a driving force in his thinking and art in the 1950's. In many ways, he anticipates the strong emphasis on *écriture* and textuality in postmodernist criticism. Recall his fondness for the Kabbala and its equation of God and text. In an essay entitled "On the Cult of Books," he notes:

> At the beginning of the seventeenth century, Francis Bacon declared in his *Advancement of Learning* that God offered us two books so that we would not fall into error: the first, the volume of the Scriptures, reveals His will; the second, the volume of the creatures, reveals His power and is the key to the former.

Borges was not afraid to use his political insights to read important books of the past as revelations of political tendencies long in the making. In 1949, he looked closely at Thomas Carlyle and Ralph Waldo Emerson and saw beyond their similarities to the essential difference between them: Carlyle's need for great men encouraged fascism; Emerson's "representative" men were Everyman in democratic dress. This somewhat oversimplified analysis must be read as an allegorical critique of the Perón regime that intervened directly in Borges's life by forcing him from his profession as a librarian and harassing his family. In the same year Borges wrote a thoughtful essay, "From Allegories to Novels," in which he tipped his hat to the superiority of literary symbolism but tried to make a case for allegory by suggesting that its signs were not always as flat or as one-dimensional as the champions of symbols would have us believe. Here again, Borges was ahead of his time. Thirty years later, deconstructionist theorists led by Paul de Man would reverse priorities and raise allegory to the top of the heap.

In 1955, Borges went blind, an event that, ironically, coincided with fame. In the next two years, he became the director of the national library and a professor of English and American literature at the University of Buenos Aires. Prizes rolled in, and his work was simultaneously translated in six countries. He could, however, no longer write complex prose, and he returned to poetry, which he could compose in his head. Besides poetry, his principal creations were spoken, including lectures that usually took the form of a spontaneous monologue on a given subject, interviews, and conversations.

The coming together of Borges's blindness and his international reputation suggest a kind of self-diffusion, almost a transcendence of the ordinary weight of experience. In a dictated prologue to a selection of Walt Whitman published in 1969, Borges maintains that there are three Walt Whitmans: the modest journalist and resident of Long Island, New York, the "loafing, carefree traveler," and, finally, "the changing, successive reader." All three are blended in the speaker of *Leaves of Grass* (1855). Still true to his earliest disavowal of subjectivity, Borges insists on the transcendent universal and asserts that a rhetorical vision, the "I" of Walt Whitman, is in fact not a self at all but rather a trinity in disguise, a universalizing force.

In an important lecture on "The Argentine Writer and Tradition" which he gave in 1951, a few years before his vision was totally impaired, Borges closed by suggesting that no writer should confuse his authenticity with a kind of programmed and willful ethnic, racial, or national identity. Borges would have had difficulty with what we today would call a multicultural intention for the creative writer. To embody, intentionally, a cultural identity would have struck Borges as the pursuit of a collective subjectivity, an idea of self far more dangerous than the Romantic illusion of heroic individuality. He had seen enough of this sort of thing in its fascist manifestation under Hitler and Perón, and, besides, he had long ago learned that the mind could be in so many different places in so short a time that it was folly to freeze its spirit in tribal ice. The closing lines of his lecture speak directly to humanity's condition in a modern era:

We must not be afraid; we must believe that the universe is our birthright and try out every subject; we cannot confine ourselves to what is Argentine in order to be Argentine because either it is our inevitable destiny to be Argentine, in which case we will be Argentine whatever we do, or being Argentine is a mere affectation, a mask.

I believe that if we lose ourselves in the voluntary dream called artistic creation, we will be Argentine and we will be, as well, good or adequate writers.

Peter Brier

Sources for Further Study

Booklist 95 (August, 1999): 2010.
Publishers Weekly 246 (July 12, 1999): 80.

SELECTED POEMS

Author: Jorge Luis Borges (1899-1986)
Edited by Alexander Coleman
Publisher: Viking Press (New York). 861 pp. $40.00
Type of work: Poetry

This important collection brings together Borges's poetic canon in one volume for the first time in both English and Spanish

New York University professor emeritus Alexander Coleman has provided the literary world a valuable and distinctive volume of Argentine writer Jorge Luis Borges's verse, collecting all previously published poetry from 1923 to 1986 in one superlative edition. Overseeing a bilingual project that includes Borges's nearly two hundred poems in both Spanish and English, Coleman drew on the talents of outstanding translators, including the work of Robert S. Fitzgerald, W. S. Merwin, Mark Strand, John Updike, and Charles Tomlinson, to give the collection a variety of approaches and styles. This collection is the second in Viking's trilogy of Borges's writing in definitive, matching volumes that began with *Collected Fictions* (translated by Andrew Hurley, 1998). For the first time, all of Borges's significant work will finally be published in English, which will undoubtedly lead to rediscoveries, new interest, and new appreciations of a most singular talent in twentieth century letters.

Such new appraisals will likely center in North America, where Borges has long been primarily known for his short stories, which are largely allegories using fantasy and detective story conventions in an elegant, innovative style. Notable examples include "Pierre Menard, Author of the *Quixote*," "The Circular Ruins," "The Lottery in Babylon," "The Secret Miracle," and "Tlön, Uqbar, Orbis Tertius." His most inventive prose appeared in the innovative *Inquisiciones* (1925; inquisitions), *Historia universal de la infamia* (1935; *A Universal History of Infamy*, 1972), *El jardín de senderos que se bifurcan* (1941; the garden of forking paths), *Ficciones, 1935-1944* (1944; English translation, 1962), and *Nueva refutación del tiempo* (1947; a new refutation of time).

While the bulk of Borges's fiction was written during the years of World War II, he was first recognized for his poetry. It was to poetry he returned in the postwar years claiming it was better to tell a story succinctly rather than draw out truths in overlong, emotional plots. Thankfully, this new collection chronologically traces Borges's poetic development book by book, including the important prologues that serve as the benchmarks in each stage of the poet's career.

In one sense, tracing Borges's steps is also following the course of South American literature in the twentieth century. After Spanish philosopher Miguel de Unamuno y Jugo called for a resurgence in Spanish-language literature in the then-new century, Latin America responded with a series of luminaries including Pablo Neruda, Carlos Fuentes, Alejo Carpentier, and Gabriel García Márquez, among many other notables. However, it is clearly Borges who enjoys the reputation of being the brightest light in

Latin American letters. This deserved appreciation was earned not only for the depth and originality of his work but also for the diversity of his efforts as reflected in the need to publish three volumes of his work in three separate genres. In addition, as director of the National Library and professor of English at the University of Buenos Aires, Borges as critic and teacher was the dominant figure shaping successive generations of writers and thinkers in his home of Argentina as well as surrounding Spanish-speaking countries. A significant benefit to having his work accessible in English is that he demonstrates his universality on a variety of levels, and no lover of verse should be without this landmark collection.

At the outset of his career, Borges was largely a regional writer, capturing his Buenos Aires vernacular, flavor, and history in his earliest book, 1923's *Fervor de Buenos Aires*. In these poems, Borges shapes his verse on street and building imagery to give his meditations a framework based as much on experience as his readings, a formula that would be reversed in much of his later material. During this period, he was a leading figure in the literary movement, Ultraismo, an offshoot of Modernismo, a turn-of-the-century movement built on the works of French symbolists and Parnassians led by Nicaraguan poet Rubén Darío. Ultraismo, known both for its use of surrealism and for its emphasis on pure imagery, championed the superiority of metaphoric free verse. Participation in this school provided Borges early mastery of the prose poem, which would serve him well in both fiction and verse efforts. In later years he would praise free verse while claiming his own voice fell naturally into traditional meters and line structure, a reflection of his lifelong interest in studies on technique.

While his verse begins with deeply localized concerns, during the period when Borges stated he was under the influence of Unamuno y Jugo, his vista quickly expanded both globally and metaphysically. He retold legends from South America ("General Quiroga Rides to His Death in a Carriage," "The Mythical Founding of Buenos Aires" "A Page to Commemorate General Suarez, Victor at Junin"), Europe ("Parable of Cervantes and Don Quixote," "Alexander Selkirk," "To a Sword at York Minister," "Poem Written in a Copy of Beowulf"), and Jewish Kabbalists ("The Golem"). His interests were also deeply rooted in North American culture, reflected in his "Texas," "Jonathan Edwards," "Emerson," "Camden, 1892," and "New England, 1967," but Borges remained grounded within himself and the unique perceptions of his own musings, synthesizing his worldview into a personal voice as in "Simplicity for Haydée Lange":

> I am familiar with the customs and the souls
> and that dialectic of allusions
> which any gathering of humans weaves.
> I need not speak
> nor claim false privileges;
> those who surround me here know me well,
> know well my afflictions and my weakness.

In *Luna de enfrente* (1925; moon across the way) and *Cuaderno San Martín* (1929; San Martin notebook), he elegized South American military leaders while praising Western writers including Joseph Conrad, Robert Louis Stevenson, William Shakespeare, Robert Browning, William Blake, Herman Melville, and especially Walt Whitman, his acknowledged primary mentor. Having learned English at an early age, followed by readings in Latin, German, and French, Borges became something of a cosmopolitan synthesis which he called "a blind library." Ultimately, his expansionist and inclusive allusions, particularly to Protestant authors, have helped broaden his appeal in the international market and made him more accessible to non-Spanish readers. Among his eulogies and tributes to his influences are verses demonstrating his keen interest in leading philosophers such as Emanuel Swedenborg, Ralph Waldo Emerson, and Baruch Spinoza. His verses based on biblical texts ("Luke XXIII," "Matthew XXV: 30," "John I: 14," "Christ on the Cross") interweave Borges's need for consolation with his modern skepticism of traditional theologies, clearly marking him as a poet of his time.

His changes in vision are perhaps best noted in the various prologues that introduce each collection of verse, moving from youthful self-abasement to learned advice for younger poets such as espousing the use of ordinary language instead of surprising diction. In his prologues, he also repeatedly refers to literature as a collaborative art requiring the reader to make words immortal, so that a writer's identity expands into the words on the page as well as into the next generation of book lovers. To this unborn audience, Borges apologized for writing verse before readers had the chance to write it for themselves. This question of the writer's identity would become a recurring theme in Borges's mature work ("The Self and the Other," "Borges and I," "The Borges," "I Am," "My Whole Life"). His multiple-layered points of view made him an important precursor to the later postmodern movement led by his fellow Latin American, Gabriel García Márquez.

On one level, this collection is unified by Borges's use of repeated favorite imagery: tigers, guitars, daggers, the moon and stars, and especially, mirrors. Mirrors are both metaphoric and personal, particularly when Borges writes of his encroaching blindness in *El hacedor* (1960; the maker), *El otro, el mismo* (1969; the other, the same one), and *Elogio de la sombra* (1969; *In Praise of Darkness*, 1974). Blindness offered both form and substance to Borges's work; his most creative period resulted from his composing largely through memorized stanzas and chants, allowing him to rely on his studies of cadence and metered line structures. In the title poem of *The Maker*, and especially that volume's "Poem of the Gifts," he repeatedly points to the irony of owning thousands of volumes and administrating university libraries he could no longer personally enjoy:

> From hunger and from thirst (in the Greek story),
> a king lies dying among gardens and fountains.
> Aimlessly, endlessly, I trace the confines,
> high and profound, of this blind library.

> Cultures of East and West, the entire atlas,
> encyclopedias, centuries, dynasties,
> symbols, the cosmos, and cosmogonies
> are offered from the walls, all to no purpose.

These poems, as in "A Rose and Milton" from *Para las seis cuerdas* (1965; for six strings), are Borges's most intimate images in lines more heartfelt than bookish, clearly his most powerful moments in literature. Other tropes are developed as well, notably in the poems in *In Praise of Darkness*, which expanded his subject matter into old age and the possibility of ethics ("The Labyrinth," "Things," "Rybaiyat"), an important theme in his latter works.

By *El oro de los tigres* (1972; translated in *The Gold of Tigers: Selected Later Poems*, 1977) and *La rosa profunda* (1975; the unending rose, translated in *The Gold of Tigers: Selected Later Poems*, 1977) in Borges's seventh decade, it was clear the poet's powers were waning, as he admitted in the prologue to *The Gold of Tigers*. In the last poems, Borges resorted to aphorism ("Susana Bombal," "The Blind Man"), and heavy-handed allusions to Greek and Roman classical literature ("Tankas"), and the old imagery became tired and provincial. His once magical mirrors are empty and have become like "Iron Coins," the title poem of his 1976 collection *La moneda de hierro*. In *Historia de la noche* (1977; the history of the night), visions of immortality become complaints about insomnia ("Alhambra," "Music Box," "I Am Not Even Dust"), and he dives into regret, imagining himself a disappointment to the dreams of his father. Borges disparages his old mentor Whitman and spends much time theorizing about his dislike of literary theory. He summarizes his feelings in "The Mirror," noting that old age has become more revealing than the poet would like:

> Now I fear the mirror may disclose
> The true, unvarnished visage of my soul,
> Bruised by shadows, black and blue with guilt—
> The face God sees, that men perhaps see too.

Writing of Iceland and Geneva, Switzerland, in *La cifra* (1981; the limit) and *Atlas* (1984; English translation, 1985), Borges finds himself isolated from his birthplace and finds language and metaphysical concerns both fleeting and forgettable ("Two Forms of Insomnia," "Acquiring an Encyclopedia," "Note for a Fantastic Story"). It is difficult to believe the author's disclaimer that his poetic references to blindness were more doleful than he actually felt, and such claims reveal that the poet remained uncertain about the distinctions between his personal and artistic selves. Still, his final, short 1985 collection, *Los conjurados*, in which he calls himself "tired earth," contains two final breaths of originality. "Clouds" and "Leaves on the Cypress Tree" reconnect his fragmented dreamworld with understandable imagery. These final chapters will undoubtedly be of more interest to scholars than general readers, a fate akin to the latter works of most writers who survive past their mature, prolific periods.

Once the Viking trilogy is completed, the publisher might perform one more useful service in its effort to make Borges's verse more accessible to the reading public. A smaller, English-only edition at a more economical price could prove useful for the classroom and for a wider range of personal libraries. Until then, readers should not miss the opportunity to explore this important verse now available in Borges's beloved second language. This collection will be of considerable value to those interested in the poet and his culture and to readers of poetry in general.

Wesley Britton

Sources for Further Study

Booklist 95 (April 1, 1999): 1379.
Commentary 108 (July, 1999): 89.
Publishers Weekly 246 (March 29, 1999): 97.

SELECTED WRITINGS
Volume 2, 1927-1934

Author: Walter Benjamin (1892-1940)
Translated from the German by Rodney Livingstone and others
Edited by Michael W. Jennings, Howard Eiland, and Gary Smith
Publisher: The Belknap Press of Harvard University Press (Cambridge, Massachusetts). Illustrated. 870 pp. $37.50
Type of work: Essays and diaries
Time: 1927-1934
Locale: Moscow and Western Europe

A translation of 141 miscellaneous selections—reviews, essays, diary entries, travel writings, radio talks—from Benjamin's Gesammelte Schriften *(1974-1985)*

Walter Benjamin was a distinguished literary and cultural critic with close ties to the Frankfurt School, especially to his friend Theodor Adorno. He received a doctorate summa cum laude from the University of Berne in 1919. In a short "Curriculum Vitae (III)" he explains his critical approach: "Such an analysis would regard the work of art as an integral expression of the religious, metaphysical, political, and economic tendencies of its age, unconstrained in any way by territorial concepts." Good examples of this approach are found in this volume in the pieces on Johann Wolfgang von Goethe, Karl Kraus, and Franz Kafka. Although he was attracted to the accomplishments of the Russian Revolution, he maintained his distance from Moscow to ensure his freedom as a thinker.

The contents of this second volume are arranged chronologically and grouped by year with representative headings. The topics are diverse and range in length from the three-line "Everything Is Thought" to substantial commentaries on writers and places. Several subjects recur (such as toys, children, hashish) and others are strikingly original, such as "Chambermaids' Romances of the Past Century" and "Hitler's Diminished Masculinity." The thirty-three-page chronology that concludes this volume could profitably be read as an introduction, for it summarizes Benjamin's activities during the eight years here represented and traces his intellectual exchanges with his good friend Gershom Scholem.

Benjamin went to Moscow early in December, 1926, following Asja Lacis, a Bolshevik actress he had met on Capri. The essay he wrote about his seven weeks there in a freezing city struggling through great changes is vivid and observant. Seeing Berlin through Moscow, he observes, is to see a city of luxury but one that is barren compared to the "fullness" of the Moscow streets. The children's festivals impress him, especially the vendors of toy carts and spades: "All these carved wooden utensils are more simply and solidly made than in Germany, their peasant origin clearly visible." The children fascinate Benjamin, with their organization into a "Communist hierarchy" leaving the gangs of delinquent war orphans, *besprizornye*, to menace night strollers. Generally, Benjamin is pleased with the evidence he sees of the workers appropriating bourgeois culture and of how "the liberated pride of the proletariat is matched by the emancipated bearing of the children." Benjamin fully approves the didactic cultural innovations, noting such Tretyakov Gallery works as *A Conspirator Surprised by the Police* and *The Poor Governess Enters Service in a Rich Merchant's House*, and he concludes that for a worker or a child, education in art is not dependent on masterpieces but on "topical works that relate to him, his work, and his class." In "pedagogical theater," several hundred people crowd into a room where the traditions and values of peasants and industrial workers are dramatized. In the scene that Benjamin witnessed, a peasant midwife was tried for the death of a woman in childbirth, but although she was found guilty, she was given a light sentence that recognized her mitigating historical circumstances and stressed the need for modern hygiene.

In a city where the law permits each citizen a mere thirteen square meters of living space, petty-bourgeois private life has disappeared. Cafés have disappeared because abolishing free trade and free intellect has taken away their patrons, and so only the office is left for social life in an environment "for which nothing counts except the function of the producer in the collective." Constant meetings preoccupy each citizen, creating tremendous competition in a culture in which Russians betray complete indifference to time and schedules. The taverns remain, however, outposts of "intoxicating warmth" where tea-drinking patrons indulge their "most secret winter lust" on frigid nights.

Benjamin's colorful sketch of Moscow in a Stalinist winter ends on a note that will grate on many readers' sensibilities. When describing the Russians' worship of Vladimir Ilich Lenin, Benjamin poses him bent over a table conning *Pravda*: "When he is thus immersed in an ephemeral newspaper, the dialectical tension of his nature appears: his gaze is turned, certainly, to the far horizon; but the tireless care of his heart, to the moment." Karl Kraus edited the satirical magazine *Die Fackel* (*The Torch*) from 1899 until his death in 1936. Benjamin's essay on Kraus in 1931, although studded with obliquities ("To fail to recognize the beauty of feminine stupidity was for Kraus always the blackest philistinism"), is an acute analysis of Kraus's vision of the corrupting influence of bourgeois technology. Kraus assaults journalism for its "empty phrase," "journalism being clearly seen as the expression of the changed function of language in the world of high capitalism." In Kraus's mind, the miracle of nature has succumbed to the laws of science, and "the fact that mankind is losing the fight against the creaturely is to him just as certain as the fact that technology, once deployed against creation, will not stop short of its master, either." In his regard for creation and the "creaturely," Kraus is "cosmic man."

Kraus is also "demon" in that he springs from the "primeval world." Kraus's style "is attained chiefly by the cardiac strength of great thoughts, which drives the blood of language through the capillaries of syntax into the remotest limbs." As a mimic, the demon Kraus "insert[s] the crowbar of his hate into the finest joints of their posture" and "probing between syllables, [he] digs out the larvae that nest there in clumps." This is the Kraus who is driven by "a nature that is the highest school of aversion to mankind and a pity that is alive only when interlaced with vengeance." The demon gives way to something worse when his "semihuman or subhuman traits are conquered by a truly inhuman being, a monster." These quotations suggest the frequent richness of Benjamin's language as he portrays a Kraus who went "berserk" seeking to change the world beginning with his own class in Vienna and finally gave up to place "the matter back in the hands of nature—this time destructive not creative nature." Of this essay, Kraus himself remarked, "I can only express the hope that other readers have understood his writings better than I have. (Perhaps it is psychoanalysis.)"

The 1934 essay on Kafka approaches that author's inkblot fictions with much ingenuity. Benjamin notes the correspondences between Kafka's officials and his fathers, the way in which they are both punishers and accusers. The accused seem guilty of "a kind of original sin," of some transgression that is "not accidental but fated." The laws in Kafka's world are written in the law books, but the books are secret, enabling the prehistoric world to exercise its power "all the more ruthlessly." Besides the accused, there is that strange group of figures identified as "assistants," whose role is to move among the other figures as messengers. As creations, they are "unfinished," and as such there is hope for them; but their place in the world is insecure, for in their world there is no hierarchy, only fluidity.

Benjamin makes much of a childhood photograph of Kafka posed absurdly against palm branches in an "upholstered tropics." In this embarrassing photo Benjamin sees the sadness of the boy who ardently wished to be a "Red Indian" "on a galloping horse, leaning into the wind. . . ." Kafka's *Amerika* (1927; *America*, 1938) fulfilled this wish. When Karl Rossman reads the announcement for the great Nature Theater of Oklahoma (really a racetrack), he knows that happiness awaits him. Rightly or wrongly, Benjamin links the Nature Theater to Chinese theater, which makes significant use of gestures, and because many of Kafka's shorter pieces are best seen as acts in the Nature Theater of Oklahoma, it seems "that Kafka's entire work constitutes a code of gestures which surely had no definite symbolic meaning for the author from the outset; rather, the author tried to derive such a meaning from them in ever-changing contexts and experimental groupings." Benjamin then stresses the importance of how Kafka saw the organization of life and work, even to the point that he could have "defined organization as destiny."

Benjamin rejects both naturalistic and supernatural readings of Kafka, the "psychoanalytic and the theological interpretations." Kafka's prehistoric world bred in him a presentiment of guilt which he envisioned as a judgment in the future. Shame, Benjamin says, is Kafka's "strongest gesture," and he quotes Kafka's confession that he "feels as though he were living and thinking under the constraint of a family." Benjamin cannot identify this family but is certain that "it is this family that forces Kafka to move cosmic ages in his writings." Benjamin connects these themes to Kafka's many images of men bent over with their heads on their chests, illustrating "the prototype of distortion: a hunched back." Benjamin traces this motif to the folk song "The Little Hunchback," thus enabling a rather tenuous connection between Kafka's profoundest depths and "the ground of folk tradition."

In his "Notes from Svendborg, Summer 1934," Benjamin recounts conversations with Bertolt Brecht about the Kafka essay, with which Brecht apparently was not impressed. Brecht's own judgment on Kafka deserves quoting: "The images are good. The rest is just mystery-mongering." So much for Benjamin's learned exegesis.

Not all of Benjamin's analyses are as critically daunting as those on Kraus and Kafka. One engrossing piece is entitled "Books by the Mentally Ill," in which he comments on unusual books in his own library. His "Library of Pathology" includes Daniel Paul Schreber's *Denkwürdigkeiten eines Nervenkranken* (1903; *Memoirs of My Nervous Illness*, 1955). In Schreber's original theology, only God could safely approach corpses; God was certainly familiar with railways; and the basic language of humanity is "a somewhat old-fashioned, but vigorous German." Other people's existence was difficult for Schreber to imagine, and consequently he used terms such as "casually improvised men" and spoke of those who had been "magicked away." Astonishingly, Schreber, who was a judge, was declared cured after ten years of hospitalization, and he returned to his family. For truly startling conceptions, however, it is hard to exceed Carl Gehrmann's *Körper, gehirn, seele, Gott* (body, brain, soul, God), published in three volumes in Berlin in 1893. Some of the fantastic case histories include "The broken reed is raised up again" (the complete Case 1) and the note in Case 7 concerning "reduction in size as the starting point for perfecting the form of the blueberry." A previously ignored insight was developed in Case 13: "Effect of sweaty feet on the sexual and respiratory systems." Gehrmann's elaborate anatomy of the brain identified such sites as those of "Fear of moral sin" and "Abyss."

"Chambermaids' Romances of the Past Century" (1929) will serve to close this sampling. Benjamin looks to these cheap romances for knowledge of the "relations of production" in literary history. One recounts the story of a woman called the Hyena of Paris, who keeps a collection of human heads on her kitchen shelves. Benjamin's conclusions about these works are in keeping with his description of himself as a materialist critic: "But let us not forget that books were originally objects for use—indeed, a means of subsistence. These were devoured. Let us use them to study novels from the point of view of their food chemistry!"

There are many other pleasures in this huge volume—the chronicles of Berlin and Paris, for example—as well as some trivial pieces well ignored, but the sheer variety of subjects and the grace of a style that shines through even in translation make this a satisfying collection from one of the twentieth century's shrewdest commentators on literature and culture.

Frank Day

Sources for Further Study

Booklist 95 (May 15, 1999): 1661.

Library Journal 124 (June 1, 1999): 111.

The New York Times, May 29, 1999, p. A19.

Publishers Weekly 246 (May 3, 1999): 61.

SEX AND SOCIAL JUSTICE

Author: Martha C. Nussbaum (1947-   )
Publisher: Oxford University Press (New York). 476 pp. $35.00
Type of work: Philosophy, women's issues, ethics, and sociology

A unique and comprehensive feminist analysis of the sociocultural factors influencing uses and misuses of sexual diversity, causing massive inequities in the treatment of women, especially those of the Third World, and of lesbians and gay men

Martha Nussbaum is an Ernst Freund Professor of Law and Ethics at the University of Chicago. She writes about classical literature, philosophy, divinity, law, politics, feminism, economic development, psychology, educational reform, and human emotion. Not surprisingly to those who know her, she does an admirable job with all of these subjects because she is a brilliant philosopher and a prolific writer with the gift of making the most complex and even arcane subjects readable and tantalizing without sacrificing analytic rigor or scholarship. The hallmark of her intellectual brilliance is her uncanny interdisciplinary ability to bring balance to dichotomous and seemingly irreconcilable philosophical ideas and social dilemmas. *Sex and Social Justice* is a prime example of such intellectual dexterity. She has dealt with similar issues in her previous works, such as *Women, Culture, and Development* (1995) with Jonathan Glover and *Sex, Preference, and Family* (1997) with David Estlund.

In *Sex and Social Justice*, Nussbaum applies her deep-rooted humanism and well-rounded liberal feminism to the international scene, especially to women's issues in the Third World. She offers detailed accounts of women's suffering and stifling living conditions to elaborate the complexity of sexual realities as practiced in various cultures with diverse political contexts and religious moralities. Sex is an integral part of patriarchal power relations and thus the root cause of one of the most egregious examples of injustice in the world. Her book consists of fifteen interdisciplinary chapters on diverse feminist concerns in a densely packed text that features ample use of empirical studies. This book has a sensibility similar to Michel Foucault's three-volume study of the history of sexuality without its Nietzsche-like adolescent cynical relativism and contains a clear and determined sense of liberal justice like that of John Rawls's *A Theory of Justice* (1971).

Nussbaum's international feminism is influenced by acute moral sensibilities emanating from her years of work with the United Nations World Institute for Development Economics Research, dealing with transnational comparative studies in living standards. She is deeply concerned with the suffering of women around the world who exist in wretched conditions, victimized by unjust local rules and conventions. Therefore, she rejects utilitarianism and relativism but skillfully engages with both and uses some of their principles to form a reconciliation between liberal and radical feminism in favor of a responsible, international feminism. She considers U.S. feminism, with less pressing issues such as eating disorders and notions of femininity, an intellectual luxury.

The main concern of her version of feminism is human respect and dignity in sexual spheres, adequate assurance of social justice, equal rights, and a basic safety net for women, lesbians, and gay men everywhere throughout the world. She forces us to imagine a transformed world that is different from our own, where sex is not a reason for discrimination, humiliation, and abuse. In this world, men and women coexist in mutual dignity and respect, and women's bodies are not misused as "great erotic vessels," even if some women actually want it that way. She advocates fundamental changes in all spheres of human endeavor regarding sex, namely the kind of changes that evolve over generations as a result of dismantling old, detrimental beliefs and habits, not by mere changes in policy.

Nussbaum's philosophical underpinnings for her work have sources from both the ancient Greek philosophies and the modern liberal ones. She is well known for her erudition in Greek philosophy, especially in its connection with modern sexual controversies. Socrates, Plato, and Aristotle did not condemn sex between men, although they abhorred certain homosexual practices as distasteful or even immoral, and they never thought there was anything irrational about it. This was the line of argument Nussbaum used in testimony against the Colorado antigay legislation, which was eventually overturned by the Supreme Court. With similar erudition and skill, she also invokes John Stuart Mill's distaste for mistreatment of women, Immanuel Kant's views of humans as ends in themselves, and Rawls's theory of social justice. Both philosophers and laypersons would enjoy Nussbaum's philosophical excursions with her distinctive and complex brand of feminism.

What is at issue for Nussbaum with regard to sex and gender are concerns such as these: What is the basic structure of equality and justice? How do we reconcile the gender differences and sexual differences? How should we apply principles of equality for women in entrenched, unjust cultural and religious contexts? Do we take these differences as part of human complexity as liberals do or as mere constructions of social oppression that are, at best, temporary mistakes that must sooner or later be corrected?

She creates her unique liberal feminist theories, which include elements of radical feminist theories, such as those of Catherine MacKinnon, author of *Toward a Feminist Theory of the State* (1989) and Andrea Dworkin, who wrote *Pornography: Men Possessing Women* (1981). At the same time, she does not agree wholeheartedly with certain sophisticated arguments, such as MacKinnon's belief that misogynist pornography should be criminalized or Dworkin's enraged denunciations of the way men regard and treat women. Nussbaum walks a fine line between liberal and radical feminism, exposing the strengths and weaknesses of both. She avoids the extreme egotism and militant individualism of postmodern feminists, such as Alison Jaggar. On the other hand, she calls for individual responsibility and conscientiousness in opposition to Christina Hoff Sommer's complacent attitude about what women really want, such as wanting to be housewives and mothers all their lives or porno stars to gain economic advantages.

Nussbaum presents a solid, Neo-Aristotelian liberal view with strong commitment to egalitarian philosophies inspired by thinkers such as Susan Okin, Amartya Sen, and Rawls. Like Aristotle, she always strives to find the appropriate mean between extreme positions. She carefully and successfully balances global concerns and those of local, public, and private equality and freedom, state prevention, and individual rights. She is at once commonsensical and scholarly, open-minded and committed, theoretical and concrete. She balances the need to address some feminists' exclusive concern about the victimization of women based on unequal power relations with her personal concern to include women from around the world.

Accordingly, she modifies the notion of cultural relativity in favor of universal principles, such as human dignity and freedom. She critiques the subordination of and cruelty toward women in many cultures in the name of religious and local conventions and customs where male members of the family, including husbands, brothers, and fathers, rule over women's lives and administer inhumane punishment for acts, such as working outside the home. No local convention is sacrosanct when it licenses outrageous cruelty toward women and children. Nussbaum's critique of unjust local customs is expressed without her falling into the all-too-familiar chauvinistic or imperial attitudes toward other cultures. She is neither obsessed with freedom of choice nor does she disregard it entirely. She advocates some of its elements that illuminate her theory of international feminism.

Through her international work, she has discovered that sexual attractiveness and sexual happiness are the least justly distributed of all human goods and among the cruelest practices against women, such as in pornography, genital mutilation, and prostitution. The effects of religion on women's rights can be just as devastating and unjust. Here, Nussbaum leans toward views espoused by radical feminists, such as Dworkin and MacKinnon, who believe that patriarchal domination translates into cruel sexual attitudes and practices toward women. Most religions accept this view, authorizing men to dominate women sexually, economically, politically, and in all other realms. This view has implications on how women are treated in cases of marriage, domestic violence, rape, and sexual harassment. The failure to criminalize marital rape serves a case in point.

Nussbaum is at her best when she explains how so-called abuses of women become socially accepted when they become indistinguishable from the so-called normal uses of women. Violence and rape are a deeper unconscious expression of what the male-dominated, heterosexual world implies. Men's role as assertive individuals becomes aggressive and oppressive, and women's role as passive individuals becomes submissive and oppressed. The nature of social justice in a given culture shapes the sexual attitudes, feelings, and practices of the members of that culture. She recounts certain practices in Islamic and Hindu culture, under the guise of religion, as glaring examples of inequality, even sadism, in matters of marriage, divorce, property rights, and child custody. She offers milder examples from Jewish and Christian teachings and practices that deny sexual freedom to women and deny homosexual couples an equal chance of forming successful sexual partnerships similar to those heterosexual couples enjoy.

Here again, Nussbaum walks a fine line between religious toleration as a hallmark of modern democracy and freedom and most religions' disregard for human rights violations, such as the widespread practice of clitoridectomies in Africa, which she labels as "female genital mutilation." Choice is quite necessary here: the choice of refusing to submit to genital mutilation or of leaving the religion and even the region that practices such atrocities. As in many cases of sexual inequality, genital mutilation is designed for the male members of the community to maintain power by monopolizing sexual pleasure. Declitorized women can also be trusted to leave the house and work in the field, apparently with no sexual desires to lead them astray.

Elsewhere in some Third World countries, such as India, women who are widowed or have incapacitated husbands have a choice between starving to death within the confines of the home or venturing outside, against tradition, to work in the fields to survive and, subsequently, pay the consequences for breaking tradition. Nussbaum tells the sad story of Sarah Begum, one such woman's struggle in Bangladesh.

Nussbaum's most heart-wrenching examples of abuse of women's sexual, social, and economic rights come from Islamic theocracies, such as those in Iran, Afghanistan, and Sudan. Women in some parts of these countries are virtual prisoners of their husbands or other male relatives. In Pakistan, another Islamic country, to convict a rapist the court demands four male witnesses. If the woman's accusation is not successfully substantiated, she herself is accused of fornication, which results in severe physical punishment and social ostracism.

Similar kinds of injustice are practiced against lesbians and gay men around the world. Nussbaum is equally eloquent and illuminating with regard to discrimination and violence against homosexuals. She gives extensive attention to the infamous Amendment II, which made it an article of the Colorado state constitution to discount discrimination against homosexuals on the basis of their sexual orientation. Nussbaum argued against Amendment II and in favor of homosexuality as rationally tenable and a socially acceptable alternative lifestyle.

Although *Sex and Social Justice* is a tour de force of cultural analysis of sexuality, Nussbaum neglects to include in her comprehensive analysis of feminism some of the important women's movements, such as those conspicuous in psychoanalysis, postcolonialism, and various feminist literary criticism orientations. Also surprisingly, she excludes serious talk about the role of history in the formation of cultural mores and dispositions on sexuality, thus rendering her own valuable and astute position ahistorical.

Nevertheless, Nussbaum, as a public intellectual and one of the most influential philosophers of our time, has produced a work of momentous importance, at once passionate and level-headed, erudite and creative, open-minded and morally committed. *Sex and Social Justice* is a major accomplishment. It is a generous intellectual feast for philosophers, researchers, and laypersons, and it should be widely read.

Chogollah Maroufi

Sources for Further Study

Library Journal 123 (December, 1998): 140.
National Review 50 (December 7, 1998): 73.
The New Republic 220 (March 8, 1999): 33.
The New York Times Book Review 104 (March 14, 1999): 16.
Publishers Weekly 245 (December 21, 1998): 45.

SHAKESPEARE
A Life

Author: Park Honan (1928-   )
Publisher: Oxford University Press (New York). Illustrated. 479 pp. $30.00
Type of work: Literary biography
Time: 1564-1616
Locale: Stratford-upon-Avon and London, England

Honan's life of Shakespeare shuns the mythology that has grown up around the playwright and places him in the context of his age

Principal personages:
WILLIAM SHAKESPEARE, a poet and playwright
JOHN SHAKESPEARE, William's father
MARY ARDEN SHAKESPEARE, William's mother
ANNE HATHAWAY, William's wife
RICHARD BURBAGE, an actor
BEN JONSON, a playwright and actor
CHRISTOPHER MARLOWE, a dramatist and poet
HENRY WRIOTHESLEY, the third earl of Southampton, Shakespeare's patron
QUEEN ELIZABETH I, the ruler of England
KING JAMES I, the ruler of England and Scotland

Every biography is a palimpsest, written over the biographies that preceded it, and in turn to be covered by the texts that succeed it. Honan's life of Shakespeare rests above a series of lives dating back at least to Thomas Fuller's *History of the Worthies of England* (1662). Fuller could not discover the date of Shakespeare' s death, but he began the unending process of eking out limited information with mythology. Fuller's brief account of the playwright tells of "the wit combats betwixt [Shakespeare] and Ben Johnson [sic]," a pleasant but unverifiable anecdote. From Nicholas Rowe's forty-page preface to his 1709 edition of Shakespeare onward, fact and fiction, or at least unconfirmed anecdote, have melded inextricably in biographies of England's premier dramatist and poet.

Honan seeks to banish the unproved, or at least to subject it to careful scrutiny. This skepticism begins with Honan's treatment of Shakespeare's birthday. Shakespeare's death date is known: April 23, 1616. So, too, is the date of Shakespeare's baptism, April 26, 1564. A birth date of April 23 would lend symmetry to the life, and April 23 is St. George's Day, the festival of England's patron saint. Hence, many a biography and reference work, indulging in a bit of wishful fact-making, cites April 23 as the date of Shakespeare's birth. Honan refuses to accept so welcome an attribution and instead chooses to leave the date, like so much else of Shakespeare's life, a mystery.

Similarly, he will not endorse Russell Fraser's claim in *Young Shakespeare* (1988) that in 1575 John Shakespeare took his eleven-year-old son to see the royal reception that Robert Dudley, earl of Leicester, gave Queen Elizabeth at Kenilworth, a short distance from Stratford. On July 18, Leicester entertained the queen with a pageant that included Triton riding on a mermaid and Arion bestriding a dolphin. In *A Midsummer Night's Dream* (c. 1595), Shakespeare's Oberon recalls,

> once I sat upon a promontory
> And heard a mermaid on a dolphin's back
> Uttering such dulcet and harmonious breath
> That the rude sea grew civil at her song. (II, i, 149-152)

Is Shakespeare recalling a scene from his childhood? In the absence of evidence, Honan discounts Shakespeare's firsthand knowledge of the spectacle.

E. A. J. Honigmann (*Shakespeare: "The Lost Years,"* 1985) and Eric Sams (*The Real Shakespeare: Retrieving the Early Years, 1564-1594*, 1995) have argued that Shakespeare spent part of his youth in Lancashire as a servant in a Catholic household, where he was noticed by Henry Stanley, fourth earl of Derby; Derby's servants are known to have performed some of Shakespeare's early plays. Honan carefully assesses the evidence, but he maintains, rightly, that the case remains unproved.

Yet what remains if one strips away the traditional accounts and surmises? Prior to Robert Greene's reference to Shakespeare's *Henry VI, Part III* (pr. c. 1590-1591), documents show Shakespeare's baptism, his marriage to Anne Hathaway on November 30 or December 1, 1582, the baptism of Shakespeare's three children—Susanna on May 26, 1583, the twins Judith and Hamnet on February 2, 1585—and his involvement in an unsuccessful 1588 suit brought by his parents against his aunt and uncle, Edmund and Joan Lambert. Honan manages ninety-two pages, nearly a quarter of his book, from this unpromising paucity of information.

He does so by focusing on Shakespeare's milieu. What would he have heard and seen and learned as a young man growing up in a market town of some 240 families? Shakespeare's father dealt (illegally) in wool. In *The Winter's Tale* (pr. c. 1610-1611) the old shepherd knows exactly how much wool a sheep yields and how much wool costs. The sheep-shearing festival in that play, set in Bohemia, recalls celebrations at Stratford. The French forest in *As You Like It* (pr. c. 1599-1600) more closely resembles the Arden north of Stratford than the Ardennes. In *The Merry Wives of Windsor* (pr. 1597) Shakespeare assigns to the aptly named Justice Shallow a coat of arms with twelve white luces (pikes), recalling the three silver luces insignia of Sir Thomas Lucy, whose fine estate, Charlecote, stood four miles north of Stratford. Shallow has come to Windsor to complain of Sir John Falstaff's poaching his deer. Rowe reported that Shakespeare killed one of Lucy's deer and, when Lucy prosecuted him too severely, wrote a caustic ballad against his antagonist. Lucy's anger then forced Shakespeare to flee Stratford for London and the theater. Honan rejects the poaching story, but he observes that the Lucy coat of arms, displayed in the Charlecote windows, could have lingered in the playwright's mind.

Even Honan cannot embrace absolute Pyrrhonism, though. Rowe was the first to report that Shakespeare attended the King's New School on Church Street, Stratford. The records are lost for the period of Shakespeare's supposed attendance, but the plays abound in references to the texts the future dramatist would have used in his classes.

Charles G. Smith (*Shakespeare's Proverb Lore*, 1963) found more than two hundred references in Shakespeare's plays to just one such work, Leonhard Cullman's *Sententiae pueriles* (1540). Honan assumes, certainly correctly, that Shakespeare attended the local school, where he received a grounding in at least the Latin classics. Rowe claimed that Shakespeare left school early because of John Shakespeare's declining fortunes. Honan maintains that Shakespeare left school at the standard age of about fifteen.

By 1592 Shakespeare was in London, writing and acting in plays. How he effected the transition from son of a glover to popular author remains a mystery. Many other children sat in grammar schools in market towns without turning into writers. Geniuses are, as the word implies, sui generis, unique, inexplicable; Honan is to be commended for not trying to explain.

As Shakespeare's career developed, references to him increased. Still, much remains unknown. Just as Honan fleshes out Shakespeare's youth by examining sixteenth century Stratford, so this biography seeks to shed light on the dramatist by focusing on the Elizabethan and Jacobean theater. Honan demonstrates how precarious this occupation of actor/playwright proved to be. Players constantly faced the hostility of Puritan officials in London and, when companies were forced to tour, in the provinces. Plague repeatedly forced the closing of the theaters. Shakespeare's star had just begun to rise in 1592 with his plays about the reign of Henry VI; the diary of impresario Philip Henslowe reveals that *Henry VI, Part III* earned more than any other play Henslowe produced. However, late in 1592, plague struck London, and the theaters did not reopen for nearly two years. By the time the playhouses reopened, old companies had disappeared, and new companies had formed. Among the latter was the Lord Chamberlain's Men, with which Shakespeare would remain until his retirement.

While the theaters were closed, Shakespeare turned to poetry, dedicating *Venus and Adonis* (1593) and *The Rape of Lucrece* (1594) to the young third earl of Southampton. In *The Poetical Register* (1719), Giles Jacob reported,

> For the Former of which Dedications, that Noble Lord gave him a Thousand Pounds, which uncommon Bounty Mr. Shakespeare gratefully acknowleg'd in the Dedication to the Latter.

Honan dismisses this long-repeated tale that supposedly explains how Shakespeare became a shareholder in his acting company. A share in the Lord Chamberlain's Men, Honan notes, would have cost about fifty pounds, a fee probably waived in exchange for Shakespeare's writing two plays a year for the troupe. Honan observes that in 1594 Southampton would not have been in any position to make a munificent gift anyway, because the earl was facing financial difficulties. Among these was a five-thousand-pound fine for refusing to marry the woman his guardian in chancery, William Cecil, Lord Burghley, had chosen for him (Burghley's granddaughter).

In the early 1600's Shakespeare also began writing his sonnets. The first 126 are addressed to a fair youth, generally assumed to be Southampton, the remainder to a dark lady who, *pace* the late A. L. Rowse's *Discovering Shakespeare: A Chapter in*

Literary History (1989), remains unidentified. These poems, so seemingly confessional, have been a siren song for many a biographer of Shakespeare (not surprisingly Oscar Wilde), luring them to declare Shakespeare homosexual and otherwise to discover therein the truth about the playwright's emotions. Honan's disclaimer is thus refreshing: "I shall solve no puzzle here and advance no major theory." Yet even he cannot so tightly lash himself to the mast of uncertainty that he does not see in these poems a dissatisfaction with the theatrical profession Shakespeare had chosen.

In fact, Shakespeare need not have returned to the theater in 1594. His two poems addressed to Southampton were immensely popular: By the end of the decade *Venus and Adonis* had gone through six editions, and *The Rape of Lucrece* went through six editions in Shakespeare's lifetime. One could not in the sixteenth or seventeenth century make a living directly from the sale of one's books; the publisher owned the copyright, and payment was slight. John Milton, for example, received five pounds for the first edition of *Paradise Lost* (1667) and another five when the work went into a second edition seven years later. However, lesser writers than Shakespeare sought and received patronage from aristocrats like Southampton or Edward de Vere, seventeenth earl of Oxford. Shakespeare devoted his energies to the stage rather because he loved the theater. By 1600 he had earned enough money to buy his father a coat of arms and himself the second best house in Stratford. The plays of the next decade, which include all his major tragedies, are not the work of someone merely going through the motions of composition. In his last years his productivity declined, but in 1613 he bought a residence in London, and the next year he collaborated with John Fletcher on the lost *Cardenio*.

Even with Shakespeare, the Lord Chamberlain's Men could face hard times. In 1597-1598 several of Shakespeare's plays appeared in print. Honan links this phenomenon to the company's falling on hard times and having to sell their playbooks. In 1597 Giles Allen refused to renew the company's lease on the land where their playhouse, the Theatre, stood. A heavy investment in the Blackfriars, an indoor theater, failed to yield immediate returns when local residents successfully petitioned to keep adult players from performing there. Only the ruse of dismantling the Theatre and moving the timbers across the Thames, where Cuthbert and Richard Burbage, the carpenter Peter Streete, and others reassembled them as the Globe, saved the troupe. King James's choice of Shakespeare's company as his own servants in 1603 did not guarantee financial security, either. For much of 1603-1604 the theaters again were closed because of plague. James gave his company thirty pounds, and the King's Men's performances at court earned them another £150. The total is about half what the player-shareholders might have earned had the Globe been opened during that time.

Still, Shakespeare prospered, and he sought in his will to ensure that his fortune would remain intact. Whatever his relationship with his wife, he left her little. Honan does not try to explain away the bequest of the second-best bed. Rather, he suggests that the intent was to keep Shakespeare's money away from the Hathaways. Susanna apparently was his preferred daughter—Hamnet had died in August, 1596—and to her he left the bulk of his property. Shakespeare's last direct descendant died in the seventeenth century; in the eighteenth his home, New Place, would be torn down, though the Birthplace remains. His greatest legacy is, of course, preserved in the First Folio, published seven years after his death. In these works the true Shakespeare, or as much as one can know of him, resides. The writer vanishes; the writings remain. Even the best biographies, and Honan's is among them, can do no more than shine a faint ray of light into the jungle where the tiger's heart, wrapped in darkness, beats forever hidden.

Joseph Rosenblum

Sources for Further Study

Booklist 95 (February 1, 1999): 957.
The Economist 350 (February 6, 1999): 89.
Library Journal 124 (February 15, 1999): 150.
New Criterion 17 (June, 1999): 78.
The New York Times Book Review 104 (February 28, 1999): 26.
Publishers Weekly 246 (January 18, 1999): 320.

SIGNS AND WONDERS

Author: Melvin Jules Bukiet (1953-)
Publisher: Picador USA (New York). 376 pp. $26.00
Type of work: Novel
Time: A few months at the end of 1999
Locale: Germany

At the end of the millennium, a new messiah arises from the wreck of a prison ship off the coast of Germany and leads his fellow inmates across the German countryside in a pilgrimage to found a new religion

Principal characters:
BEN ALEF, the new messiah and former prison inmate on the *Farnhagen*
SNAKES HAMMURABI, an inmate who becomes Ben Alef's interpreter to the masses
THE PEDDLER, Snakes's former boss and father figure, who runs various criminal enterprises in Hamburg
DIETRICH EISENHEIM, an inmate and the unrepentant former Nazi commander at Bergen-Belsen
ASHER ROSE, a famous Holocaust survivor who denounces Ben Alef in a bid to save him
MAX VETTER, a fisherman who witnesses the first miracle and becomes a disciple of Ben Alef

Melvin Jules Bukiet teaches writing at Sarah Lawrence College. He received the Edward Lewis Wallant Award for the best Jewish-American Fiction of 1992 for *Stories of an Imaginary Childhood* (1992). He has also written *After* (1996) and *While the Messiah Tarries* (1995), and his stories have appeared in such publications as *Antaeus* and *The Paris Review*.

In the brief prologue to *Signs and Wonders*, Bukiet considers the concept of the end of the millennium. He examines the arbitrariness of the calendar that measures the centuries and notes how so many people, from the hopeful to the waggish, are using the concept of the millennium to define otherwise ordinary human events. He even includes a list of ten things that the reader can expect to have happen during the coming millennium, including the death of computer mogul Bill Gates and war in the Middle East. With that introduction, he begins a tale in which even the most cynical characters await a dramatic close to the end of the millennium.

Signs and Wonders is definitely a man's book, in which the few women who appear are assigned the sexist roles of either Madonna or whore (or both). Perhaps Bukiet limited his main characters to men so that he could focus on the subjects of faith and loyalty without the added complications of male/female relationships. The result, however, is a book that at best is one-sided and, at worst, denies women any importance in the mysterious events that are taking place. Women fulfill very limited, specific roles and do nothing of importance to the plot. That said, the novel does present an interesting portrait of human beings' need to find hope and eagerness to believe in old-fashioned miracles in a modern, corrupt age. The novel also shows how corrupt and cynical the results can be. The criminals follow Ben Alef against their own better judgments when they could instead be free to escape; in a sense, they have never left the confines of their cell and the fate that brought them together.

The setting of the opening scene, definitely an all-male environment, is a cell on the prison ship *Farnhagen*, anchored off the north German coast. Newcomer Snakes Hammurabi confronts his eleven fellow inmates as they size him up, and he negotiates his position in their hierarchy. He relates the criminal trespass that has brought him to the *Farnhagen*—using a church altar as a urinal. Although he has been exposed to several bizarre religious sects by his father, a spiritual seeker whose diplomatic job took his family across the globe, Snakes has no religious beliefs of his own. He has made a living as the favored son of The Peddler, carrying out various criminal tasks to support the latter's varied enterprises, which are conducted from his home base, a private club called the *Kastrasse*. We learn that Snakes's parents legally changed his name just before they died in a snake-handling session on a U.S. military base. Snakes learns the crimes of the other inmates, among whom is the former commander of Bergen-Belsen, Dietrich Eisenheim, an aging Nazi who still believes fervently in the führer's cause. The exception is the mysterious Ben Alef, who never speaks. No one has seen him eat or sleep, either, and no one seems to remember when he arrived among them.

Once the inmates' crimes and attitudes are delineated, Bukiet disrupts their miserable, forgotten existence with the fury of a storm unlike any seen before on the northern German coast. At first the prisoners are merely neglected, and in their growing hunger, they begin to consider cannibalism. The silent Ben Alef is menaced by Anton Barsch, who is serving time for killing a police officer, but Ben Alef produces a hard-boiled egg out of thin air, and it is eaten instead. This is an interesting parallel to the Catholic mass, wherein believers consume the symbolic flesh and blood of Christ, and the egg itself has the connotations of life offered by the Christ figure. That night, the storm intensifies, and the prisoners realize that the Farnhagen is sinking; they hear screams as the lower decks are flooded. Ben Alef suddenly speaks, moaning about showers as the rain washes the grime from his body, and lightning strikes the ship, liberating the prisoners from their cell and striking dead Eisenheim, who had attempted to touch Ben Alef.

The first miracle that the prisoners cannot explain rationally is witnessed by Max Vetter and occurs after they leave the sinking ship. At first the men sprawl on the rubber covering from the ship, but then Ben Alef leads them toward the shore, walking across the water until they reach the sandy beach. He insists that they bring the body of Eisenheim with them, and after they have arrived on shore, he apparently brings Eisenheim back to life. With the addition of Max, the number of Ben Alef's followers matches exactly that of Christ's disciples.

Max, who has fished this bay for decades, believes in Ben Alef because he knows there is no sand bar that could have supported their walk. Max considers himself blessed to be the sole outside witness to this miracle, and he becomes a disciple, traveling with the prisoners as they journey across the countryside. Beginning with this incident and continuing throughout the book, Max writes letters to his sister

Frieda—letters that are never posted. Although this is an intriguing mystery, Bukiet never lets the reader know whether Frieda actually exists. There is a possibility that Max Vetter is the most depraved criminal among them, even though he did not come from a prison cell.

Although the order of Ben Alef's miracles does not follow the order set forth in the New Testament for Christ's miracles, they are similar in nature. Ben Alef first makes himself publicly known at a wedding, where he performs two miracles. The band of pilgrims comes upon a wedding about to take place, but the food for the wedding feast has been stolen, possibly by the pilgrims themselves. Ben Alef causes a flood of fresh corn to fall from a makeshift pavilion his men hold over the bride and groom, and later he seems to turn water into wine. Bukiet portrays these miracles as straightforward. Although he explains them through the opposing character of Father Immaculato reporting the story to the pope, those who actually witness the events have no doubts that they are genuine, and Bukiet does not give any indications that they are not.

As Ben Alef and his men move through the countryside on their way to Hamburg, more and more believers, who name themselves "Alefites," join them. The Alefites adopt corn as their food of choice, and citizens along the way leave food for them as they pass through the towns. An aspiring reporter who was lucky enough to witness the aftermath of the wedding miracles reports on each stage of their journey, even as the media seize on this wild new religious group and pursue the Alefites in search of a story. A mysterious limousine shows up, and Snakes Hammurabi recognizes his old boss, The Peddler. In this newfound faith, Snakes at first rejects The Peddler's advances, but when at last they arrive in Hamburg, the escaped prisoners are promptly arrested and jailed. This leads to a religious fury of self-mutilation by burning and sexual orgies in the parking lot below the jail where the Alefites have gathered.

This new religion is troubling to local authorities, the German chancellor, and the pope in Rome. Bukiet clearly shows how eager people are to believe in someone who promises hope and performs miracles, as well as how easily they create and justify their own responses to the messianic message. The fact of the approaching millennium date contributes to the hysteria and the rapid growth of the Alefites, first in Germany, and then across the globe.

After The Peddler helps the prisoners escape from jail, he takes them to the *Kastrasse*, where a deeply troubled Snakes takes them on a tour of the criminal activities taking place. Ben Alef is attracted by one young woman, who is being taken off to be abused by a client, and he causes her to be rescued from this fate, similar to the New Testament redemption of Mary Magdalene. She joins his followers. Ben Alef continues to perform miracles in Hamburg, and The Peddler changes his criminal operations to a money-making scheme involving Ben Alef as the messiah. One of Ben Alef's mysteries is the blue tattoo on his arm that seems to link him to the Nazi death camps, although he is much too young to have been in one. This tattoo is revealed to be a fraud by the young reporter. Incredibly, this does not shake his followers' belief in him, and when one of his aging hippie followers recognizes Ben Alef as the illegitimate son she lost track of years earlier, this madonna-whore mother is also revered by the Alefites.

The ecclesiastical and civil authorities plot against Ben Alef, sending Asher Rose, a distinguished Holocaust survivor and spokesperson, to speak against him. Instead, Asher Rose recognizes Ben Alef as the messiah and is shocked to realize that Ben Alef is his own son and that The Peddler is his long-lost brother. In a father's attempt to save his son from what Rose believes is certain assassination, Asher Rose denounces Ben Alef. The outraged Alefites crucify Asher Rose and sack Hamburg. During the mass riot, the prisoners begin to die in cruel ways that are linked to the crimes that brought them to the *Farnhagen*.

Although the Holocaust is not the subject of this novel, the characters often make allusion to it. The synagogue in which Asher Rose is killed had been restored at great expense by the Germans, even though there scarcely remained enough Jews in the city to fill it for services. German guilt at the destruction of the Jews is constantly raised by examples of how careful modern Germans are to deny such prejudices. Dietrich Eisenheim alone continues to assert that the Nazi plan was right, and because Ben Alef endures him, no one attempts to silence him. Everyone from the prisoners to the Alefites to the authorities accepts Ben Alef as a Jew, as they would expect the messiah to be.

As the end of the millennium approaches, only four of the prisoners are still alive, including Ben Alef himself. Max Vetter and the two women, Ben Alef's mother and the woman he rescued from The Peddler, also remain in the group. Ben Alef leads them on a final journey, to EuroDisney, and this is where the novel becomes confusing. Up until this point, the narrative had been fairly straightforward and linear. As miraculous as the events surrounding Ben Alef were, they were told in a realistic manner. Suddenly, in chapter 24, Bukiet relates the story of Pluto, Mickey Mouse's dog in the Disney cartoons, as if this animated character were a real being. This character, somehow displaced by Goofy, becomes a vicious killer. He is supposedly the doom that awaits Ben Alef at EuroDisney. This change in the narrative is difficult to comprehend, and the resolution of the novel does not adequately account for it. Although Bukiet's depiction of the synthetic materialism of the Disney franchise as the center of belief in the modern age is understandable, his giving the animated characters a mysterious reality does not work. It is never quite clear who or what Pluto is supposed to be, although allusions to an evil figure are given in memories from Snakes's past. Welcomed by the staff of EuroDisney, Ben Alef is called upon to resurrect the frozen Walt Disney, father of Mickey. This turns into a horrible scene of melting ice and rotting corpse, and Ben Alef is killed by Max Vetter dressed in a Goofy costume after Eisenheim's assassination attempt fails. Readers are denied the explanation of Vetter's action, although they are told that it had something to do with "dear Frieda." Snakes Hammurabi, the only remaining disciple, bitterly denounces any future belief in God.

Patricia Masserman

Sources for Further Study

Library Journal 123 (December, 1998): 152.
The New York Times Book Review 104 (September 26, 1999): 20.
Publishers Weekly 246 (January 18, 1999): 326.
The Wall Street Journal, October 15, 1998, p. A20.

SLEEPING WITH EXTRA-TERRESTRIALS
The Rise of Irrationalism and Perils of Piety

Author: Wendy Kaminer (1949-)
Publisher: Pantheon Books (New York). 278 pp. $24.00
Type of work: Current affairs
Time: The late 1990's
Locale: The United States

A caustic critique of what the author considers America's irrational and too-evangelical culture

Wendy Kaminer is a Public Policy Fellow at Radcliffe who is also a contributing editor at *The Atlantic Monthly* and has published articles and reviews in *The New York Times*, *Newsweek*, *The Nation*, and *The New Republic*. This is her sixth book, with much of her previous work devoted to various aspects of the women's movement.

Sleeping with Extra-Terrestrials consists of eight essays in which Kaminer attacks a number of targets that are usually considered untouchable. Her primary subject is Western religious faith, which she prefers to term "supernaturalism." Her own position is that of a liberal agnostic, although her arguments can well be deemed those of an atheist. She does admit that organized religion can offer people psychological comfort and community, as well as needed social services, but fiercely opposes its assaults on public policy and secular government. She balances the benefits of religious belief, such as courage, compassion, confidence, and stoic endurance of hardship, with the horrifying malevolence of religious wars, intolerance demonstrated by book burnings, inquisitions, witch and heretic burnings, endorsement of slavery in nineteenth century America, and terrorism in the Middle East today. She proudly calls herself a secularist, determined to maintain an impenetrable wall between religion and the state.

Kaminer's favorite sage is H. L. Mencken (1880-1956), who attacked religion and the clergy in scathing terms that no commentator will proffer today. He called religious belief "a peculiarly puerile and tedious kind of nonsense." Challenges Kaminer, "Name one widely published intellectual today who dares to write like that. Name one mainstream journal that would publish Mencken's assault on religion today." She also yearns for outspoken philosophers in the vein of Bertrand Russell (1872-1970), who declared the absence of God and an afterlife a virtual certainty.

These days, she says, both Russell and Mencken would be dismayed at the suffusion of public discourse with piety. Conservatives routinely invoke "Judeo-Christian" ideals (thereby excluding other faiths and unbelievers), while many liberals call themselves communitarians, regarding religious affiliations as essential wellsprings of morality. Virtue is commonly presumed to derive exclusively from religious teachings, with character often seen as a function of religiosity. She cites surveys taken in the 1980's that show only one quarter of the adult population willing to protect the right of atheists to oppose religion in public places, with intolerance of atheism even stronger than intolerance of homosexuality.

According to polls taken in the 1990's, 95 percent of Americans profess a belief in

God, 46 percent credit the biblical account of Creation, and three quarters rate their chances of going to heaven as excellent or good; only 4 percent expect to end up in hell. Yet both conservatives like William Bennett and liberals like Yale law professor Stephen Carter charge that liberal intellectual elites disdain belief in God, opt for moral relativism, and are biased against religion. Kaminer has tried in vain to identify even one class of atheistic intellectuals exhibiting such intolerance.

She regards religious belief as an exceedingly powerful social and political force which has largely escaped critical examination, let alone satire. She notes that when she wrote a 1996 *New York Times* op-ed article on Hillary Rodham Clinton's "conversations" with Eleanor Roosevelt,

> I was not allowed to observe that while Mrs. Clinton was criticized for talking to Eleanor Roosevelt, millions of Americans regularly talk to Jesus, long deceased, and that many people believe that God talks to them, unbidden. (At least Mrs. Clinton didn't imagine that Mrs. Roosevelt answered back.)

This citation fairly represents Kaminer's tone and attitude: She is iconoclastic, witty, tart, and provocative, eager to pound her computer keys against what she considers unexamined piety, spiritual smugness, and mental vapidity.

She scorns the popular view that people cannot be good without gods, preferring Mary McCarthy's (1912-1989) observation that "Religion is only good for good people." From her liberal perspective, organized religions sometimes brand homosexuality and family planning as sinful, encourage gross discrimination against homosexuals and heterosexual women, condemn racial integration, demand censorship of the arts, and fear science, sex, and untrammeled human creativity. Thus religions will sometimes divide humankind and even make hatred seem holy. Balancing the scale, she allows that some religions have also been forces of liberation, as in the civil rights and abolitionist movements, resistance to the Vietnam War, and the maintenance of social welfare programs. She resolutely refuses, however, to accept the proposition that religion is a source of our values; after all, secularists have values, too.

Kaminer fervently defends the wall between church and state, which is enshrined in the First Amendment's prohibition on establishing a state religion. She worries about Stephen Carter's advocating, in *The Culture of Disbelief* (1993), that the government extend preferences akin to affirmative action programs to religious groups, and abandon the policy of strict neutrality toward them. Such religious accommodation would countermand the views of Thomas Jefferson (1743-1826) and James Madison (1751-1836), both of whom argued that freedom of religion in a secular state was essential to a free society. Surely, she concludes, if God cares about human beings and wants to save their souls, "He'll manage without any help from the government."

In the 1990's, Kaminer notes, attacks on secularism began to enjoy a broad appeal beyond the right-wing conservatism of Christian evangelism. Widespread, nonsectarian anxiety about social change, a declining faith in government, and an increasing pop spirituality generated demands for new infusions of religion into public life. Separation of church and state has been widely misinterpreted as the banishment of religion from public life, rather than insurance that sectarian beliefs will not be imposed on a pluralistic society.

Ironically, she notes, while conservative organs like *The Wall Street Journal* bemoaned the hostility of judicial elites toward religion, the Supreme Court in 1995 issued a remarkable decision requiring state support for religious activities. In *Rosenberger v. University of Virginia*, the Court held that private religious groups are entitled to direct public funding. In a 5-4 decision, it declared that the denial of a public university's financial help to a campus newspaper, *Wide Awake*, constituted "viewpoint discrimination." Kaminer points out that *Wide Awake* was an evangelical paper engaged in pure proselytizing, with a mission not to inform but to cleanse and convert. This was the first case mandating direct state funding of religious inducement.

The fundamentalist attack on evolution, in states such as Kansas and Tennessee, relies on the description of religion as a "viewpoint"; that issue was central to the Rosenberger case. Champions of creationism are now demanding equal time for the teaching of "creation science" with evolution in the public schools. So far, the Supreme Court has rejected this view of creationism as an alternative scientific theory, rejecting a mandate to teach "creation science" in a 1987 case.

Kaminer strongly opposes the use of vouchers for school children. Virtually no possibility exists that vouchers will create an alternative private system to public schooling that would be open and accessible to everyone. Instead, they threaten to worsen educational opportunities for the millions of children left behind in public schools. Public schools in Milwaukee, for example, face a potential loss of seventy million dollars a year pursuant to a voucher program approved in 1998 by the Wisconsin Supreme Court (which the U.S. Supreme Court declined to review). By directing government funds to parochial schools, vouchers will entangle government in sectarianism, forcing taxpayers to support religious ideas and practices that may be anathema to them. Kaminer concludes that religious schools and faith-based social service programs are developing an unprecedented entitlement to public support. She points out that religious organizations are exempted from federal antidiscrimination laws, even when they dispense federal funds. Churches serving as publicly funded welfare providers can legally fire employees for heresy, even employees who are essentially on a federal payroll.

Kaminer grants that religion may at times be a civilizing and moral force, but regards sectarianism as vicious. In Alabama, for instance, Governor Fob James in 1997 organized resistance to a federal court order prohibiting officially sponsored religious activities in the public schools. He also threatened to call out the National Guard to back a local judge who refused to recognize the state court's order as the law in his county. In Alabama's Pike County public schools all children were required to attend Christian sermons, where Jewish children who did not worship Christ were told they would burn in hell. One Jewish boy was forbidden to wear the Star of David around his neck: The principal considered it a "gang symbol."

Pop spirituality and New Age therapies provide inviting bull's-eyes for Kaminer's acerbic rationalism. Too often, she points out, the question, "How do you feel?" is regarded as more important than, "What do you know?" while repression of emotions is considered more problematic than ignorance. Angels are seen as better parents than the arbitrary, abusive Old Testament God. An enormously popular book in the early 1990's, *The Celestine Prophecy* (1993), assures readers that what humans imagine as death is a happy transition to a higher spiritual plane. The preoccupation with celestial life also includes speculations, in some books' convictions, about extraterrestrial visitations, as reported in *Communion* (1987), *Abduction* (1994), and other recent texts. These authors specializing in spirituality contemptuously view skepticism as the refuge of the unenlightened. *The Celestine Prophecy* insists that science, born of the secularization of human culture, is useful in mapping our material world but useless as a guide to the nonmaterial universe of interpersonal energy. The appeal of these books is that of a promise of bliss: no fear, loneliness, pain, or death. The belief systems of pop spirituality demand very little of people. A good attitude is an acceptable substitute for good works, while self-absorption is a spiritual imperative. Kaminer dismisses these mass-market spirituality books as "offensive gibberish."

Kaminer examines the public's extravagant reaction to Princess Diana's death as an example of cultish frenzy reminiscent of public response to Elvis Presley's death. The tearful protestations, amounting to mass hysteria, signified the loss of two pop redeemers. To many of his devoted followers, Elvis is a Christ figure who never really died. Diana, in death, was reinvented as a great humanitarian with emerging spiritual power, who has now entered the millennial discourse. Today, popular culture has formed an alliance with religion, as television increasingly has used religious themes in such series as *Touched by an Angel*. Celebrities become pop divinities, while Deepak Chopra's advice is admired by the likes of Barbra Streisand, Donna Karan, Oprah Winfrey, and Demi Moore.

In her essay "Junk Science," Kaminer reports her discouragement that 44 percent of Americans prefer the biblical story of Creation to Charles Darwin's theory of evolution. In the late 1700's, the Austrian physician Franz Anton Mesmer (1734-1815) claimed that a universal force, or fluid, coursed through bodies and through the atmosphere. While his claims were debunked by a commission of scientists headed by the chemist Antoine Lavoisier (1743-1794), his work nonetheless greatly influenced spiritualists and alternative healers. At the turn of the millennium, practitioners of therapeutic touch claimed that they could scan the body's energy field and redirect its energy flow without ever touching the patient. Kaminer sees Chopra as exemplifying the use of junk science in the service of New Age alternative healing. What he offers his enormous following is wish fulfillment or magical thinking, as he advocates a "fourth dimension" where the body is a mere illusion, and promises to take his readers or listeners to a land where old age, senility, infirmity, and death do not exist. Faith, not reason, is the engine of such pseudoscience.

Kaminer attacks the drug war waged by U.S. authorities as an egregious example of pseudoscience. A 1997 study by Columbia University indicates that 21 percent of violent felons in state prisons committed their crimes while under the influence of alcohol alone; only 3 percent were high on cocaine, and only 1 percent on heroin.

Since Americans learned long ago that prohibition of alcohol failed, why does the country not, sensibly, end the useless prohibition of drugs, which pose far less danger to public safety? Kaminer suggests a reason: because the war on drugs is a faith-based antivice crusade driven by moral fervor, not pragmatism or reason. Its subdivision, the battle against "crack babies," plays to "racist anxiety about a presumptively sociopathic, less-than-human, African-American underclass."

In a somewhat rambling final essay, "The Strenuous Life," Kaminer asserts that the freedom and opportunity for inventiveness offered by a godless world are traded by religionists for the security of a divine, benevolent despotism. She considers the notion of God as irrelevant to her behavior; she has abandoned metaphysical speculation as rationally insoluble, yet insists on having a strong, secular sense of moral sensibility: "Doubting the existence of God has never led me to doubt that murder is wrong." Her rational critique of varieties of irrational thinking will be a tonic for thoughtful people fed up with a culture awash in irrational pieties and intolerant beliefs.

Gerhard Brand

Sources for Further Study

The New York Times, November 16, 1999, p. B8.
The New York Times Book Review 104 (October 24, 1999): 18.
Publishers Weekly 246 (August 23, 1999): 33.

SONNY LISTON WAS A FRIEND OF MINE
Stories

Author: Thom Jones (1945-)
Publisher: Little, Brown (Boston). 312 pp. $23.00
Type of work: Short fiction
Time: 1960-1995
Locale: Vietnam, Hawaii, Illinois, and Michigan

In his third collection, Jones tells more breakneck stories of Vietnam, boxing, and psychic distress

Principal characters:
MATTHEW, an unemployed forty-year-old who finds his mother's dead body
JOHN HAROLD HAMMERMEISTER, an assistant principal at an urban high school who keeps a tarantula on his desk to intimidate students and faculty
FELIX, a Marine who sets a roadrunner on fire in one story and slowly burns to death when a grenade pin is pulled out in another
KID DYNAMITE, a young boxer
FRANKIE DELL, an usher at a movie theater
ANSON, a short man with a hump who is fired from his engineering job and becomes obsessed with mice
WILLIAM, a man who feels that the emptiness in his life has been filled when he meets the woman of his dreams
MOLLY BLOOM, his lover, who has recently been released from a mental institution

After three well-received collections of stories, Thom Jones's own story is well known: a hitch in the Marines in the 1960's, a stint at the Iowa Writer's Workshop in the 1970's, failure to write and sell stories in the then-popular Raymond Carver mode, and ten years as a high school janitor. Then, one day he saw a successful old friend on television and, in envy and despair, sat down to write "The Pugilist at Rest" in his own manic voice; the story was picked out of the slush pile at *The New Yorker* and won an O. Henry Award in 1993. Jones once sold three stories in a day, and his first book *The Pugilist at Rest* (1993) was a finalist for the National Book Award. It makes for a good story, and Jones has ridden the wave of it, hailed as, according to rhapsodic reviewers of that book and his second, *Cold Snap* (1995), "a major talent with great promise."

One has a right, then, to expect that the "great promise" would be fulfilled by his third book. However, what Jones delivers in *Sonny Liston Was a Friend of Mine* is, to quote an old rock-and-roll lyric (one of Jones's favorite devices), "the same old song." It is a generous book in length, by the standards of short-story collections, at more than three hundred pages; as Jones said in an interview, he likes to give his readers their money's worth. However, it is not such a generous fulfillment of Jones's "great promise." The themes and voices in most of the stories are much the same as in the first two collections. Although that in itself is not a crime—after all, a writer must be allowed to weave his or her own unique figure in the carpet—overall these stories are not as strong as those in his previous books. Granted, that weakness may be due to the fact that what was a unique voice in 1993—a hyped-up, dangerous, wild-man alternative to the well-made stories cranked out by so many Carver-copying M.F.A. graduates—now seems a bit strained and overdone, mainly because Jones himself has done it so many times. Perhaps the book is so generous in length because Jones loves the sound of his own voice and thus never seems to get where he seems to be going.

The other problem with Jones's stories in this collection is that his characters are not very likable; character flaws are forgivable if they are interesting, but most of Jones's characters are selfish, self-indulgent, and meaninglessly mean. The most obnoxious is Matthew, an out-of-work man who, as the title indicates, is "40, Still at Home," and whose idea of a "commendable feat" is to sleep for twenty-two out of twenty-four hours. When he finds his cancer-racked mother's dead body in bed, he searches her safe and is as delighted to find a prescription for morphine as he is to find her money. To avoid probate, he zips her in a sleeping bag, puts her in the freezer, takes some morphine and hops back in bed, feeling "absolutely, positively, right-on-the-money cap-ee-tal." This is supposed to be comic, but it comes off as quintessential adolescent meanness.

In "Tarantula," thirty-eight pages are devoted to making life hell for John Harold Hammermeister, an ambitious, admittedly not very likable, young academic who takes the job as assistant principal at W. E. B. Du Bois High School in urban Detroit. Hammermeister, who has big plans of climbing the ladder to the position of state superintendent, keeps a tarantula on his desk to intimidate students and faculty, but he meets his comeuppance from a janitor who reads Joseph Conrad and who stabs the tarantula with a pencil. Then, with the help of another janitor, he puts duct tape over Hammermeister's eyes and mouth and beats his legs, knees, and elbows with a baseball bat. These events are portrayed with great satiric fun, with former janitor Jones self-indulgently enjoying himself.

The Vietnam stories in this collection are predictable and seem to be excuses for brutality; they do not add anything to an understanding of that complex conflict and the men who were victimized by it. "The Roadrunner" is an account of Marines stationed at Oceanside, California, going to Tijuana for obvious and not interesting encounters with prostitutes, concluding with one of the men pouring gasoline over a roadrunner and setting it afire. While the act suggests the kind of cruelty and barbarism required to go to Vietnam and do the dirty work to be done there, and echoes the images of that war in which many were immolated by napalm, one must ask whether the story illuminates those atrocities or merely trivializes them.

Payback time, a favorite Jones plot ploy, takes place in the next story, "A Run Through the Jungle," complete with the usual Vietnam War story references to "slopes," "klicks," "toe-poppers," and "dinks." Although the plot focuses on the efforts of Break on Thru Company (featured in earlier Jones stories) to kill a North Vietnamese officer, the story ends with Jones's idea of moral justice and resultant philosophical wisdom. Felix, the man who immolated the roadrunner in the previous story, falls, unpinning a phosphorus grenade on his chest and dying horribly of internal combustion within three minutes. "What goes around, comes around," says one of the men, and they all feel good because, although it hardly needs to be said, "Christ! I was alive."

Two of the better stories in the collection, the title story and "I Love You, Sophie Western," deal with adolescent males who try to find some heroic or romantic meaning in the world. Although Sonny Liston is not really a friend of Kid Dynamite, the young boxer in the title story, he does meet him once (as Jones says he himself did as a young man) and Liston signs a picture for him, "To the Kid, from your friend, Sonny Liston." The story is an engaging combination of young boy stuff—throwing snowballs at school, being awkward with a girlfriend, trying to cope with a stepfather—and adult stuff—fighting in the Golden Gloves, trying to establish a career, coping with a dangerous nemesis. Although the Kid wins his big fight by a split decision, he loses in the long run because a cut over his eye puts him out of the tournament. The story ends with the inevitable realization that "the real world, which had seemed so very far away all these years, was upon him."

"I Love You, Sophie Western," the other young man story in the collection, focuses on Frankie Dell, who works as an usher at a movie theater and gets adult advice from the projectionist, a pedophile with a clubfoot. Frankie drops acid, has been in a mental institution, and is on medication, but he likes reading Charles Dickens's *Great Expectations* in his high school English class. When the theater shows the 1963 film *Tom Jones* (a sly reference to the author himself), Frankie falls in love with the character of Sophie Western, played by Susannah York. He takes one look at her and, thinking what a great world she inhabits, so unlike his own, knows that "his life had been changed irrevocably." It is the signal for which he has been waiting; he needs to change and he knows that he can. Frankie seems transformed, quoting seventeenth century poetry to a girl in his geometry class, vowing never to masturbate again, swearing that he is off dope. However, his grand ideals are not to be; he is beaten and has his pants pulled down in front of the girl by a schoolyard enemy. The projectionist advises him that he needs to quit school and get a fancy car if he wants to get the girls and that he can get the car faster if he performs fellatio on him. The story ends with Frankie doing what he is asked, looking up at the pedophile with sheep eyes and swallowing.

Another story that works better than most in this collection is "Mouses," in which Anson, a short man with a hump, is fired from his engineering job and becomes obsessed with mice. Catching one and naming him Al, Anson puts him in a cage, sympathetically identifying that the mouse was trying to get by, like everyone else. In a parody of scientific investigation, Anson sets up various experiments with the mice in which they are as controlled as he feels he has been. Consistent with Jones's sense that although what goes around comes around, one does not get what one earns, the story ends with Anson luckily getting a job that he likes and burying the mice one by one as they die. The story ends with undergraduate philosophical ruminations, such as there is a dark side to intelligent beings, a craving for destruction and defilement.

Anson thinks happiness is like Yukon gold, coming not in chunks or boulders but only as tiny grains, claiming that he is content to take what comes, a grain here, a grain there. "What more can you ask for?"

The cover flap of this book promises that Jones is now working on a novel. Then again, the cover of *The Pugilist at Rest* made the same promise. If one wonders what a Thom Jones novel would look like, the last story in this collection, "You Cheated, You Lied," at over seventy pages his longest so far, may give one an idea. Taking his title from a rock-and-roll song by the Shangri-Las, Jones begins the story in the waiting room of a neurology clinic in his hometown of Aura, Illinois. The hero, who is there for temporal lobe epilepsy (a malady suffered by many other Jones heroes), is reading Arthur Schopenhauer (a Jones favorite) when in walks, just released from a mental institution, the future love of his life, named Molly Bloom after James Joyce's memorable heroine in *Ulysses* (1922). The hero, William, feels that the hole in his life, "the great empty abyss," has been filled.

The rest of the piece is a love story, at least as Thom Jones conceives a love story. It involves sex between the lovers, sex with others, and dropping acid, then a trip to Hawaii where there is more sex between the lovers, sex with others, and dropping acid. There is even a brief appearance by ballet dancers Rudolph Nureyev and Dame Margot Fonteyn at a Diamond Head party. There is jealousy, the inevitable breakup of the lovers, depression, a return to the mental institution, and finally, full circle, the reunion where the story started, in the waiting room of the neurology clinic. The story ends with Molly and William referring to each other as Estragon and Didi, from Samuel Beckett's *Waiting for Godot* (pb. 1952), saying silly romantic things. William realizes that "if ever a romance had less than a snowball's chance in hell, it was ours," but concludes that he and Molly are more in love with each other than any two people he has heard about since the dawn of humankind.

Although it may be true in the world of Thom Jones, as one of his characters says, that "the whole world is a neurology ward," it may also be true that readers do not need to be reminded of that fact repeatedly. Although Jones may have provided a bit of welcome, ragged, rough-edged relief to the clean lines of M.F.A. storytelling at the end of the 1980's, too many stories in this collection are characterized by rambling rant, artistic carelessness, and personal self-indulgence or hatefulness.

Charles E. May

Sources for Further Study

Booklist 95 (November 1, 1998): 451.
Boston Globe, February 4, 1999, p. E2.
Library Journal 123 (December, 1998): 159.
New Statesman 129 (February 26, 1999): 57.
The New York Times Book Review 104 (March 14, 1999): 38.
Publishers Weekly 246 (January 18, 1999): 329.

SOUTH OF THE BORDER, WEST OF THE SUN

Author: Haruki Murakami (1949-)
First published: Kokkyo no Minami, Taiyo no Nishi, 1992
Translated from the Japanese by Philip Gabriel
Publisher: Alfred A. Knopf (New York). 213 pp. $22.00
Type of work: Novel
Time: 1951-1988
Locale: Japan

After having several affairs in his life, Hajime realizes how much he has hurt people who love him

Principal characters:
HAJIME, the narrator and central character
SHIMAMOTO, Hajime's childhood sweetheart, who develops from a shy girl with a disability into a mysterious, alluring woman
YUKIKO, Hajime's wife and mother of their two daughters
YUKIKO'S FATHER, who finances Hajime's nightclub but uses his name as cover for shady business transactions
IZUMI OHARA, Hajime's first girlfriend, whose heart he breaks
IZUMI'S COUSIN, a woman who engages in a wild, two-month affair with young Hajime

At its core, Haruki Murakami's novel *South of the Border, West of the Sun* is about the central character, Hajime, who proves unable to make moral decisions and, instead, yields to various temptations. While Hajime realizes late in his teens that he is "a person who can do evil," he is curiously passive when it comes to acting on his insights. He knows that he could easily hurt others again, including those who love him, should the opportunity arise.

Hajime presents a character who is not easily likable yet has a hauntingly complex nature. Murakami's protagonist powerfully affects others yet is oddly powerless when it comes to setting directions in his own life. This contrast between Hajime's power over others and his lack of control over his own future creates much of the dynamic tension in this provocative novel.

Because of its realism, straightforward narrative, and generally nonpolitical nature, *South of the Border, West of the Sun* did not immediately find an American publisher. The book is a different work from, for example, Murakami's widely acclaimed *Nejimaki-dori kuronikuru* (1994-1995; *The Wind-Up Bird Chronicle*, 1997), which mixes surreal elements in storytelling with political concerns about Japanese war crimes in China during World War II. This novel also does not contain the elements of science fiction or magical realism that characterize much of Murakami's previously translated fiction in English. Yet, with its tale of a morally shiftless narrator adrift on an ocean of waxing and waning affection and desire for various women in his life, *South of the Border, West of the Sun* represents a subtle literary achievement that can very well stand on its own.

When the narrator is born January 4, 1951, his parents name him Hajime, which means "beginning" in Japanese. On a literal level, Hajime muses that this is because his birthday fell on "the first week of the first month of the first year of the second half of the twentieth century." His name may also allude to the new beginning of a postwar Japan that had just overcome the worst of the war's effects. Hajime's father survived life as a soldier and prisoner of war to become a manager, and his hometown quickly rebuilt what American bombing had destroyed.

Hajime grows up in a home built before the war, and there is a sense that, with the exception of him being an only child and thus different from most of his classmates of conventionally large families, his living situation is a metaphor for the postwar Japanese mindset of trying to pick up from a point in history before military expansionism brought on ultimate disaster, defeat, and surrender.

Yet, Murakami suggests that the price for collectively trying to forget the troubling past and to live with a kind of historical amnesia is a general lack of moral stamina and direction in life. Just as Hajime lets desire overpower him, Murakami's novel implies that his country appears to have lost some deeper sense of history and direction. These social and political undertones appear only on a very indirect, subtle level in the novel and require some effort on behalf of the attentive reader to detect them.

Hajime grows up as somewhat of an outsider because he comes from such a small family. He becomes the close friend of Shimamoto, a girl who moves into his neighborhood and attends the same class in elementary school, which lasts for six years in Japan. Childhood polio damaged Shimamoto's left leg, which gives her a disability in a society that, until recently, did not treat people with disabilities sensitively. While Hajime and Shimamoto do their homework, they listen to her father's Western records. These include Nat King Cole's song "South of the Border," which, to them, symbolizes a vague longing for an exciting, exotic future.

Hajime reveals his morally diffident nature when, after his family moves to another school district, he stops visiting Shimamoto. He explains to himself that he feels slightly awkward to visit her without the pretext of shared homework.

Content to go with the socially acceptable flow of things, he acquires Izumi Ohara as his girlfriend and tries to sleep with her. When Izumi proves too shy, he arranges a date with her cousin away in Kyoto, who, at age twenty, is three years his senior. Hajime's relationship with the cousin develops into a purely sexual, torrid two-month affair. His refusal to divulge the name of his lover is clearly indicative of their one-dimensional view of each other. As Hajime notes, "It never occurred to either of us that we might want to become long-term lovers."

When Izumi finds out, she is devastated. Shocked by his power to destroy another person, Hajime confides, "In truth, I damaged Izumi beyond repair." While he goes to college in Tokyo, Izumi stays behind and never recovers. Years later, she sends him an anonymous postcard when her cousin dies; a common friend tells Hajime that she is still unmarried and has lost some of her beauty at thirty-six. When Hajime finally encounters Izumi by chance at the end of the novel, he is terrified that "her face showed me nothing . . . an infinite blank." His betrayal has let her die inside. Yet while Hajime is humbled by the experience, he feels helpless to change and unable to say that he would never act as badly again.

Typical for the novel's theme of the lack of direction in contemporary, postwar Japan, Hajime fails to find much professional and personal fulfillment. There is an attitude of defeat and exhaustion, reminding a reader of the literature of the European existentialists or the New Novel in postwar French literature.

"My four year of college were pretty much a waste," Hajime confesses. Neither politics, education, nor career development capture his interest. When he enters the workforce, "the job was a total bore," and his life becomes a "tedious existence."

Change occurs when he meets Yukiko on a rainy day while on vacation. After they get married, her father, who owns a construction company, provides Hajime with the start-up capital to open his own nightclub. For once, Hajime feels that "the possibilities were intriguing." Yet even this relationship has a darker side, since his father-in-law uses his name to cover some unscrupulous business. Nevertheless, for the next eight years, Hajime dedicates himself to his business, opening a second club and raising a family.

Murakami's detailed description of Hajime's nightclub operation may owe something to the author's own experience. For some years in the mid-1970's and 1980's, Murakami and his wife managed a bar in Tokyo. In interviews, Murakami has said that what he enjoyed most about this period were the stolen moments when he would sneak off to read books; Hajime, at one point, is engrossed in a book about "the Sino-Vietnam border conflict after the Vietnam War."

Yet after Shimamoto surprisingly reenters and then departs his life forever, Hajime becomes disillusioned with his position as proprietor and provider of good times. "[W]hat lay before me was a typical noisy bar—artificial, superficial, and shabby. A stage setting, props built for the sole purpose of getting drunks to part with their cash." This cynical insight connects Hajime to the sad mood of many postmodern protagonists and relates to what Marxist critics, such as Fredric Jameson, would call the cultural crisis of late capitalism. Murakami's connection to international literary topics and concerns becomes starkly visible.

Hajime's greatest crisis occurs when his childhood sweetheart Shimamoto unexpectedly turns up in his club. In a scene deliberately modeled after Hollywood's *films noirs*, among which Michael Curtis's *Casablanca* (1942) is directly mentioned in the novel, Hajime falls for the elementary school friend who has transformed herself into a beautiful, seductive, and tragically alluring woman. Given Murakami's fascination with American culture and his often stated belief that Japanese literature should turn to America for inspiration, Hajime's Humphrey Bogart-like self-fashioning adds spice and dark forebodings to the climax of the novel.

Betraying his wife Yukiko for his longing for Shimamoto, Hajime takes her at a moment's notice to a remote river where she lets go of the ashes of her dead baby daughter. The two nearly consummate their affair when their Tokyo-bound plane is delayed but not canceled. Typically, Shimamoto disappears for a while, leaving

Hajime racked with despair and unable to let go of his fascination with his childhood friend.

In the end, Shimamoto and Hajime spend only one night together. Before they make love, Shimamoto plays the old Nat King Cole record and relates the strange tale of Siberian farmers, who begin to wander west in a futile pursuit of the sun until their strength leaves them and they die of exhaustion in the frozen tundra. Her story, alluded to by the novel's title, is not the only symbolism at play here. Like the book, Shimamoto's life is defined by the longing expressed in the lyrics of an American jazz song and the obsession with a self-destructive journey toward an impossible goal.

As Hajime wakes up from a night of lovemaking in his mountain retreat, Shimamoto has left without a trace. Back in Tokyo, he realizes that she had originally planned to kill him and commit suicide on their return drive but inexplicably changed her mind to let him live. Acknowledging his affair, he reconciles with Yukiko, whose grace in accepting him back saves Hajime from despair.

In the end, *South of the Border, West of the Sun* offers a fascinating insight into the mind of a deeply postmodern character. Hajime perceives his professional life as shallow, and his character is inherently unable to resist any temptation. The ease with which he accepts an end to his life with Yukiko and his two daughters, if Shimamoto had wanted him to live with her, is described with a frightening self-awareness of his own flawed character. To what degree Hajime's dilemma and attitudes are exemplary of the lovelessness of contemporary society is left to the reader to decide. Murakami's novel, however, will challenge its audience to rethink the circumstances of their own lives.

R. C. Lutz

Sources for Further Study

Booklist 95 (November 1, 1998): 452.
Library Journal 124 (February 15, 1999): 184.
The New York Times Book Review 104 (February 14, 1999): 8.
Publishers Weekly 245 (November 23, 1998): 57.

SPINOZA
A Life

Author: Steven Nadler (1958-)
Publisher: Cambridge University Press (New York). Illustrated. 407 pp. $34.95
Type of work: Biography, philosophy, and history
Time: 1632-1677
Locale: Holland

A biography of seventeenth century philosopher Baruch Spinoza that examines Spinoza's social and historical setting, as well as his ideas

Principal personage:
BARUCH "BENEDICTUS" SPINOZA, a philosopher

Baruch Spinoza's first name means "blessed" in Hebrew, an ironic name for a man who was excommunicated with curses from the Jewish synagogue in Amsterdam when he was only twenty-three years old and who was condemned as an atheist by Christian writers during and after his life. Since his time, his work has provoked widely varying responses, including both blessings and curses. Some have argued that he was indeed an atheist because he maintained that nature was a closed chain of entirely determined causes and effects. Others have claimed that he was one of the most profoundly religious thinkers in history. Spinoza did identify nature with God, but his God has always seemed utterly unlike the God of traditional Christianity or Judaism. Spinoza saw God or nature as containing all things, completely impersonal, and without any power of choice or decision. Was he naturalizing God or deifying nature?

Steven Nadler's biography of Spinoza does not solve the riddle of the true meaning of Spinoza's philosophy, but it does provide an introduction to the man and his thinking. It is also a meticulously researched and absorbing examination of the social and historical setting of Spinoza's work. One of the greatest difficulties for the biographer is the lack of information on the philosopher's childhood and adolescence. Nadler deals with this absence of data by concentrating first on the rise of the Jewish community in the Dutch Republic and then on Spinoza's family. The reader occasionally has the feeling that the first third of Nadler's book looks at everyone who knew or might have known Spinoza, while Baruch himself hardly appears until it is time for him to be blackballed from the Jewish community. Still, biographers can only work with the sources that they have, and readers will be familiar with Spinoza's surroundings by the time they are fully introduced to the thinker as a grown man.

Nadler, a member of the University of Wisconsin's Center for Jewish Studies as well as a professor of philosophy, might be expected to take a special interest in Spinoza's Judaism. However, Spinoza does not appear in these pages as a particularly Jewish thinker. While he did come out of a Jewish tradition and engaged in interpretations of the Old Testament, his thinking was much closer to currents in liberal Dutch Christian thinking than to the thinking of other Jewish philosophers or theologians. This may have been one of his problems. As Nadler convincingly argues, many of the

Jews of the Netherlands were immigrants from Spain and Portugal. In their native lands, they had been pressured to convert to Christianity. The more tolerant political climate of the Netherlands enabled them to return to their ancestral faith, and they did so with all the zeal of new converts. At the same time, the intellectual awakening of seventeenth century Europe, exemplified by individuals such as Belgian philosopher René Descartes (1596-1650), posed challenges to traditional perspectives. Heretics such as Spinoza threatened the rediscovered Jewish faith.

Nadler manages to reconstruct Spinoza's educational background. He provides documentary evidence that Spinoza did not, as legend has sometimes recorded, train to become a rabbi. In fact, the future philosopher did not complete the higher grades of Hebrew education, probably because he was needed as a merchant in the family business. Although he did have a good foundation in Scripture, his passion for learning led him to seek the kind of education that we would refer to today as "liberal arts." Some time in his early twenties, Spinoza enrolled in the Amsterdam Latin school of Franciscus van den Enden. It was at about this time, also, that Spinoza began using the Latin form of his name, "Benedictus," in a symbolic move toward the Latin culture of gentile Europe. Van den Enden's school existed to provide the sons of prominent families with the skills they would need to enter university, and Spinoza must have been much older than his fellow pupils. Van den Enden was a radical adherent of republican government, as well as a humanistic educator. Late in life, Spinoza's former tutor was executed in France for plotting to overthrow French king Louis XIV and replace the French monarchy with a republic. Spinoza's own republican ideals must have been encouraged at van den Enden's school.

After his study with van den Enden, Spinoza became a lens grinder, grinding the glass lenses used in telescopes and other optical instruments. The legend of Spinoza portrays him as a philosophical hermit, eking out a living from his craft and spending his days alone with his thoughts. Nadler offers evidence that this legend is wrong on two counts. First, although the philosopher did keep his expenditures to a minimum, he did not need to grind lenses to maintain himself. Grants and pensions from friends and admirers supported him. Spinoza ground lenses mainly for his own optical experiments, not to earn a living. Second, Spinoza's life was far from solitary. He was unmarried and apparently had few ties to his family after his excommunication, but he enjoyed numerous social and intellectual connections. Many of these were with members of the various Christian groups known as the Collegiants. These were small sects of relatively free thinkers, who formed discussion groups and favored religious liberty and individual interpretations of Scripture. Nadler also examines Spinoza's international connections. He devotes attention to the philosopher's long correspondence with Henry Oldenburg, secretary of England's Royal Society. This correspondence was interrupted, but not ended, by the wars between England and the Netherlands. The young Gottfried Wilhelm Leibniz (1646-1716), who would himself become a famous philosopher and mathematician, wrote Spinoza. Spinoza's fame also led the University of Heidelberg to offer him a chair in philosophy. He rejected this offer, fearing possible limitations on his freedom of thought.

Although Spinoza was widely known in his lifetime, he was often controversial and frequently misunderstood. As Nadler shows, many of Spinoza's admirers, including Oldenburg, seem to have misunderstood the radical nature of the philosopher's thinking. This thinking, most completely expressed in Spinoza's *Ethica* (1677; *Ethics*, 1870), expressed a view of the universe that was utterly deterministic. Everything that happens must happen. The famous phrase "*Deus sive natura*" ("God or nature") expressed Spinoza's apparent view that "God" and "nature" are interchangeable terms. This identification of God with nature, as well as Spinoza's denial of free will, made the philosopher a dangerous heretic or atheist in the eyes of many Christians, as well as Jews. The thinker's dislike of controversy probably, Nadler suggests, led him to publish relatively little during his lifetime and to put off the publication of *Ethics* until after his death.

Nadler spends relatively little time on the problems raised by Spinoza's thinking. The biographer identifies his goal as an investigation of the philosopher's life, rather than an analysis of the work. Still, readers might have benefited from a brief recognition of some of the more obvious logical questions posed by the approach taken by Spinoza. *Ethics*, for example, seems to argue that ethical behavior is a matter of seeing the completely deterministic nature of the universe and acting in accordance with it. Once one sees things *sub specie aeternitatis* ("from the perspective of eternity"), one sees that all things must happen as they do, and one will think and act in harmony with the universal nature of things. If, however, nature or God contains all things, including people, then how is it possible for people to see things from the perspective of God? If there is no free will, moreover, people cannot choose how they will think or act. They simply act as they do.

Some discussion of these difficulties might have helped readers see more clearly the intellectual context of Spinoza's thought and how Spinoza's thinking contrasted with that of Descartes. The seventeenth century was a time when mechanistic views of the world were becoming more common. Rising currents of scientific thought presented a universe that could be understood as causal relationships among material objects, like the workings of machines, and that could be represented through the necessary relationships of logic. This view of things, however, both challenged traditional religious ideas and raised questions about how human beings could really understand or experience anything if thought was simply a matter of mechanical relations. Descartes's response to the problem was to pull humans out of the mechanical and material world. Descartes presented a dualistic nature that consisted of mechanical connections among objects and free spirits acting on objects. In his writings on Descartes, Spinoza attempted to present the Belgian thinker in a more rigorously logical form, rewriting Descartes's work as sets of geometrical propositions. Spinoza's rejection of dualism and of a separate realm of the spirit may be seen as the same sort of logical rigor. For Spinoza, the world is a set of necessary causal relations, and thought is a set of necessary logical relations. This view, however, overlooks the very problem addressed by Descartes's dualism: How are human experience and decision making possible if there is no mind separate from mechanical necessity? This question continues to trouble philosophers, and a biography of Spinoza is an appropriate place at least to acknowledge it.

Spinoza continues to be an important philosopher. Albert Einstein, among others, greatly admired him. The Norwegian philosopher Arne Næss has based his teachings on deep ecology on Spinoza's view that human beings are a part of an all-encompassing Nature and should exist in accordance with this Nature. Despite his continued relevance, though, Spinoza has been the subject of few biographical studies. Most of the biographies of him that exist rely on questionable legends about his life. In 1998, Margaret Gullan-Whur published *Within Reason: A Life of Spinoza*. Gullan-Whur's work made a useful contribution, but the author's dedication to feminism led her to concentrate heavily on Spinoza's attitudes toward women. She succeeded in demonstrating that the philosopher, like most men of his time, accepted the male domination of society. This attitude was inconsistent with his egalitarian republican ideals, but it may be too much to demand twentieth century views from a seventeenth century figure. Gullan-Whur also claimed that Spinoza's philosophy was greatly influenced by a failed romance with Clara Maria van den Enden, daughter of Franciscus. Nadler offers a convincing argument that this supposed romance never happened.

One of the many strengths of Nadler's biography is the attention the biographer gives to Spinoza's *Tractatus theologico-politicus* (1670; *A Theologico-Political Treatise*, 1862). This short work was not only a compelling argument for religious liberty but also a much briefer and clearer statement of Spinoza's thinking than the complex *Ethics*.

Both general readers, seeking an introduction to Spinoza, and professional philosophers or intellectual historians, seeking insight into the biographical development of Spinoza's thought, will benefit from this well-written, carefully researched new book.

Carl L. Bankston III

Sources for Further Study

Booklist 95 (February 15, 1999): 1005.

Library Journal 124 (February 1, 1999): 93.

The New York Times Book Review 104 (July 18, 1999): 20.

A STAR CALLED HENRY

Author: Roddy Doyle (1958-   )
Publisher: Viking Press (New York). 343 pp. $24.95
Type of work: Novel
Time: 1902-1921
Locale: Dublin and rural Ireland

Born into the crushing poverty of Dublin's slums at the beginning of the century, Henry Smart from an early age makes his own way on the streets until, aided by his wits and good looks, he finds himself an actor in the great events leading to Irish independence

Principal characters:

HENRY SMART, the protagonist; born into poverty, early orphaned, swept into the Easter Rising of 1916, he finds that the streets and wonderful good looks are the right training for a revolutionary and lover
HENRY SMART, SR., the peg-legged bouncer at a brothel and a gangster's hit man; his brief contact with his son gave the lad invaluable skills
MISS O'SHEA, young Henry's schoolteacher for three days; later his wife and partner in revolution
GRANNY NASH, Henry's grandmother; the only remnant of his childhood, she spends all her time reading novels by female authors
PIANO ANNIE, a woman whom Henry meets during the Easter Uprising and lives with for a while until her husband returns from World War I
IVAN, a farm lad whom Henry recruits for the Irish Republican Army (IRA) and who later uses his power in his own self-interest
JAMES CONNOLLY, a historical figure who led the Irish Citizens' Army which took over the General Post Office in Dublin on Easter Monday, 1916
MICHAEL COLLINS, another historical figure; he led the campaign of violence against the British in the Anglo-Irish war, 1919-1921
JACK DALTON, Henry's old friend from early days in the uprising; his paranoia and his powerful position among the Dublin revolutionaries make him dangerous
DAVID CLIMANIS, a Latvian Jew, friend to Henry
ALF GANDON, the gangster who once employed Henry's father; he later comes to power in newly independent Ireland

A Star Called Henry represents Roddy Doyle's departure from fiction in contemporary settings and, in part, from the comic tone that has characterized his work since the late 1980's. However, in some of his work—*Paddy Clark, Ha Ha Ha* (1993) and *The Woman Who Walked into Doors* (1997)—Doyle portrays not only urban poverty but its inherent tragedy, two themes that are important in *A Star Called Henry*. This novel's greater innovation lies in its use of historical events—particularly Dublin's Easter Rising of 1916 and the violence of the years that followed—as a background for its fictional central character, Henry Smart. As the first volume of a proposed historical trilogy, *A Star Called Henry* covers only the first twenty years of Henry Smart's life, beginning in 1902 and ending on the eve of the 1921 treaty, which created an independent Ireland except, as it worked out, for the six Protestant northern counties.

This work follows the tradition of the picaresque novel, the episodic adventures of a rogue hero. Thus the novel's first section is devoted to Henry's first seven or eight years. He is born to Melody and Henry Smart, a couple doomed by their desperate poverty. Henry is their second son, the first, also Henry, having died in early infancy. This Henry, however, is notable for his glowing health and beauty, qualities that remain with him through his adolescence. Now his mother often shows him the star that she believes represents his brother. In fact, many of Henry's siblings die, even his favorite little brother, Victor, with whom he makes a sort of life on the streets for several years after their father, a one-legged bouncer in Dolly Oblong's brothel, abandons the family and their mother sinks into depression and madness.

Henry teaches Victor what he knows of stealing and cadging food; he even gets him into school for a few short days, thanks to the generosity of Miss O'Shea, a teacher rebellious enough to recognize Henry's ability and to sneak the boys past the school's regulations. The high point of this time is the sudden appearance of Henry's father when the boys are about to be trapped by an angry mob after they have disrupted a state procession for Edward VII, on the occasion of his visiting Dublin.

Henry, Sr., sweeps the boys out of the crowd and carries them to safety through the Dublin sewers, a territory he knows well from his work as a hit man. He has found the sewers an excellent place to dispose of bodies, as well as to make his own escapes. The pull of underground water—Dublin's streams as well as sewers—remains with Henry for the rest of his life and helps him make several close escapes. Henry receives another legacy from his father—the old man's wooden leg, which he keeps at his side through most of his adventures, a talisman and, more important, a weapon.

The second section is set during the Easter Rising of 1916. Henry has been recruited into the Irish Citizen Army, outfitted (and taught to read) by James Connolly, who has recognized his abilities and who now heads the ragged crew who have taken over the General Post Office. Henry is an able and resourceful fighter (thanks to his years on the streets), but he has no interest in Irish independence. "I didn't give a shite about Ireland," he says, but he does feel the excitement of great events, and he likes the violence. As he fires his rifle at the surrounding businesses, he feels as if he is shooting all the possessions denied to him and to all of his class. At the post office, he is present for historic proclamations of independence by national heroes including James Connolly and Patrick Pearse.

Also at the post office he finds his old teacher, Miss O'Shea again. She has left teaching for the life of a revolutionary, although she chafes at the way the men dismiss the women's abilities out of hand, relegating them to supplying tea and sandwiches. At the very moment the post office undergoes its first bombing, she and Henry are having epic sex in the basement (their coming together is so intense that Henry says her nipples left two pock marks on his forehead for the rest of his life).

The Rising is a military failure; English troops and weapons easily overpower the Irish, although it raises Irish consciousness. Henry remains oblivious to the issues. He moves in with Piano Annie (so named for her habit of playing popular songs on her partners' backs during lovemaking) and scrounges work on the docks until Annie's husband returns from the trenches of World War I and Henry himself is brought into the IRA by Jack Dalton. Thus he begins his real career as a terrorist, recruiting youth across the rural countryside and training them in the ways of guerilla warfare. When he and Miss O'Shea find one another again, they marry and become a terrorist team, always accompanied by the elder Henry's wooden leg. Henry refuses to learn his wife's first name.

Throughout their activities, however, Henry acts on his own agenda as well. He wants to know more about his father, and whenever he has the opportunity he bribes Granny Nash with books (she often reads two at a time), for she is his sole source of family history. She doles out facts parsimoniously, but gradually he realizes that his father worked not only for the brothel keeper Dolly Oblong but for Alfie Gandon, a thug who has now become involved in Irish politics. His father had imagined that Gandon and Dolly Oblong were really the same person, and was moved by romantic notions of Dolly's double life, but in fact, Henry realizes, his father had merely been Gandon's pawn, and when he was no longer useful, Gandon had killed him.

At the same time, Henry has become friends with David Climanis, a Latvian Jew, who seems like one of the last decent men in Dublin. Henry is shocked when Jack Dalton defends the killing of Climanis, claiming he was a spy. The last straw falls when Henry realizes that one of his recruits, Ivan (now called Ivan the Terrible), has become a sort of pirate, using terror to manage his district for his own gain.

Henry concludes that he has been a dupe, the stooge of the power bosses in Dublin who have used him and countless others like him not to promote the cause of independence but to manipulate the cause to further their power. They hold that power by terrorizing the innocent, and Henry and his wife have played into their hands. It is no accident that Alf Gandon, who used Henry's father before him, has now modified his name to O'Gandúin to appear more Irish, and is said to be running the country from a jail cell.

In the midst of the civil war that follows the creation of the Irish Free State, Henry renounces violence. He says farewell to his infant daughter and to his wife (in jail for terrorism) and strikes out for Liverpool at the age of twenty.

As a character, Henry Smart is an oddly compelling combination of terrorist, lover, and comedian. Despite his quick hand with revolver or wooden leg, Henry maintains a generous heart (that, along with his good looks, accounts for his appeal to women); witness his efforts at the General Post Office to find soldiers' pay for the destitute wives of men fighting for England in World War I or his fondness for David Climanis and his family. Despite his initial cynicism about the rebellion, he comes to have genuine hopes for the cause and grieves when they are dashed. Despite his braggadocio about his looks and his conquests—both military and amorous—Henry always maintains a central honesty that allows him to see into the heart of things, and always he has a core of good humor that takes the reader with him through blood, poverty, and disillusionment.

Like Doyle's earlier work, *A Star Called Henry* is full of the everyday grit of the lives of the poor, the taste of bad food, the odors of Dublin's sewers and polluted air, the clamorous sound of their voices. Indeed, the re-creation of everyday speech is one of Doyle's great strengths. It wobbles only when he recounts his thoughts as an infant (difficult to carry off, even with Henry's exuberant style).

Doyle's portrayal of the deterioration of the cause of Irish freedom into a sort of power politics played by amoral thugs has been commented on by some reviewers who have noted that such a picture contradicts the usual Irish understanding of their revolution. No people want to see their national heroes portrayed as scoundrels, but in fact the actual historical figures in this novel are rather remote after the General Post Office scenes, and the evils that attend the cause seem to come from the human failings of all the warriors rather than originating with the leaders. Even an ordinary farm boy like Ivan can develop a lust for power in the right circumstances, Doyle seems to suggest, and even the most hardened yobbo of the lot can grow disgusted with himself, get a new suit, and head for Liverpool.

Ann D. Garbett

Sources for Further Study

Booklist 95 (June 1, 1999): 1741.
Library Journal 124 (August, 1999): 137.
New Statesman 128 (September 6, 1999): 54.
The New York Times Book Review 104 (September 12, 1999): 7.
Publishers Weekly 246 (July 12, 1999): 70.
Time 154 (October 4, 1999): 102.

STIFFED
The Betrayal of the American Man

Author: Susan Faludi (1959-   )
Publisher: William Morrow (New York). 652 pp. $27.50
Type of work: History and psychology
Time: World War II to the end of the twentieth century
Locale: The United States

A cultural critique of the new cultural definitions of masculinity and the inadequate legacy of fathers toward sons in the post-World War II period

Susan Faludi is the author of *Backlash: The Undeclared War Against American Women* (1991) and a Pulitzer Prize-winning journalist. Her previous work dealt with the magnitude of men's resistance to women's struggle for equality and independence. This work starts with the query, "Why do men resist women's gains?" but quickly shifts focus to explore the new nature of manhood in a media-driven age.

Faludi introduces her subject with an allegory of a father-to-son inheritance: an artificial star, or satellite, appearing in the heavens before the joint gaze of the father and son (out of the reach of the mother in the kitchen), marveling at the newest frontier to master. It appeared that these World War II "fathers had made their sons masters of the universe," passing on an ethic of community responsibility, loyalty to job and family, and a clear set of skills to the sons. In the days of World War II, the real heroes were the ones honored in journalist Ernie Pyle's dispatches from the front (where he was killed by enemy fire shortly before the war's end). They were not the glamorous "flyboys" with silk scarves posing by fighter plane cockpits, but "little guys" who rose to acts of magnificent courage in the service of a common goal. By century's end this image of masculinity had morphed to a media-induced "ornamental culture" which valued only celebrity, the appearance of masculinity now defined by name recognition rather than by skilled production, and devoid of any larger social purpose.

Faludi chooses her definition of masculinity from a mix of New Deal social responsibility and the paternal mentoring of apprentices in the skilled trades, combined with a healthy mix of community participation, or, as one of my male friends put it, a female's ideal of what men should be. And, it should be clear from the outset, Faludi is in no way repudiating her feminism, or her critique of male and media attacks on women's modest gains in the workplace and the family. Rather, she is turning her journalist's skill to defining the experience of "the other side," that is, men, who certainly do not feel powerful or secure in their positions.

The bulk of this book consists of her interviews with selected men, which serve to illustrate the corruption of the masculine image, but they seem almost randomly chosen. Why, for example, has she devoted 70 pages to the story of loyal fan Big Dawg's despair at the Cleveland Browns leaving Cleveland in 1995, prefaced with a thumbnail sketch of economic indicators like the continued downsizing, corporate restructuring, and drop in men's real wages during that period? Or why has she chosen the young men of the Spur Posse (a gang-type group of Los Angeles youths whose claim to fame was their violent sexual exploits) to show the hollowness of "the sons'" aspirations? She pairs this exploration of American youth with the cadets at the Citadel (the all-male military academy in South Carolina that was forced to admit a young woman), whose violent, sexually charged sadistic hazing of junior classmen had already become a symbol of perverse masculinity run amok. Both groups spoke of loyalty and the dependency of the individual on the group as a prime virtue, but Faludi disavows their predatory behavior as a valid exemplar of masculinity. In *Backlash*, she noted that the prevailing definition of masculinity until the 1980's had been "good family provider," which was even then being undermined by economic facts of life: plant closings which put blue collar men on unemployment lines and then in service sector jobs paying only a fraction of their former wages. By the mid-1980's, another group of discontented, angry younger men had emerged in the pollsters' sights, men who were angry about their economically precarious position, and who blamed women for it. In *Backlash*, she handily debunked the claim that men's shrinking ability to be the good provider was attributable to women's taking "men's jobs"; women's gains were mainly at the lower-paid, female end of the labor force, and women were victims of these same economic shifts. Women became the scapegoats onto which society projected all of its fears.

In *Stiffed*, by contrast, she appears to blame "culture" for men's ills. Culture in this sense is a protean concept that seems to have no clear boundaries. The United States has changed, she states, from "a society that produced a culture to a culture rooted in no real society at all." The connections among this culture, economic forces, and social-psychological dynamics of father-son malaise seem ill-defined. Although she never loses sight of economic forces, they are "only surface symptoms," masking a deeper "crisis at the core, the need for a guiding father." The "fathers" to whom she refers are the fathers of the World War II generation, who could not prepare their "sons" for the transformation from a utilitarian to an "ornamental" culture where media image has become reality, usurping the role of real accomplishment, of making something tangible. Women have long been objectified by the culture, and the women's movement's response was to challenge it. Men now also are expected to present the appearance of masculinity, defined by a consumerism that depends on display. Men are not used to this, however, which has been associated with femininity, and have no way of naming or confronting it.

Faludi is at her best when she is telling these men's stories: members of the Christian Promise Keepers, the soldier present at the My Lai massacre during the Vietnam War, who refused to participate in the killing, a male porn star who was turning softy, actor Sylvester Stallone. However, she sets the scene for each of these personal histories in such overwhelming detail that it becomes difficult to see the relevance of each to her overall thesis. These oral histories seem to be used as epigrammatic of her theme rather than as evidence for it, and her historical vision goes back only as far as World War II. Pervading her description of each of these men's lives is an overwhelming sense of longing for a past (even one less than a decade ago), when things were different and they could feel pride in their crafts and their place as men. If one goes back to the late nineteenth century, however, Thorstein Veblen's scathing social commentary in *The Theory of the Leisure Class* (1899) made the distinction between productive and useful activities of industry and the conspicuous consumption and uselessness of the upper class. Veblen valued the "real work" of the engineer and the craftsman, who actually created something, and mercilessly mocked the foibles of the rich, whose only purpose was to show off their wealth. Faludi shares his nineteenth century disdain for ornament, and his notion of "real work," but not his link with an upper class as the basis for them. Rather, she extends the concepts to our entire culture, drawing on the pervasive drive for name recognition via the mass media.

The one group of men that epitomizes her ideal of the true masculine ethic of production is the Long Beach, California, naval shipyard workers. She provides readers with images of the immense machinery and utilitarian function of producing the great carriers of World War II, which buoyed a masculine identity based on the builder, not the warrior. These men (and now, some women also) were a mixture of racial and ethnic backgrounds; they referred to their relations on the job with father-son metaphors, and their loyalty to the job and the shipbuilding enterprise was betrayed by a mix of post-Cold War policies and private sector political clout that resented their productivity. As the shipyard closed, these men clung to their pride in workmanship. These "utility men" she then contrasts with men at McDonnell Douglas Aerospace, who also experienced layoffs in the early 1990's, but who, she contended, lacked the sense of utility that came from "real" production. The men she interviewed there were middle managers, who seemed unsure of what their real function had been. With the layoffs, they were consigned to reporting to the Outplacement Center, where they hung out all day as if they were still working. Some reported that they had not even told their wives they were not working; others were facing divorce. Men described their shame at not being able to support their families, at not being able to feel like men any more, of feeling castrated, emasculated. Faludi contrasts the frequently racist attitudes of these men, which "buttressed a masculinity based on exclusion and privilege," with the Long Beach shipyard workers' "ethic of inclusion and community."

The betrayal to which Faludi refers, however, is not the betrayal by a corporate class that used its workers, both blue and white collar, and then abandoned them when they became unnecessary to profits. Nor is it the misdirected scapegoating she amply documents (and deplores) that drives the homophobia and misogyny of the cadets at the Citadel. Rather, it is the loss of the "good father," who was a teacher of important skills, and who gave the sons opportunities to develop their own abilities. The refrain that she picks up is the men's plaint that their own fathers had somehow let them down—even when their fathers did play sports with them, they somehow felt empty—but the fathers of many of the men she interviewed had been simply absent, or even violently abusive.

For feminists of her era, she stated, it was easy to find "the enemy" and to work for change because the injustices were palpable to them. On the other hand, men were supposed to be privileged, the dominant group, in control of things. Yet men do not feel dominant or in control. Men in the domestic violence counseling group Alternatives to Violence certainly did not feel in control, except when they were abusing their partners. The downsized, the men rendered irrelevant, whose stories she chronicles here, certainly felt loss of control over their lives. For men now, however, there is no tangible enemy to fight. The men whose fathers did show them by example "how to be a man," were the ones who did so by "leading a meaningful life," such as by struggling against racism and social injustice. Although Faludi is an articulate opponent of race-based discrimination, and disapproves of the homophobic and antiwomen views many of these men expressed, she is less willing to name class as a cause of men's (and women's) desperation, despite all her talk about downsizing. For her, too, naming a problem is being well on the way to taking action to change it.

She takes issue with what represents only one strand of the feminist movement, which sees men as the enemy, and which she then disputes to show that men also are victims of a culture that denies them a socially meaningful identity. For many feminists, however, the problem lies not with men per se, but with a society supporting inequality based on class as well as on race and gender. Faludi's larger purpose here is to enlist both men and women in pursuit of a common goal. In places she almost names it: to bring about social transformation, based on an ethic of caring and social responsibility, which transcends gender.

Susan Lehrer

Sources for Further Study

Booklist 96 (September 15, 1999): 194.
The Economist 353 (November 13, 1999): 5.
Library Journal 124 (October 15, 1999): 90.
Maclean's, November 1, 1999, p. 70.
New York 32 (October 4, 1999): 53.
The New York Review of Books 46 (October 21, 1999): 25.
The New York Times Book Review 104 (October 3, 1999): 8.
Publishers Weekly 246 (September 13, 1999): 69.
Time 154 (October 4, 1999): 100.

T. S. ELIOT
An Imperfect Life

Author: Lyndall Gordon (1941-   )
Publisher: W. W. Norton (New York). 719 pp. $35.00
Type of work: Literary biography
Time: 1888-1965
Locale: St. Louis; Cambridge, Massachusetts; and London

A heavily revised and updated edition of the two-volume biography that made Gordon one of Eliot's most sensitive interpreters

Principal personages:
T. S. ELIOT, a poet
CHARLOTTE ELIOT, his mother
HENRY WARE ELIOT, his father
VIVIENNE ELIOT, his first wife
VALERIE ELIOT, his second wife
EMILY HALE, his close friend
EZRA POUND, his friend and adviser
BERTRAND RUSSELL, his teacher and Vivienne's lover
MARY TREVELYAN, his close friend
JOHN HAYWARD, his close friend and adviser
VIRGINIA WOOLF, one of his close Bloomsbury friends

Lyndall Gordon's previous volumes on T. S. Eliot, *Eliot's Early Years* (1977) and *Eliot's New Life* (1988), were hailed as a significant advance in the understanding of his life and work. *T. S. Eliot: An Imperfect Life* does not merely combine the earlier volumes; rather it is a rewriting of Gordon's understanding of Eliot, which takes advantage of new material (especially letters) that was not previously available. The result is a reconceived biography that probes the poet's character and his poetry even more deeply than did the earlier volumes.

Subtitles to biographies can be neutral ("a life") or provocative ("the untold story") or descriptive ("early years"). Gordon's choice of "an imperfect life" is both provocative and descriptive. It might also be deemed redundant. What life is not imperfect? In Eliot's case, however, the subtitle is apt. He was obsessed with his life, with all human life, as imperfection. He aspired to the rank of saint. He deplored his fallibility and the fact that he never attained a mystical vision of God, never experienced beatitude except in the most fleeting instances. Eliot found it difficult to tolerate his fellow men and women, to accept the world as it is with all its imperfections. As man and poet he strove to transcend time, to focus his imagination on the eternal. Life, in many ways, was a torment for him because it was so imperfect.

Eliot grew up in St. Louis, but he thought of New England as his spiritual home. The Eliot family had, in fact, a dark and distinguished history in Massachusetts. Like Nathaniel Hawthorne, Eliot was related to one of the judges at the Salem witchcraft trials. Like Hawthorne, Eliot grew up keenly aware of the ambiguity of human actions and distrusted the sincerity of human motivations. If anything, Eliot retained more of his Puritan background than Hawthorne did. As a young man, he regretted his family's decline (as he saw it) from the strict religious and moral code of Puritanism to a more relaxed and tepid Unitarianism. Gordon shows that Eliot's decision to join the Church of England was almost an inevitable outgrowth of his journey back to the seventeenth century, in which the religious imperative structured an individual's life. Indeed, the Church of England was not always structured enough for Eliot, who spent many years in a London flat saying the rosary each night.

Gordon's biography reveals how misunderstood Eliot was as a poet. Although he wrote in the modernist tradition, he was not a modernist who turned conservative. Rather his concern with modernity was always essentially religious. He was using modernist techniques such as stream of consciousness to expose the contemporary world as a wasteland filled with hollow men. He despised writers like H. G. Wells (1866-1946) and D. H. Lawrence (1885-1930) who celebrated human love and looked toward a future centered on the development of human consciousness alone. Man was incapable of creating utopias—sexual, political, or of any other kind—Eliot emphasized. As he wrote his first successful play, *Murder in the Cathedral* (1935), he thought of the characters called the evil tempters as writers like Wells and Lawrence.

The first part of Gordon's biography is a little congested with her analyses of Eliot's early verse. There is very little narrative drive until she enters upon his years in England. As soon as he meets and marries Vivienne Haigh-Wood, the biography takes on a verve and bite that is quite engrossing. Gordon presents a very detailed and moving portrait of Vivienne. A nervous woman, she was a talented writer who contributed excellent work to Eliot's journal, *Criterion*. Eliot often said that if not for Vivienne, he would have returned to Harvard, defended his Ph.D. dissertation, become an academic, and given up poetry. Vivienne, however, had faith in Eliot as a poet and convinced him that his future lay in the literary world in England.

Yet the marriage was not a success. Vivienne could not settle down, and the couple were not sexually compatible. Eliot seemed to cringe from the sexual act. It reminded him too much of his mortality and his imperfections. It distracted him from his quest for eternal truths. At the same time, he was hardly a prude. He wrote a good deal of dirty poetry, some of it racist and misogynistic, not to mention anti-Semitic. Gordon does not mince words about this deplorable side of Eliot.

The high-strung Vivienne drove Eliot into isolation. The more she wanted from him, the less he seemed able to give. She turned to other men, particularly to Bertrand Russell, who, in the guise of trying to help her, seduced her. Eliot thought his former teacher a scoundrel and often criticized him in print. However, he put up with Vivienne's mental breakdowns for more than eighteen years, and he did what he could. Not until he was invited to teach at Harvard did he decide to desert her, having his attorney write her a formal letter announcing a separation. Vivienne never could quite believe he had abandoned her, and she never stopped believing in him as a great poet. All her attempts to see him were foiled, save for one excruciating public confrontation at a poetry reading.

Eliot sought solace in a Boston friend, Emily Hale. He had apparently wanted to marry her before meeting Vivienne, but something in Hale's behavior led Eliot to believe she did not want him. After resuming a friendship with Hale in the 1930's he realized his mistake. He should have courted and married her. Now he felt it was too late. His feelings were very complicated. While Hale still expected him to marry her one day, Eliot felt he was not meant for marriage—or rather that the moment had passed him by (as he makes clear in his great poem *Four Quartets*). He felt guilty about Vivienne. It is not as though he simply thought he was at fault, but rather the wrecked marriage was one more sign of the imperfection of life. Although Emily Hale seemed to hold out the promise of a new life, Eliot evidently decided it was only an illusion.

With Hale keeping her hopes up, Eliot reconfigured his life in the 1940's, sharing a flat with the literary critic John Hayward and befriending Mary Trevelyan, an outgoing Englishwoman who also hoped to marry Eliot. There was no romantic relationship, however, and Eliot made clear he wanted none. He was celibate. Virginia Woolf (1882-1941) and Ezra Pound (1885-1972), among others, found this aspect of Eliot a mystery. Why did he pretend to be such an old fogy? Why did he behave with such elaborate courtesy? What was the basis for his stilted manner? Gordon shows that he feared too much human contact and that he was genuinely ascetic. He was a man perpetually trying to cleanse himself of sin and almost a parody of the Puritan—as Eliot himself well knew when he wrote the line "How unpleasant to meet Mr. Eliot."

After Vivienne died in 1947, Emily Hale thought that surely the time to marry had come. Eliot balked and eventually became belligerent, breaking off his relations with her. It is a very sad story. In part, Hale misperceived his attentions to her; in part, he seems not to have made his true intentions (a desire for intermittent companionship only) clear. Gordon sensitively reveals the breakdown of their love as a complex human story, so that there is no need to take sides.

Although Eliot continued to see Mary Trevelyan and enjoy her company, he also withdrew from her when their relationship seemed to get too intense. The more she pursued him, the more he withdrew. Eventually, as with Hale, the friendship failed. During this period (the late 1940's and early 1950's) Eliot thought of himself as a burned out case. His life was over. He had no more poetry to write. His plays were for a popular audience and represented a different (lesser) order of creation. He had, rather, his career as critic and public figure to uphold as a kind of civic and literary duty. It was a joyless life.

Then the remarkable event happened. It must have seemed to Eliot like a miracle. He fell in love with his young secretary Valerie. She had grown up reading his poetry. She had always wanted to work for him at his publisher's, Faber & Faber. Even after getting the job, however, she held back, giving the poet no inkling of her feelings. Gradually, however, as he grew to appreciate her competence and tact, he began to confide in her. It took eight years, but in that time the couple fell deeply in love, a fact Eliot kept from even his closest friends.

A photograph of Eliot and Valerie in Gordon's biography supports the cliché that a picture is worth a thousand words. The man is simply happy—perhaps for the first time in his life—completely happy, and it was a surprise to him and perhaps as much a mystery to him as it is to his biographer. It is no flaw in Gordon's book that she cannot say exactly how it is that Eliot came out of his shell and gave so much of himself in the last years of his life. Perhaps he felt he had done his penance. Perhaps Valerie's youth, enthusiasm, seriousness, and intelligence overwhelmed him with joy, and he saw that she would be the perfect caretaker of his estate as well as a loving wife. She came with no baggage, and with her he was frank about his own. She has said that he was the perfect husband, never a burden, and nothing like the cold, remote figure that other women found. It might almost be said that Eliot finally permitted himself a moment of love. In poor health, he knew he did not have much time left.

There are so many ways in which Eliot seems alien from his time, so many ways in which he is not very likable. Gordon does not blink at these facts. Indeed, she sometimes speaks simply as a woman who finds Eliot's behavior despicable, yet in her role as biographer she presents a story that is more complex than her own feelings about it. It is an extraordinary performance: to see the biographer on the page as a person who makes judgments and then steps back to say that in a biography such judgments are not appropriate or have to be transcended in the narrative of the book itself.

Gordon's biography, then, is a fine contribution not only to an understanding of Eliot but to an understanding of what is best in contemporary biography as well.

Carl Rollyson

Sources for Further Study

Booklist 95 (March 15, 1999): 1282.
Film Comment 35 (July, 1999): 68.
Library Journal 124 (May 15, 1999): 97.
The New York Times Book Review 104 (April 18, 1999): 10.
Publishers Weekly 246 (April 26, 1999): 65.
The Times Literary Supplement, January 17, 1997, p. 4.

TELLER OF TALES
The Life of Arthur Conan Doyle

Author: Daniel Stashower (1960-)
Publisher: Henry Holt (New York). Illustrated. 472 pp. $32.50
Type of work: Literary biography
Time: 1859-1930
Locale: Great Britain

An authoritative biography of Doyle, creator of the Sherlock Holmes detective stories and numerous other works

Principal personages:
ARTHUR CONAN DOYLE, famous writer and creator of the Sherlock Holmes stories
JEAN DOYLE, his second wife and a spiritualist

Arthur Conan Doyle is best remembered as the creator of the fictional "consulting detective" Sherlock Holmes and as the author of sixty mysteries featuring that character. This is no small honor, as Doyle's Sherlock Holmes stories have been popular with readers for more than one hundred years. The character of Holmes is almost universally recognized throughout the English-speaking world and beyond, with the stories translated into dozens of languages and Holmes's image appearing in newspaper advertisements and cartoons, on playing cards, as figurines, and through other media. The stories are a genre unto themselves and have inspired numerous writers to add their own Holmes stories alongside Doyle's "canon." Scores of plays, radio programs, and movies about Holmes also have been created, as have games, college courses, and songs. The character of Holmes is so embedded in literary folklore that many people believe that he actually lived.

The Holmes stories made Doyle famous in his day. That work helped make the author wealthy and even played a role in securing for him a knighthood in 1902, but Doyle was a remarkable man who accomplished considerably more than creating and writing the character of Sherlock Holmes. Indeed, Doyle frequently bemoaned the fact that Holmes's wild popularity obscured the author's "higher" and "more substantial" works.

Daniel Stashower's *Teller of Tales: The Life of Arthur Conan Doyle* portrays the writer in a way that Doyle himself would probably have appreciated. Only a small number of the 444 pages of text directly discuss what is sometimes called "Sherlockia": the origin of Holmes's name, the archetype of Holmes's character, the relationship between the character of Dr. Watson and Doyle himself, and other well-established trivia concerning the Holmes tales. Instead, Stashower seeks to present Doyle's life as he lived it, devoting relatively little time to the writing of the Holmes stories and focusing instead on his historical novels, his patriotic crusades, and in his later life, his spiritualism.

In examining these other aspects of Doyle's life, Stashower removes the Holmes creator from the shadow of his creation. Stashower presents in bold relief a complex, remarkable man whom Sherlock Holmes fans often dismiss as merely the "literary agent" of the writings (supposedly written by Dr. Watson). Doyle is shown to be an ambitious and talented individual, whose strong values, sense of purpose, and unbending chivalry made him a popular and influential person in Victorian and Edwardian Britain.

After very briefly describing Doyle's lineage (he came from a family of successful artists, although his father was an alcoholic who was eventually committed to an asylum) and his childhood (impoverished), Stashower details Doyle's training as a medical doctor, his efforts at writing during the long spells between patients, and his eventual transition to a full-time writer. The Holmes stories make up only a small portion of Doyle's written work, which also includes historical novels, science fiction, poetry, nonfiction monographs, plays, pamphlets, and other writings. Some of these enjoyed a good measure of popularity, including his novels *The Exploits of Brigadier Gerard* (1896) and *Sir Nigel* (1906).

Doyle remained a prolific writer for most of his adult life. With fame and wealth (provided largely through the Holmes stories), Doyle devoted his energies to a number of causes. For example, through public statements and writings he sought (with some success) to overturn the conviction of a man whom Doyle believed to be wrongly convicted of mutilating cattle and later was able to do similar service for a convicted murderer. In both cases, Doyle was seen as applying "Sherlockian" methods to clarify mysteries, prompting international attention to the cases and increasing his own reputation in the process.

With similar earnestness Doyle wrote pamphlets and essays to urge policy initiatives by the British government: encouraging the adoption of certain safety devices for the navy, calling for greater military preparations against the nascent threat of submarine attacks, opposing human rights abuses in the Belgian Congo, pronouncing on the negative consequences of the women's suffrage movement, and suggesting ways for managing Irish demands for home rule, among various other issues. A staunch defender of his country, Doyle wrote patriotic tracts supporting Britain's side in the Boer War and World War I. These were not merely armchair exercises: He served as a surgeon in South Africa for a time during the Boer War (after being rejected for military service), and he established a volunteer regiment to help defend Britain during World War I. He even ran twice for Parliament, though both times without success.

Doyle's fame, energetic drive, and talent in part led to his encounters with many Victorian literary and political giants. Oscar Wilde, George Bernard Shaw, Harry Houdini, James M. Barrie, Bram Stoker, Agatha Christie, David Lloyd George, Arthur Balfour, and many others passed through Doyle's orbit. Some became his friends, and some engaged in heated public disputes with him, but clearly Doyle had earned access to the highest circles of literature and social criticism.

All the more tragic, then, is the steady alienation of Doyle's friends and acquaintances as he became increasingly absorbed with spiritualism during his later years. Spiritualism was a kind of pseudoreligion that became popular around the beginning of the twentieth century, founded on the belief that the spirits of the dead continue to live in an afterlife and that those spirits can communicate with the living. Such communication is supposedly conducted through "mediums," sometimes accompanied by paranormal phenomena such as levitation, spectral appearances, and disembodied voices. In addition, mediums at times claimed the ability to use communication with spirits to divine secrets and to learn of future events.

Doyle's interest in spiritualism began rather early in his life, driven in part by his general fascination with the paranormal and supernatural, his strong desire to find purpose and meaning in life, and the death of his father, first wife, and children. At first Doyle's interest was that of a somewhat dispassionate researcher. He attended séances and read spiritualist literature, identifying possibilities for fraud and noting alternative explanations for seemingly supernatural actions. By the time of World War I, however, Doyle came to accept spiritualism with a faith that attends the most fervent religious believers. This conversion was abetted by his second wife, Jean, who claimed to possess the ability to channel spirit messages into writing through her own hand. Stashower speculates that Jean's discovery of her "gift" might have been prompted by a desire to comfort her husband in the face of a disbelieving world. Yet in this way Jean also virtually ensured that her husband would never again question spiritualism's truth, as he could never even imagine that his wife was capable of deceiving him.

Doyle's conversion to spiritualism provoked head-shaking disbelief that this man of common sense and keen reasoning should join a movement populated by charlatans, cranks, and dupes. To be sure, Doyle admitted that many "mediums" were undeniably frauds, but he argued that this fact should not indict all mediums. Doyle recognized the skepticism most people felt about spiritualism, but this knowledge merely increased his sense of missionary zeal. He devoted the final decade of his life almost entirely to promoting spiritualism.

Doyle's writings during this period essentially became propaganda for spiritualism. Even a final installment of his popular "Professor Challenger" stories was merely a thinly disguised tract to encourage a belief in spiritualism. Critics largely dismissed his work as unworthy of his earlier efforts, and newspapers such as *The Times* of London and *The New York Times* wondered aloud whether Doyle was going soft in the brain. These suspicions would increase with each new pronouncement by Doyle that a particular medium he had observed was unquestionably genuine, despite widespread evidence to the contrary. Perhaps the final straw was Doyle's pronouncement, after much examination and testing, that a photograph taken by a young girl depicting fairies at play was absolutely authentic. Doyle went on to write a book, *The Coming of the Fairies* (1922), which marshaled "evidence" of the existence of fairies. Doyle was now shunned by all but his most steadfast friends and family. Even many of his spiritualist allies now abandoned him as an embarrassment to the movement.

After mounting heart problems in his final months, Doyle died on July 7, 1930, at seventy-one years old. He was physically active and promoted spiritualism until the end. His death was followed by a flood of "messages" from Doyle, supposedly communicated to mediums. At the time, Doyle's passing seemed almost a merciful end to a life that had come to represent pathos, pain, and diminished greatness.

Daniel Stashower's recounting of Doyle's life is steadfastly sympathetic. While not avoiding the less flattering aspects of Doyle's life, such as his affair during the final years of his first marriage and his obsession with spiritualism, Stashower continuously reveals Doyle's true spirit. The reader can sense Doyle's unimpeachable honesty, integrity, humaneness, and chivalry. From start to finish Doyle's life was larger than life, but his heart is always grounded in such simple elements as family, community, and faith.

Overall, Stashower presents an authoritative, engaging, and entertaining biography of Arthur Conan Doyle. His thorough research involves numerous sources, including letters, manuscripts, interviews, and news articles. He writes in a polished, smooth style, with an underlying sense of warmth and humor. The book includes a select bibliography and an extensive index.

The biography is marred only by Stashower's need to apologize repeatedly for some of his subject's nineteenth century beliefs. Assuming that modern readers hold superior and near-unanimous beliefs about homosexuality, race, sexuality, gender relations, warfare, and other topics, Stashower either attempts to provide extenuating circumstances to excuse Doyle's pronouncements on these matters or tacitly emphasizes that Doyle's views are not being endorsed by the biographer. Doyle's purported offenses against late twentieth century political correctness are hardly felonious, and one would think that a modern reader naturally allows some latitude in word choice and social values for a denizen of a past century. Stashower's readiness to side against Doyle's "offensive" beliefs is all the more odd given that he treats Doyle's belief in spiritualism and fairies with kind, if somewhat condescending, tact.

That criticism aside, *Teller of Tales* is a valuable work for those interested in nineteenth century literature and culture, fans of the Sherlock Holmes stories, and general readers looking for an entertaining and thought-provoking story about a remarkable, very human, man. It is a valuable addition to the dozen other biographies on Doyle that have been written over the years, including two by Doyle himself.

Steve D. Boilard

Sources for Further Study

Booklist 95 (July, 1999): 1917.
The Economist 352 (July 17, 1999): 12.
Library Journal 124 (July, 1999): 89.
The New York Times Book Review 104 (September 12, 1999): 26.
Publishers Weekly 246 (July 5, 1999): 51.

THE TESSERACT

Author: Alex Garland (1970-   )
Publisher: Riverhead Books (New York). 273 pp. $24.95
Type of work: Novel
Time: The late 1990's
Locale: The Philippines

A variety of characters pursue their different interests only to meet in a violent climax

Principal characters:
SEAN, a British sailor alone in Manila
DON PEPE, a gangster who controls shipping in and out of Manila
JOJO,
TEROY, and
BUBOT, Don Pepe's bodyguards and henchmen
ROSA, a physician
RAPHAEL and
LITA, Rosa's children
CORAZÓN, Rosa's mother
ALFREDO, a psychologist who is studying the dreams of Manila street boys
TOTOY and
VINCENTE, subjects of Alfredo's research

In a note at the end of *The Tesseract*, Alex Garland writes: "Some definitions of a tesseract describe it as a hypercube unraveled, and others as the hypercube itself. I chose the version used here only because I happen to prefer it." This is not only a definition of the title of this novel; it is something of a description of its structure. Unfortunately, the meaning of the term is clear only to those with a prior knowledge of esoteric terms in mathematics. A title should clarify for the reader, not obfuscate. In this novel, it is clear only that several disparate elements meet in violent collision at a point where they intersect for no apparent reason.

At the beginning, a British merchant seaman named Sean is alone in a room in a shabby hotel in Manila, waiting for the arrival of Don Pepe, a mestizo gangster who extracts a fee from every ship that enters or leaves the port. The first mate of Sean's ship has sent him to plead with Don Pepe for free passage, since the ship cannot afford to pay the usual fee; Sean is to promise that in the future the ship's passage will be paid.

The sailor grows increasingly nervous as the time for the meeting comes closer. He is especially disturbed by the fact that the peephole in the door to his room has been covered, so the room's occupant cannot see anyone who might be outside. As he grows more nervous, he becomes more and more fixated on the pistol he carries. Don Pepe, in his limousine with three bodyguards, is on time for his appointment with Sean, despite a delay caused by a collision with a stray cat. Jojo the chauffeur has been ordered to kill the injured animal, and his shirt is splattered with blood as he does so. He thinks that Don Pepe has not noticed the incident, but in fact the Don has seen it all. The cat will assume greater significance later in the novel.

The Don and his three henchmen enter the hotel and knock on the door to Sean's room. By this time the sailor is in a state of panic. When the Don's aide knocks a second and then a third time, Sean appears in the doorway, firing his pistol. Don Pepe and Bubot are killed at once, and Sean makes his escape through the rotten wall of his room and down a corridor parallel to the one where Teroy and Jojo are firing shot after shot into Sean's room. Once they realize that he is no longer there, they set out on a mission of revenge, as if Don Pepe were still giving orders.

The second section of the novel concerns Rosa, a physician, her two children, her husband Sonny, and her mother Corazón. It is a domestic scene in which Rosa bathes the children, Raphael and Lita, while Sonny, driving home from work, is delayed by a flat tire, inflicted by two mischievous street boys. They will later appear as major characters, Vincente and Totoy.

Much of the section centering around Rosa is devoted to flashbacks (the book contains many of these) concerned with her earlier life on a small island in the Philippine archipelago. Her parents were poor but she was determined to get an education. Her parents sent her to stay with relations in Manila when she became infatuated with a young fisherman. Like other characters in the novel, including her son Raphael, the object of her love carries a disfiguring scar on his chest. In contrast with the passionate feelings Rosa bears for the scarred fisherman, those she has for her husband are not. Nevertheless, Rosa is one of the most sympathetic and admirable characters in the novel, nurturing her children and caring for her annoying mother, Corazón, while carrying on a career devoted to healing the sick.

The third set of characters in *The Tesseract* is a trio consisting of the psychologist Alfredo and two street urchins, Vincente and Totoy. Alfredo is a lonely man who pays the two boys to tell him their dreams, the most interesting of which are Vincente's. Another of the novel's many flashbacks makes clear that he has been brought to Manila by his father, who has left him, telling the boy to wait for his return, an event which never happens. There are suggestions that the father has been killed, although how, when, and for what reasons are unclear; the experience of being abandoned strongly affects the content of Vincente's dreams. Totoy is less valuable to Alfredo because he is prone to feed the investigator invented fantasies instead of actual dreams.

The two boys function as connecting links to the other stories. It is they who, as a prank, slash the tires on Sonny's car. Sonny, therefore, gets home late to Rosa and misses the gunplay; the boys' prank probably saves his life. In the same scene in which they slash Sonny's tires in their race on foot across the city, pursuing the gangsters who are pursuing Sean, an interjection from the anonymous narrator asks who would kill a cat, and provides several answers. The individuals listed are as disparate a group as the principal characters, including first a rich college boy, who is knocked off of his motor bike by the sudden appearance of the cat in his headlights and angrily shoots it with a gun given to him by his father. His only connection to any other part of the story is that he encounters the cat in the same quarter of Manila as the hotel where Sean shoots Don Pepe.

The others mentioned act from differing motives. A bitterly disillusioned policeman shoots a cat on his way to committing suicide. A crazed woman shoots any cat she sees because her child died from an infection caused by a scratch. A drug addict is ready to demonstrate his power by killing anything that moves. Finally there is a bare list of those characters, stripped to a single motive or way of living: "A cat hater. A mouse lover. A rat protector. A gangster's chauffeur."

The cat is obviously several cats, since a single cat could not die several times, despite the proverbial nine lives attributed to felines. The cat killed by Jojo on the orders of Don Pepe is the only one whose death is described in detail and therefore represents the deaths of all the cats and by extension of all living things. Further, since the cat which Jojo so brutally, if reluctantly, kills is dispatched before any human is killed, its death is a precursor to the deaths of Don Pepe and the others which follow.

These deaths are at the hands of Jojo and Teroy, thoughtlessly following a code that dictates that they shall exact vengeance for the death of their chief, not realizing that there is no reason for them to do so. They do manage to kill Sean, but their wild shooting also kills Corazón, Rosa's mother. Rosa herself is used by Sean as a human shield and narrowly escapes with her life, while Vincente, after a long chase after Jojo and Teroy, appears to be dead, but is not.

Garland is speculating, in *The Tesseract*, about chance and fatality, and reaches the same bleak conclusions that he arrived at in his earlier novel, *The Beach* (1996). In his world there is no justice; people do not earn or deserve what happens to them. There is no connection between behavior and fate. Neither does Rosa's early love affair with a young fisherman win her education, her release from poverty, or her career, nor does the illicit nature of that relationship earn her punishment. Further, as a dialogue with her daughter makes clear, her career does not make her a hero. The fact that she is spared while Sean uses her as a shield from the guns of gangsters is in no way a reward for heroism or virtue. It is dumb luck.

Garland compiles an impressive roster of the dead: Don Pepe and Bubot, Sean, a number of cats, Corazón, and Rosa's young lover. It is surprising that the psychologist Alfredo, whose only activity seems to be reading, is not on the list, since his life is so barren, but in the end he even accepts a demanding invitation from a friend, which will amount to a blind date. For no discernible reason, he is spared even an encounter with the gangsters. Don Pepe and Bubot, evil as they are, no more deserve death than does Corazón or Rosa's former lover, who somehow wanders into the story toward the end. All events are random; the only law which operates is chance.

Garland's earlier novel won praise for the depth of its thought and his intelligence; this may have influenced him in unfortunate directions. The story, the sense of dread that hangs over the characters, and the crispness of some of the characterizations are evidence of an imposing talent, one which does not require the obfuscation provided by the title and the author's failure to explain it.

John M. Muste

Sources for Further Study

Booklist 95 (February 1, 1999): 958.
Library Journal 124 (February 15, 1999): 152.
National Review 51 (May 31, 1999): 68.
The New York Review of Books 46 (November 4, 1999): 25.
The New York Times Book Review 104 (May 2, 1999): 34.
Publishers Weekly 246 (March 15, 1999): 41.

THE TESTAMENT

Author: John Grisham (1955-   )
Publisher: Doubleday (New York). 435 pp. $27.95
Type of work: Novel
Time: 1996-1997
Locale: Washington, D.C., and the Pantanal region of Brazil

An eccentric billionaire starts a family feud and an enormous legal battle by leaving his entire estate to a previously unknown daughter, said to be a missionary living among aboriginal Brazilians

Principal characters:
TROY PHELAN, a ruthless, lecherous, self-made billionaire
NATE O'RILEY, a forty-eight-year-old Washington, D.C., trial lawyer facing ruin because of acute alcoholism and career burnout
RACHEL LANE, Troy Phelan's middle-aged illegitimate daughter, heir to his entire estate, who is working as a missionary-physician in the Brazilian jungle
JOSH STAFFORD, Phelan's trusted lawyer, executor of his eleven-billion-dollar estate
JEVY, Nate O'Riley's powerful, happy-go-lucky, young Brazilian guide, who speaks both Portuguese and English
HARK GETTYS, one of the attorneys contesting Phelan's will on behalf of Phelan's six legitimate children
MALCOLM SNEAD, Troy Phelan's personal assistant for the past thirty years

The Testament is a change of pace for popular legal-thriller writer John Grisham. His latest novel takes the reader deep into the jungles of Brazil, where a devout, middle-aged missionary-physician, who has turned her back on civilization, is unaware that she is heir to an eleven-billion-dollar estate, which is growing at about two million dollars a day. Nate O'Riley, once a dynamic trial lawyer, is released from the sanatorium where he is recovering from yet another relapse into dipsomania and given the assignment of finding Rachel Lane, illegitimate daughter of Troy Phelan. No one even knew that Phelan had an illegitimate daughter until he named her his sole heir in a holographic will just before leaping out his fourteenth-floor office window to his death.

The old tycoon had six legitimate children from three marriages. They range from Troy Phelan, Jr., who is in his late forties, to Ramble Phelan, an obnoxious, aspiring punk rocker who is only fourteen. They consider themselves the only rightful heirs, and all hire lawyers to contest their father's will. The lawyers gather like hyenas around a fresh carcass. Some of them are eventually eliminated by infighting, while the survivors join forces behind Hark Gettys, who is smarter and more unscrupulous than any of the others. They agree they must contest the will on the grounds that Phelan was mentally incompetent when he signed the document in the presence of many witnesses, including three reputable psychiatrists who all found him completely sane, and then committed suicide because he had just gotten tired of living. The lawyers have agreed to pay Malcolm Snead, Phelan's chief assistant for the past thirty years, five million dollars for falsely testifying that the old man had been growing increasingly insane for several years before composing his final testament. They are hoping that if they put up a strong enough fight, the executor of the estate, Joshua Stafford, will offer to settle out of court. All six legitimate children and their three mothers are portrayed as parasites who have already wasted most of the millions they were able to get from Phelan during his lifetime. Phelan felt he had already given them more than they deserved, and he certainly did not want any of them to have a hand in running his corporate empire.

The narrative alternates between the flooded, mosquito-infested, infernally hot Pantanal region of Brazil and the plush, air-conditioned homes and offices of Washington, D.C., and its sprawling suburbs. By the time Nate O'Riley makes it to Corumbá, a polyglot boomtown of ninety thousand on the Paraguay River, he has come to realize that his biggest problem will not be in finding Rachel Lane but in staying sober. He still has an irresistible craving for liquor. He demonstrates this by nearly killing himself with a bottle and a half of cheap vodka on the night before he is scheduled to start upriver.

After a series of misadventures on a bewildering labyrinth of rivers filled with alligators and anacondas, Nate finally gets to meet Rachel Lane. She is a slender, softspoken, compassionate woman in her early forties, who has lived among the same dwindling population of Ipicas for the past eleven years. She is not the least bit interested in money, and Nate cannot persuade her to sign a document accepting Phelan's bequest. In fact, he cannot even get her to discuss the estate because of her bitterness toward her father. She does enjoy spending time with Nate, however, because she has no opportunities to speak English among the Ipicas, a population virtually unknown to the rest of the world. A platonic love relationship develops between a man who thought he was interested only in money and a woman who is interested only in serving God by serving humanity.

The rivers are infested with clouds of mosquitos, many carrying malaria and dengue fever germs. When Nate starts back toward Corumbá in a small, open boat (the larger craft that carried him upriver having sunk in a storm), he is seized with chills and fever. He has succumbed to dengue fever, a disease deadlier than malaria. While he is lying near death in a primitive hospital, Rachel Lane appears at his bedside and assures him that he is not going to die, because God has plans for him. When he finally recovers, he searches the town for the missionary but can find no trace of her. Everyone assures him he must have been having hallucinations.

The viewpoint character—and the only character in the novel who changes—is Nate O'Riley. His dramatic conversion after his brief encounter with the dedicated missionary seems incredible. It is reminiscent of the spiritual transformation that supposedly occurred to journalist Henry Morton Stanley when he found British missionary Doctor David Livingstone on the shores of Lake Tanganyika in 1871 and greeted him with the famous words, "Doctor Livingstone, I presume." Stanley, however, spent many months with Livingstone in Africa, whereas Nate manages to spend only a few hours with Rachel in the Brazilian jungle. Nevertheless, such is the charismatic missionary's spiritual influence that Nate feels completely disgusted with his old life when he gets back to Washington, D.C.

> At some undefined point in his life, pushed by his work and his addictions, he had lost decency and shame. He had learned to lie, cheat, deceive, hide, badger, and attack innocent witnesses without the slightest twinge of guilt.

Even without Rachel's signed authorization, Nate takes it upon himself to defend her interest against the greedy, desperate relatives and their unscrupulous attorneys. This, he decides, will be his last case. He will find some other way of earning a less glamorous but more honest and more satisfying living. He will also try to reestablish some sort of relationship with the children of his two broken marriages. Somewhat miraculously, he has lost his craving for alcohol. During a lull in the court case, he drives across the country to visit his two younger children in Salem, Oregon, and then goes on to Evanston, Illinois, where he has a far less satisfactory meeting with his college-aged son. His grown daughter deliberately stands him up in Pittsburgh; she feels so bitter that she does not want to have anything more to do with him. Finally he is summoned back to Washington, where Josh Stafford has arranged a meeting with all six of Phelan's legitimate children and their representatives to try to work out a financial settlement.

The emotional upheaval aroused by his experiences with his own children has made Nate more sympathetic toward the children of Troy Phelan. Like Nate's children, Phelan's six offspring grew up with an absentee father who was totally absorbed in materialistic enterprises and thought he could substitute money for affection. They are hardly to blame for the way they turned out. Nate, posing as Rachel's representative, surprises everyone by agreeing to a settlement more generous than their greatest expectations. He quickly gathers all the necessary signatures on the dotted lines—all except for Rachel's. Now Nate has to go back to the Brazilian jungle and try to persuade the obstinate woman to accept an estate worth at least five billion dollars after the relatives, their lawyers, and the Internal Revenue Service collect their shares. Nate thinks he can persuade Rachel to accept the inheritance because she could build hospitals, purchase badly needed medicine and equipment, and create schools, not only for her own flock but for all the dwindling indigenous populations in the Pantanal. As his chartered helicopter heads for the isolated village where he first encountered the dedicated missionary, Nate is in for the surprise of his life.

Characterization, as critics have often pointed out, is not Grisham's strong suit. Most of the money-hungry lawyers remain two-dimensional figures, as do the bickering heirs. Grisham does not consider himself a great writer but merely a competent professional who provides commercial entertainment for the masses. He does, however, manage to create strong identification with his renegade hero, Nate O'Riley, and this is sufficient to keep the reader turning the pages right up to the surprise ending. The term most often used by reviewers to describe a Grisham novel is "page turner."

The millions of Grisham addicts can always count on the emotional payoff of a surprise ending as well as a good story.

Grisham's first novel, *A Time to Kill*, was published in 1989 and sold millions of copies after getting off to a slow start. Since then he has been turning out novels at the rate of about one per year, and every one has been a best-seller. Grisham's books have been translated into thirty-four languages and have been number-one best-sellers in eight countries. Many of his novels, including *The Firm* (1991) and *The Client* (1993), have been made into films and have featured such stars as Tom Cruise, Gene Hackman, Ed Harris, Julia Roberts, Denzel Washington, Susan Sarandon, and Tommy Lee Jones. *The Testament* had a first printing of 2.8 million hardcover copies and a second printing within the first week. The book's cinematic potential, with the Brazilian jungle and the inside look at the skulduggery of Washington, D.C., is obvious.

Critics have complained that Grisham writes the same novel over and over again. It features the crusading outsider fighting a desperate battle against a horde of legal sharks motivated by greed and a passion for notoriety and conspicuous consumption. One of the secrets of Grisham's truly phenomenal success is that even though he was a lawyer and a politician himself, he shares the same low opinion of lawyers and politicians held by the person on the street. He is able to articulate the contempt that his readers feel intuitively, and he can provide documentation to support it.

In *The Testament*, however, Grisham seems to be trying to move in a new direction, as well as to turn out a book that does something more than merely entertain. He is using the "bully pulpit" he has earned as one of the world's most widely read authors to call attention to the destruction of the Brazilian rainforest and its native inhabitants. These pathetic people, who have nothing, are being driven to extinction by powerful lumbering, mining, and agricultural interests. When Portuguese explorer Pedro Alvares Cabral first entered Brazil in 1500, there was an estimated native population of five million, speaking 1,175 languages. Five hundred years later, only 270,000 native peoples survive, speaking 170 languages. They died of smallpox, measles, yellow fever, influenza, and tuberculosis, all diseases brought by colonists. They were enslaved, slaughtered, or driven off their land. In 1967, it was reported that Indians were deliberately murdered with chemical and bacteriological weapons. They were bombed with deadly bacteria from airplanes and helicopters. The agency in charge of native populations was issuing clothing deliberately infected with smallpox and tuberculosis germs.

The world already knows about the terrible ecological implications of destroying the irreplaceable rainforests of South America, but it knows little, if anything, about the plight of the native inhabitants. They are regarded by the encroaching entrepreneurs as little better than alligators, anacondas, or monkeys, who will have to be exterminated in order to turn the virgin forests into lumber and packaging materials and in order to clear the land for cattle destined to be served as hamburgers. Part of Grisham's mission in *The Testament*, it appears, is to testify to these injustices.

Bill Delaney

Sources for Further Study

Booklist 95 (January 1, 1999): 831.
Library Journal 124 (January, 1999): 148.
New Statesman 127 (September 4, 1998): 48.
New York 32 (February 15, 1999): 59.
The New York Times Book Review 104 (March 7, 1999): 12.

TIME, LOVE, MEMORY
A Great Biologist and His Quest for the Origins of Behavior

Author: Jonathan Weiner (1953-)
Publisher: Alfred A. Knopf (New York). 300 pp. $27.50
Type of work: Biography and history of science
Locale: University and other biological research laboratories in the United States and elsewhere

A compelling narrative of Seymour Benzer's search for the connection between genes and behavior

Principal personages:
SEYMOUR BENZER, a physicist, biologist, geneticist, and cofounder of molecular biology
SIDNEY BRENNER, a biologist
FRANCIS CRICK, the codiscoverer of the deoxyribonucleic acid (DNA) double helix
MAX DELBRÜCK, a Caltech biologist
JEFF HALL, an early postdoctoral student of Benzer and cocloner of *period*
DEAN HAMER, a molecular biologist at the National Institutes of Health
RONALD J. KONOPKA, the discoverer of the *clock* mutants
EDWARD LEWIS, a researcher of fly mutants at Caltech
BARBARA MCCLINTOCK, a plant geneticist and Nobel laureate at age eighty-one
THOMAS HUNT MORGAN, a biologist and Nobel laureate
CHIP QUINN, a biologist who researched memory in flies
MICHAEL ROSBASH, a molecular biologist
ERWIN SCHRÖDINGER, a German quantum physicist
GUNTHER STENT, a cofounder of molecular biology
ALFRED HENRY STURTEVANT, a discoverer of gene mapping
JAMES D. WATSON, a cocreator of the double helix model of DNA
EDWARD O. WILSON, a Harvard sociobiologist

A simple glass milk bottle, the so-called fly bottle, that common and unglamorous tool of many research biologists, has been the scene of some of the most significant discoveries of the twentieth century in genetics and molecular biology. *Time, Love, Memory: A Great Biologist and His Quest for the Origins of Behavior* recounts the story of the work of many scientists but especially that of Seymour Benzer, who did basic research using genetic dissection, an approach that he "had started . . . with single genes . . . working up to behavior" in a fly room at the California Institute of Technology (Caltech). He invented the "countercurrent machine," a panpipe arrangement of nesting test tubes that would allow the flies to sort themselves according to the persistence of their attraction to light, a behavior that made *Drosophila* "the perfect creatures with which to found a new science, an atomic theory of behavior." This approach revealed the connection between genes and behavior and, along with the work of scores of his students and fellow scientists, established the science of molecular biology, one of the two most important sciences of the twentieth century.

Benzer was one of a handful of scientists who began to look seriously at the question, what are the connections, the physical connections, between genes and behavior? Jonathan Weiner crisply narrates the stories of Benzer and a host of other biologists, a number of whom, like Francis Crick and Benzer himself, began their scientific careers as physicists. Their work has brought molecular biology to the point at which the Human Genome Project is nearly complete and the promise (or threat) of determining the behavioral and physical traits of nearly any—perhaps all—species is a reality.

Weiner's book traces the development of molecular biology from the beginning of the twentieth century to the present in a narrative packed with good science; fascinating personal profiles of scientists, students, and scholar-adventurers; and stories of triumph and failure. Weiner is an excellent scientific writer, splendidly informed and fully engaged in his topic. To research this topic he interviewed more than 150 scientists, participated in seminars at Princeton University, and read hundreds of papers published by the men and women who created molecular biology. Led by James D. Watson, Francis Crick, and Seymour Benzer, biologists working variously with *E. coli*, *Drosophila*, nematodes, and birds sought to answer basic questions about an organism's behavior and whether instinct was actually hardwired at the level of the gene or, even more specifically, at the level of the atom.

The story of the invention of molecular biology, the discovery of the gene, and the proof of the connection between behavior and genetic anatomy is, throughout, the story of people. One of the facets of this book that is especially appealing is the reiterated instances of the close mentoring bond that existed between and among so many of the scientists and their students. Thomas Hunt Morgan's student, Alfred Sturtevant, created the first genetic map and followed Morgan from Columbia University to Caltech; Max Delbrück's student Salvador Luria worked on bacteriophage. By 1953, when workers had worked out a nearly complete map of the phage chromosome, Benzer, still nominally a physicist at Purdue University, created a brilliant experiment in which he infected a plate of bacteria with two strains of the defective *r* mutants of the phage virus, splitting the *rII* and leading to "the explosions of genetic mapping and genetic engineering that now dominate biology." By the summer of 1956 he had created from his replications of this simple but elegant experiment a version of the code of codes, a gene map of the fine structure of the *rII* region of a phage chromosome. He kept the map rolled up like a Torah scroll and would dramatically unroll it at conference presentations. It is this mapping that has grown to the nearly finished Human Genome Project, the Manhattan Project of biology.

Benzer's work with phage kept him busy for ten years before he became bored and looked for some new interest to catch his fancy. That turned out to be his search for the "atoms of behavior," the connection of the molecules of the gene to personality, the traits of character and instinct. How is behavior inherited? To answer this question he turned to reading everything he could find about the inheritance of behavior, as did his friends Sidney Brenner, Gunther Stent, and Delbrück, who wanted "to take instincts apart the way Benzer had taken apart the gene."

Benzer in particular wanted to build on the genetic foundation so well prepared by physics, chemistry, genetics, and ethology to find "something new about some of the oldest cornerstones of human experience—time, love, and memory—and the oldest cornerstones of heredity, nature, and nurture." He wanted to work "from the gene to the neuron to the brain to behavior," having already successfully dissected the gene. He wanted "to go from the gene to the kinds of instincts that ethologists studied out in the wild. . . . the imprinting of goslings on geese, the mating dances of ducks." Benzer's invention of the countercurrent machine in 1966 at Caltech, and Edward Lewis's suggestion that he use a poison called ethyl methane sulfonate, a popular mutagen, gave him the means by which he could create huge numbers of mutants and quickly sort them on the basis of their attraction to light. He found the experiments interesting, but he had no goal in mind, no idea where such work could lead. However, that sorting led to his identification and location of a phototropic gene and, within a few years, to the identification of other genes such as *clock* (discovered by Benzer's student Ronald J. Konopka), *period*, *fruitless*, and many others. Chip Quinn and Benzer discovered that *Drosophila* could be "educated," that is, some of the flies could be trained to avoid light; others, however, could not. This observation led to the mapping of *dunce*, a gene that "lies on the far left tip of the X chromosome, just a few map units from *white* and from the mutants of Konopka, the mutants that lost the sense of time." The importance of this discovery was that it gave researchers a "point of entry into the mechanisms that allow each of us to accumulate histories and apply the lessons we have learned at our choice points," a quality that many religious thinkers call "agency." For Jonathan Weiner, the most amazing quality of these extraordinary discoveries was that Seymour Benzer allowed his students to leave his lab with his mutants in their pockets, so to speak, to build careers on them, each gene opening extraordinary views into the behavior of the human family.

Perhaps even more astounding was the discovery of P elements, genes "that do not stay in one place in chromosomes" or "jumping genes." They act as shuttles carrying other DNA into other chromosomes. Geneticist Barbara McClintock earned a Nobel Prize at age eighty-one for her work with purple, white, and spotted kernels of maize at Cold Spring Harbor. "Then molecular biologists discovered jumping genes in *E. coli*, *Drosophila*, and human beings," including *mariner*, first discovered in *Drosophila*. Building on this and similar discoveries in molecular biology, Michael Rosbash and Jeff Hall were able to explore "the molecular links between genes and behavior." By constructing a complete DNA library of "snipped DNA ribbons, so that they could inject each fragment of DNA into a single fly egg and test the fragments one by one," they then injected *period* into time-blind flies. In 1984 Hall and his students decided that "they had done it; they had injected the first piece of behavior into the genes." Papers announcing this achievement were published in 1984 and 1985; the implication was that such genetically engineered behavior could be injected into any species. Understanding behavior at the molecular level therefore comes down to metabolism regardless of the behavior or the species.

Benzer, who had started this research, could have been the sort of champion for the atomic theory of behavior that Watson had become for genetics after he and Crick had built the double helix model for DNA in 1953, but he had moved on again, studying more and more deeply the nervous system of the fly, discovering that although human brains are fancier than fly brains, "they are made of the same stuff." In 1978 Delbrück gave the commencement address to Caltech's seniors and argued that the atomic theory of behavior was a grand but ultimately futile attempt to unite behavioral biology and the humanities. Yet the Human Genome Project may prove Max Delbrück wrong. Further work in the late 1980's developed tools to enable researchers not only to map genes to their chromosomes but also to discover what protein each gene makes.

What makes Weiner's book so fascinating is, of course, not just the facts of the scientists' work on this or that aspect of the science. With his clear exposition, narrative power, and capacity for characterizing the human players in this ongoing drama, Weiner makes the reader see the full scope and sweep of each discipline as it developed and led into the next. For example, Carol Benzer's work on Alzheimer's disease depends in part on Seymour's fly stains and perhaps on the work of his Korean postdoctoral student, Kyun-Tai Min, who has used that super tool, the electron microscope, to try to find fly brains and human brains with similar problems. Another team has attacked the problem of memory, successfully defining at the molecular level the steps involved in making lasting memories. In the 1990's, another researcher, Dean Hamer, discovered that somewhere "within about four million base pairs on the tip of the long arm of the X chromosome there might be a gene that might somehow relate to the sexual orientation of the men in his particular study." Despite Hamer's very qualified and tentative findings, his story lit up the news media in sensational fashion, as did his announcement in 1996 of his discovery of a "happiness gene." And so it goes. Thus, Weiner offers the caution of Edward O. Wilson that we are ignorant "of the meaning of human existence in the first place" as check on the too exuberant rush to anoint biogenetics in any of its forms as the key to human happiness. Each experiment, each discovery, reminds one of the reality of moral dilemmas and decisions, no matter that they may be constructed as mechanically as the "patterns that were laid down first by the genes and the growing nerves in the embryo, then by a lifetime of choices inside that gray-brown sheet." Francis Crick has even begun to reflect on the possibility that genetic dissection of the brain's frontal lobes may provide the "answer to the problem of free will" and why humans make the choices they do.

Time, Love, Memory continues Jonathan Weiner's excellent work in making a scientific field accessible to a wider audience without condescension or distortion. Perhaps this book will, like Sinclair Lewis's *Arrowsmith* (1925), James D. Watson's *The Double Helix: A Personal Account of the Structure of DNA* (1968), or even Erwin Schrödinger's *What Is Life? The Physical Aspect of the Living Cell* (1943), inspire young scientists to follow their passionate curiosity into further discoveries.

Theodore C. Humphrey

Sources for Further Study

Christianity Today 43 (August 9, 1999): 70.
Los Angeles Times, March 9, 1999, p. E1.
The New York Times Book Review 104 (April 4, 1999): 17.
Newsweek 133 (February 15, 1999): 65.
Publishers Weekly 246 (February 1, 1999): 78.

'TIS
A Memoir

Author: Frank McCourt (1930-)
Publisher: Charles Scribner's Sons (New York). 367 pp. $26.00
Type of work: Memoirs
Time: The 1950's to the 1980's
Locale: New York City and Ireland

This sequel to McCourt's 1996 memoir Angela's Ashes *chronicles the writer's return to New York*

Principal personages:
FRANK MCCOURT, the author and narrator
ANGELA MCCOURT, his mother
ALBERTA MCCOURT, his wife
MALACHY,
MICHAEL, and
ALFIE, his brothers
MAGGIE MCCOURT, his daughter
EMER, an Irish girl who jilts the author

In *'Tis*, Frank McCourt's sequel to his immensely popular candid memoir *Angela's Ashes* (1996), young McCourt has finally made it back to the United States. As the previous book stated, the author was born in post-Depression Brooklyn, New York, and brought by his bankrupt Irish parents to Limerick, Ireland, where things go from bad to worse in this gray city by the disease-ridden Shannon River. McCourt spends his younger years in abject poverty, enduring starvation, disease, his drunken father's abandonment, the malnutrition deaths of younger siblings, his mother's begging on the streets, and the mean-spirited, repressive Catholic Church. Throughout, he looks toward America as the garden of paradise, using all his wits to return to her golden shores.

For the overwhelmed nineteen-year-old, however, 1949 America does not nearly live up to his mystic visions. McCourt's first loss of innocence centers on a Catholic priest who befriends him on his voyage from Ireland. Reluctant to leave the youngster alone in New York City, the priest takes him to dinner, then a hotel room where he attempts a sexual encounter. Dismayed, the bewildered youth lands on his feet and soon finds a job cleaning the lobby of the New York Biltmore Hotel, thanks to the powerful Irish Democrats. Deeply ashamed of his appearance—a chronic eye condition and rotten teeth—McCourt suffers acute embarrassment, especially around the young American college girls who gather in the lobby to meet upper-class boyfriends. As he did as a child in Ireland, McCourt finds refuge in the library reading, in particular, Fyodor Dostoevski's *Crime and Punishment* (1866). After sending most of his wages home to his mother Angela in Ireland, the youngster finds a room in a boardinghouse where a landlady watches his every move and monitors even his use of the electric light. He spends his first American Christmas in the drunken company of this Swedish landlady and her demented glug-drinking sister. As McCourt points out, no one in Limerick would believe his first American Christmas.

The Korean War serves as the catalyst that boosts McCourt's step up the American social ladder. After Army basic training, he is stationed in Germany as a military dog trainer. The young man learns more about life, realizing in postwar, poverty-stricken Germany that Ireland does not hold a monopoly on misery. Here, the women sell themselves for a pound of coffee or a few packs of cigarettes. Forced to give up his canine unit, McCourt learns to type, as he claims, faster than any other Army clerk in Europe. Germany's proximity to Ireland allows a visit while on furlough. Wearing his American Army uniform, he earns accolades from his old Limerick neighbors, but he still finds his family almost in the same depths of poverty as when he departed. Before he leaves, McCourt makes a brief visit to Northern Ireland to see his father, who abandoned the family when the author was ten years old. However, the young soldier leaves in great consternation when he discovers that his family in the north blames his mother for his drunken father's unconscionable behavior. Before he leaves Ireland, the McCourts move into newer accommodations. After his discharge, he returns to New York ready to settle down with an Irish girl with whom he corresponded during the war.

However, the romance with Emer fails to ripen. McCourt, working now as a warehouse laborer, spends much of his time, and most of his money, drinking with his chums. Living in another run-down rooming house owned by an Irish, holier-than-thou landlord, McCourt becomes increasingly despondent. Emer wants an educated man and a good provider, but McCourt's lack of initiative excludes him from the running. After she takes up with an insurance man, the jilted young man decides he will don a suit and work 9 to 5 in the insurance industry to win her back. All this happens to no avail, as McCourt quits in disgust. However, the effort brings him one step closer to the education he needs to realize his real calling as a gifted English teacher at Stuyvesant High School and city colleges. In a particularly heroic gesture, McCourt walks into New York University with the G.I. Bill in hand. Without a high school diploma, he is placed on probation and begins his studies.

In college, McCourt feels lost for a while. Deeply ill at ease, he finds it difficult to tell if the professors praise or ridicule him. Ashamed of his looks and his Irish brogue, he keeps to himself, attempting to remain invisible at any cost. However, his ability to write soon posits him squarely in the spotlight when a professor reads his work to the class. Now, everyone knows about his background in Irish poverty. This works out well when an especially attractive classmate approaches him. Mike, otherwise known as Alberta, is a stunner. McCourt and Alberta have their ups and downs, moving in and out before eventually marrying.

Before they marry, however, McCourt acquires his degree and becomes a teacher in a Staten Island vocational school, where, initially, he feels entirely uncomfortable. Up to this point, his students have been neglected thoroughly by a retired predecessor who neither distributed books nor graded papers. Gaining authority and confidence for McCourt remains problematic for a while. In this venue, the demoralized McCourt finds his dreams once more shattered, as he assumes the job of day care worker rather than teacher and feels increasingly disconnected from life. This low-paying job seems to ensure his continuance in poverty. At one point, the electricity in his cold water flat is disconnected because he failed to pay the bill, though an upstairs neighbor plugs in an extension cord for him so he can continue to use his electric blanket for warmth.

By this time, his younger brother Malachy McCourt, author of *A Monk Swimming* (1997), owns a popular Manhattan bar and has become a radio and television celebrity. Understandably, McCourt feels jealous, especially because his efforts to educate and improve himself have been fruitless. Another McCourt brother, Michael, has by now made his appearance in New York. Admirably, all three sons take turns supporting their mother and younger brother Alfie back in Limerick, Ireland. After a few years, Alfie and McCourt's mother Angela pay a visit to New York—and never go home. Troubles surface with the mother, who, although loved deeply, has a difficult time getting along with her sons. As the author tells the reader, her face becomes pinched and she turns up her nose in the face of the slightest adversity. Like many older people, she finds it difficult to make sense out of anything new. For instance, she views tea bags as abominations. Undoubtedly, this ongoing familial strife has its origins in the family's very sad past. No one can please her, and she winds up living a lonely existence in a tiny New York apartment, which causes the author grief.

McCourt's father also represents a sore memory for the author. Throughout *'Tis*, he recalls his early-childhood father who cared lovingly for him and rails against the drunk who embarrassed and starved him. At one point, the author's father comes to New York, hoping after years to reconcile with the family he abandoned for the bottle. Family rumor has it that he stopped drinking. However, the brothers practically roll him off the ship, and his visit is a nightmare, especially for McCourt's mother who deeply considered giving the only man she ever loved one last chance to provide her with comfort in her old age. The end of *'Tis* closes the circle commenced in *Angela's Ashes*. Upon her death, the family decides to have their mother cremated, so they can readily transport her back to Ireland where she is buried in a particularly moving scene in an abbey graveyard outside Limerick, Ireland.

Ultimately, McCourt does not find much happiness. He takes the ferry back and forth to Staten Island for eight years, dwelling many times on the Statue of Liberty and all the immigrants who came before him. If the reader reads between the lines, it becomes apparent that his increased drinking causes turmoil in both his work life and his family life. His greatest happiness comes from his work. When his students respond to J. D. Salinger's *The Catcher in the Rye* (1951) and to Shakespeare's plays, he is jubilant. Clearly, he is doing what he was born to do. A particularly poignant section of the book involves a class of nontraditional students, including wives and mothers who return to school to learn English composition. As McCourt notes, his was the only white face in the room. These remarkable students may be in school to learn, and they certainly do, but McCourt is the one who walks away with the deepest knowledge about life in America.

Only two other morsels of happiness are presented to McCourt in America: his daughter Maggie and his teaching position in Stuyvesant High School in Brooklyn. He adores his daughter and deeply enjoys his role as father, though, unfortunately, his marriage does not last. After years as a substitute teacher, an older, wiser McCourt finds his niche in the school for gifted students. He pares back the tough outer skin of these students and illuminates the dark passages of their minds with the light of literature.

Early on, when McCourt reads *Crime and Punishment*, the reader cannot help but see McCourt mirrored in Dostoevski's Raskolnikov, the shabby, half-starving, street-wandering young man who dreams of glory. The literary allusion works for a while, but the author carries it much too far. Like Raskolnikov, McCourt has a distant mother who pesters him to make good so he can financially support her. Similarly, both young men share watchful, overbearing landladies, and his New York landlady's demented sister mirrors Raskolnikov's other victim. After a rocky start, the book improves. Perhaps the reader can attribute this to a foggy memory that becomes clearer with time's passing. The voice heard later, although pained, especially in sections concerning his mother, is poignant and thus, real.

'Tis is indeed a sequel and cannot stand alone. Although the language, at times magical, rings with rhythmic Irish cadences, the child's voice that was so compelling in the Limerick slums is not nearly as engaging as the awkward adolescent walking down 68th Street in Manhattan. Furthermore, while the circumstances McCourt earlier faced on the banks of the Shannon are tragic, indeed tear-provoking, the East River is not nearly as evocative. By all means, the youngster who was fresh off the boat must have experienced great heartache and dark moments alone in post-World War II New York, but McCourt fails to balance the dark with even a glimmer of light. He may be down and out, but he can after all indulge in lemon meringue pie, a big step up from his earlier days when he used to lick grease off the fish-and-chips newspaper wrapping. He can take daily showers, a far cry from Limerick's Roden Lane's overflowing communal street toilet. Although he complains repeatedly about the state of his eyes, which is no small thing, indeed, especially to an adolescent, he is far from the Limerick typhoid ward. America, the land of his dreams, is a continual nightmare for the young McCourt. In short, the book needs balance. While in Germany, he fails to see the beauty of the Bavarian mountains. In New York, he fails to notice the grandeur of the city. He constantly regurgitates the misery endured by earlier immigrants but never considers the wonders they encountered nor the heights of glory they reached.

M. Casey Diana

Sources for Further Study

Booklist 95 (March 1, 1999): 1102.
Library Journal 124 (May 15, 1999): 122.

Los Angeles Times Book Review, July 25, 1999, p. 9.
The New York Review of Books 46 (June 24, 1999): 14.
New York Times Book Review 104 (May 2, 1999): 33.
Publishers Weekly 246 (April 5, 1999): 230.
Science 284 (June 25, 1999): 2096.
Scientific American 280 (June, 1999): 98.

TRAVELING MERCIES
Some Thoughts on Faith

Author: Anne Lamott (1954-)
Publisher: Pantheon Books (New York). 275 pp. $23.00
Type of work: Religion, autobiography, and essays
Time: The 1950's to the 1990's
Locale: The United States

A collection of twenty-five short essays recounting Anne Lamott's quirky journey of faith from nonbeliever to born-again Christian, and how her belief shapes her life today

Novelist and columnist Anne Lamott is the author of seven books, including the highly acclaimed *Bird by Bird: Some Instructions on Writing and Life* (1995) and *Operating Instructions: A Journal of My Son's First Year* (1993). A memoir of her son Sam's first year of life, *Operating Instructions* traces Lamott's struggles as she deals with single motherhood within the context of her Christian faith. In *Traveling Mercies*, Lamott tells the story of how she became a believer and offers moving reflections on how her faith helped her deal with aging, problems with self-esteem, coping with the deaths of loved ones, parenting, and recovery from drug and alcohol abuse. Her witty, irreverent, and searingly honest account offers a compelling portrait of a modern seeker's quest for a meaningful spirituality.

Lamott's spiritual autobiography opens with a striking metaphor. She compares her progression from nonbeliever to born-again Christian with stepping from one lily pad in a pond to another: "Each prepared me for the next leaf on which I would land, and in this way I moved across the swamp of doubt and fear." The beginning of her quest was anything but promising. She came of age in the 1960's in California when the hippie movement was just beginning to influence American culture. Her parents were liberal intellectuals whose lifestyle encouraged Lamott's growing fondness for alcohol and drugs. They were also strident atheists who thought that religion was only for the stupid, ignorant, and "uncouth," and they raised Lamott and her two brothers to believe in "books and music and nature." Still Lamott secretly prayed—although she did not know to whom or why. Her spiritual longing, coupled with the damaging effects of the emotional fallout from her parents' shaky marriage, caused her to feel like an outsider in her own home. She compares herself to a "ridiculous palm tree" that grew down the street from where she lived: "It did not belong, was not in relationship to anything else."

Lamott's lily-pad experience continues as "chosen mothers" unwittingly shape her nascent spirituality. An Italian Catholic woman and a Christian Scientist, both mothers of friends, treat her as an adopted daughter and provide glimpses of God as they share their religious traditions with her. In one of the most amusing scenes from the book, a group of Jewish girls welcome her as one of their own and conduct a mock Bat Mitzvah in her honor. Finally, a college philosophy professor introduces her to Søren Kierkegaard's *Frygt og Bæven* (1843; *Fear and Trembling*, 1939), which proves to be a spiritual turning point for Lamott. After a class discussion of Kierkegaard's retelling of the story of Abraham's near sacrifice of Isaac, Lamott perceives God is real and, in "a lurch of faith," she "crosses over" from doubt to belief.

Yet Lamott's newfound faith is not strong enough to keep her life from spiraling out of control. Alcohol and drugs continue to dominate her. When an affair with a married man ends, she learns she is pregnant and has an abortion. Several nights after the procedure, she drowns her sadness in alcohol and suddenly becomes aware of a presence in the room with her. She knows that it is Jesus Christ, and the realization causes her to sober up quickly. She is appalled that she may be having an honest-to-God religious experience. The reality of the divine presence does not pale in succeeding days. She continually perceives God gently but relentlessly following her like a little cat demanding attention. Finally she can stand it no longer and sighs in surrender, "F— it: I quit. . . . All right. You can come in."

Although some readers may be put off by Lamott's frank and sometimes profane language, her directness is part of the book's appeal. Her conversion is no less real because of the way she expresses herself. She feels her faith deeply and strives to live according to what she understands God's will to be. She does not try to hide her faults and concedes that she is a "bad born-again Christian." She also admits that she is sometimes embarrassed about openly confessing her faith. However, her innate honesty does not allow her to sidestep the issue, and she declares with characteristic wit:

> I am a believer, a convert. I'm probably about three months away from slapping an aluminum Jesus-fish on the back of my car, although I first want to see if the application or stickum in any way interferes with my lease agreement.

Lamott's conversion eventually aids her in conquering the destructive effects of alcohol, drugs, and bulimia, but it does not transform her into someone she is not. She remains a political and social liberal, as well as a feminist. She has discovered, however, that faith can act as a common denominator to bridge the gap between opposing points of view. In the essay "Knocking on Heaven's Door," Lamott finds herself sitting on a plane next to a man who is reading—and clearly enjoying—a book about the apocalypse by a right-wing Christian novelist. She had reviewed the book and denounced it as "hard-core right-wing paranoid anti-Semitic homophobic misogynistic propaganda—not to put too fine a point on it." The man seated next to her sizes her up as well and reluctantly accepts her as a Christian, but one who is misguided at best. It seems that the battle lines are drawn until a crisis on the plane helps them recognize each other for what they are—fellow believers who may be on opposite sides of the political fence but, paradoxically, are one in their faith.

Unlike many "feel good" books about Christian living that gloss over life's troubles, *Traveling Mercies* does not shy away from big questions and tough situations. For example, the chapter entitled "Ashes" begins as a meditation on the meaning of Ash Wednesday and ends as a reflection on mortality, love, and friendship. Lamott begins by describing a heated argument with her young son, Sam, when he refuses to forgo watching television on Ash Wednesday. Her anger is nearly uncontrollable and her sense of guilt deep:

> I went for several walks, and I thought about ashes. I was sad that I am an awful person, that I am the world's meanest mother. I got sadder. And I got to thinking about the ashes of the dead.

She continues her reverie and remembers the funeral of her best friend, Pammy, who died of breast cancer a few years earlier. In one of the most poignant passages of the book, Lamott describes what it felt like to hold a handful of Pammy's ashes in her hand before she scattered them in San Francisco Bay. Her graphic description of the gritty, sticky texture of the ashes conveys an intimacy with death that may make some readers uncomfortable: "I licked my friend's ashes off my hand, to taste them, to taste her, to taste what was left after all that was clean and alive had been consumed, burned away. They tasted metallic, and they blew every which way." Her grief is tangible and profoundly moving, grounded in physical as well as spiritual reality. At the close of the chapter, Lamott reflects on her own son's mortality, recognizing that in the distant future someone who loves Sam may be scattering his ashes to the wind. Her painful recollections acknowledge the lack of order in life—that things do not always turn out as one would wish, but she also affirms the notion that one can often find a tinge of joy in the midst of profound sorrow.

Some of Lamott's most engaging essays deal with the joys and pitfalls of parenting. In "Mountain Birthday," she relates the tug of war she and Sam had when a paragliding instructor invites Sam to take a ride in honor of his seventh birthday. Sam is eager to go and shamelessly targets his mother's insecurities as he tries to manipulate her to decide in his favor: "Then he tried sweet talk. I became 'wonderful perfect thin mother,' as in 'Let me get you some water, wonderful perfect thin mother.'" Lamott is understandably nervous about Sam's request. She fears for his safety but does not want to be overprotective. She seeks advice from her friends, who tell her to pray. She does so but is still undecided. She complains to God, "Would it be so much skin off your nose just to give me a sign?" and receives no definitive answer. Her confusion once more illustrates one of her predominant themes—life is a process of discovery, is rarely neatly packaged, and offers no easy answers. Finally she decides to act on the advice of a friend who is also a priest—to listen to the deepest feelings of her heart because that is frequently how God speaks.

Sam's "sweet talk" skillfully plays upon one of Lamott's constant obsessions: self-image. From the time she was a child, she felt insecure about her weight and appearance. She was particularly frustrated by her frizzy hair, which elicited teasing and cruel remarks from friends and family. Over the years, she tried all sorts of methods to straighten her hair in an effort to fit in with the latest fashion. As she recounts in her essay "Sister," two black friends try to convince her to let them weave her hair into dreadlocks. Lamott demurs at first. She feels that as a white person "it was presumptuous to appropriate a black style for my own liberation." She changes her mind after seeing the film *The Shawshank Redemption* (1994). The movie's ending helps her put her hair fixation into perspective when she realizes that "if I were the prisoner being baptized by the torrential rain, half my mind would be on how much my bangs were going to shrink after they dried." When she accepts the mother and daughter's offer to style her hair, Lamott discovers the experience to be sacramental:

> I felt the connection and the tenderness, the reciprocal healing offered by the laying on of hands. . . . Marlene worked with a grave sense that we were doing something meaningful—politically, spiritually, aesthetically.

After the three women complete the ritual, Lamott does indeed feel liberated from her self-loathing. She looks in the mirror and sees someone "beautiful—royal, shy, groomed. Beautiful. Strange. Mulatto." The experience chisels away at her former insecurities and reveals her true self—a self that she can accept and value.

Tough and tender, witty and wise, Lamott's spiritual memoir is grounded in real-life events yet moves beyond them to point to some of life's most challenging questions. She does not present God as an "I'll fix everything" deity, but as a trusted friend who walks alongside her, helping her cope, overcome, learn, and grow. Never dogmatic or preachy, she does not try to convince the reader to believe as she does. Instead, she merely offers snapshots from her own existence as examples of how faith can illuminate the dark patches we all encounter on life's road. Occasionally, her reflections seem self-absorbed, especially when she writes about her weight and hair. However, her self-deprecating humor and candor redeem these passages, saving them from tediousness and transforming them into delightful moments of grace revealed. Although written from a Christian perspective, the issues addressed in *Traveling Mercies* are common to us all. Lamott's book will appeal to believers and nonbelievers alike because her insights are firmly grounded in human nature and everyday life.

Pegge Bochynski

Sources for Further Study

The Atlantic Monthly 284 (October, 1999): 104.
Booklist 95 (August, 1999): 1981.
Commonweal 126 (October 22, 1999): 24.
New York 32 (September 27, 1999): 82.
The New York Times Book Review 104 (September 19, 1999): 7.
Newsweek 133 (September 27, 1999): 66.
Publishers Weekly 246 (July 26, 1999): 73.
Time 154 (October 4, 1999): 104.

TRUE AT FIRST LIGHT

Author: Ernest Hemingway (1899-1961)
Edited by Patrick Hemingway
Publisher: Charles Scribner's Sons (New York). 320 pages. $26.00
Type of work: Memoirs
Time: 1953-1954
Locale: Kenya

A fictionalized memoir of Hemingway's last visit to Africa in 1953-1954

Principal personages:
ERNEST HEMINGWAY, the author and narrator
MISS MARY, his wife
POP, Philip Percival, a white hunter
DEBBA, Hemingway's Wakamba "fiancée"
G. C., a game warden and friend of the author
NGUI,
KEITI, and
CHARO, some of the African staff for the safari

Every reader of *True at First Light*, which Ernest Hemingway's heirs and publishers report is the last of his posthumous works, should be reminded of John Updike's comments on the publication of *Islands in the Stream* (1970). In words that apply to each of the works that have been issued in Hemingway's name since his death, Updike wrote:

> This book consists of material that the author during his lifetime did not see fit to publish; therefore it should not be held against him. That parts of it are good is entirely to his credit; that other parts are puerile and, in a pained way, aimless testifies to the odds against which Hemingway, in the last two decades of his life, brought anything to completion. It is, I think, to the discredit of his publishers that no introduction offers to describe from what stage of Hemingway's tormented later career *Islands in the Stream* was salvaged, or to estimate what its completed design might have been, or to confess what editorial choices were exercised in the preparation of this manuscript. Rather, a gallant wreck of a novel is paraded as the real thing, as if the public are such fools as to imagine a great writer's ghost is handing down books intact from Heaven.

The odds to which Updike refers are now well known: Hemingway's last years can only be described as a tragedy. A lifetime of hard drinking, courting physical danger, ricocheting between periods of mania and depression, and coping with the frenzy of renown had begun to affect him by the mid-1940's. The wounds, concussions, and broken bones had all taken their toll. Then, when he was returning in January, 1954, from the six-month stay in Africa that *True at First Light* recounts, two plane crashes and a brush fire within a single week left him with two spinal disks cracked and impacted, his liver and one kidney ruptured, a dislocated right arm and shoulder, a concussion and a cracked skull that leaked cerebral fluid for several days, and first-degree burns on his face, arms, legs, chest, and back. Physically and mentally debilitated, he returned to his home in Cuba but would never be the same. The prescriptions and self-medications that he took to treat the aftereffects of all this, together with his increasing consumption of alcohol, eventually led in 1960 to a mental breakdown and paranoid delusions. As a result, he was hospitalized at the Mayo Clinic—where he was given electroshock treatments that affected him like a series of new concussions, leaving his memory weak but his delusions intact. On July 2, 1961, he committed suicide in his Ketchum, Idaho, home.

In the weeks and months that followed, his widow Mary discovered that he had left fifty pounds of unpublished manuscripts—thousands of pages, hundreds of thousands of words. As executor of his estate, she was left with the responsibility of sorting this all out and determining what, if anything, from this cache of manuscripts deserved to be published. Ultimately, she (and, later, his sons) determined that every one of the works that he left behind deserved to be published—the letters that he had specifically directed them not to print, the stories he had chosen not to publish or collect, and each of the long works that he had been unable to shape into a finished form that satisfied him.

There are still no introductions that respond to Updike's questions for any of the books that have been published since Hemingway's death. However, thanks to Hemingway biographers such as Carlos Baker and Michael Reynolds, and to Rose Marie Burwell's comprehensive examination of the postwar manuscripts and the books eventually drawn from them in her indispensable *Hemingway: The Postwar Years and the Posthumous Novels* (1996), people do know much more about how the posthumously published books evolved.

Hemingway returned to Cuba after the Allied victory in Europe intent on writing an epic about World War II. He failed; but between 1945 and 1961 he never stopped writing. The last two books that he published, each of which grew out of longer works that he had begun in the 1940's, included one of his worst and one of his most highly praised. *Across the River and into the Trees* (1950), the remains of his original plan to write a novel about World War II, was variously described by reviewers as a parody, a travesty, an embarrassment, trash, and worse. Hemingway was clearly finished, many of them said. *The Old Man and the Sea*, which appeared two years later, surprised even the naysayers and was generally hailed as a small masterpiece.

In the last nine years of his life he published no more books, but he worked compulsively on five different projects: a novel set in the south of France during the 1920's (published in 1986 as *The Garden of Eden*); another novel, consisting of four major sections, about a painter named Thomas Hudson in Bimini and Cuba (*Islands in the Stream*); an African book (*True at First Light*); a bullfighting book (published in 1985 as *The Dangerous Summer*); and, finally, a book of reminiscences about Paris in the 1920's (published in 1964 as *A Moveable Feast*).

A Moveable Feast was by far the most successful of these projects: Several months before his death Hemingway delivered an all-but-complete manuscript to his publishers, indicating that he was still working on a final chapter and a title. Each of the other projects was left unfinished. In each of these later works the narrator or main character is an artist or writer; in three—*True at First Light*, *A Moveable Feast*, *The Dangerous*

Summer—the artist is Hemingway himself. In *The Garden of Eden* and the Paris memoir he is looking back, mining his past to make sense of his present; in the African and bullfighting books he is returning to places that had been almost sacred to him earlier, only to find them diminished or inaccessible. Each of these four books seems to have involved an effort to return to earlier sources of inspiration in the hope of recapturing a mastery that Hemingway knew had disappeared. *The Garden of Eden* draws on the same period and the same autobiographical sources as *The Sun Also Rises* (1926). *Islands in the Stream* recalls elements of *To Have and Have Not* (1937) and *For Whom the Bell Tolls* (1940). *The Dangerous Summer* returned to the bullfighting of *The Sun Also Rises* and *Death in the Afternoon* (1932). *True at First Light* was an attempt to recapture the spirit of *Green Hills of Africa* (1935) and the inspiration behind "The Snows of Kilimanjaro" and "The Short Happy Life of Francis Macomber."

As he worked on each of these projects at various points during the last fifteen years of his life, moving from one to the other, unable to finish or totally abandon any of them, writing, always writing, he lost his way and each work began to grow exponentially. As the books grew longer, Hemingway tried to see their length as a virtue. He began to keep obsessive daily counts of the number of words he was writing and began to brag about the counts in his letters to his publisher, editor, and friends. He worked as if quantity were the same as quality, or loquacity were a virtue in a writer whose reputation was based on his radical paring of language down to its absolute essentials. Where once Hemingway had prided himself on his "iceberg theory" of literature—the idea that nine-tenths of his writing was beneath the surface of the carefully chosen words that were actually on the page—in these manuscripts he repeatedly told his readers much more than they wanted to know. Where once he had used repetition for effect, he now began to repeat himself endlessly.

None of these manuscripts can fairly be described as "aimless," but all of them turned out to be endless, all of them metastasized. When he set them aside, *The Garden of Eden* stood at 200,000 words, *Islands in the Stream* at 182,000, *The Dangerous Summer* (a 10,000-word assignment from *Life* magazine) at 120,000, and *True at First Light* at 200,000. When they were eventually published by his estate, each was drastically cut—*True at First Light* by 75 percent, *The Garden of Eden* and *The Dangerous Summer* by two-thirds, *Islands in the Stream* by about one-third—without any explanation to readers of who did the cutting, how, or why.

Hemingway's son Patrick is credited with editing *True at First Light*, but neither his almost incoherent introduction nor the egregious "Cast of Characters" that he appends to the book convince readers of his competence to make aesthetic choices about his father's manuscript. He does not mention that a 50,000-word excerpt from the manuscript was serialized in several issues of *Sports Illustrated* in 1971-1972, does not explain how this book relates to that excerpt, and does not tell what was eliminated.

What readers are left with here—as was the case with *Islands in the Stream*, *The Garden of Eden*, and *The Dangerous Summer*—cannot fairly be described as a book "by Ernest Hemingway." Hemingway did not complete it, did not decide it was ready for publication, did not edit it, did not order its parts, and, therefore, did not create its emphases. It would be more accurate instead to describe *True at First Light* and these other books as "drawn from the writing of Ernest Hemingway."

In the case of *True at First Light*, the result is a first-person account of several parts of a trip to Africa that Hemingway took with his last wife, Miss Mary. The subjects of the fragments that are collected here are the threat to the Hemingway camp posed by a handful of Mau Mau warriors who have escaped from jail, Miss Mary's quest to shoot a lion, her plans for a Christmas celebration, Hemingway's bantering friendships with the hunter Philip Percival, a game warden known as G. C. and his gun-bearer Ngui, and Hemingway's relationship with a native Wakamba girl named Debba, whom he describes as his "fiancée."

The dialogue ranges from stilted and embarrassing to very humorous and sharp; the descriptions of Africa range from powerful to hackneyed. Hemingway "goes native"—shaving his head, dying his clothes the burnt orange of the Wakamba tribe, carrying a spear, acting as an elder of the tribe and the fiancé of Debba—and the conversations that he and Miss Mary have about this are often hilarious. At times he presents himself with a self-deprecation and a consciousness of his own pretensions that is appealing and unusual in Hemingway's work; at others—especially in all the conversations about the "new religion" that he and his friends have invented—he loses all sense of those pretensions and appears at his self-indulgent worst. He talks too much, tries to think deeply but mostly fails, and ultimately recognizes that his fantasy of escape among the Wakamba is doomed to fail.

Readers will never know what Hemingway might have made of this or his other unfinished books if he had been granted the time or the health to work on them further. That he could follow *Across the River and into the Trees* with *The Old Man and the Sea*, could write *A Moveable Feast* after all that he had suffered, at least suggests that he might have turned these books into works that he would have wanted to publish.

As it stands, *True at First Light* is not worthless—none of the posthumous books are—but it is also not a book that anyone could seriously recommend to a reader who is interested in discovering the work of Ernest Hemingway.

Bernard F. Rodgers, Jr.

Sources for Further Study

Booklist 95 (January 1, 1999): 820.
The Christian Century 116 (July 28, 1999): 742.
Christianity Today 43 (February 8, 1999): 76.
Library Journal 124 (January, 1999): 105.
Newsweek 133 (May 3, 1999): 71.
The New York Times Book Review 104 (March 7, 1999): 19
Publishers Weekly 245 (December 7, 1998): 43.

TRUFFAUT

Authors: Antoine de Baecque and Serge Toubiana
First published: 1996, in France
Translated from the French by Catherine Temerson
Publisher: Alfred A. Knopf (New York). Illustrated. 462 pp. $30.00
Type of work: Film and biography
Time: 1932-1984
Locale: Primarily France and the United States

The definitive biography of François Truffaut, noted film critic and film director, whose films are directly related to his life

Principal personages:
FRANÇOIS TRUFFAUT, French film critic and film director
ROLAND TRUFFAUT, his adoptive father
JANINE DE MONFERRAND, his mother
GENEVIÈVE DE MONFERRAND, his grandmother
MADELEINE MORGENSTERN, his first wife
ANDRÉ BAZIN, a film critic and mentor to Truffaut
JEAN-LUC GODARD, a film director, friend turned rival
JEAN-PIERRE LÉAUD, an actor who portrayed Antoine Doinel in Truffaut's films
HELEN SCOTT, Truffaut's American agent

Authors Antoine de Baecque and Serge Toubiana are both affiliated with *Les Cahiers du Cinéma*, the film journal for which Truffaut wrote for as a film critic. They had, of course, ready access to all his film essays, his correspondence, and his notes for an unpublished autobiography. In addition to perusing published Truffaut interviews, they interviewed many of Truffaut's associates, friends, and lovers. As a result, their work draws from a considerable amount of research and may be considered the definitive biography of Truffaut. The book also contains a filmography, an exhaustive bibliography, copious notes, and dozens of well-chosen photographs of Truffaut, his associates, and his work (stills and film scripts).

De Baecque and Toubiana stress the close relationship between Truffaut's life and his work, which they read as primarily autobiographical. Truffaut's "clandestine childhood," also the title of their first chapter, provides the key to understanding his films and to defending, even justifying, his behavior. The illegitimate child of Janine de Monferrand, he was unwanted and unloved, living with a wet nurse until his grandmother Geneviève de Monferrand took him in. When he was almost two years old, he was legally adopted by Roland Truffaut shortly before Roland married Janine, but the couple did not really want Truffaut to live with them. It was not until his grandmother passed away that the ten-year-old Truffaut would live with his parents. Then he was "left to his own devices in a more indifferent, not to say hostile, world." Attracted to his mother, who did not return his love, he began to turn to young women and had his first sexual experience at fourteen. Throughout his life he was a philanderer incapable of fidelity, and he had his first case of syphilis at seventeen. When he learned that Roland Truffaut was not his biological father, he also began a search for a surrogate father, a role played by writer and rebel against bourgeois morality Jean Genet, with whom he had much in common, and by André Bazin, a mentor responsible for furthering his career in film criticism.

His childhood, according to the authors, also motivated two quite different kinds of behavior. On the positive side, his interest in reading, fostered at his grandmother's home, became a means of escape when he went to live with his parents. In addition to becoming a voracious reader, he became an avid filmgoer, attending two or three movies every day at the age of twelve. Film became another means of escape as he identified with screen actors. These two interests led almost inevitably to his career as a film critic and, eventually, a director. On the negative side, his awareness of himself as unwanted and unloved led to his behavior problems at school, chronic lying, petty theft, desertion from the army, and, eventually, two suicide attempts before he was twenty years old. For Truffaut, "life was the screen" in a double sense: He lived film, but his troubled childhood also became the content of his first film, *The 400 Blows* (1959), just as many of his experiences were incorporated into his other films.

Becoming a film director was almost inevitable for Truffaut, who, with friend Robert Lachenay, wrote film notes, traded in stolen film stills, and organized Cercle Cinémane, a film club that failed financially. Despite personal and financial disasters, Truffaut was becoming well known in film circles, which his biographers describe in great detail, stressing his relationships with other film aficionados, many of whom became famous film directors (Jean-Luc Godard, Claude Chabrol, as examples). André Bazin, who hired him as his personal secretary at Travail et Culture, helped him make additional contacts. After writing for *Elle*, a women's magazine, he began in 1953 to write film criticism for *Les Cahiers du Cinéma*, a job with which Bazin also helped. In fact, he wrote so many pieces for the journal that he published some of them under pseudonyms, one of them Robert Lachenay. His most significant essay at *Les Cahiers du Cinéma* was "A Certain Tendency in French Cinema" (1954), in which he attacked the French tradition of adapting literary works to films, an attack that plunged him into critical debate.

Truffaut, a "hitchcocko-hawksian" (Bazin's term), began writing essays about his beloved American films and his favorite directors: Alfred Hitchcock, Howard Hawks, and Orson Welles. These led to his celebrated *politique des auteurs* (the auteur theory), which makes the film director the "author" of a film. De Baecque and Toubiana thoroughly dissect the development of the theory, its application, and the critical controversy it aroused. While Truffaut continued to write film criticism for *Les Cahiers du Cinéma* and *Arts*, his interest was turning to film directing. While he was moved by Henri-Pierre Roché's novel *Jules et Jim* (1953; *Jules and Jim*, 1963), he put that project aside and instead adapted Maurice Pons's short story "Les Mistons" ("The Brats") to film. In discussing this film, de Baecque and Toubiana establish a precedent for their subsequent discussions of all of Truffaut's films: They cover production details, problems on the set, and personal relationships between actors and filmmakers. The most important of these matters was Madeleine Morgenstern, Truffaut's future bride, convincing her father to finance Truffaut's film and to set up a production company, Les Films du Carrosse, for him. By the end of 1958 Truffaut's short film had won a director's prize at the Festival du film Mondial in Brussels; he had married Madeleine Morgenstern (he was accused of mercenary motives); and he "became a spokesman for a culture that had been scorned up to then, the culture of film devotees."

In *The 400 Blows*, the film that established him as a film director, Truffaut introduced the character of Antoine Doinel, his "creation and alter ego." He modeled Doinel's character after his own childhood experiences, an action that understandably upset his parents, but Doinel is "part Truffaut, part [Jean-Pierre] Léaud," the boy who played him. According to Truffaut, he and Léaud recognized in Doinel "traits they both shared." The tie between Truffaut and Léaud was close: Léaud became part of the Truffaut family, and the authors regard Truffaut as Pygmalion figure, older brother, and father figure to the younger man. Léaud appeared in several of Truffaut's films, often as Antoine Doinel; the Léaud/Doinel cycle of films includes *Antoine et Colette* (one of five brief vignettes released in 1962 as *L'Amour à Vingt Ans*, or *Love at Twenty*), *Stolen Kisses* (1968), *Bed and Board* (1970), and *Love on the Run* (1979). In fact, Truffaut commented that in *Stolen Kisses* he hoped to "'liberate' Léaud from Doinel" so that Léaud could go on to other roles and further his career, but he continued to cast Léaud as Doinel until 1979. After completing the last Léaud/Doinel film, Truffaut was "emancipated" from Doinel. De Baecque and Toubiana claim that the break "made Truffaut feel lonelier, almost like an orphan."

This tie between his films and his family relationships is a pervasive theme in *Truffaut*. A subsection of the chapter on New Wave cinema is entitled "Parallel Families." The authors assert that Truffaut had "two families, the one he started with Madeleine, and his professional one, centered around Les Films du Carrosse." Apparently Truffaut had difficulty separating the two families, for many of his films are autobiographical, and often he plays out his affairs through the plots of his films. He even casts leading men (Jean-Louis Trintignant, for example) who physically resemble him. As the authors claim, Truffaut's films are his life. This may explain his practice of sleeping with the female leads in his films: "He was perpetually unfaithful, more out of a need to seduce and be loved than out of Don Juanism." For Philippe Labro, Truffaut "was not a hollow Don Juan" because "what counted most was his work, the idea of imposing his own style and his own world, the desire to exhibit all his talent." The details about Truffaut's affairs would seem to be material for sensational news journals, but Truffaut's affairs directly affected his films: Plots and characters were altered, often modeled on his past or current life. Occasionally, the desire to control resulted in his not only directing but also acting in his own films (*The Green Room*, 1978, for example).

Truffaut is presented as a tireless worker, who wrote, directed, acted, and totally involved himself in his films; and, because he had his own production company, he had the opportunity to be a true auteur director. His biographers describe his contributions to his films, but they also portray him as a prodigious networker and promoter of his films. Maintaining a correspondence with influential people all over the world,

Truffaut kept his films and himself in the public eye. He was extremely popular in the United States, where he frequently traveled and where he met his idol, Alfred Hitchcock. With the help of Helen Scott, who served as agent and translator, he published his extensive interviews with Hitchcock. Because he had exhaustively researched Hitchcock's work, his questions elicited frank and revealing responses about the films. The book, *Hitchcock* (1967, revised and expanded 1984), helped make him an international, rather than a French, filmmaker and critic.

Truffaut became the leader of the New Wave, but he never became, as did Alain Resnais and Jean-Luc Godard, an experimenter or theoretician with a political edge. Truffaut's films have been, for the most part, critical and popular successes; and his unwillingness to adopt Godard's "militant, revolutionary cinema," unpopular with the filmgoing public, led to a confrontation between the former friends and two of the most critically acclaimed French directors. De Baecque and Toubiana provide their readers with the 1960's political context and explain how politics brought about a final break between the two directors. After Godard attacked Truffaut's *Day for Night* (1973) for being thoroughly middle class and then asked him to finance his next film, Truffaut launched a violent counterattack in which he accused Godard of elitism and hypocrisy and suggested that he only posed as a subversive artist. Truffaut's role, his biographers claim, was to situate himself "at the center of French cinema, or rather 'at the extreme center,' independent though working within the system."

De Baecque and Toubiana describe their subject as a man shaped by a loveless environment, driven to find in books and films an escape from turbulent teen years, and determined to exert control over his life and films, which often seem identical. Truffaut seems to have relished his role as a misfit (in school, army) and marginalized figure (after discovering that his biological father was Jewish, he declared that "he had always felt Jewish," even as he saw himself as the "'Jew' of the Truffaut-Monferrand family"). On the other hand, Truffaut is very much the misfit who succeeds and who stands, somewhat safely and securely, at the "center" of filmmaking.

Thomas L. Erskine

Sources for Further Study

The Atlantic Monthly 284 (August, 1999): 93.
Booklist 95 (April 15, 1999): 1452.
Library Journal 124 (May 1, 1999): 79.
The New York Times Book Review 104 (July 11, 1999): 15.
Publishers Weekly 246 (May 10, 1999): 53.
Time 154 (July 5, 1999): 76.

THE TWENTY-SEVENTH KINGDOM

Author: Alice Thomas Ellis (1932-   )
First published: 1982, in Great Britain
Publisher: Moyer Bell (Wakefield, Rhode Island). 159 pp. $22.95
Type of work: Novel
Time: 1954
Locale: Chelsea, London

Life at a bohemian British boardinghouse is changed forever by the arrival of the enigmatic Valentine, a young postulant on leave from a Welsh convent who is said to have the ability to perform miracles

Principal characters:
VALENTINE, a Roman Catholic postulant from the West Indies
AUNT IRENE, the Russian émigré who owns the boardinghouse
KYRIL, Irene's nephew, an art dealer
AUNT BERTHE, Irene's sister, Mother Superior of the convent
MRS. MASON, Irene's belligerent housekeeper
MRS. O'CONNOR, a friend and neighbor with criminal connections
FOCUS, Irene's Persian cat

What do you get when you combine a traditional British comedy of manners, dark-humored surrealism, a metaphysical allegory, and a cast of characters that includes a philosophical Persian tomcat named Focus? The answer is Alice Thomas Ellis's appealing, offbeat novel *The Twenty-seventh Kingdom*. First published in Great Britain in 1982, the novel was a runner-up for that year's prestigious Booker Prize. Especially notable is the fact that it is one of five published books to date by Ellis, who did not begin writing until her forties, after giving birth to seven children.

The book's central character, Aunt Irene, is one of the last survivors of an upper-class Russian, Roman Catholic family who, over generations, fled political persecution in the Ukraine, Lithuania, Austria, Turkey—"or, as the story-tellers would have it, across 27 lands and 30 countries until they came to the 27th kingdom." No longer wealthy, Irene operates a small, rundown boardinghouse in Chelsea, and her sister Berthe has ended up as Mother Superior of a convent in Wales. The two have never been particularly close, but as the story begins, Irene's and Berthe's lives are intersecting in an unexpected way.

The Mother Superior writes to ask a favor of Irene: Will she take into her house, for an indefinite period, a young nun who needs to "test her vocation" before receiving her vows? The details are fuzzy, only that the postulant is a West Indies native, an orphan, and that her name is Valentine. Irene agrees, though she has no vacant rooms. To make space for Valentine, she decides to throw out a current lodger, a neurotic loner referred to as "little Mr. Sirocco," who is conveniently away on holiday at the time.

Mr. Sirocco is not the only resident of Dancing Master House, as Irene's building is known, to have his careful routine thrown into disarray by the exotic, dark-skinned visitor. Irene's nephew Kyril, handsome and obnoxious, has two goals regarding

Valentine: to offend her religious sensibilities and to seduce her, in no particular order. Kyril has his work cut out for him. Valentine takes no offense at his constant jabs:

> Aunt Irene glanced at her quickly. The girl was smiling—she didn't mind Kyril at all. And she isn't sad, thought Aunt Irene. She isn't the least bit sad. She's quiet because she's happy. How extraordinary. Aunt Irene felt quite giddy with surprise and had to suppress a wish to reach out and touch Valentine as though she were a talisman. Perhaps it was the sun that made people happy. Her own people were mostly miserable. They wrote long glum books and sang glum songs and went on glumly about the extent of winter and the sound of the rivers freezing and the shortage of meat—not just the serfs who had had every reason to feel thoroughly depressed, but the rich and privileged. They worried about their souls and stared deeply and hopelessly into the depths of themselves. . . .
>
> Kyril scowled. It looked as though Valentine wasn't going to play his game, didn't know the rules—didn't even know there was a game. Kyril was extremely fond of winning, and he always won, because he was prepared to go beyond the bounds of the acceptable, but you couldn't win against a person who wasn't playing.

Valentine's serenity and otherworldliness affect everyone she meets, with varying results. At one point, she even inspires a local girl, who was not theretofore religious, to take her vows at the convent. The housekeeper Mrs. Mason, on the other hand, takes offense at Valentine's joining the household: "I don't think it's right for me to clean the bedroom of a half-caste," she proclaims at one point. Valentine is unfazed by the racism: "Valentine shrugged. She had seen evil before. She didn't like it, but it neither alarmed nor surprised her."

As the repercussions of the girl's stay continue to mount, the other characters have their own problems to deal with as well. Irene is stalked by a threatening, mysterious man she believes is trying to arrest her for long-delinquent income taxes. Focus is taunted by an amazingly agile rat that remains just out of his grasp. Kyril's attempted seduction of Valentine strikes out in a major way.

When Irene returns late one evening from the racetrack, she surprises Valentine and Kyril sitting intimately on the floor, laughing and playing dice. Knowing her nephew as she does, she suspects the worst:

> Kyril turned his amazing gaze upon her, his expression mellifluous and calm, and Aunt Irene realised with a horrible lurch of her internal organs that Kyril was intent on seducing Valentine. He was always like this when he had his eye on a new victim—reasonable and wise and quite assured of his own irresistibility. It was afterward that he became devilish, fragmented, and unsafe. Kyril wasn't like other men, in whom doubt and frustration wrought havoc. It was fulfilment that was Kyril's undoing. I should have thwarted him sometimes, thought his aunt. Now it's too late.

Too tired and rattled to intervene, Irene flees upstairs under the pretext of indigestion. And as she feared, it is not long afterward that Kyril makes his move:

> When his aunt had limped upstairs, Kyril prepared to pounce. He had never found it necessary to employ any particular technique in these circumstances. Whereas plainer men would offer champagne, flattery, meaningful glances, Kyril would merely remark in Anglo-Saxon that he was now ready, and the object of his desire would instantly comply with his wishes.
>
> He untied the sash of his robe and turned to Valentine. But she had gone. Somewhere someone was laughing, and for the life of him Kyril couldn't tell who it was.

Very thoughtfully he retied his sash. He was thinking that no one should ever hear of this. Not because he had been rejected, but because he didn't understand, and he had been quite sure that life could hold no surprises for him. He saw himself as one of those unusual and fortunate men who were able to understand and fully exploit the new insights that were being developed in every field of human endeavor, both scientific and philosophical. Comte, Darwin, Freud, Einstein had, each in his own way, done his bit to soothe Kyril's conscience and smooth his path toward untroubled self-indulgence. Kyril now knew that there were no gods or ghosts, only taboos and neuroses and $E = MC^2$, and very nice too. The watches of the night held no terror for Kyril, for were not all things concrete and clear, and all mysteries explained?

Unbeknown to the crestfallen Kyril, the embarrassing incident has been observed after all—by Focus, who is hiding under the stairs:

Focus was rolling about in catty paroxysms of delighted mirth. He'd never liked Aunt Irene's kitten, Kyril, who was always complaining about finding white cat hairs on his clothes and in his bread and butter; and he'd morosely witnessed Kyril's numberless conquests, comparing him with the neighbourhood's dominant tom, a scratty looking object who stalked Cheyne Row. Focus had been made a eunuch for the sake of the sweetness of the air in Dancing Master House. He was glad, because it enabled him to take a removed and measured view of affairs—human, feline and, indeed, divine.

The subplots and intrigues continue to swirl and coalesce. Aunt Irene makes a fateful decision to accept Mrs. O'Connor's offer of having her thug sons beat up the secretive tax man. Mrs. O'Connor, lighting a candle in church after Benediction, catches a glimpse of Valentine in the building's doorway, literally walking on air: "dark as a painted saint against the gilded evening, just for a moment the light that outlined her outlined her completely and Mrs. O'Connor could see light beneath her feet." Mrs. O'Connor rushes to tell her family about it, but her son Victor sums up the reaction: "You're nuts."

Readers learn that it was Valentine's tendency to levitate that resulted in her removal from the convent, the kind of thing that Mother Superior Berthe considers too disruptive of the sisters' daily routines to be permitted. "How the vulgar loved portents, prodigies, and the untoward," Berthe thinks. "Only the religious knew how embarrassing they could be—and quite beside the point."

The last straw for Berthe was the day that Valentine returned alone from the convent orchard, having somehow picked a basket of the best apples from the tops of the trees where the other nuns' ladders could not reach. Berthe keeps one of the apples in her desk drawer, both as a talisman and a reminder of the necessity for sending Valentine away. The fruit remains supernaturally fresh and shiny, and in an ominous foreshadowing Berthe decides she will not let the girl return to the convent until the symbolic apple rots.

The pleasures of *The Twenty-seventh Kingdom* are not in the story alone but also in the texture of Ellis's writing—its ever-inventive punning and wordplay, the rightness of her individual characters' voices, and Irene's droll asides on topics ranging from human (and feline) nature, to religion, to fate. "Most women and some men found him irresistible," she observes of Kyril, "which had proved bad for his character. Men who didn't find him attractive often wanted to beat him up." Of Mrs. O'Connor's bad-seed son Victor, Irene muses:

> Victor had much in common with the late Fuhrer. For instance, he thought that many problems could be solved by shooting a lot of people—in particular the working classes, homosexuals, and the Royal Family (except for the Queen Mother, whom he quite liked). This would leave the upper and professional classes and Victor to run the country. And the Queen Mother, of course.

The dramatic climax of the story, while not unsatisfying, raises enough questions about all that has gone before ("Thus it was that the Major was the last person to see Valentine fly . . . ," the section begins) that many readers will be led to reopen the slim volume to page 1 and, with the gift of hindsight, watch the disparate pieces of *The Twenty-seventh Kingdom* come together, so fluidly, again.

Carroll Dale Short

Sources for Further Study

The New York Times Book Review 104 (October 24, 1999): 22.
Publishers Weekly 246 (July 26, 1999): 62.

THE UNDISCOVERED MIND
How the Human Brain Defies Replication, Medication, and Explanation

Author: John Horgan (1955-)
Publisher: Free Press (New York). 326 pp. $25.00
Type of work: Science, technology, medicine, and history of science
Time: The twentieth century
Locale: The United States and Western Europe

A captious scrutiny of the scientific quest to understand the mind

When John Horgan, a journalist who has been called the enfant terrible of modern science, published *The End of Science* (1996), the book provoked much discussion and controversy. The discussion centered on what Horgan called "ironic science," speculations about the world that can be neither verified nor falsified by actual experiments. The controversy brewed over his claim that the scientific enterprise was exhausted, that every great scientific discovery that can be made has been made, and the remaining task for scientists is filling in these big pictures with increasingly trivial details. When asked what he thought of Horgan's arguments, Stephen Hawking, a renowned physicist immobilized by Lou Gehrig's disease who communicates by spelling his words on a computer, gave the succinct response, "garbage."

Like Hawking, John Maddox, longtime editor-in-chief of the journal *Nature*, strongly disagreed with Horgan's ideas and even published a book, *What Remains to Be Discovered* (1998), to prove that scientists have a long agenda of achievement ahead of them, including discoveries that will change their ideas as radically as Charles Darwin's and Albert Einstein's discoveries changed past ideas. While these criticisms have not made Horgan happy, the critics irritating him the most were certain scientists studying the human brain, "mind-scientists" who felt that they were starting, rather than ending, a period of important scientific discovery. Even though those scientists are involved in what they and Horgan consider humanity's most significant scientific endeavor, he thinks that they have become lost amid the overwhelmingly complex interconnections of the brain's ten million synapses. He began investigating the major accomplishments and limitations of neuroscience in *The End of Science*, but, because the mind is essentially who we are, he sees *The Undiscovered Mind* as a much more important book than *The End of Science*.

For both books he interviewed principal researchers and theoreticians, visited university laboratories and research institutes, and attended meetings of relevant professional organizations. He has also read the chief articles and books of his interviewees. However, his methods warrant some criticism. He restricts himself primarily to Western scientists, and even within this limited group, most of the scientists are American. Furthermore, he often characterizes his subjects unfavorably with regard to their appearance, habits, and personalities, which will likely taint the unwary reader's views of what these talented men and women are trying to say. A cursory reading of the history of science is sufficient to reveal that ugly and cantankerous scientists have made more than their share of great discoveries. Indeed, these unflattering descriptions tell the reader more about Horgan than they do about the scientists.

Horgan's purpose in *The Undiscovered Mind* is to give his readers an overview of the important mind-sciences, but this overview is often colored by his negative evaluations. For example, one of his principal themes is the "explanatory gap" between physiological theories of the mind and the psychological phenomena they try to explain. Despite some successes, neuroscientists have failed to unify the data derived from brain research in the way that Isaac Newton's theory of gravity unified the motion of matter in the universe. However, neuroscientists might legitimately respond that this explanatory gap does not mean that an objective chasm exists between brain and mind. Moreover, gaps have existed in science before, and Newton himself was forced to call upon the world's creator to account for some of the erratic planetary motions in his theory of the solar system. These and other gaps were not bridged until the discoveries of Einstein.

Also troubling Horgan is the reductionism that he sees as endemic among mind-scientists. He calls their fragmentation of the brain into the functioning of its neurons the "Humpty-Dumpty Dilemma," because these scientists are adept at breaking the brain into many pieces, but they have no idea about how to reconstruct them. They can picture millions of neurons firing at the same time, but they do not even know which signals are associated with a person moving an arm, much less how the brain integrates the disparate workings of its highly specialized parts to create the unity of perception and thought that constitutes the mind. Even when researchers focused on particular mental functions, Horgan experienced difficulties in relating specific neuronal activities, as revealed in the sacrificed brains of macaque monkeys, to such general ideas as memory and decision making. The scientist doing this work thought the explanatory gap was in Horgan's own head.

Individual human brains do exhibit enormous variability, which became obvious in the early history of neuroscience when brain-damaged patients were studied. In honor of Phineas Gage, whose brain was severely damaged in 1848 when an explosion drove an iron bar through his head, Horgan has called this field "Gagian neuro-science." Eventually, Gage's personality deteriorated. Because his frontal lobes had been damaged, some neuroscientists identified them as the seat of moral reasoning. However, numerous cases since then have shown that people who suffer similar forms of brain damage often exhibit very different traits and behaviors. Horgan uses these results to attack the theory that modules of the brain are linked to very specific functions.

Several decades after the Gage accident, Sigmund Freud, the founder of psychoanalysis, worked on brain-damaged patients, but he had doubts about how valuable neuroscience would be in understanding the human psyche. He therefore abandoned his search for the physiological causes of mental disorders and began to develop psychoanalysis, a purely psychological model of the mind. Since Freud's time, numerous controlled studies have failed to verify Freud's ideas, and modern psychiatrists tend to prescribe drugs rather than talk therapy for such ailments as depression. For his part Horgan thinks that Freudian psychology is not very different from other psychotherapies, and psychoanalysis has survived mainly because scientists have not developed a clearly superior model of the mind.

Psychoanalysis was one of a small number of therapies used in the nineteenth century, but by the end of the twentieth century more than four hundred forms of talk therapy existed. With the multiplication of behavioral and experiential therapies, Horgan asks if any of them work. His answer is contained in the "dodo hypothesis" derived from Lewis Carroll's *Alice's Adventures in Wonderland* (1865). The book describes a race in which a dodo declares that all participants win and all will receive prizes. For Horgan, all psychological therapies for mental disorders are equally effective, and claims for the superiority of one over another are futile, exemplifying an allegiance effect. That is, researchers have the tendency to find evidence for the therapy they practice.

Scientists who favor drugs in treating the mentally ill fare no better in Horgan's analysis than psychotherapists. He thinks that such drugs as Thorazine (chlorpromazine) and Prozac (fluoxetine) are no more effective in treating emotional disorders than old antidepressants or even placebos. He also fears a "chemo-fascism," in which medical personnel use drugs to control behavior they find undesirable, reminiscent of Nurse Mildred Ratched in Ken Kesey's *One Flew Over the Cuckoo's Nest* (1962). Some critics have found Horgan's attack on pharmaceuticals overblown because these drugs have allowed numerous mentally ill patients, who were formerly confined to asylums, to function effectively in society. Furthermore, scientists are creating new drugs that are more selective in their activity and less harmful in their side effects than the drugs Horgan attacks.

Despite this criticism, Horgan believes that drugs have been oversold. They may benefit some people some of the time but so, too, do other therapies. Similarly, he finds that behavioral geneticists exaggerate their claims to measure the relative contributions of nature and nurture to the human personality. He is particularly concerned about the hyperbolic rhetoric of scientists who state that they have found genes for manic depression, schizophrenia, alcoholism, heroin addiction, and a host of other ills. These "gene-whiz" scientists give people false hopes that behavioral geneticists will soon have the solutions to many medical and social problems. In Horgan's view no scientist has unambiguously proved that a specific gene is linked to a complex behavioral disorder. The scientists who proclaim that "genes rule" minimize the effect of parenting, education, and other environmental facts that actually shape a human person.

In the background of Horgan's critique of behavioral genetics is his historical knowledge of how Adolf Hitler and the Nazis used genetic information to kill millions of people they believed defective or inferior. A similar fear underlies his discussion of evolutionary psychologists, because they view the mind as a complexus of skills programmed into the brain by natural selection. According to Horgan, evolutionary psychology has had few successes, even failing to explain such basic human traits as altruism.

Toward the end of his book, Horgan discusses the possibility of machines mimicking the human mind. Artificial intelligence (AI) enthusiasts can certainly point to some successes, such as the IBM computer Deep Blue's defeat of chess champion Gary Kasparov in 1997. On the other hand, Horgan agrees with those critics of AI, who hold that the mind will never be simulated because no algorithmic process is able to reproduce such conscious phenomena as understanding, free will, and the self.

At the end of *The Undiscovered Mind*, as at the end of *The End of Science*, Horgan makes an ascent into the mystical. He describes himself as a "mysterian" when faced with the conundrum of consciousness. Mysterians believe that the mind is an insoluble mystery that is forever beyond the reach of science. Horgan's views may well anger those scientists who feel that the inability to understand something now in no way precludes the possibility of understanding it later. As a lapsed Roman Catholic, Horgan seems to have retained a longing for the transcendent, hence his obvious displeasure with reductionists who see the human brain as nothing but a pack of neurons, genes, adaptations, or computational modules. He even likens belief in these reductionisms to the doctrinal faith of traditional religions. For many scientists, this goes too far, because the methodologies of science are essentially different from those of religion.

For Horgan, those awaiting a Newton of the mind-sciences are destined to wait in vain. Refusing any reductive resolution of the mind's riddles, he adopts a wryly skeptical stance. He realizes his views will be unacceptable to most scientists who, by habit, have the future in their minds and hearts. They will never be able to abandon their quest for ideas that increasingly help humanity understand the world. Many scientists are optimistic that they will find the answers to the questions that have piqued their curiosity. Horgan and his critics certainly disagree about where the mind-sciences are in their evolution—either at the start of the development of what will lead to many new and exciting ideas or at the end of what will be a deep morass of frustrating limitations. All can agree that the basic mysteries of the human mind will continue to intrigue, delight, disconcert, and fascinate its investigators. On the other hand, if Horgan is right, if the human mind is, in fact, irreducible to anything else, then mind-science may truly be science's final frontier.

Robert J. Paradowski

Sources for Further Study

Booklist 96 (September 15, 1999): 208.
Library Journal 124 (October 15, 1999): 101.
The New York Times Book Review 104 (October 31, 1999): 30.
Publishers Weekly 246 (August 2, 1999): 63.

VENONA
Decoding Soviet Espionage in America

Authors: John Earl Haynes (1944-) and Harvey Klehr (1945-)
Publisher: Yale University Press (New Haven, Connecticut). Illustrated. 487 pp. $30.00
Type of work: History
Time: The 1940's and the 1950's
Locale: The United States

A very well researched study of the full extent of Soviet espionage in America during the 1940's and the 1950's as revealed in the decoded Venona cables, which the United States government released in 1995

Principal personages:
EARL BROWDER, a Soviet spy and head of the Communist Party of the United States of America (CPUSA) from 1930 to 1945
LAUCHLIN CURRIE, a White House aide who spied for the Soviets in the 1940's
KLAUS FUCHS, a British scientist who was imprisoned for revealing atomic bomb secrets to the Soviets
THEODORE HALL, an American scientist who revealed atomic bomb secrets to the Soviets
ALGER HISS, an American diplomat and Soviet spy, who was imprisoned for perjury
JULIUS and
ETHEL ROSENBERG, Americans executed in 1953 for giving atomic bomb secrets to the Soviet Union
HARRY WHITE, a Soviet spy and assistant secretary of the Treasury in the 1940's
VASILY ZUBILIN, the head of *Komitet Gosudarstvennoi Bezopasnosti* (KGB) activities in the United States during World War II

Although the United States and the Soviet Union became allies against the Nazis after the German invasion of the Soviet Union in June, 1941, the Soviets conducted extensive industrial, scientific, and military spying against the United States throughout the 1940's and the 1950's. The full extent of Soviet spying in America and the active collaboration of more than three hundred Americans with Soviet intelligence agents was not revealed to the public until the 1995 release by the United States government of the Venona cables.

In 1939, officials in American and British intelligence began intercepting coded messages sent to the Soviet Union from Soviet embassies in the United States and Great Britain, but until 1942 American and British intelligence agents were more concerned with deciphering coded messages sent from Nazi Germany and Japan to their military commanders. By 1942, British and American cryptanalysts, or codebreakers, had successfully broken the German Enigma code and the Japanese military code, and thus the Allies were able to read all secret military messages sent by the Nazis and Japanese from 1942 onward. Neither Germany nor Japan ever knew that the Allies had broken their codes, and they continued to send messages in the same codes. The deciphering of the German and Japanese codes enabled the Allies to learn of enemy military strategy in advance of battles, and the work of these cryptanalysts contributed significantly to the Allied victories over Germany and Japan in World War II.

In 1943, President Franklin D. Roosevelt began to suspect that Joseph Stalin, his ally against the Nazis, was conducting espionage in the United States. He ordered American intelligence organizations, such as the Office of Strategic Services, the Federal Bureau of Investigation (FBI), and Army Military Intelligence, to begin investigating the extent of Soviet spying in America. In February, 1943, Colonel Carter Clarke, who was then the chief of the Special Branch of the Army Military Intelligence Division, instructed his colleagues to begin examining the coded messages sent from Soviet embassies in the United States. This extremely secret undertaking was called the Venona Project. Work on deciphering these messages proceeded very slowly, but by 1946, Americans had successfully broken the Soviet code and were able to read messages sent by Soviet spies in America to their superiors in Moscow. American cryptanalysts also deciphered messages sent before 1946.

Thanks to the efforts of these diligent cryptanalysts, it became abundantly clear to United States government officials that there were many Soviet spies operating in America as well as Americans within and outside the United States government who had betrayed important military, atomic, and industrial secrets to agents of both the KGB (the chief security service of the Soviet Union) and the GRU (the Soviet military intelligence agency), which had entered the United States either illegally or as diplomats. American intelligence agents soon discovered which Soviet diplomats in the United States were KGB or GRU agents. It also soon became clear to American intelligence officials that the extent of Soviet spying in America and the number of American traitors were much larger than had been previously suspected.

In response to this very real threat to American security, President Harry S Truman created the Central Intelligence Agency (CIA) in 1947 and issued in the same year an executive order establishing an extensive screening program for government employees and banning members of the CPUSA from employment with the federal government or in defense industries. Until the release of the Venona cables in 1995, many people questioned President Truman's actions, which they viewed incorrectly as an excessive invasion of individual rights. Such critics, however, did not understand that the CPUSA had cooperated fully with the KGB and GRU in order to recruit and train overt and covert American communists for espionage in America. Almost all American spies identified in the Venona cables were members of the CPUSA. The loyalty of American communists was to the Soviet Union and not to the United States.

When congressional investigations in 1947 and 1948 began to reveal the reality of Soviet spying on America and the existence of American traitors in high governmental positions, the American public reacted with anger. Many American spies invoked their Fifth Amendment protection and refused to testify about their criminal activities and their membership in the CPUSA. Their stonewalling persuaded Americans that Soviet spying was much more extensive than was actually the case. Those government employees who refused to testify before congressional committees, such as the House Committee on Un-American Activities, were dismissed from their jobs and barred from further employment by the federal government or in the defense industry.

The American public did not know whom to believe and for very good reasons. President Truman and his successor, President Dwight D. Eisenhower, concluded that it would not be advisable to reveal the existence of the Venona Project or the source of information obtained from the decoded Venona cables because they did not want the Soviets to know that Americans were reading their most secret messages. Shortly after the end of World War II, the Soviet Union occupied most of Eastern Europe and became the main enemy of the United States. The reality of the Cold War and the military danger that the Soviet Union posed to the United States became obvious, especially after the Soviet Union exploded its first atomic bomb in 1949. The decoded Venona cables proved that the Soviet Union had produced and detonated an atomic bomb quickly because spies such as Klaus Fuchs, Theodore Hall, and the Rosenbergs had furnished KGB and GRU agents essential atomic secrets, which enabled Soviet scientists to develop the atomic bomb more quickly than would have been otherwise possible.

The American public became enraged upon realizing that these spies had betrayed the United States not for money but for ideological reasons. Spies such as the Rosenbergs, Alger Hiss, Lauchlin Currie, and Theodore Hall demonstrated clear contempt for American democracy. Although their guilt was proven beyond a reasonable doubt, they remained unrepentant because, in their minds, they had done nothing wrong.

The successful prosecution of Soviet spies was difficult for American prosecutors because they chose not to reveal in court any information obtained solely from the Venona cables. These decoded messages were, however, essential for prosecutors because they served as independent corroboration of statements given by former Soviet spies, such as Elizabeth Bentley and Igor Gouzenko, who gave much useful information about Soviet spying in North America to American and Canadian intelligence agencies. Many Americans who spied for the Soviets escaped prosecution entirely, whereas others were convicted of lesser crimes such as perjury simply because the American government did not dare reveal the truth about the decoded Venona cables.

During the decade immediately following the end of World War II, Americans did not know what to believe. The Alger Hiss case illustrates very nicely the complexity of the situation for Americans. Until 1938, Whittaker Chambers had directed the espionage activities of a covert communist spy named Alger Hiss. In 1938, however, Chambers decided to turn against communism, and he stopped spying for the GRU. In 1939, he informed the FBI of Hiss's support for Communism, but for reasons that are still not clear, the FBI did not take seriously the danger to American security posed by communist spying in America. In defense of the FBI, one should remember that the FBI's responsibility for investigating espionage was not clearly spelled out until late in World War II. In 1948, Chambers testified before the House Committee on

Un-American Activities, about the communist activities of Hiss, his former subordinate. Hiss testified under oath that he had never been a communist. Congressman Richard M. Nixon played an active role in these hearings, and Hiss was later convicted of perjury for lying to this congressional committee about his communist past. Chambers had been an alcoholic and several people expressed doubts about his veracity, but until the revelation of the Venona codes in 1995, it was still defensible for people to side with Hiss against Chambers. However, the Venona codes proved that Hiss was both a communist and a spy. Although Chambers was not a sympathetic individual, he did tell the truth when he testified in 1948 that Alger Hiss had been a communist. For decades after Hiss's conviction and imprisonment for perjury, many people criticized Chambers and defended Hiss. The release of the Venona cables in 1995 proved that Hiss had been both a communist and a spy, and served to rehabilitate posthumously Chambers's reputation.

The research conducted by John Earl Haynes and Harvey Klehr, in America and in recently opened Russian archives, significantly improves our understanding of the nature and extent of Soviet spying in the United States from the 1930's to the 1950's and answers several questions which were never fully resolved in the years immediately following World War II. Despite adamant denials by communists and communist sympathizers in America during the Cold War, the guilt of specific American spies such as Julius and Ethel Rosenberg, Alger Hiss, Theodore Hall, Gregory Silvermaster, Lauchlin Currie, and more than three hundred others has now been demonstrated beyond a reasonable doubt. Since the release of the Venona cables, it has become clear that there was factual proof for the numerous charges leveled against many American traitors in the 1940's and 1950's by various congressional committees and federal prosecutors. Although certain politicians, such as Senator Joseph R. McCarthy, made unsubstantiated and irresponsible charges by claiming that General George C. Marshall and Secretary of State Dean Acheson were communist sympathizers, the various House and Senate committees, which in the 1940's and 1950's investigated communist activities against American security, correctly understood and demonstrated the seriousness of the threat created by Soviet spying against America both during and after World War II. This is a fascinating and well-documented historical study that demonstrates clearly that more than three hundred American traitors endangered American national security by betraying for ideological reasons essential American military, atomic, and industrial secrets to the KGB and GRU.

Edmund J. Campion

Sources for Further Study

The American Spectator 32 (September, 1999): 67.
Booklist 95 (April 1, 1999): 1370.
The Economist 352 (August 28, 1999): 67.

Library Journal 124 (April 15, 1999): 116.
The New Republic 220 (July 5, 1999): 29.
The New York Times Book Review 104 (May 9, 1999): 34.
Time 153 (June 7, 1999): 66.

VÉRA (MRS. VLADIMIR NABOKOV)
Portrait of a Marriage

Author: Stacy Schiff
Publisher: Random House (New York). Illustrated. 456 pp. $27.95
Type of work: Literary biography
Time: c. 1923-1977
Locale: Europe and the United States

The story of a woman's fifty-five-year marriage to a brilliant but self-centered poet and novelist

Principal personages:
VÉRA EVSEEVNA NABOKOV, née Slonim, wife of Vladimir Nabokov
VLADIMIR VLADIMIROVICH NABOKOV (alias VLADIMIR SIRIN) poet and novelist
DMITRI NABOKOV, son of Véra and Vladimir
DOLORES HAZE, a twelve-year-old starlet

Stacy Schiff describes her latest biography, *Véra (Mrs. Vladimir Nabokov): Portrait of a Marriage*, as "the story of a woman, a man, and a marriage." More accurately, it is the story of Vladimir Nabokov's married life. It joins five other, less covert, biographical studies of the Russian-born author of *Lolita* (1955): Andrew Field's trilogy *Nabokov: His Life in Art, a Critical Narrative* (1967), *Nabokov: His Life in Part* (1977), and *VN: The Life and Art of Vladimir Nabokov* (1986); Brian Boyd's more scholarly *Vladimir Nabokov: The Russian Years* (1990); and Boyd's *Vladimir Nabokov: The American Years* (1991). Schiff's ostensible focus on Véra allows her to probe previously unexplored nooks and crannies of the novelist's life and show his utter dependence on his wife, who seems to have had "some trouble discerning where she ended and her husband began." Vladimir Nabokov, alias Sirin, alias "VN," became Véra's life and career; the reader is told that she elevated "the role of wife to a high art." She was his agent, his muse, his classroom assistant, his typist, his learned corrector, his best reader, and his biggest fan. According to one much repeated anecdote, Véra even saved *Lolita* from the incinerator (actually, a flaming trash barrel in the Nabokovs' backyard). The story of her devotion and sacrifice seems to be the story of Vladimir Nabokov's success.

Though it has ten chapters, Schiff's biography divides itself more effectively into four major sections, corresponding roughly to the stages or temporary residences in the Nabokovs' lifelong migration: Berlin; Paris; Ithaca, New York; and Montreux, Switzerland. Véra and Vladimir both managed to escape Russia moments before the Old World permanently collapsed. They met and married in Berlin, and it was there that their son, Dmitri, was born. A decade later, the couple was again on the move, this time fleeing Berlin for France just as the Nazis were intensifying their campaign against Jews. Véra was Jewish but escaped the tragic fate of some of her Jewish friends and neighbors. Nabokov's brother, Sergei, was a homosexual and would later die in a concentration camp. Paris was less inviting to Véra than to Vladimir, who was able to hobnob with the French intelligentsia; he quickly began to earn an international name for himself. Shortly before Paris fell to the Nazis, the Nabokovs set sail for America, where Vladimir eventually found a permanent teaching position at Cornell but still made time, at Véra's expense, to write some of his most important English-language works. After the publication of *Lolita*, which catapulted Vladimir to celebrity status, the Nabokovs made one more major move in their lives, this time to Switzerland, where they took up permanent residence at a hotel in Montreux.

The first chapter of Schiff's biography does not begin with Véra's birth and childhood, as one might expect, but unchronologically with the meeting and early courtship of the future Nabokovs in Berlin. Mask imagery runs through this section of the chapter, because Véra was supposedly wearing a mask at their first appointed meeting. She seems to have been the aggressor in this case, he the alluring poet fighting off women. In a sense the mask becomes a metaphor for their relationship. Vladimir's love poetry to Véra abounds with references to masks and masking. His pseudonym, V. Sirin, functioned as a "little silk mask." After their marriage, he began to publish under his real name. Schiff writes, "So disassociated was Vladimir from his family name after his years as Sirin that when first he saw Nabokov in print he read it as 'Nobody.'" Similarly, Véra transformed herself when she assumed her married name, which functioned "almost as a stage name." These masks stayed with them for life, even as others were created. Vladimir would use "VN" in later years; one of Véra's later epistolary pseudonyms was J. G. Smith. According to Schiff, Véra's "whole being was to constitute a mask" for her husband, allowing him to speak through her and allowing her to hide in "full view."

The title of Schiff's biography seems to promise an unmasking: "Véra" followed by "Mrs. Vladimir Nabokov" in parentheses. This is an inversion of Véra's practice in the 1950's of signing business letters as "Mrs. Vladimir Nabokov" and then typing "Véra Nabokov" in parentheses above her married name. The book's subtitle, *Portrait of a Marriage*, however, immediately muddies the waters by shifting the focus away from the woman. Can it be that there was no Véra independent of Mrs. Vladimir Nabokov? Is the reader to believe that the story of this woman's life is neither more nor less than a portrait of her marriage? The answer seems to be yes. Their marriage was such a partnership, albeit a one-sided partnership, at least on the surface, that it is not possible or desirable to separate Véra completely from Mrs. Vladimir Nabokov. In 1925 Nabokov wrote to his sister that "in love you must be Siamese twins, where one sneezes when the other sniffs tobacco." In this marriage Vladimir was the sniffer, Véra the sneezer—always.

Underlying their relationship was a remarkable fluidity of identity: They could not be pinned down easily for study by critics or biographers. Statements would be made by one and denied or corrected by the other. In his passion Vladimir would embellish, while Véra in her precision would quibble. Shown an account of their first meeting that Vladimir gave in an interview, Véra noted that there were at least three factual errors in the first sentence alone, but she would not say what they were. These games mirrored the games in Vladimir's fiction, which made mincemeat of the boundaries between life and art. On more than one occasion, Nabokov appropriated episodes from Véra's life and gave them to characters in his novels. One of Schiff's modi operandi is to draw parallels between female characters in the novels and Véra in real life. The reader is reminded, for example, that Clare in *The Real Life of Sebastian Knight* (1941) is particularly "Véra-like." These parallels are seldom endorsed by the Nabokovs. When asked whether a character was modeled after her, Véra would usually scoff at the suggestion and deny any similarity.

This fiction-making, which extended into real life, is the source of some anxiety for Schiff. She realizes how easy it is for a biographer to fall into one of the Nabokovs' many traps. She is also aware that her biography would not have pleased Véra, who is no longer alive to defend herself. In one footnote Schiff writes,

> The biographical account [that Véra] would have found most acceptable would doubtless have resembled Mrs. Shade's entry in the *Pale Fire* index: "*Shade, Sybil, S*'s wife, *passim.*"

Schiff notes how distasteful Véra would have found the long entry for Véra Evseevna Nabokov in the index of Boyd's second biography. Not surprisingly, Véra's entry in Schiff's index is even longer. In another footnote, Schiff uses first person and no quotation marks to voice Véra's objections to Schiff's own comparison between Véra and Zina in Nabokov's *Dar* (1952), translated as *The Gift* (1963). Schiff clearly sees herself as the latest in a line of Nabokov biographers. In narrating the Nabokovs' last trip to Ithaca in 1964, she gives Andrew Field's version, then Boyd's version, and finally her own version, demonstrating that the same episode benefits from multiple perspectives. How does Schiff's "portrait" stack up against Field's and Boyd's biographies? More effectively than the others, which focus directly on Vladimir, Schiff's "portrait" conveys a strong sense of how important the marriage was to Vladimir's teaching and writing.

Chapters 5 and 6, titled "Nabokov 101" and "Nabokov 102," offer perhaps the best exegesis of their marriage. These two chapters cover the Ithaca years, when Vladimir was teaching at Cornell. Véra would attend class with him and sit nearby as he lectured, serving as his "assistant" (his term). Her duties included fetching things from his office, erasing the chalkboard, operating the light switch, prompting his memory, getting him back on track at times, and protecting him from attractive coeds. She would grade his bluebooks and monitor his conferences with students, cautioning him to be more gentle in his responses to their writing. It was in Ithaca that Vladimir wrote *Lolita* as well as *Pnin* (1957), the story of an absent-minded professor. Véra encouraged him at every turn. She retrieved discarded pages from the waste basket and saved them for later publication. As his "agent," she found a publisher for *Lolita* in France after the novel had been rejected by several American publishers.

Véra made her husband's success and fame possible. This seems to be the prevailing message of Schiff's book. In the early years of their marriage, she supported him and their son while Vladimir traveled and gave poetry readings. Though she fell in love with him because of his poetry, she later encouraged him to switch to prose; she also encouraged him to abandon Russian for English at a crucial point in his career. In the

United States, where butterflies and coeds were abundant, Véra did her best to keep Vladimir focused on his writing. She freed him from much of the academic drudgery at Cornell. She dissuaded him from giving up on *Lolita* to write a novel about the love life of Siamese twins. In her mind, not all of her suggestions turned out for the best. She later regretted persuading him to translate Alexander Pushkin's *Evgeny Onegin* (1833) as *Eugene Onegin* (1964), a decade-long project that she felt had cost Vladimir "a few titles of his own." She not only typed but also critiqued his works in progress. His manuscripts are laced with her corrections and substantive comments—not all of them heeded. Yet the only work in which Vladimir overtly acknowledges Véra's contributions is his Pushkin translation. As Schiff writes, "She was more than a typist, less than a collaborator." Sadly, this seems to be Véra's memorial, along with "She was just a wife."

Not including the cursory recounting of Véra's childhood in chapter 1, Véra's life without Vladimir is given precisely seventeen pages at the end of Schiff's 374-page narrative (456 pages, counting the back matter), yet Véra lived for more than a decade after her husband's death in 1977, overseeing his empire of reprints, translations, and some new publications and assisting his critics and biographers. It is not accurate, therefore, to call this a biography of Véra. It is "a portrait of a marriage," with a greater interest in the novelist than in his wife. The book is valuable because it offers a perspective on Vladimir Nabokov that complements the several biographies by Andrew Field and Brian Boyd.

Edward A. Malone

Sources for Further Study

Booklist 95 (February 15, 1999): 1003.
Boston Globe, April 18, 1999, p. E1.
Library Journal 124 (April 1, 1999): 98.
The New York Times Book Review 104 (April 25, 1999): 34.
Publishers Weekly 246 (March 22, 1999): 81.

VICE
New and Selected Poems

Author: Ai (1947-   )
Publisher: W. W. Norton (New York). 256 pp. $25.00
Type of work: Poetry
Time: The late twentieth century
Locale: The United States

This award-winning collection provides a gallery of Ai's most shocking and memorable portraits of real and imaginary people

Many selected poems of relatively young poets seem premature; this one does not. A collection of selected poems is appropriate once a poet has a group of anthologized, widely discussed, often-quoted and often-cited poems that span several books. *Vice* gives the essence of this unique and powerful poet's work. Ai's characteristic dramatic monologues have won for her wide acclaim. In this book, readers hear from silenced individuals who exist on the margins of American culture as well as from figures in the political and entertainment worlds. The imagined thoughts of American icons give new interpretations of their public words and acts, while the anonymous speakers show the pain, desires, and resourcefulness of the disadvantaged. This book received the highest recognition: It was honored with the National Book Award for Poetry in 1999.

This award is only one of many received by Ai; her honors include the Lamont Poetry Award for *Killing Floor* (1979) and an American Book Award for *Sin* (1986). In addition, before this collection Ai had published three other books: *Cruelty* (1973), *Fate* (1991), and *Greed* (1993). *Vice* includes selections from all five previous books as well as her newest poems. Her titles indicate that the interior landscapes she describes are not picturesque. Dominated by violence, lust, rage, and exploitation, they display the darkness she finds at the center of the human personality.

A somewhat mysterious poet, Ai has been a speaker for the disenfranchised since her first book. She points out that her name means "love" in Japanese; it is appropriate that in French, "Ai!" is a cry of pain. Of mixed-race background, Ai speaks for all those who have been overlooked by the system, whatever their background or race. She commented that her father was Japanese and her mother, "a Black, Choctaw Indian, Irish and German woman from Texas." However, she does not limit her subject matter to any group; her speakers come from all likely and unlikely places.

The cover of *Vice* is a good key to the contents—it shows two men in black uniforms being hauled away in what appears to be a police van; they are covering their faces with their black hats. The voices in the book, particularly in the last or "new poems" section, will emanate from behind the hats. It is most appropriate that *Greed*, *Fate*, *Cruelty*, and *Sin*—with *Killing Floor* thrown in for good measure—should combine into *Vice*, which suggests a habitual, aware violation of human decency and the social contract.

Ai's poems have always been strikingly original, memorable for their clashes and dissonances, their violence, their startling and often unpalatable insights. The theme is the human capacity for destruction, but the poems are not nihilistic. With the drive to destroy comes the drive to love, and sometimes the two are indistinguishable. She once said something to the effect that if a new work did the same thing as a previous one, she would tear it up, even if it was good. Yet, although each work does something new, there is always an underlying voice of pain, outrage, and growth, and it would be easy to identify an Ai poem. Her poetry is shocking, but not gratuitously so—it aims to jolt the reader out of complacency, and its kicks are well placed.

Ai's earliest work gave voice to suffering rural people, often women, who had to survive by any means possible. These tended to be shorter poems but still persona poems, casual dramatic monologues that give a good glimpse into life on the edge. Many of Ai's characters are women with the odds stacked against them. In her first poems, these women are colorful outlaws or outcasts, filled with desire and need, victims and/or perpetrators of violence. The speaker of the frequently anthologized "Everything: Eloy, Arizona, 1956" has a jaunty vitality that makes her a survivor rather than a victim, even though nothing positive appears on her horizon:

> Tin shack, where my baby sleeps on his back
> the way the hound taught him;
> highway, black zebra, with one white stripe;
> nickel in my pocket for chewing gum;
> you think you're all I've got.

She also has the trucker she is expecting to come along, who will affirm her sensuality and sense of self even though the relationship has no future and she knows it.

> He's keys, tires, a fire lit in his belly
> in the diner up the road.
> I'm red toenails, tight blue halter, black slip.
> He's mine tonight. I don't know him.
> He can only hurt me a piece at a time.

Other women speak, briefly and forcefully, in "Twenty-Year Marriage," "Why Can't I Leave You?" "The Country Midwife: A Day," and others. Desire, love, and violence mingle convincingly in the poems.

After her first work, the poems become longer, more complex. They also begin to explore social issues more fully. The speakers seem to step out of the pages of history, black-and-white grainy photographs suddenly turning three-dimensional, vivid with color. Some readers will find the pungent and sometimes bellicose poems distasteful, but true slice-of-life poetry does not present neatly carved vignettes. The power of Ai's work is that it brings to life individuals for whom living is a struggle, and it forces one to identify with them—an identification readers are reluctant to accept.

Yet to be passive, to refuse life's vital, violent élan in the world Ai describes, is to die. Indeed, what it takes to survive in this world is a zest for life as well as enough violence within to counter the violence without. Thus readers cheer for "The Cockfighter's Daughter," who, after an abusive home life and failed marriage, comes back home to the violent old man. When he dies, "face down, in his homemade chili," the speaker looks at the fighting cock, her inheritance: his symbol and hers. The fighting cock had once torn a hunk out of her father's flesh.

> When the old man stopped the bleeding,
> the rooster was waiting on top of the pickup,
> his red eyes like Pentecostal flames.
> That's when Father named him Preacher.

The speaker drives her car down into the river, but then jumps out at the last minute, choosing to live as her father's heir rather than to die. She drives off in his truck with Preacher the cock, intending to follow her father's schedule of fights.

Also characteristic of Ai's later work is her tendency to enter boldly the minds of people in high places, showing that the motives and desires are the same on top as on the bottom, but that the situations are complicated by issues of power and money. One of the most striking of her monologues does not involve the power figure but a victim—Mary Jo Kopechne, the woman who drowned at Chappaquiddick. This poem, entitled "Go," tells of the incident in Kopechne's voice and makes of Edward Kennedy, her companion who failed to save her, a symbol of the corruption of Camelot idealism. Kennedy, "grown fat and jowly/ at the table where no feast is ever served," is contrasted with the mythic Kennedys who died young, their images unsullied. Part of the effectiveness of the poem is the way—as the waters did with their victim—it sucks the reader in with its fairy-tale beginning:

> Once upon a Massachusetts midnight,
> under a sky smoothed of light,
> as if wiped by flannel,
> a car sailed off a bridge
> but did not float.
> Then the water, the dark gray water,
> opened its mouth
> and I slid down its throat.

Many of the most recent, previously uncollected poems leap from news headlines, although many of them are carefully labeled "a fiction." They give interior glimpses of adulterous presidents, paparazzi, other national figures. If some of them are not as compelling as the earlier ones, then it may be that the events are too current to be recast as poetry even by Ai—there is something about the Clinton scandal that cannot be separated from "yesterday's news." Moreover, her most persuasive, most intensely real characters tend to be women. The men she creates are interesting, too, but they are more likely to provide insights into a political or social situation than create a new friend or enemy for the reader that cannot be shaken loose easily.

The most striking poems in this last section are often about historical situations that Ai has personalized by giving it "a local habitation and a name." Thus the speakers in "Chance" and "Rwanda" make the injustices described in the poems real to the reader by forcing him or her to participate. "Chance" tells the story of a young girl whose family vacation resulted in her father's cancer, because of nuclear tests conducted on unsuspecting civilians in the 1950's. "Chance" portrays the ordinary, innocent activities of the family, who have been selected by chance (and by an irresponsible agency) for tragedy. "Rwanda" is one of the handful of poems that does not reflect life in the United States. It has as its speaker a girl whose family is killed by a neighbor who is a part of the terrorists. This poem has a colorful and misleadingly hopeful beginning:

> My neighbor used to come to our hut,
> bringing melons so sweet
> I thought I should not eat them,
> because I would die
> and haunt my family like a ghost
> with hard, black seeds for eyes.
> One day, he brought his uncle and two friends
> and they asked my father to go outside with them.
> I thought he had come to get permission to marry me
> and I was glad because I loved him, . . .

But the intent is murder, not marriage, and the neighbor kills the father and mother and later rapes the speaker, who is left with a son she does not kill only because her mother's bones tell her that killing is a sin. The poem moves toward closure with despair that reaches beyond the speaker's own situation:

> but in my heart I know
> both his mother and father died long ago
> and left this orphan to grow like a poisoned flower
> beside the open grave that was my country.

The poems included here have been thoughtfully chosen; most of Ai's most frequently anthologized poems are here, but this is a modest-sized book, containing seventy-six poems: eighteen new ones, and the rest from her five previous collections. *Vice* is a fierce, cutting, and insightful commentary on the times and places it records and reimagines. It clearly demonstrates that Ai is a skilled narrator and master monologuist as well as an adept spokesperson for the marginalized, especially the rural American poor, of the middle to late twentieth century.

Janet McCann

Sources for Further Study

American Visions 14 (October, 1999): 35.
Booklist 95 (February 14, 1999): 1028.
Library Journal 124 (April 15, 1999): 100.
Publishers Weekly 246 (March 29, 1999): 97.

VITA NOVA

Author: Louise Glück (1943-   )
Publisher: Ecco Press (Hopewell, New Jersey). 51 pp. $22.00
Type of work: Poetry

An intense, poetic exploration and reexamination of lost love in the myths of Dido and Aeneas and of Orpheus and Eurydice

The title of Louise Glück's latest collection of poems, *Vita Nova*, suggests that it is a work built on the structural theme of renewal by love in Dante's famous sonnet sequence. However, the new life of which Glück speaks in these poems is not only a renewal of life but also an acceptance of death; it is closer to a *lebenstod* or love-death song than the discovery of a transcendent love. In addition, Glück uses myths and allusions from classical literature, especially Dido and Aeneas from Vergil's *Aeneid* (c. 29-19 B.C.E.; Eng. trans., 1553) and Orpheus and Eurydice in this book; in contrast, she uses only a few allusions to Dante or his *La vita nuova* (c. 1292; *Vita Nuova*, 1861).

The poems are written in a spare style that is simple and direct in language and often ironic and mocking in tone; that simplicity is very intense and each poem is filled with startling natural images, especially those dealing with light. There are also many voices in the poems, and Glück uses an interrogator of her own and such mythic speakers as Eurydice and Dido. This creates a dialogue within her own poems that adds to the complexity of the poems and the book as a whole.

"Vita Nova" is the first poem in the collection, and it does have some Dantean overtones. It begins with renewal: "You saved me, you should remember me." The "you" is, perhaps, similar to Beatrice in Dante's poem. However, the savior "should" remember the speaker of the poem and does not. This line is followed by images of renewal, of "apple blossoms," and of feelings from childhood. A beautiful scene from "Lugano" and a memory of a joyful moment intensify this renewal: ". . .so that I woke elated, at my age/ hungry for life, utterly confident." The poem evokes such "moments" again and again in these poems; this allows Glück to use juxtaposition and questions that produce various resolutions to the apparent renewal provided by such glowing moments.

The last stanza announces the renewal: "Surely spring has been returned to me this time." However, the discovery of renewal in spring is not, as it is in Dante, associated with a "lover" but with "a messenger of death." The speaker of the poem welcomes this discovery: "yet/ it is still spring, it is still meant tenderly." The embrace of death is as tender as that of a lover and is "still spring." This notion is a clear revision of the tradition and the source of this poem.

"Aubade" varies the poetic genre as well; an aubade is an ancient song that speaks of the parting of two lovers with an announcement of dawn. Glück's poem is instead a return to the dawn of one's life, childhood; however, that blissful time is shattered by the acknowledgment of "time," the "tragic dimension." Images of a room and especially those of light bring back the ideal time with "the self at the center." In this evocation of a beautiful moment, there is still something unsatisfying, "time stirring, time/ crying to be touched, to be/ palpable." Earlier in the poem, "time" was "tragic," whereas now it is a way out of "stasis." The poem ends with an interesting resolution of these opposites. The speaker returns to childhood "in the presence of riches"; however, "I didn't know what the riches were made of." The common desire to return to a time of innocence is qualified by the fact that any return must be accompanied by the full weight of experiences of a later time. The poem is a complex interrogation of some of the most common romantic themes.

"The Queen of Carthage" is the first of a number of poems that deal with Dido's rejection by Aeneas and subsequent suicide. Glück once more unites love and death. The poem is primarily a recitation of the memories of the coming of Aeneas and his bringing the gift of "passion." Dido describes the coming of Aeneas and her release in passion in terms of "the Fates." Again, the focus is on the moment:

> . . . What difference
> between that and a lifetime: in truth, in such moments,
> they are the same, they are both eternity.

Dido accepts "suffering" as she had accepted the "favor" of love; the dual nature of love and suffering is clearly a major theme of the book.

The next poem on Dido, "The Burning Heart," has an interrogator who doggedly questions the feelings of Dido: "Ask her how he touched her." Dido's reply includes many of the traditional descriptions of the visitation of Eros: "His gaze touched me/ before his hands touched me." The interrogator prods: "Asks her if the fire hurts." He is referring, of course, to the fire of passion and to the fire of Dido's pyre on which she is burned. Her reply stresses the union of the lovers. They are first together, and gradually Dido realizes the differences as well: "though neither of us ever moved/ we were not together but profoundly separate." The last question is "Do you regret your life?" Dido reaffirms the truth of love in spite of her terrible fate: "Even before I was touched, I belonged to you;/ you had only to look at me." The gaze of the beloved has the power to enthrall as it does in Dante and Shakespeare.

"Roman Study" is an ironic portrayal of Aeneas, who betrayed love for empire. It begins with Aeneas longing for the passion of the Greek Aphrodite instead of the Roman Venus. However, this longing is quickly replaced by a "contempt" for Greece and its "light." He moves toward a life of reason and watchfulness. He rejects the "predictable, routine" quality of tragedy for the worldly claims of empire. The speaker of the poem is Aeneas, and Glück exposes his rational and rationalizing nature in his own self-justifying words.

"The New Life" is written not from the male viewpoint of Dante, but from that of a female speaker who assesses her life. This takes the form of a confession:

> I have been in my other lives
> too hasty, too eager,
> my haste a source of pain in the world.

The speaker is similar to Dido, who accepts her punishment as the logical fulfillment of passion. She has ". . . died having answered for/ one species of ruthlessness." That "ruthlessness" is, of course, this passion of love which Glück sees not in sentimental but classical terms; the visitation of Aphrodite is filled with terror.

"Formaggio" at first seems to deal with different themes. It speaks of the world and the speaker's relationship with and acceptance of it. A group of stores on Huron Ave. in Cambridge becomes her "place of safety." It is a place where the "salespeople" are "kinder than parents." The poem then shifts from a place of rest to the troubled self. The speaker, again, has had "many lives." She uses a metaphor to define those lives in time: "Above the hand/ the branching future, stems/ ending in flowers. And the gripped fist" is the "self in the present." She deliberately, almost desperately, holds on to the saving details of the present rather than retreat to blessed moments of the past, as many of the early poems in this book do.

"Orfeo" is the first of a group of poems using the Orpheus and Eurydice myth; here, Orpheus speaks of his grief for his lost Eurydice. His focus is, however, more on his art than his grief. His glorious music comes from "real grief." The treatment of Orpheus is interesting: Glück sees the artist as using grief to perfect his or her art. He will be remembered by Dis, the god of the underworld; he has achieved fame for the power of his song, a reward for which all artists search. The love that he has lost is, of course, sacrificed to the perfection of his art.

"Immortal Love" and "Earthly Love" are paired poems that touch on one of the important themes of Dante's *Vita Nuova*. In "Immortal Love," the soul is stepping outside and venturing "at the invitation/ of any desire." This unholy action is questioned by one of Glück's interrogators: "Promiscuous one, how will you find/ god now?" The resolution is ironic. The interrogator then asks if the soul has "no home, since god/ never meant to contain you?" The soul apparently is freed from the body to seek love.

"Earthly Love" is an ironic treatment of love. It begins by speaking of love as one of the "Conventions of the time." This love diverged from such conventions; it was "voluntary, alive." However, "true happiness" is only possible with "self-deception." The ending brings together all of the contradictions of the poem. The speaker will "repeat these errors" even if they are built on "illusion"; "And in either case, it will end." Earthly love is temporary and filled with illusion and delusion, but the speaker accepts it and defines its nature.

"Eurydice" is a reply to the earlier Orpheus poem. Eurydice has arrived at the moment when she returns forever to the underworld. The "Transition is difficult" and the passage filled with "regret." The ending, however, focuses on a longing for what she must leave behind, "an image of earth's beauty." The last stanza touches on a deeper regret, the nature of love: "But to live with human faithlessness/ is another matter." Earthly love had been defined as imperfect and transitory earlier, and it is now embodied in the betrayal of Orpheus. Human love in this book does not produce a Dantean transfiguration; for Glück it is a "faithlessness" we live with, although its pains are deeper than the loss of life.

"The Winged Horse" is an amusing poem that uses metaphors from racing genealogies to define the mythical horse associated with poetry. The speaker asks for Pegasus to visit her: "Come, Abstraction/ by Will out of Demonic Ambition:/ carry me lightly into the regions of the immortal." That ambition is contrasted to a life lived in "Reality"; its final reward is ironically a "Dream Out of Blind Hope."

"The Golden Bough" alludes to the mythical fruit that Aeneas uses for his safe passage into the underworld. Aeneas is the son of Venus, so his "sacrifice of love" is "less painful than for the other heroes." In contrast to Dido's passion, his mind is "clear." Because "beauty/ ran in his veins," the legacy of Venus, "he had no need/ for more of it." Possessing "beauty" within him, he is self-sufficient; he has no need of love or passion, only a "taste for empire." Glück's treatment of male lovers is mocking and bitter; they do not give in to the power of love but are led by other needs such as art or politics.

The last poem in the book, also called "Vita Nova," is less mythic and rooted in the contemporary world. It begins by speaking of "the splitting up dream" of lovers who are separating and arguing about possession of the dog, Blizzard. It ends with an evocation of passion: "Never/ will I forget your face, your frantic human eyes/ swollen with tears." However, the ending turns away from Dido's pyre and Eurydice's retreat to the underworld: "I thought my life was over and my heart was broken./ Then I moved to Cambridge." So in the last poem of the sequence, the speaker moves from heartbreak to a new life in the ordinary world.

Louise Glück's *Vita Nova* is an impressive book of poems. She revises and interrogates the ancient myths of Aeneas and Dido and of Orpheus and Eurydice and gives a new meaning to Dante's *Vita Nuova*. The poems are powerfully written and structurally complex with their reversals, reconciliations, and questioning of their own premises. Glück has used myth in her poems before, but this book shows a full reexamination of the nature and use of ancient myths in contemporary poetry.

James Sullivan

Sources for Further Study

Booklist 95 (February 1, 1999): 959.
Library Journal 124 (March 1, 1999): 88.
Publishers Weekly 245 (December 21, 1998): 62.

WAITING

Author: Ha Jin (1956-   )
Publisher: Pantheon Press (New York). 308 pp. $24.99
Type of work: Novel
Time: The mid-1960's through the mid-1980's
Locale: China

A novel about life under the iron rule of communism in the Chinese People's Republic, focusing on three people who are all helpless victims of that country's tumultuous political and social evolution

Principal personages:
LIN KONG, a Chinese army doctor
SHUYU, his first wife
HUA, their daughter
MANNA WU, an army nurse who becomes Lin's second wife
BENSHENG, Shuyu's brother

Waiting is a good title for Ha Jin's novel because it has multiple associations. Not only is Manna Wu waiting for Lin Kong to get permission to divorce his first wife, but the people of China are waiting for the good things in life that they have been promised as well. Meanwhile, the whole world is waiting to see what political, economic, and social changes will take place in this mysterious land of 1.5 billion people—whether it will become a peaceful member of the family of nations, or a lucrative market for the Western world, or whether it has a hidden agenda that will turn it into an aggressive monster that could bring on an apocalyptic third world war.

Jin does not criticize the Communist government. He does not suggest that there is corruption in high places or that the higher-ranking members of the party enjoy a more luxurious lifestyle than that of the common people. His characters are too humble, too subdued, and too regimented to think of questioning the bureaucracy regulating every aspect of their lives. Like the reader, they seem to realize that with the enormous population pressure, the Chinese people are lucky to have a plain but adequate amount of food, decent clothes, clean beds in shared living quarters, and books, plays, and films heavily weighted with propaganda for entertainment. Furthermore, they are kept in ignorance of the outside world, so they have no basis for comparison. Possession of foreign books could ruin a budding career. The Communist bureaucrats have the power to send anyone anywhere and to appoint them to any occupation they choose. Lin Kong owns a small collection of relatively innocuous books like Leo Tolstoy's *War and Peace* (1865-1869) that he keeps out of sight, and he has bound them all in plain wrapping paper to hide their titles.

For nearly eighteen years, Lin Kong and Manna Wu have been waiting to be free to marry. Lin's wife Shuyu remained behind in tiny Goose Village when he went off to the city to work as an army doctor. She symbolizes the old China. She even has bound feet that are only four inches long. The two were never in love but were united by an old-style marriage arranged by their parents in accordance with ancient Chinese tradition. Shuyu became a devoted wife who bore Lin a daughter and faithfully cared for both of his aged parents until their deaths. She is humble, obedient, and industrious, and has come to worship her husband; he, however, has become so citified that he no longer has anything in common with her. He has fallen in love with an intelligent, relatively liberated woman who might be said to represent the new China. They work together, but Manna Wu remains a virgin because their activities are so carefully monitored that they are not even able to go for walks together outside the grounds of the hospital where they work.

Lin regularly applies to the village court for permission to obtain a divorce. Shuyu obediently accompanies her lord and master, but cannot bring herself to tell the judge that she no longer loves her husband or that she willingly agrees to the divorce. Instead she breaks into tears. The judge can find nothing in her conduct to justify a divorce; on the contrary, she has been such a model wife that she makes Lin look like a monster of ingratitude. Shuyu's cunning, avaricious brother Bensheng always accompanies his sister to the court and speaks in her behalf. He is opposed to the divorce because it would affect him financially. He has been able to borrow money from his brother-in-law on a regular basis, partly because Lin is a soft touch and partly because he feels guilty for virtually abandoning his wife and daughter.

Year after year the application for divorce is summarily rejected. Lin and Manna can only wait for eighteen years to elapse, after which time he will be free to obtain the divorce unilaterally. In the meantime, everyone connected with the hospital takes it for granted that Lin and Manna are virtually the same as an engaged couple; she has no chance of attracting another mate, especially as she grows older and new crops of attractive young nurses arrive every year. When Lin visits his home on periodic leaves, he does not sleep with his wife. He is forced to remain celibate while waiting for his divorce and marriage to the woman he loves. The reader is made to feel great pity for all three of these simple, honest people whose lives are being ruined by an inflexible bureaucratic system that knows no pity but only rules and regulations. Without intending to do so, the author reminds the reader of such Western works as George Orwell's *Nineteen Eighty-Four* (1949), Aldous Huxley's *Brave New World* (1932), Henry James's short story "The Madonna of the Future" (1873), and even Franz Kafka's *Der Prozess* (1925; *The Trial*, 1937). Francine Prose, who reviewed *Waiting* for *The New York Times*, referred to Jin as "the Isaac Babel of the Chinese Army."

Ha Jin is a professor of English at Emory University in Atlanta. He was born in Liaoning, China, and served for six years in the People's Liberation Army. Since coming to the United States in 1985, he has published six books, including two collections of poetry, *Between Silences: A Voice from China* (1990) and *Facing Shadows* (1996); two collections of short stories, *Ocean of Words* (1996) and *Under the Red Flag* (1997); and his first novel, *In the Pond* (1998). *Ocean of Words* won the PEN/Hemingway Award and *Under the Red Flag* won the Flannery O'Connor Award for Short Fiction. *Waiting*, his second novel, was a winner of the National Book Award. These are impressive achievements for a man who has only been in the United States for fifteen years and for whom English is a second language. No doubt his success is partly due to the fact that he writes with authority about the hearts and minds of the modern Chinese people, a subject of increasing interest to the Western world because they outnumber the populations of the United States, Europe, and Russia combined.

Jin's prose has a faintly foreign flavor. He writes in short, simple, declarative sentences and evidently does not have a broad English vocabulary. Like Ernest Hemingway, he makes the most of common words and never tries for verbal pyrotechnics. The very first sentence in *Waiting* is a good example of Jin's style: "Every summer Lin Kong returned to Goose Village to divorce his wife, Shuyu." The effect of such simple language is to make the reader feel as if he or she is in China, living among common people who are far less sophisticated than typical Westerners.

Although the novel holds the reader's interest through sympathy with the principal characters and through the insights it provides into life in modern China, there is very little in the way of suspense or drama. The reader knows from the outset that Lin and Manna are not going to be married for at least eighteen years, so the annual visits to the court do not hold out any hope for Lin to end his frustration or for Manna to realize her dream of having her own home and family. The only really dramatic incident occurs when Manna is brutally raped by an officer, who then dares her to report him to the authorities. Here Jin displays his ability to evoke strong emotions in the reader without deviating from his simple language.

The officer is correct: Manna decides against charging him with rape. It would be only her word against his, and he would truthfully claim that she came to his quarters of her own free will. She would be disgraced, because it is still a very serious matter for an unmarried woman to lose her virginity. She might even lose the affection of Lin Kong, who might wonder whether she was more attracted to the virile warrior than to the sensitive, bookish doctor who was willing to do without sex with either his wife or his mistress for eighteen years. The fact of the matter, as Manna must admit to herself, is that she actually did find the brutal soldier sexually attractive, especially since she had had no experience with sex except in her fantasies.

There is a great deal of talk about food in the novel. Food is a subject of the utmost importance to a country that has one and a half billion mouths to feed. Evidently the Communist Party had succeeded in coping with China's oldest problem. There is enough for everyone, but they have to use their culinary ingenuity to make the most out of grains and vegetables—garlic, crab apples, turnips, cabbages, carrots, rutabagas, corn, sorghum—occasionally flavored with a little pork. Ration coupons are issued for many kinds of food as well as for manufactured goods. Even obtaining a bicycle requires waiting for a hard-to-obtain ration coupon. Yet people are aware that life is better for the average person than in the old days. They continue waiting and waiting for conditions to improve further, waiting for the goods and services that Americans take for granted.

After waiting for eighteen years, Lin and Manna are finally free to marry. She turns out to have an insatiable appetite for sex, partly because she has waited so long to indulge in her fantasies and partly because she is a relatively liberated, new type of woman who feels entitled to have as strong desires as a man. Poor Lin finds it difficult to satisfy his headstrong new wife and begins to change his attitude about the humble, devoted, tradition-bound Shuyu, who demanded so little of him. He even wonders whether he was ever really in love with Manna or whether his feelings were affected by the fact that she represented forbidden fruit.

Eventually Manna gives birth to twins. This should be a joyous occasion, especially in China, where it is hard enough to obtain permission to have even one child. The long wait, however, has taken its physical and psychological toll on Manna. She is now approaching middle age. Childbirth is a terrible ordeal for her, and motherhood does not give her the satisfaction it would have done when she was young. She is becoming a querulous, chronically dissatisfied wife who blames most of her troubles on her patient, hard-working, well-meaning husband. She too has come to doubt whether she ever loved Lin and wonders if she was only a victim of circumstances that led to such an interminable period of waiting. She feels that he is not really much of a man. He is not an especially satisfactory lover, and if he had had more strength of character he might have been able to do something to prevent her from waiting eighteen years for the fulfillment of her dreams.

In order to be able to provide financial support for Shuyu, as required by the divorce decree, Lin has had to sell his ancestral home in Goose Village. Shuyu has moved to the city and obtained a factory job. She lives with her daughter, Hua, now a grown woman. Both find that they prefer city life to the drudgery and boredom of life in the country. Hua has the potential to acquire an education and a professional career. At the end of the novel, Lin is staying away from home more and more frequently and paying visits to his first family in their one-room quarters. Shuyu treats him with the same consideration, as if they are still man and wife and will always remain so in spite of any government decrees.

Bill Delaney

Sources for Further Study

Library Journal 124 (October 15, 1999): 105.
The New York Times Book Review 104 (October 24, 1999): 9.
Publishers Weekly 246 (November 1, 1999): 46.
Time 154 (November 8, 1999): 144.
The Wall Street Journal, October 22, 1999, p. W8.

WALKER EVANS

Author: James R. Mellow (1926-1997)
Photographs by Walker Evans
Publisher: Basic Books (New York). Illustrated. 654 pp. $40.00
Type of work: Biography
Time: 1903-1975
Locale: New York and Lyme, Connecticut

A massive biography of a photographer whose work illuminated the times in which he lived and changed the very definition of his art

Principal personages:
WALKER EVANS, a twentieth century American photographer
WALKER EVANS, JR., his father, an advertising man
JESSIE BEACH CRANE EVANS, his mother
JANE SMITH NINAS EVANS, his first wife
HANNS SKOLLE, a painter, a longtime friend of Evans
RALPH STEINER, a New York photographer
JAMES AGEE, the author of *Let Us Now Praise Famous Men* (1941)
HART CRANE, a poet and a friend of Evans
LINCOLN KIRSTEIN, another friend, a wealthy patron of art and literature

The untimely death of James R. Mellow brought an end to a distinguished career. Mellow edited books and periodicals, wrote criticism of art and literature, and produced several impressive literary biographies. Each of them, he said, was meant to be not only a faithful portrait of his subject but also an accurate re-creation of an era. Mellow thought of his trilogy *Charmed Circle: Gertrude Stein and Company* (1974), *Invented Lives: F. Scott and Zelda Fitzgerald* (1984), and *Hemingway: A Life Without Consequences* (1992) as a history of the lost generation and its writers. His book *Nathaniel Hawthorne in His Times* (1980) was the first in a projected series about nineteenth century Americans, which would also have included biographies of Margaret Fuller, Henry David Thoreau, and Ralph Waldo Emerson.

Because Walker Evans is best known as a photographer, rather than as a writer, one might be tempted to compare this life with the monographs Mellow wrote for the Pace Gallery, *Jim Dine, Recent Work* (1980) and *Picasso, the Avignon Paintings* (1981). It is true that art criticism is an important component of *Walker Evans*. Whenever Mellow mentions one of the many photographs by Evans that are included in the book, he not only notes when, where, and under what circumstances it was taken but also points out how elements in the design produce the intended effect. Sometimes he speculates as to what kind of camera Evans may have used for a particular shot or explains how Evans overcame practical difficulties in order to get the picture he wanted—for instance, posing his wife in front of the camera while with a right angle lens he photographed his unsuspecting and thus unselfconscious subject.

However, in format and in overall purpose, *Walker Evans* closely resembles Mellow's four literary biographies. Like them, it begins with an incident in the subject's life, in this case the only meeting between Evans and Mellow. At the time, neither of the men had any idea that Mellow would someday write a biography of Evans. As the author admits in his prologue, in 1974, when *The New York Times* asked him to interview Evans, Mellow knew something about his photographs but almost nothing about the man, not even enough to guess the significance of Evans's tossing down tumblers of brandy while they talked. Only after the interview appeared in *The New York Times* on December 1, 1974, did Mellow learn about Evans's alcoholism, which his friends had hoped he had under control. In any case, Mellow did not have a chance to pursue this slight acquaintance with the famous photographer. During the winter, Evans's health declined rapidly; he died of a stroke on April 10, 1975.

In the years that followed, Mellow moved on to other projects. However, it was almost inevitable that his interest in American cultural history would eventually lead him back to the photographer, who, like the men in the literary biographies, both reflected and influenced the times in which he lived.

After giving readers a glimpse of Evans near the end of his life, Mellow goes back to the beginning and, as in the literary biographies, proceeds chronologically from there on.

Interestingly, he devotes only one chapter, and a very short one at that, to Evans's early years. After pointing out that both his mother and his father had New England roots, the biographer establishes the fact that the first Walker Evans, the photographer's grandfather, lived in St. Louis, Missouri, and married a girl from Mexico, Missouri, where Evans's father, Walker Evans, Jr., was born. It is suggested that Jessie Beach Crane, the poet's mother, was from the same area. Although there are some photographs of her as a young woman, the reader is told almost nothing about her background or her interests.

Walker Evans III was born in St. Louis; however, because his father worked in advertising, the family moved frequently. Young Walker attended schools in Kenilworth, Illinois, near Chicago; in Toledo, Ohio; and in Windsor, Connecticut. After a brief period at Pennsylvania's Mercersburg Academy, he spent two years at the famous preparatory school in Andover, Massachusetts, Phillips Andover. Subsequently he attended Williams College, but he dropped out after one year. Mellow hypothesizes that Evans's passion for fixing time and place in photographs may have arisen out of the rootlessness of his early years.

Evans always dated his career as a photographer as beginning in 1928, five years after he left college. Previously, he had planned to become a writer, and with that end in mind, after he had worked in New York for three years, Evans persuaded his father to finance a year's study in Paris. While he did see some magnificent photography in Paris and even took some snapshots himself both there and on his travels through France and Italy, for some time Evans did not admit to himself that photography was any more than a diversion from his real vocation. However, after Evans returned to New York, some of his friends, the painter Hanns Skolle, for example, saw that he had not yet found the right outlet for his creative impulses. Mellow quotes Skolle as recalling one day in particular when he complimented Evans on his eye for composition and suggested that he photograph the Brooklyn Bridge, where the two men often walked. Evans soon had a series of pictures of the bridge and its surroundings. In 1930, three of them were published in a volume containing the "The Bridge," a long, mystical poem by a new friend of Evans, Hart Crane.

However, even before completing his Brooklyn Bridge series, Evans had made a sensible decision. Because photography was not just a casual interest but a real passion, and because, as Skolle had assured him, he evidently had the eye of an artist, Evans would forget about a literary career and concentrate on photography. He already had studied photographic technique with the highly respected New York photographer Ralph Steiner, and he had learned a great deal about the visual arts through his association with Skolle and the artists in his circle. Even during these years of relative obscurity, Evans was making important friends, Lincoln Kirstein, for example, the wealthy founder of the quarterly *Hound and Horn*. Kirstein essentially became his patron, introducing him to the most influential cultural leaders in America.

Although it would be some years before he was financially secure, during his first decade as a photographer Evans won recognition often enough to prove to himself that he had chosen the right profession, and he received commissions often enough to survive. His work appeared in *The Architectural Record*, *Creative Art*, and *Hound and Horn*; he had exhibitions in various New York galleries; and in 1933, he became the first photographer to have a one-man exhibition at the Museum of Modern Art, or MOMA. The subject of that series was Victorian architecture. Two years later, Evans was asked to take five hundred photographs for MOMA's "African Negro Art" series. Evans also took pictures of wealthy tourists on a yacht trip to Tahiti, of ordinary Cubans in prerevolutionary Havana, and, for *Fortune*, of communists at a summer camp in Florida. Admittedly, at that point in his life, Evans could not pick and choose; even a small commission could mean the difference between eating and going hungry. If he was less than enthusiastic about the yachting socialites, who were living in luxury while in New York men sold apples on street corners, and if he was appalled at what greed had done to the unspoiled islands they visited, Evans had to keep his political opinions separate from his art.

However, Evans's detachment was not just a matter of necessity; it had to do with the way the photographer defined his art. Mellow points out that even though Evans is best known as the coauthor of *Let Us Now Praise Famous Men*, in which James Agee described the desperate existence of sharecroppers in Depression-era Alabama, the photographer had no political agenda or sociological purpose. Above all, Evans was a realist. He believed that the function of photography was to capture people and places at a particular moment in time and, in the process, to point out the unique beauty of a person, an object, a cast of light. In later years, when he was so well established that he could choose his own assignments, Evans produced portraits of African Americans in Mississippi and of New Yorkers in the subway, but he also photographed golfers at the prestigious St. Andrew's course in Scotland and the social elite at the Henley Royal Regatta in Cambridge, England. He found empty main streets and quiet family cemeteries as captivating as the Chicago River or the New Orleans French Quarter.

Evans was as complex a person as he was an artist. His long, stormy affair with Jane Smith Ninas, who eventually married him, would provide all the material for a best-selling novel; his friendship with James Agee and his involvement with Agee's women would supply enough scandal for another. At times, however, one cannot help wishing that the author had found some way to compress *Walker Evans* or at least to have diminished the details. Having researched his subject so thoroughly, examining all of the correspondence he could obtain and interviewing everyone who was in any way associated with Evans, Mellow seems compelled to share so much with his readers that sometimes the text is just one quotation after another. Moreover, the narrative, which in itself is fascinating, proceeds by stops and starts. Whenever a name is mentioned, the author pauses, inserts a biographical sketch, and explains at length why that person was significant. However, not only are these faults almost inevitable in standard biographies, but as one presses on through the book, it becomes evident why Mellow felt it necessary to use so much detail. If he is to present a complete picture of Evans, he must explain how friends like Skolle, Crane, Steiner, and Kirstein influenced the direction of his career, and if, like Mellow's other biographies, this book is to provide insight into cultural history, it must include accounts of Evans's encounters with Ernest Hemingway and Georgia O'Keeffe and even such information as the fact that his photographs appeared in books by Sherwood Anderson and Richard Wright.

Unfortunately, Mellow died before he could finish his monumental work. Therefore the last eighteen years of Evans's life had to be covered in a brief, year-by-year summary, based on Mellow's notes and on other books. However, extensive notes, a chronology, a bibliography, and an index are included. In an excellent introduction, Hilton Kramer suggests what he believes Mellow would have said in his final chapter and also sums up Mellow's own achievement as a historian of American modernism. Even unfinished, Kramer concludes, *Walker Evans* is "a landmark work on the life of Walker Evans as well as an extraordinary chronicle of the art of our time."

Rosemary M. Canfield Reisman

Sources for Further Study

Booklist 95 (April 15, 1999): 1499.
Choice 37 (December, 1999): 709.
Library Journal 124 (April 1, 1999): 92.
The New York Times, June 18, 1999, p. B39.
The New York Times Book Review 104 (July 18, 1999): 8.
Publishers Weekly 246 (April 26, 1999): 63.

WALKIN' THE DOG

Author: Walter Mosley (1952-   )
Publisher: Little, Brown (Boston). 260 pp. $24.95
Type of work: Novel
Time: Contemporary
Locale: Los Angeles

Mosley's protagonist Socrates Fortlow, a former convict, works to stay alive in contemporary Los Angeles, but he also must learn how to accept the thanks of those he helps and, finally, their help

Principal characters:
SOCRATES FORTLOW, a sixtyish former convict trying to hold onto his life in South Central Los Angeles
DARRYL, his informally adopted son
MARTY GONZALEZ, his boss at Bounty Supermarket
HOAGLAND MARS, an alcoholic trumpet player whom Socrates saves
BELLANDRA, Socrates' late aunt and the source of much wisdom
IULA, Socrates' sometime girlfriend, the owner of a diner on Slauson Avenue

Socrates Fortlow spent twenty-seven years in prison for murder, and has been out for nine, but life is hardly any easier for him free at sixty. He lives in an abandoned house off an alley in South Central Los Angeles, holds a marginal job at a supermarket in a better neighborhood, and spends each day straddling the two worlds and trying to stay alive. Socrates lives on the edge of life: His thoughts are filled with memories of prison, what it has done to him, and how easy it would be to return, and yet he is always on the brink of exploding in rage at the violence and injustice and inhumanity around him. Prison is now inside him.

There is more to Socrates Fortlow than his profile shows, however, and Walter Mosley's powerful novel reveals just what this hero is made of—and how he can change that makeup. Actually, as Mosley has said in interviews about the work, *Walkin' the Dog* is really "twelve stories straining to be a novel," but the dozen short fiction pieces are so similar in setting and character, tone, and plot development, that they easily fulfill the requirements of a novel. In the first story or chapter, Socrates nearly fights his black supervisor at work and is only saved by the appearance of Marty Gonzalez, the boss. Marty wants to move Socrates up from bagger to produce manager, but Socrates is not yet ready for that responsibility. The course of the twelve chapters or stories of *Walkin' the Dog* reveals Socrates Fortlow moving to a place where such responsibility is possible.

Readers realize in this very first chapter that there is more to Socrates Fortlow than his statistics reveal. He cares for other people and has a powerful instinct to help them. His informally adopted son Darryl is clearly close to flunking out of high school, but Socrates helps to get him a new living situation that keeps him in school. He aids Darryl; at the same time he is himself unable to accept help from others; he is the true loner, living in his illegal house with only the two-legged dog Killer as a companion. Real change is precipitated when a young woman is killed and dumped in his alley, and the police jail the ex-convict Socrates as a likely suspect. Socrates has the stoic demeanor, learned from decades in prison, to handle anything the police can do to him, but he does not know how to handle the people who help him in this situation; "I don't know how to act when people get all in my business," he confesses when friends get him released. "Socrates felt big and angry. . . . Like Killer, his two-legged dog, who for no reason sometimes in the middle of the night sat back on his legless haunches and cried for all he was worth." Like his dog, Socrates is a survivor, but he has been crippled by his collisions with life, and they have left him deeply scarred. *Walkin' the Dog* follows Socrates as he learns to live with those scars and to move beyond them.

In the second chapter, Socrates suddenly recalls a promise he made to a friendly cellmate, and he plants an African tree in his yard and makes love to a beautiful woman in memory of the convict. Another ex-convict searches out Socrates, trying to find the secret of dealing with the guilt for his crimes, and Socrates tells him, "We got to see past bein' guilty. We already been there." Lydell Samuels does not have Socrates' strength, however, and ends up killing himself. Right Burke was Socrates' best friend years before, and Socrates helped him to die with dignity. Now he overcomes the hostility of Burke's survivor, Luvia, and accompanies her to the grave to pay homage to Burke. The connection later leads to another act of charity, when Socrates finds the trumpeter Hoagland Mars drunk on the street and takes him to Luvia's house for rehabilitation. When a huge mugger confronts Socrates in his alley one night, the former convict kills him with a stone and then awaits the police. When they do not come, he atones for his act by helping to embalm Ronald Logan and going to his funeral. Each chapter or story thus reveals another aspect of Socrates' humanity unfolding as he slowly sheds the prison of his own life and mind.

Socrates spends a lot of time trying to figure out how to live in this violent, racist world that surrounds him. It seems "like every time somethin' gets serious or important you got to put up blood and freedom just to stay in the game," Socrates complains to his girlfriend Iula. He attends a Wednesday night discussion group and talks with other blacks about their plight; what he learns is that they all have problems, but that they do not have to take them out on others. As he tells Iula one night, "' . . . you can be hungry but you don't have to be mad.' A wave of emotion choked off the end of his sentence." He also learns that it is all right to be scared and unsure, and, finally, he accepts his own terrible anger.

> I mean I been thinkin' about bein' mad at white folks lately. I mean I'm always mad. But bein' mad don't help. Even if I say somethin' or get in a fight, I'm still mad when it's all over. One day I realized that I couldn't stop bein' mad. Bein' mad was like havin' an extra finger. I don't like it, everybody always make fun of it but I cain't get rid of it. It's mine just like my blood.

Slowly Socrates pulls himself out of his own prison and into a better and brighter place. He eventually accepts the produce manager's position at Bounty Supermarket from Marty; he gets his first refrigerator, and a phone, and he begins to reach out, not only to Killer and Darryl and Iula, but to others. When a development company tries to evict him from his home, he fights and wins, and gets money from the corporation after moving to a better place. When he is put in jail a second time during this eviction struggle, he is finally able to thank the lawyer who helps to free him. He even hosts the discussion group in his new house—although the place lacks furniture.

Socrates Fortlow, in short, becomes a new man, or an old man with a better, gentler inside. In some ways, *Walkin' the Dog* is a kind of initiation novel—of a sixty-year-old man. As William Shakespeare in *King Lear*, Ernest Hemingway in *The Old Man and the Sea*, and countless other writers have long known, characters can gain knowledge and insight at any age, can change their lives. Socrates Fortlow has always been tough; buying his new refrigerator, he sees a Mexican and recognizes their similarities: "a toughness, a solitary self reliance. The nod they shared was the consolation of heroes home from a war that was lost." What Socrates needs are the skills that will go beyond that toughness and self-reliance and help him to win a few battles. In the twelfth and final story or chapter of the book, Socrates stalks a policeman, Cardwell, who has killed black children, but then discovers a newfound freedom in not killing him but, instead, parading in front of the police station wearing a sandwich board listing the policeman's crimes. Socrates is symbolically crucified, and arrested for his act, but neighbors emerge to back him up, and their relations with the police change. Because of Socrates Fortlow, the black neighborhoods of Los Angeles are better places in which to live. He has become the hero of a war that this time he has won, and in the process he has gained true freedom.

Walkin' the Dog is what once was called an existential novel, a work in which a hero finds the means to preserve his own identity and freedom in a world where both are constantly threatened. (Ralph Ellison and Richard Wright wrote earlier black versions of this genre in the 1950's, in *Invisible Man*, 1952, and *The Outsider*, 1953, respectively.) Socrates Fortlow has to carve out his own morality in an immoral world, where the institutions that are supposed to provide order (like the police) are themselves corrupt and corrupting. Socrates kills a bad man, but is never caught by society's laws—or rewarded by law enforcement—and he atones for the act in his own way; he threatens the greedy development company officer who is trying to evict him, and is successful in extorting money from him. Morality, Mosley posits, is a day-to-day construction, and each man must make up his own and live by it. Socrates Fortlow is doing just that, and in the process, he makes himself a better person. He learns to control his anger, and, in the process of helping others, he learns how to accept their help. As he remembers his Aunt Bellandra saying—and her wisdom is often in his head—"The chains on a black man go down through the centuries. They once made us slaves to the plantation but now they make us slaves to the slaves we was." Socrates shows readers the ways to break free of those chains. Walter Mosley is no optimist, but in the gritty world he renders, readers can find a cautiously positive worldview.

Walter Mosley is best known for his earlier detective novels featuring Easy Rawlins as the black hero (*Devil in a Blue Dress*, 1990, is probably the best known, for it was made into a successful film.) The Socrates Fortlow character, seen first in *Always*

Outnumbered, Always Outgunned (1997) is an equally captivating character and in some ways a much more realistic protagonist, for he is not trapped in the conventions of the detective novel genre, but dwells in his own city and his own mind. These are the real streets of Watts that Socrates walks; he views a terrible city from the bus he takes from work each day, one split by real racial divides. Socrates is a realistic character struggling in this modern hell to save himself and to free himself and others from the fear and anger and history which trap all this city's residents. In language sometimes harsh but often poetic, Mosley renders Los Angeles for all its residents, black and white, and acts as a cultural mediator between them.

David Peck

Sources for Further Study

Booklist 95 (July, 1999): 1896.
Boston Globe, October 22, 1999, p. C15.
Library Journal 124 (August, 1999): 141.
The New York Times Book Review 104 (November 7, 1999): 9.
Publishers Weekly 246 (August 9, 1999): 338.

WALKING ON WATER

Black American Lives at the Turn of the Twenty-first Century

Author: Randall Kenan (1963-   )
Publisher: Alfred A. Knopf (New York). 670 pp. $30.00
Type of work: History and sociology
Time: 1991-1994
Locale: The United States

An African American novelist and short-story writer with a background in the social sciences interviews African Americans from all walks of life as he crisscrosses the country over several years

Early in Randall Kenan's compendious collection of interviews with African American men and women, the reader meets Jack Guilles, a muscular, blond student at the University of Vermont who calls the writer "homey" and who swears that despite the color of his skin, he is a black man. Born to parents whose racial identity is never mentioned and brought up with a black family living in Brooklyn, Jack grew up as a black man, and although he initially resists, the writer eventually accepts him as one. An irresistible young man who in his speech mixes cursing, joking, and complaining with social awareness, Jack is only one of the many fascinating people Kenan brings to life on the page. That is the good news. The bad news, unfortunately, is pretty much the same as the good. However compelling is the wealth of material that Kenan presents, there is a bit too much of it, and it has not all been shaped to its best advantage; a flood of voices begins to drown out the timbre of each.

The task Kenan has set for himself is admirably quixotic. Defining himself as a nonessentialist on issues of racial definition, he quite logically goes looking for the essence of black life where he is least likely to find it. Because the large urban centers dominate so many of the conventional and better-known images of black life in America, Kenan keeps his visits to Chicago and Los Angeles brief; New York, his adopted home, serves as an interior location to journey to and from, rather than as a destination. As he explains when he cuts short his trip to Chicago, "Why add to the trillions of words when so much of the country had yet to be written about?" Far better to take to the road as a black Charles Kuralt or a contemporary version of anthropologist and novelist Zora Neale Hurston, exploring black lives off the state highways and in the seminar rooms of the nation's campuses.

Kenan himself has an engaging personality. He is as interested in *Star Trek* as in military history, in science fiction as in alternative drama, and he easily calls upon these and other sides of his multitudinous self to draw out his subjects. His method is to give the reader the background and setting of the interview, then allow the subject to speak for himself or herself with as little interference as possible, and the stories tumble out. Listen to William Lee, an Air Force major stationed in Grand Forks, North Dakota, talking about how his father was killed for the crime of having demanded gas at a "whites only" gas station:

> We used to live in a rural area. A guy needed some help on the side of the road. He stopped. Helped the guy. They jumped him, they stabbed him, and left him there to bleed to death. He was able to gain enough strength to drive in his car about two or three odd miles down the road. Pulled into the first place he could, which was a juke joint. . . . These were all black folks. And they watched him as he was dying in the middle of the floor in a pool of blood. . . . I'm six years old, Christmas, 1960.

Kenan listens to this story in profound respect for the depth of human tragedy that he has uncovered. Scratch the "ordinary" lives of black people living anywhere in the United States, the book suggests, and extraordinary tales of history and personal determination are revealed.

How is one to link them together? Kenan's central point is that there is no single African American tale which is told again in the lives of black people. Rather, there is a multiplicity of stories. A writer devoted to an angry thesis might be tempted to dismiss the lives of upper-middle-class, black New Englanders as not representative of black America. Kenan would rather point out that there is no history of black people in America deeper or richer than that in New England. Rather than dismissing them, he would much rather talk to them and hear what they can tell him, especially after meeting Dora Grain on Martha's Vineyard. A mother and former labor organizer who once had the opportunity to travel to Africa to interview W. E. B. Du Bois, Ms. Grain passes along the formula for bringing up children who are black in a culture dominated by whites that was passed along to her: "*Teach them never to trust them.*" This chilling formulation is not motivated by hate, she assures Kenan, but by the practicalities that black people have to face about the limits of most white people they will meet.

Kenan is obviously a voracious, omnivorous reader, and lengthy quotations gush from his pages. One would not say he wears his erudition lightly; rather, he shares it generously, with all of the freshness of an undergraduate discovering ideas for the first time. As such, although the main task of his book is not to tell the stories of the movers and shakers but of the lovers and doers of black life, it is no surprise that when he gets to Chicago, the two people he hopes to meet are Gwendolyn Brooks and her friend, Haki R. Madhubuti. Regarding Ms. Brooks, he was to be disappointed, but he was lucky enough to interview poet and activist Madhubuti (who at one time was also known as Don Luther Lee). In the spirit of a world-weary traveler consulting a wise man, Kenan approaches Madhubuti saying, "I keep hearing that black culture is dead. And if it's not dead it's dying." Madhubuti replies with a thoughtful summation of how black life and culture have and have not improved over the years, but ends by looking for hope at the bottom. He has been working with getting literature into prisons he tells Kenan, and many of the black prisoners tell him,

> my problem was nobody never introduced me to ideas that were life-giving and life-saving. For the first time in my life, here I'm in prison. I got nothing else to do but think, and I really didn't realize how precious thought was until I had to do it. I just need some literature to keep feeding my mind. So that's the option.

This is not another argument that literature can save the world, only that the lack of it will destroy lives.

Inevitably, his quest brings him back to his old stomping grounds, the Southeast, and though his discussion of North Carolina is curiously brief and almost listless, his account of visiting Georgia around the time of the Rodney King riots is riveting. While there, he meets the leaders of a group calling themselves the Students for Afrikan American Empowerment (SAAE), who have based the group on the original Black Panther party (both in terms of its revolutionary ideology and in terms of its commitment to community involvement). They are determined to avoid what they see as the mistakes of the Civil Rights movement. Kenan reacts with both alarm and admiration as he watches them go through self-defense drills and take mandatory target practice and listens to their concerns about the African American future. Though he is aware of the distance that separates his middle-class life from their radical activism, his high regard for their dedication is apparent; in them, he believes, the tradition that stretches from Frederick Douglass to Thurgood Marshall has found a new home.

The chapter that deals with the SAAE is "Walking on Water," the title chapter, a phrase which comes from the story of Ibo Landing. In this story, based loosely on a historical event, slaves who are new arrivals at St. Simons Island off the coast of Georgia revolt and determine to walk back to Africa; if the god of the water wants them to drown, they will drown. As told as a folktale, some versions have them marching off to freedom across the "river" Atlantic, while some have them all drowning. Kenan's research suggests that about twelve of them probably did drown, and the rest were returned to slavery. This image of having to do the impossible to achieve freedom not only serves as the central image of what the author clearly hopes is nonetheless happening in life but also serves as a figure for what Kenan himself is trying to find. Though there may not be a definable essence that determines who is more or less black than another person, there may be a shared task: Through whatever magic might be available, African Americans at the close of the twentieth century need to find the secret and the courage to walk into a world that might drown them, but might also allow them to pass through to freedom. Appropriately, then, near the end of his journey, he interviews Ana Bel Lee Washington, an artist whose painted version of the story of the Ibo Landing shows the freed slaves arriving in Africa. "Ibo Landing? It's fact," she tells Kenan. Her version might be fantasy, but it is necessary fantasy.

This conjoining of two stories of African American warriors makes for a powerful chapter, but it is not as powerful as it should be. The effect is somewhat muted by the other material Kenan has included in the chapter. It is not that the story of Lori Hewett, a college student working on her second and third novels (all of which are published eventually) is uninteresting—far from it. However, Kenan does not convince the reader that the material fits, one of the book's major creative flaws. At 650 pages, it is too ambitious by half. A firm editor might have trimmed the book down to 425 pages and produced a better book. Kenan's persona throughout is that of a studiously casual and self-reflective observer, and while this consistent narrative persona and his many thoughtful asides do much to enrich the book, little would have been lost had he condensed some of his digressions and asides or exercised greater authorial privilege in shaping the material that emerges from his interviews. Simply telling the reader how someone felt instead of reporting that he asked about her feelings cuts out inessential material, and the reader would realize that he must have asked about her feelings.

Though fascinating, glimpses into how his hundreds of subjects have answered the question "What does it mean to be black in America today?" do not add up to a book that is significantly more than the sum of its parts. Nonetheless, if this work lacks the clarity of *A Visitation of Spirits: A Novel* (1989) and *Let the Dead Bury Their Dead and Other Stories* (1992)—two books about a small black community in North Carolina—the movement toward a larger canvas certainly speaks of the artist's own growth. It will be a surprise if it does not prove to be a major turning point in Randall Kenan's own development. This is a book the author had to write, and one suspects he is writing not to everyone, but to those who will find they have to read it.

Thomas Cassidy

Sources for Further Study

Booklist 95 (February 15, 1999): 1010.
Library Journal 124 (February 1, 1999): 111.
The New York Times Book Review 104 (March 14, 1999): 28.
Publishers Weekly 246 (January 4, 1999): 79.

WALTER BENJAMIN AT THE DAIRY QUEEN
Reflections at Sixty and Beyond

Author: Larry McMurtry (1936-)
Publisher: Simon & Schuster (New York). Illustrated. 204 pp. $21.00
Type of work: Memoirs
Time: The twentieth century
Locale: Texas

A series of rambling autobiographical essays from one of the preeminent writers of the American West—reflections on family, history, geography, and a lifetime of reading and writing

With his steady stream of novels and screenplays, from *The Last Picture Show* (1966) to *Lonesome Dove* (1985) and *Texasville* (1987), Larry McMurtry is arguably one of the most popular authors writing about the American frontier. Here in this curious new volume, however, an extended and digressive rumination on endings, he does not so much celebrate the mythic West of his writing and upbringing as lament its passing. Largely elegiac, occasionally just plain cranky, McMurtry reflects not only on the end of a way of life that his West Texas family has known since the nineteenth century, but also on the end of a larger Western tradition, the European West, its modernist art and culture. Again and again he finds correspondences between these two "Wests"; if there is a spine to the book, something connecting its meandering, repetitive essays, it very likely has to do with the tension this writer has felt over the years as he has tried to free himself from one landscape and read himself into another. Land and literature—those are his recurrent interests in these pages. McMurtry claims he did not in fact set out to write an autobiography (though he has clearly done so), but rather to describe the distance that separated him from the European writers and historians he has spent a lifetime reading.

Certainly reading is the primary event here, the crucial activity throughout McMurtry's life. The box of nineteen books given him by an older cousin going off to war launched the young Texas boy into a world quite different from the harsh, featureless High Plains of his childhood. Reading became an imaginative escape, a way to remove himself from the restricted, ultimately doomed life of ranching that was his legacy, and to create for himself a wider, richer, less constrained existence: a community not of cows and taciturn cowhands but of stories and voluble storytellers, a world of books. As he discovers, however, this new world of literature, the colorful and congested European cosmopolitanism that held out such heady promise for a boy brought up on silence, isolation, and empty spaces, is itself in decay. The catastrophe of World War I and the closing of the American frontier—each produced, at roughly the same time, a deep and disabling sense of cultural loss. Moreover, McMurtry cannot quite shake that feeling, the sense of everything winding down. Dissolution permeates his four essays, even if the chapter titles themselves only hint at it: "Place and the Memories of Place," "Reading," "Book Scouting," "The End of the Cowboy—The End of Fiction." Sad or irritated, fearful or bluff, his tone of voice may vary, but what does not alter is his sense that literary traditions, family rituals, professional customs, regional ways of life are passing, and for McMurtry that is clearly not a happy fact of contemporary existence.

What triggers these poignant retrospections on art and life is a reading of Walter Benjamin's 1936 essay "The Storyteller." It is summer, 1980, a summer of record high temperatures in Archer City, Texas (familiar to his readers as the fictional Thalia). As McMurtry sits sipping on a cool lime Dr. Pepper in the Archer City Dairy Queen, he is struck by the German writer's lament for the "diminution of the power of oral narrative in our twentieth-century lives." Reading this, he is stirred to examine Benjamin's critique: where *are* the stories and the storytellers now? what *has* become of that elemental exchange of experience, the oral tradition? Looking around the Dairy Queen he can say that here, in these small, clean, fast-food institutions from the 1960's, there is at least a *place* where folks can meet and talk, where gossip can be exchanged, where stories can be told. For this reason, as a potential locus for storytelling, he champions the homely West Texas "DQ," though on further reflection he is forced to recognize that Benjamin's assessment is nevertheless probably accurate. Even here, storytellers are nearly extinct, because it takes more than a place; it takes a particular way of being curious about experience and of valuing practical memory to make for a powerful oral tradition. These, he fears, have indeed fallen away, or have more likely been eroded by a nonstop barrage of technological innovation that has smothered curiosity and made memory obsolete. Given the constant stream of information from television sets, people have no time to be curious. Given the prodigious memory banks in computers, what do people really need to be able to remember anyway? Yet without the galvanizing effect of curiosity or the creative power of memory, what hope is there for stories? McMurtry's grandfather, struggling to survive on the bleak frontier, needed to remember where water holes were, what weather signs meant. It was a matter of success or failure, practically of life or death. Now people can dial up almost anything and need to carry almost nothing with them. Even more than that, McMurtry suggests, the media have not only supplied memories but shaped and edited those memories as well. Someone else is making the stories while people passively consume the universally packaged product as information. Benjamin knew that information is the enemy of the story, and though he may not have seen the developments this far down the road, McMurtry is inclined to think that he would have understood the change—and lamented the loss.

To a certain extent these autumnal reflections are the product of a man in late middle age who has, as he describes it, survived a serious health crisis. He writes as a "new" man, one who has come through coronary by-pass surgery but who cannot quite go back to seeing himself or the world as they once appeared. Though he recovered quickly from the immediate physical trauma, McMurtry confides that the emotional trauma was far more grave and took him a full two years to get past. The index of this is the fact that for those two years he was, for the first time in his life, unable to read for pleasure. The single most enjoyable, most necessary act of his entire conscious life was no longer possible for him. The last two major works he had read were Marcel

Proust's (1871-1922) twelve-volume novel *À la recherche du temps perdu* (1913-1927; *Remembrance of Things Past*, 1922-1931) and the five-volume *Diary of Virginia Woolf* (1977-1984), both products of the great modernist impulse in literature, both celebrations of mischievous curiosity and exhaustive memory, both examples of how life, the gossip of everyday things, can be transmuted into art by a storyteller of genius. Now he was unable to lift a page. He had relocated his book business to Archer City, moving 200,000 volumes from his Washington, D.C., store, along with 20,000 of his own, to a small Texas panhandle town, and now, surrounded by all of this, he could not read.

From the moment he read his first work of world literature—Miguel de Cervantes's *Don Quixote de la Mancha* (1605, 1615), as it turns out—he realized that what he derived from literature was a feeling of independence. Reading separated him from the other men working cattle alongside his father. It was essentially a private activity, his "equivalent of the cowboy's dream," an escape from the tedium of long days and flat land. Before long it became a hunger, a craving which led him to Houston, where there were bookstores, and Rice University, where there were libraries, then to graduate school at Stanford, where there were exhilarating opportunities to read and write. Once he became a practicing, then a published writer, he realized that he would always feel the irresistible tug of reading, always feel reluctant to put down a book to pick up a pen. So when he was unable to read, his world clearly had changed.

Even when it is finally possible for him to read for pleasure again, he seems not to have regained his former joyous abandon in the act. He reads as voraciously, if not as rapidly, as before and acquires books with as much avidity, but now he has a "less generous level of attention to bestow." Having lost sight of his self after surgery, he lost sight of literature for a while, too, or maybe it is as simple as that he is now all too aware of time running out. He is in his middle sixties, he has had a major health crisis; he will never be able to read all the books he wants to, never be able to write all the books he needs to. This would account for the melancholy cast of his reflections, his nostalgia for a time when, as he remembers, publishers were eager for new fiction, and independent booksellers were devoted experts, priests of a trade that has now become the province of corporate bottom-liners; a time when scouting for esoteric volumes was a romantic adventure involving years and taking one across continents instead of an electronic search polished off in minutes from the comfort of one's living room. In these sorts of passages, *Walter Benjamin at the Dairy Queen* feels more like a journal or a commonplace book, a compendium of fugitive entries, elliptical observations, intriguing but unconnected lists. Again and again McMurtry will glancingly comment on his reading habits (a shift from fiction to nonfiction), construct hierarchies (greatest booksellers he has encountered), produce bibliographies (scholars of the frontier he has admired), paint portraits ("Great Readers" he has emulated), deliver opinions (Jack Kerouac, 1922-1969, as a literary Huck Finn striking out for new territory). This can trail off into curmudgeonly ranting that is not particularly fresh or revealing—when he laments family meals that are no longer family meals or decries the ubiquity of television sets—but on the whole McMurtry serves up vividly appealing if fragmentary morsels. None is more engaging than his wistful remembrance of

Edmund Wilson (1895-1972), one of his so-called Great Readers (along with Susan Sontag, Joseph Alsop, and George Saintsbury) and a great lay critic of the deteriorating American values that McMurtry himself exposes. He is charmed by Wilson's insatiable literary appetite, heartened by his broadly catholic tastes. Such a reader is for him a kind of ideal, and one that is imperiled as writers and cultural journalists who might have inherited Wilson's mantle increasingly choose to pursue a superficial brilliance that is not actually grounded so much in reading as in a kind of virtuosic cultural osmosis.

To say that the book is prevalently retrospective in stance, elegiac in tone, is not to say that it is without pages of high spirits. McMurtry is too full of warm enthusiasms, is too passionate a bookman for that. The love of books, the quest for rare editions, the passing on of these gems to new generations of readers—all of this produces a wonderment that is also a feature of his writing here. He is more than capable of raising a laugh with his tales of the wildly varied, even eccentric systems that book collectors have devised for arranging their personal libraries. It is also true, however, that McMurtry writes of himself as a man who all his life has been interested in "vanishing breeds," whether it be the storyteller of Benjamin's essay or the cowboy of the herding tradition. Benjamin's literary culture has been eclipsed by a late twentieth century microchip technology inhospitable to the projects and premises of modernist art, just as the culture of McMurtry's ancestors has been extinguished by an agricultural technology they would have neither understood nor welcomed. Epochs and landscapes have passed away. In this odd, rambling, but touching book, a former cowboy sings the sad song of their demise.

Thomas J. Campbell

Sources for Further Study

Booklist 95 (August, 1999): 1982.
Library Journal 124 (October 1, 1999): 92.
The New York Times, December 13, 1999, p. B10.
The New York Times Book Review 104 (November 21, 1999): 14.
Publishers Weekly 246 (September 6, 1999): 87.

THE WAY OF THE WORLD
From the Dawn of Civilizations to the Eve of the Twenty-first Century

Author: David Fromkin (1932-)
Publisher: Alfred A. Knopf (New York). 272 pp. $25.00
Type of work: History
Time: From the beginning of time to the 1990's
Locale: The world

An interpretive historical account of the progress of humanity from the earliest times to the 1990's, primarily focusing upon developments in the West and culminating with the United States' role as the world's only superpower

David Fromkin is professor of international relations, history, and law at Boston University. His earlier publications include *In the Time of the Americans: FDR, Truman, Eisenhower, Marshall, MacArthur, The Generation That Changed America's Role in the World* (1995) and *A Peace to End All Peace: Creating the Modern Middle East, 1914-1922* (1989), a well-written discussion of the diplomatic origins of the modern Middle East that was a best-seller and a finalist for both the National Book Critics Circle Award and the Pulitzer Prize. Unlike some academics, Fromkin writes for the general reader and not just the specialist, and this book is no exception.

The Way of the World has many predecessors. Fromkin refers to one, H. G. Wells's *The Outline of History: Being a Plain History of Life and Mankind* (1920), but there are many others who have attempted to encompass all of history, from Sir Walter Ralegh in the seventeenth century to Arnold Toynbee in his twelve-volume *A Study of History* (1934-1961). Few, however, have told the story in such a limited space—just 220 pages of text. Needless to say, much "history" has been left out, but Fromkin's intent is not to relate all of history in a relatively short book; instead, he "concentrates mostly on the lives that led to the only civilization still surviving, the scientific one of the modern world and the prospects before it." Also, as might be expected from a student of international relations, his interest and thus his focus in this work is not on literature or music or even science itself but rather on what he calls the high drama of politics and war. *The Way of the World* tells a selective story of the past, choosing to highlight only what "explains" the present and suggests the future.

Fromkin's inclusion of Wells is apposite. Wells's universal history is largely the epic of human progress rather than the story of decline, which was the theme of Oswald Spengler's *The Decline of the West: Form and Actuality* (1926). Like Wells's work, Fromkin's work is also the tale of humanity's evolution and progress, and he obviously believes that the late twentieth century world and its history have reached their apogee of development—thus far. To arrive at the place where humanity resides today, *The Way of the World* takes the reader through eight milestones or turning points of history. These are presented in short chapters, roughly arranged in chronological order. "Becoming Human" deals with humanity's biological evolution from the early hominids of Africa four million years ago to the emergence of *Homo sapiens*. The second milestone was "Inventing Civilization," and here the emphasis is on the birth of civilization in the Middle East beginning with the Sumerians and Egyptians. Despite the title, unfortunately there is relatively little discussion of the origins of civilization in China, and civilization in the Indus River region gets very short shrift, which is understandable given Fromkin's opinion that those civilizations ultimately failed and lost out to the West and its scientific modernism. The origins of Western civilization were in the early Middle East, and that Western emphasis continues throughout *The Way of the World*.

Fromkin's third turning point in the evolution of human progress he calls "Developing a Conscience," and here, too, westerners receive the attention. Although he mentions—almost in passing—Lao-tzu, Zoroaster, Vardhamāna (and Jainism), Buddhism's Siddhārtha Gautama, and K'ung Futzu/Confucius, the development of Fromkin's "conscience" was primarily the result of the Jews and particularly the Greeks, and far more space is allotted to the Greek wars of the fifth century B.C.E. than any other subject in the chapter. If one desires more than a superficial discussion of Eastern religions and philosophies, one is advised to go elsewhere.

The fourth stepping stone was what Fromkin refers to as "Seeking a Lasting Peace," and here the concentration is upon the conquests and accomplishments of Alexander the Great and the development of the Roman Empire, with China's imperial history receiving only a brief mention. To Fromkin, Alexander was one of history's most significant figures because he set the standard of humanity's potential, an exemplar of how far humans might endeavor to reach and achieve. Not every reader will place Alexander at such a pinnacle, and the one source he refers to would be considered out of date by many historians, but *The Way of the World* is much more a personal and interpretive view of the past and of the future than rediscovering and understanding the past for its own sake.

"Achieving Rationality" is the fifth of humanity's crucial steps, and here Fromkin discusses the history of western civilization in the years between 1000 and 2000 C.E. Undoubtedly the most far-ranging—and disjointed—chapter in *The Way of the World*, "Achieving Rationality" seemingly covers everything from Edward Gibbon, King Arthur, St. Patrick, and Muhammad to the Black Death, the Thirty Years' War, humanism, and capitalism, but it does little in speaking directly to the chapter's title: achieving rationality.

Refreshingly straightforward, "Uniting the Planet" is the saga of European exploration and conquest and its consequences. Chapter 7, "Releasing Nature's Energies," on the scientific and industrial revolution, contains many names mentioned in brief, with Thomas Alva Edison receiving the most space, a somewhat eccentric choice perhaps. "Ruling Ourselves" begins with Woodrow Wilson's ideas of democracy and self-determination as the inspirational model for the rest of the less fortunate world. For Fromkin, America is more an idea than a nation, its history exhibiting a uniqueness, an exceptionalism, denied to others. America's revolution against Great Britain was an affirmation of the uniqueness of American individualism, but he notes that English history and political theory have contributed to America's success, referring particularly to the Magna Carta of 1215 as distilled through John Locke and subsequently influencing the Declaration of Independence and the Constitution. World War I was a turning point; the world became "modern" instead of Romantic or Victorian. Fromkin often uses terms with delightful imprecision, and he claims that "Europeanization," "westernization," "Americanization," and "modernization" are essentially the same thing. Not everyone would so readily agree, but it is America which best personifies the modern as the exemplar of the open society, with its democratic politics, universal education, a meritocracy, and the shining beacon of the consumer society, the ultimate product—at least thus far—of the scientific-industrial-technological revolution.

In the last third of the book Fromkin turns from historian to seer, and he peers into the future. He expresses some concern that there are no alternative models left—that history has conspired to put all of its eggs into a single basket, the basket of modernization best expressed in the United States. Although he warns about overconfidence, the dark side of human nature, and other unforeseen negatives, Fromkin, like Wells before him, remains the optimist. He rightly denies that progress is inevitable and suggests that a more valid key to past and future is to see it as the story of fluctuations, but his own faith is in progress. Fromkin's is a cautionary progress—how could anyone writing at the end of the often horrendous twentieth century be anything but cautious?—and he worries about the loss of social cohesion and the revolt against modern world unity. There are the numerous subnational movements, or atavistic tribalisms, appearing in the former Soviet Union, Yugoslavia, and even Belgium, Canada, and Great Britain, just to mention a few. Here, he believes, the United States, the epitome of a successful multiethnic society, which he claims has transcended both national and religious differences, can serve a model for the rest of the world. He makes the obligatory reference to terrorism, but not too seriously, and although there is a brief chapter on the possibilities of environmental disaster of one sort or another, here again optimism reigns; all the world has to do is to follow the lead of the United States and other open societies who are best equipped to solve such challenges, although why this might be so is left undiscussed.

In 1941 Henry R. Luce famously referred to the twentieth century as "the American century," and it can be admitted that that characterization is in many ways true, particularly with the demise of the Soviet Union. However, Fromkin seems to claim that American supremacy is not necessarily merely the consequence of a particular equilibrium in time, the result of two disastrous European wars which severely affected the nations of that continent, as well as the end of the Cold War, with the possible coming emergence of Asia, especially Japan and China, as alternative successful paradigms. Instead, what has made the United States supreme will likely continue into the twenty-first century and beyond. "Looking back a thousand years from now, our progeny may say that the twenty-first was the American century because in it, for the first time, American ideas were put into practice on a worldwide scale." The future does not necessarily even have to be restricted to the planet Earth; outer space, the planets, even the stars hold promise for humankind, and again the United States could well lead the way. After all, the story of America is the story of the frontier, and space might well be the final frontier, something of a combination of Frederick Jackson Turner's frontier hypothesis and *Star Trek*. American culture, American political ideas (learned and borrowed from England), American science and technology will likely prevail far into the future, at least so Fromkin forecasts.

There is an interesting conceit at the beginning of *The Way of the World* which elucidates what Fromkin intended to accomplish in this work. He imagines a shaman of tens of thousands of years ago sitting at a fire in a cave retelling to his tribal group the old stories of the tribe, including who were their ancestral heroes, where they had come from, what they had accomplished, and then projecting their future destiny. Fromkin sees himself as a modern shaman, telling humanity (at least American humanity) where it has come from and where it may be going, and it is Fromkin-as-shaman, telling his story in an evening, which justifies the brevity of *The Way of the World*. It is a not unsuccessful approach, but it does have its drawbacks.

First, a small group of humans living, surviving, and dying together thousands of years ago would undoubtedly have achieved a homogeneity, an in-group awareness and self-knowledge that they would bring to the ancient shaman's words; he could allude, refer, be brief, and they—his family, clan, tribe—would readily understand his allusions and references. That is less true in Fromkin's modern world. If the reader did not already have a substantial knowledge of the history of Western civilization when he or she opened *The Way of the World*, it is unlikely that the reader would be much enlightened, and modern America at the edge of the twenty-first century is a particularly illiterate society when it comes to knowledge of the past—just ask any teacher of history. Second, Fromkin leaves out much of the modern world in his emphasis on the history and accomplishments of the West, or rather he leaves out much of today's world that is not "modern" by his definition. Large portions of Africa, Asia, the Middle East, and Latin America, to say nothing of the former Soviet Union and parts of Eastern Europe, lack a great deal of the modern, politically, economically, and socially. Can the various religious fundamentalisms that seem to be waxing rather than waning be ignored? Fromkin envisions the rest of the world emulating the West, particularly the United States, but it is at least arguable that great portions of the world are falling further behind the consumer-driven, scientific, "rational" civilization of America and Europe. One hopes that Fromkin's shamanesque view is not too Pollyannaish and that his assessment of the twenty-first century is correct; it could be most unfortunate for all if it is not.

Eugene Larson

Sources for Further Study

Booklist 95 (January 1, 1999): 823.
The Economist 349 (December 12, 1998): 6.
Foreign Affairs 78 (May, 1999): 132.

Library Journal 123 (October 15, 1998): 81.
Los Angeles Times Book Review, July 4, 1999, p. 5.
The New York Times Book Review 104 (January 17, 1999): 9.
Publishers Weekly 245 (December 21, 1998): 41.
School Library Journal 45 (June, 1999): 158.

WHILE I WAS GONE

Author: Sue Miller (1943-)
Publisher: Alfred A. Knopf (New York). 266 pp. $24.00
Type of work: Novel
Time: The late 1960's and the late 1990's
Locale: Adams Mill and Cambridge, Massachusetts

When a man she once knew moves to her small town, a middle-aged wife and mother discovers how dangerous it can be to relive the past

Principal characters:
JOSEPHINE (JO) BECKER, the narrator and protagonist, a veterinarian
DANIEL BECKER, her husband, a minister
DANA JABLONSKI, a sculptor, once Jo's housemate at Cambridge
ELI MAYHEW, a biochemist, another housemate, now living in Adams Mill
JEAN BENNETT, his wife, a political science professor
NORA BECKER, one of the three daughters of Jo and Daniel, now in a New York film school
CASS BECKER, Nora's twin sister, a guitarist who travels with a band
SADIE BECKER, the youngest daughter, a college student

In *While I Was Gone*, Sue Miller again addresses the issues related to sexual love, maternal love, marriage, identity, and morality that she introduced in her first novel, *The Good Mother* (1986), and later explored in *Family Pictures* (1990), *For Love* (1993), and *The Distinguished Guest* (1995). Throughout her works, Miller emphasizes her belief that life is made up of a series of difficult choices and that when one makes the wrong choice, one must face the consequences. However much she sympathizes with characters like the protagonist of *The Good Mother*, who is forced to choose between her lover and her children, Miller will not perpetuate the faith that pervades this permissive era, that one can have it all.

In the first chapter of *While I Was Gone*, which serves as the prologue to the narrative, Jo Becker admits that there was a time she believed that she was an exception to the rule. It seemed that she did indeed have everything. She was the wife of a minister who loved her enough to exempt her from the usual tasks of a minister's wife, and she was the mother of three interesting if very different daughters, all of whom seemed to be proceeding satisfactorily into adulthood. Moreover, she found her career as a veterinarian fully as satisfying as her husband Daniel did his work in the ministry. However, Jo now remembers that for some time before her past came back to claim her, she had felt increasingly disconnected from her husband and from her whole comfortable but predictable world. Even though she had tried to dismiss her sense of detachment as a manifestation of the empty nest syndrome or, alternatively, as a phenomenon associated with middle age, Jo knew that it was casting a shadow on her life and diminishing what had been a very happy marriage.

After this introduction, Jo proceeds to relate her story. It begins with a telephone call in which the youngest Becker daughter, Sadie, informs her parents that the professor she most admires, Jean Bennett, is now living in Adams Mill. When Bennett brings an ailing dog, Arthur, to Jo's office, Jo discovers that Jean's husband, a prominent biochemist, is the same Eli Mayhew who was Jo's housemate some thirty years before. In the four chapters that follow, Jo relives that time when, bored with life as a medical student's wife, she fled to Cambridge, assumed a new identity, and moved into a house with six other young people. Jo became especially fond of the outgoing Dana Jablonski. When she was with Dana, Jo felt freer than she ever had before. However, for some reason, she did not admit her deceit about her identity even to Dana. It all ended on a cold day in January when Dana was found dead in the living room. The police were never able to identify the murderer, and the housemates dispersed. Jo summarizes what followed in the sixth chapter of the novel, how she went home, got a divorce, went back to school, met and married Daniel, settled down in Adams Mill, produced three daughters, and reared them successfully. She was much too busy to think much about that strange period when she had suddenly dropped out of sight and made herself into someone she was not. The chapter ends with Daniel's sermon at a funeral service for a young mother, a sermon that aroused in Jo a sense of joy and of commitment to her husband that she had not experienced for a long time.

Up to this point, Miller has handled her narrative in a fairly conventional manner. She began in the present, related an episode from the recent past and then, when the encounter with Jean Bennett made further explanations necessary, proceeded to a straightforward, chronological account of what transpired thirty years in the past, events that, Jo hints, have since come back to haunt her. However, throughout the second major segment of the novel, which begins with Eli's appearance at the beginning of the seventh chapter and concludes with Jo's rejection of him at the end of the eleventh chapter, the author maintains not one, but two story lines, each representing one of the two lives between which Jo eventually must choose. One of the narratives focuses on Jo's family, her work, and her activities within the community. Jo describes her preparations for Thanksgiving and Christmas, looks forward to having her daughters home for the holidays, worries about their tendency to quarrel when they are together, recalls incidents from their childhood, ponders their present personalities, and with obvious delight quotes some of Daniel's more memorable witticisms. However, there is another narrative thread that runs through this section, in which Jo reveals her increasing obsession with Eli and details their movement toward a sexual relationship. Unlike the other narrative, which consists of dozens of incidents, for the most part this account is psychological. Nevertheless, it seems certain to end in an act of adultery, and it is only an accident of timing, or perhaps a providential intervention, that prevents such a betrayal from taking place.

Jo's abortive affair with Eli begins innocently enough. Since Arthur is his dog, not Jean's, it is Eli who brings him back to Jo to see whether there is any possibility of him healing or whether, as it turns out, he must be put down. From the very beginning, Jo is attracted to Eli, although she is not yet obsessed with him. Jo tells herself that inviting the newcomers to a party at her house is just a matter of courtesy, and there is an added reason to do so since Sadie will be at home, and Jean is her favorite professor. Returning the courtesy, Jean and Eli invite the Beckers to their home. However, during the evening, Eli makes so vicious a verbal attack on Daniel and the beliefs that are the basis of the minister's life that there is no possibility of any more socializing between the two couples.

Jo chooses to ignore Eli's evident contempt for Daniel and agrees to meet Eli for a quiet lunch. At this point, Jo is still pretending to herself that her only reason for seeing Eli is her desire to talk over a part of her past with someone who shared it. Yet, by the time Jo telephones Eli to arrange a rendezvous at the Ritz Hotel in Boston, she can no longer tell herself that her motives are innocent. Deceiving her husband with a plausible reason for spending the night in Boston, she sallies forth, intent on adultery. Almost as soon as they meet, however, Eli confesses to murdering Dana and proceeds to recite all the distasteful details. Horrified and frightened, Jo eludes Eli, finds her car, and races back to Adams Mill, where she repeats Eli's story to Daniel. To Jo's amazement, Daniel is not particularly interested in the murder of someone he never met; what does concern him and, indeed, devastates him is Jo's betrayal of him and everything they have had together. At this point, he cannot see any hope for their marriage.

In the final section of *While I Was Gone*, Eli gradually fades into the background. Although Jo does decide to report his confession to the police, the matter is dropped for lack of evidence. After all, it is just her word against his, and even her daughter Sadie finds Jo's story hard to believe. Once Jo moves past the issue of the murder, she can focus on something that she now sees is much more important: her marriage to Daniel, which is truly in jeopardy. It takes a good deal of soul-searching on Jo's part and a massive effort at forgiveness on Daniel's, but at the end of the novel, it is evident that over time Jo and Daniel will be able to reestablish their relationship on an even more substantial foundation.

It might seem that *While I Was Gone* is primarily a story about relationships between men and women, contrasting sexual obsession, like that which drives Jo toward Eli, and real love, which Jo had experienced with Daniel. However, another important theme in the novel is the love of parents for their children and, since the narrator is a woman, specifically maternal love. One of Jo's most vivid memories is of the day her two toddlers got out onto the roof, and she had to coax them back to safety. Recalling that experience, she always had to remind herself that once her girls became adults, she could no longer protect them by persuading them to come to her. Jo worried almost incessantly about Cass, the musician, who had no fixed residence and never seemed to plan beyond her next gig. When she came home that fall, however, Cass amazed and delighted her parents by announcing that she had finally decided on a career and was off to New York to become a model. What is particularly ironic is that all the time she was worrying about Cass, Jo herself was rushing toward disaster, and since no one else knew about it, there was no one to keep her from falling off the roof.

As she tells her story, it becomes increasingly evident that until Eli came back into her life, Jo had never come to terms with her own identity. Even while she worried about Cass's feckless existence, she did not admit to herself that she herself had a much more serious problem, a habit of running away, and not only from others but also from herself. She had never known who she was; instead, she just assumed one role after another. After marrying the medical student, Jo first envisioned herself as a doctor's wife, then played the part of a waitress, and finally became the mysterious stranger whom her housemates in Cambridge could never really get to know. When in the course of investigating Dana's murder the police found out who Jo was, she ran away again.

The Jo whom readers meet at the beginning of the novel is a very different person from that confused young woman. However, the feelings of detachment she mentions in the first chapter suggest that she had once again dwindled into an actress in life, rather than a participant. She was just going through the motions, acting the part of a wife, a veterinarian, a member of the community, even that of a mother. It was therefore very easy for her to add another role to her repertory, that of mistress, and even to play all these parts at once.

At the end of *While I Was Gone*, Jo has realized that she can never again disappear from her relationship with her husband. She must somehow reconcile all the selves she has been, all the parts she has played, for Daniel cannot embrace a phantom. However, Jo also knows that individuals can never fully know each other or even themselves, and therefore they must learn to bridge the gulfs between themselves in the only way they can, through forgiveness.

Rosemary M. Canfield Reisman

Sources for Further Study

Booklist 95 (November 1, 1998): 452.
The Christian Century 116 (March 10, 1999): 267.
Library Journal 124 (January, 1999): 156.
The New York Times Book Review 104 (February 21, 1999): 10.
Publishers Weekly 245 (November 2, 1998): 68.
Time 153 (February 22, 1999): 91.

WHO DO YOU LOVE
Stories

Author: Jean Thompson (1950-)
Publisher: Harcourt Brace (New York). 306 pp. $23.00.
Type of work: Short fiction
Time: The 1980's and 1990's
Locale: Central Illinois, Missouri, Mississippi, Oregon, California, Montana, Tennessee, and New Orleans

In fifteen disturbing but intriguing stories, Thompson subtly peels back the facades that most people present publicly and reveals the true people cowering behind them

Principal characters:
SCOUT, a twenty-year-old who works in a bookstore and takes drugs
ANNIE, a twenty-one-year-old who works in a deli
BENNY, a forty-four-year-old woman who is a sculptor
PETE, a student who travels with Benny
KENNETH DACEY, a rich businessman
DR. FLYNN, a retired pathologist, a widower
THE CAMPBELLS, a couple, married eighteen months, who buy Dr. Flynn's house
EVIE, a dutiful granddaughter
GRANDMOTHER, a ninety-five-year-old woman
MARY ANNE, Evie's younger sister

One of the finest photographers in the United States, Larry Kanfer, confines his picture-taking to Central Illinois. He works out of Champaign, two or three miles from where Jean Thompson lives and works. Kanfer's landscapes capture the bigness and the loneliness of the prairie as its stark geometries stretch out toward the thin, barely perceptible line that separates land from sky. He preserves the nuances of every cloud and shadow, the simple dignity of every arrow-straight road and sentinel silo. His photographs project subtle messages. Although Kanfer's pictures seldom have people in them, one can easily surmise how such a landscape might affect anyone who lives in it.

Jean Thompson often does with words what Larry Kanfer does so strikingly with film. She creates vivid landscapes in such stories as "The Amish," but then she goes one step further: She populates her wordscapes with the middle Americans who live there. Even when she sets her stories on the Oregon coast, as she does in "All Shall Love Me and Despair," or California, as she does in "Antarctica," the people in them seem like middle Americans, Midwesterners who carry the Midwest with them like cumbersome backpacks when they land in other places.

In "The Little Heart," Pete, a twenty-six-year-old microbiology student, a hunk who accompanies the accomplished forty-four-year-old sculptor, Benny, on a trip from Illinois or Missouri to New Orleans, makes a statement that is at the heart of much of Thompson's writing: "Isn't it weird how the worst times make the best stories." As in the title of this collection, *Who Do You Love*, the words are not followed by a question mark.

The fifteen stories in *Who Do You Love*, one of five finalists for the 1999 National Book Award in fiction, are tales about people's bad times, about people who have been drawn and quartered emotionally. Their lives are in tatters, but usually they go on living. When the tedium of their daily existence overwhelms them, they pick a fight or sell a house or take a trip or, like Scout, who loved the "tidy way the needle slipped beneath the skin, took its discrete bite," get a drug fix.

Thompson focuses on many situations that make the evening news or provide fodder for radio's endless talk shows—a father's physical and sexual abuse, child snatching, post-traumatic stress in a Vietnam War veteran, drug addiction, the furtive murder of a nagging spouse, the problems of aging, facing up to life in a retirement community or nursing home.

Thompson, quite validly, is frequently compared with Raymond Carver (1938-1988), whose overall focus resembles hers. One can, however, look further back to Sherwood Anderson's *Winesburg, Ohio* (1919) for an equally accurate comparison. Anderson (1876-1941) shocked America's post-World War I reading public by revealing what goes on within the quiet houses on peaceful streets in ordinary towns in Ohio. Jean Thompson's stories will not shock an American public in a new millennium, because in the intervening years many of that public's sensibilities have been anesthetized. Very little shocks Americans of the early twenty-first century. They have heard it all. They have seen it on television.

To a large extent, this insensibility is what Jean Thompson's stories convey. Her protagonists bungle through their days, one foot ahead of the other, as they inch across the prairie toward the thin line between earth and sky, between life and death. Their expectations are not high. If they can capture hours—even minutes or seconds—of pleasure, as Scout is able to with his needle or as Benny does with her casual companion, Pete, they grab those hours and run with them, soon to fall exhausted by the wayside, like Scout fatally adrift on a stolen boat or Benny slouching behind a fish tank in the New Orleans Aquarium.

Many of the stories in this collection focus on denial, an American way of coping with things that cause discomfort: Pretend they are not there and they will cease to exist. In "Antarctica," Evie uses denial to convince her aging grandmother that she is not at death's door. More significant, however, is that Evie is so completely in denial about the physical and sexual abuse her father visited upon her and her younger sister, Mary Anne, when they were children, that she has erased these events from her consciousness. Their horrors resurface when she goes to visit her sister in Killdeer, Montana. The very name of the town suggests the slaughter of the innocent.

In one of the more convoluted of these stories, "The Widower," denial is also a controlling theme, as is the theme of personal isolation, which pervades much of Thompson's work. Dr. Flynn, a retired pathologist, lives in the house that he and his late wife inhabited for years. They decorated it to their liking, painting the living room a Wedgwood blue at the suggestion of a noted decorator. Caroline Flynn was the typical stay-at-home wife of her era. The couple appeared to have an ideal marriage for fifty-one years. It ended, according to Dr. Flynn, when Caroline suffered an aneurysm while doing the laundry in the basement.

When Dr. Flynn and his daughter agree that running the house is too much for him, they talk of his going into a retirement community. Flynn puts his house on the market, and a real estate agent, one of the more memorable minor characters in this collection, shows it to the recently married Campbells. Flynn cringes at the thought that, if this couple buys the house, they will change things that he and Caroline had done to put their indelible marks upon a house that, in the terms of the cliché-ridden agent, they had turned into a "home."

The Campbells do not rush into making an offer until after Dr. Flynn suffers a heart attack that almost overnight transforms him, in real estate terms, into a "motivated seller." The young couple buys the house for a song and have enough money left over to transform it into a "home" of their own liking. As they go about doing this, Dr. Flynn refuses to leave them alone.

He finds countless excuses to visit them, coming by with hardware that he finds among his boxes or to give them advice and, occasionally, to deliver admonitions. The wife sympathizes with this lonely old widower, who appears grief-stricken, and who, himself, is probably not far from the grave. The husband, however, is less sympathetic and finally tells Flynn that his visits and suggestions are not welcome.

During the visit in which this encounter occurs, Flynn reveals to Campbell that his marriage was not the happy, romantic idyll that it seemed on the surface. Caroline was a nag and a terrible cook. Finally, she complained so bitterly about having had to cook for the past fifty years that Dr. Flynn took over this onerous responsibility.

As a pathologist, he realizes that his wife's allergy to seafood might bring about symptoms that over time could become increasingly pronounced and might inevitably result in a fatal episode of anaphylactic shock. On Flynn's deathbed in the hospital, to which Campbell has accompanied him after Flynn has a serious heart attack while visiting his old house, the old man reveals that, as the cook, he introduced shrimp into all sorts of things that his wife ate—spaghetti sauce, meat loaf, macaroni and cheese. Caroline had small allergic reactions from this seafood, but finally one day he did her in with a mouth-watering gumbo. She was quickly seized with the anaphylactic shock that closed her airways and suffocated her.

The dialogue in this particular portion of the story is nothing short of inspired. With its underlying stratum of dark, droll wit, it becomes a model of denial. Campbell does not want to hear Dr. Flynn's confession. As Dr. Flynn confesses to murder, Campbell carries on his own conversation about Flynn's daughter, who, informed of her father's attack, is rushing to the hospital. When Dr. Flynn persists in his confession, Campbell offers him water or Sprite. Finally, when the confession pours out too forcefully for Campbell to ignore any longer, he resorts to outright denial: "You can't kill somebody that way. Macaroni and cheese."

Before he dies, Dr. Flynn makes it clear that he has no more reason to be optimistic about the Campbells' marriage than he has to be nostalgic about his own. He asks

Campbell how much his wife cost him, to which an enraged Campbell retorts that he loves his wife. The skeptical Flynn utters his last, skeptical words before dying: "Sure you do." Campbell seethes at him, "You're a sick, bitter old man consumed by jealousy," but Flynn, already dead, is deaf to Campbell's words.

Thompson's powers of observation and her detailed depiction of scenes and characters evoke memories of Joan Didion at her best. The visual qualities of Thompson's descriptions, enhanced by details that involve all the senses, are extraordinary. In "Fire Dreams," for example, she describes a neighborhood and a family that lives in it:

> The lawns are velvet, and kindly yellow light spills from the windows. On the next block are the Holidays. That's what I call them, though it's not the name on their mailbox. As regularly as a grade school, their house displays the trappings of the season. Festoons of paper hearts a month before Valentine's Day. Then eggs and bunnies, then patriotic bunting, then jack-o'-lanterns and witches. Turkeys in November, Christmas an explosion of lights and plastic Santas. Every night the premises are lit like a prison yard.

Such descriptions, intermixed with Thompson's cynicism and black humor, make poignant statements about contemporary life in mainstream America.

"Fire Dreams," "The Amish," "Mother Nature," and "Antarctica" are told in the first person, whereas most of Thompson's stories employ third-person narration. Thompson handles first-person narration well, through it achieving an immediacy and narrative intimacy that cannot always be attained in third-person narration. In "The Amish," particularly, the first-person narration permits the reader to experience the events of the story directly through the persona of a ten-year-old child.

Many of Thompson's stories peter out rather than end. They trail off as the lives of most ordinary people trail off, ending not with a bang but a whimper. Typical is "The Rich Man's House," in which Kenneth Dacey, the unnamed protagonist's neighbor, goes off for a weekend of fishing and disappears. Jesse, who looks after Dacey's house, shows the protagonist, whose husband ran off six months earlier, through the entire lavish spread, now standing unoccupied. The deserted wife goes there to feed the cat; Jesse goes there to tend to caretaking chores. Sometimes Jesse sleeps over in the house. Sometimes she does. Thompson does not suggest any romantic encounters between the two, but, with admirable subtlety, allows her readers to ink in their own endings.

R. Baird Shuman

Sources for Further Study

Booklist 95 (May 15, 1999): 1671.
The New York Times Book Review 104 (July 25, 1999): 14.
Newsweek 133 (June 14, 1999): 74.
Publishers Weekly 246 (April 19, 1999): 58.

THE WHOLE WOMAN

Author: Germaine Greer (1939-   )
Publisher: Alfred A. Knopf (New York). 373 pp. $25.00
Type of work: Women's issues and current affairs
Time: The late twentieth century

A wonderfully acerbic indictment of the oppressive character of media and multinational corporations in their oppression of women—bodies, minds, and hearts—at the turn of the millennium

Mellowed perhaps by the years since she published *The Female Eunuch* (1970) but still outrageous in her witticisms and puns, Germaine Greer, in *The Whole Woman*, takes on the whole of the industrialized world (and thus the whole world) in her indictment of the situation facing women at the end of the twentieth century. "It's time to get angry again," she writes in her opening recantation of her vow not to write a sequel to *The Female Eunuch*. Greer, professor of English and comparative literature at Warwick University, England, has made a name for herself as a witty and controversial talk-show guest, refusing to agree with either standard feminist or conservative positions.

The book shows, in Greer's inimitable style, how women are the losers in the equality game, in everything from plastic surgery to transsexualism and reproductive technology (in the "Body" section); the "Mind" section takes on the culture of work and sex roles, while "Love" and "Power" deal with relationships and backlash. In England, "women's liberation" was the operative term for the women's movement far earlier than in the United States, and Greer laments the loss of the goal of liberation, and the acceptance, instead, of a false equality. In every case, the single-word section and chapter titles play down the hard-hitting exposé of the text.

Using materials from media—newspapers, magazines, advertising, and film, as well as scientific studies and academic research— Greer critiques the industrialized world and interprets society with a vengeance. Interspersed with boxed quotations from celebrities, newspapers, talk shows, and critics, the text is bursting with an astonishing amount of information.

Tellingly, Greer begins the "Body" section with "Beauty." Here she describes the multibillion-dollar beauty industry, calling it "a global pandemic" because women in China, India, and Africa are now the market for makeup, creams, hair products, and foundation garments. Illustrative here is the Miss World contest, outmoded in the industrialized world but popular in India and Africa. Much of this section details statistics and descriptions of the pain, expense, and time involved in the lengthy surgery and recovery period for breast implants. The time and money spent on cosmetic surgery around the world are ironically juxtaposed to the rising incidence of and lack of a cure for breast cancer.

The most important body part of a woman is her womb, but it is not celebrated in the Western world or even thought to be vital (once she has given birth). Certainly, women are not as identified as female by their wombs as they are by their breasts or their genitalia. Greer devotes a large section to the shocking rise of hysterectomies in the late twentieth century, especially in the United States, and asks if it is possible that the wombs of American women are four times as unhealthy as those of Swedish women, given that American women have four times as many hysterectomies.

Greer might be criticized by radicals for her strong refusal to accept transsexuals and transvestites as women, using the argument that breasts and reconstructed vaginas do not make a woman. Why are there so many more male-to-female transsexuals than female-to-male? Perhaps, says Greer, it is because males will not accept damaged males or those who do not wish to be males. She avers that women should not accept these individuals as females either. In any case, Greer notes the conservative nature of all sex-change surgery, which serves to strengthen sex-role stereotypes and stringent gender roles. Gender reassignment disavows the mother and the socialization process. If the transsexual demands to be accepted in women's places, he is no better than a rapist, says Greer, penetrating female space.

The "Mind" section gathers material reported in diverse sources to show how, transculturally and transhistorically, women have done the majority of work in the world. She reiterates the now-usual argument that women's unpaid labor is not included in economic analysis (gross domestic product) because it is unpaid and not recognized as work (child care, water or firewood carrying, hand cultivation, meal preparation). Leisure time is seen as a masculine privilege in most cultures worldwide. Additionally, Greer claims, a woman spends any remaining time "working on her body, her appearance, her clothes." Men, she says, spend no time on this aspect, because their clothes are durable, their hair requires little maintenance, and their bodies are more acceptable, no matter the shape. Why is it, she asks, that women buy so few compact discs? Because they do not have the time to listen.

Housework has become more time-consuming and onerous, not less so, as standards of cleanliness have risen. Television commercials persuade that toilets and floors need daily cleaning, that laundry and carpets must be dosed often with detergents. Both women and men internalize these standards, thus helping to raise the divorce rate, as women cannot meet their husbands' standards of immaculate order.

Women shop, buying upward of 80 percent of all retail goods. Men do not shop; they buy things—"cars, computers, CDs, photographic, sound and sports equipment. Practically everything else is sold to women," asserts Greer. Women are trained for shopping from a young age, as girls spend hours in malls after school; even if they have no money, they learn the process. They are taught that in order to exist they must acquire.

The chapters on estrogen and testosterone are exposés of the way that pharmaceutical companies have oversold hormone replacement therapy (HRT) to doctors and to women and the current way that high testosterone is used as an excuse for male violence. In two hundred years, modern European females have experienced a rise in the average number of menstrual cycles in a lifetime from 30 to 450 (earlier menarche, fewer pregnancies, shorter lactation, later menopause). Additional estrogen adds more cycles; we do not know what this may be doing to the female body in the long term.

Women's tendency to depression is the subject of Greer's chapter "Sorrow." Citing animal studies showing that serotonin levels fluctuate according to changes in status, as well as human studies showing that successful people have higher serotonin levels than those of lower status, Greer believes we should treat the situation that causes depression, instead of altering people's reactions. She is predictably critical of the upsurge of use of Prozac and other selective serotonin-uptake inhibitors.

Greer interprets the outpouring of grief and sorrow after the death of Diana, princess of Wales, from the four-fifths of the mourners who were women as an expression of those women's own pain. If the women's movement could "harvest the energy in women's oceanic grief," asserts Greer, "we [could] move mountains."

The "Love" section begins with "Mothers" and moves through the various relationships of women. True to her style and thesis, however, Greer continues to puncture preconceived notions. Citing growing numbers of single mothers in all areas from England to the Caribbean and sub-Saharan Africa, Greer reminds the reader of the rising number of women and children in poverty, in both the industrialized and the developing worlds.

The experts' and media's blaming the mother for the problems of children, both psychologically and physically (intrauterine), has become more strident and universal. Greer wonders how long it will be before human mothers are made obsolete. The artificial uterus is already scientifically possible. Like the early twentieth century Swedish radical feminist Ellen Key, Greer proposes motherhood as a genuine career option, with a pay and benefits-rewards system. If we were willing to honor our rhetoric about family values and child care, we as a society would not hesitate to pay handsomely for children's welfare.

"Daughters" examines family sexual abuse and incest, while "Sisters" criticizes the assumption that all women, even of different generations, classes, and circumstances, are alike. As Greer notes, popular media cannot stomach contradiction, complexity, or paradox, thus "woman" must be either socially constructed or a universal essence, with no combinations tolerated.

What has happened positively since the second wave of the women's movement is that friendship between women is now taken seriously, both for adults and for girls. That observation leads to Greer's discussion on "The Love of Women." Here she is at pains to point to the differences between gay men and lesbians—in levels and kinds of sexual activity, in monogamy or promiscuity. Greer summarizes some of the inconclusive genetic research purporting to have discovered a "gay gene" and concludes that both heterosexuality and homosexuality are most likely socially constructed. She is critical of the late twentieth century emphasis on orgasm rather than intimacy for all sexual orientations and notes that such a view is inherently masculinist.

The final section, "Power," begins with a chapter on male impotence and the recent hype for Viagra. One of Greer's virtues is her continued emphasis on the similarly problematic societal expectations for men as well as for women. When "penetrative sex" is assumed to be the only real sex—in films, advertising, and other media—it is no wonder that there is a growing incidence of sexual dysfunction in both men and women. Male fertility, as evidenced by sperm count, has dropped precipitously in the twentieth century all over the industrialized world; the reasons are not known, but we do know that extra testosterone lowers sperm count.

The "Fear" chapter demystifies flashers and exhibitionists. Greer believes that women should reject the exaggerated power of the phallus, noting that violence against women often includes injuries much worse than rape. Misogyny or hatred of women is explored in "Loathing"; women's irrational belief in the batterer's protestations of love is the biggest barrier to using the existing legal and social remedies against him.

Most important are the final chapters "Equality" and "Liberation." Greer recapitulates her thesis that equality is not good for women because it posits patriarchal society as that into which women should be integrated, and that society is violent, inequitable, and tyrannical. Greer cites ridiculous but true case histories of England's Sex Discrimination Act (1975), such as the outlawing of women-only swimming sessions at health clubs and the refusal to grant a license to a female-only taxi firm.

Liberation for women means changing society: distributing the world food supply rationally, providing clean water for everyone, promoting motherhood as an acceptable career, educating women worldwide (the best way to lower population growth). The multinational corporations use women as their territory, controlling research, information, hygiene, and food. Women will be liberated only if they are able to use their adaptability to survive and change, taking power instead of spending their energy on their bodies and their possessions. That power coup, says Greer, may likely begin with the poorest women of the world—Chinese women who are divorced for bearing daughters, Thai women ruined by prostitution and AIDS, or women incensed by Islamic fundamentalist beliefs on women's education and sexuality (for example, "honor" killings for sexual infractions).

The real value of this book is its gathering of scientific and media sources on disparate subjects from reproductive technology and cosmetic surgery to sex changes and cancer, from housework to shopping and violence against women. Although most of the statistics and examples are from England, there is much information on the United States and other industrialized countries, as well as the developing world. Greer's most telling charges are reserved for the market economy of the Western world, however. Her writing is clear, concise, refreshing, and witty, although she is given to generalizations supported by only one example. Though short on notes and references, her wide-ranging polemic is wonderful for beginning discussions. The book illustrates again and again that women's issues are integrally related to the whole world; as Virginia Woolf put it in *Three Guineas* (1938), "My country is the whole world."

Margaret McFadden

Sources for Further Study

Booklist 95 (April 1, 1999): 1363.
Commentary 108 (September, 1999): 65.
Library Journal 124 (May 15, 1999): 113.
New Statesman 129 (March 12, 1999): 48.
The New York Times Book Review 104 (May 9, 1999): 19.
Publishers Weekly 246 (March 22, 1999): 76.

WHO'S IRISH?
Stories

Author: Gish Jen (1956-   )
Publisher: Alfred A. Knopf (New York). 208 pp. $22.00
Type of work: Short fiction
Time: The twentieth century
Locale: The United States and China

Eight wide-ranging tales of immigration and assimilation told primarily from an Asian American viewpoint

In *Who's Irish?*, Gish Jen, acclaimed author of *Typical American* (1991) and *Mona in the Promised Land* (1996), continues her exploration of the immigrant experience, writing from a multifaceted ethnic viewpoint. While various writers, past and present, draw on their native origins to formulate novels, short stories, memoirs, essays, and such, Jen sets herself apart by consolidating and intermingling her own Chinese roots with those of other cultures. The result is not only a greater understanding of the Chinese immigrant's experience but also a deeper discernment that no one ethnic group has a monopoly on the bewilderment inherent in the alienation and assimilation associated with American mainstream culture—the immigrant experience is universal. This realization, to go one step further, instills in the consciousness of the reader harmonious feelings of identification with other cultural groups. For instance, in the first and title story, "Who's Irish?," the narrator, an elderly immigrant Chinese woman whose daughter, a bank vice president, has married into an Irish American family, feels baffled by modern American mores. Depressed and isolated, she stands with one foot in America and the other in China until she finds solidarity and refuge with the child's other grandmother, Bess, an Irish immigrant she earlier criticized for being lazy. Jen prompts the reader to develop an understanding that both grandmothers have similar needs and longings.

Who's Irish? is Jen's debut collection of eight emotionally penetrating and enlightening short stories. These superbly crafted narratives are not, however, by any means neat little tales of initial confusion, intermediate cataclysm, and ultimate reconciliation in the formation of a new American identity. Indeed, the individual stories are complex, many-sided, and oftentimes contradictory, simultaneously, as it were, light and dark. The title story is a tale of acute tension—generational, gender-bound, and cultural. The Chinese immigrant grandmother lives with her first-generation daughter, a modern Chinese American woman, who is married to a depressed, unemployed Irish American man. To her mother's great consternation, the daughter accepts complete financial responsibility for the family. The Irish, after all, are lazy, reasons the older woman when her son-in-law fails to keep a job. Narrating in a somewhat musical, pidgin dialect, the widowed grandmother blames her grandchild's negative traits on her Irish genes. She is contemptuous of her son-in-law, who is too proud to care for his daughter Sophie. Of particular concern, it seems, is the three-year-old's penchant for removing her clothes in public. Although the grandmother is the child's primary caregiver, the parents have clear ideas of their own regarding child rearing. In particular, they do not believe in physical discipline. This belief causes cultural bedlam. On one hand, the reader's heart goes out to the elderly narrator, so emphatic regarding her Chinese ways of bringing up children—spare the rod and spoil the child, she philosophizes. On the other hand, the reader is angry because in her attempts to instill obedience, the narrator brutalizes her granddaughter, beating the child in secret despite the parents' strenuous objections. It is her duty, she rationalizes, to beat the child into submission for the child's own good; after all, millions of Chinese children, all obedient, are disciplined in this manner. Also, the narrator's superior tone and racist attitudes concerning other ethnic groups, in particular the Irish, make her at times hard to relish. The reader is relieved when the desperately unhappy woman finds a safe harbor with her son-in-law's mother after her daughter and son ask her to leave their home. In this win-win resolution, Chinese and Irish grandmothers share the mutual enjoyment of their American granddaughter.

Jen reverses the bicultural Chinese American dilemma in her fourth story, "Duncan in China." Here, second-generation Chinese American protagonist and underachiever Duncan Hsu, thirty-seven and still suffering sibling rivalry and maternal strife, escapes America (and his brother Arnie, who drives a BMW convertible) by returning to mainland China to examine his heritage. In China he believes he will discover a country of old nobility and philosophic sages. Tension and anxiety also permeate this dim tale of the American English teacher or "foreign expert," as the Chinese call him, and his various quixotic encounters with students and coworkers in a Chinese mining town. Culturally naïve, nothing in his American life prepares Duncan for post-Cultural Revolution China. His colleagues smile out of one side of their mouths and criticize him out of the other. On a trip, he comes to realize his favorite students are spies. His poverty-stricken, tubercular relatives, desperate to escape China, manipulate him and paralyze him with guilt. Ultimately, Duncan realizes that his dream of China is a nightmare. Acknowledging the life he might have led had his family not immigrated, he shudders and admits his foolishness in taking for granted the American Dream.

The author peruses the other side of the American Dream in "Birthmates," the book's second story, featured in *Best American Short Stories*, 1995. In this very short narrative, the author weaves the tale of alienated and bewildered computer programmer Art Woo, who finds himself among the low-income, mostly black residents of a welfare hotel, where he has accidentally chosen to stay. Ironically, the communications expert is entirely unable to communicate. Through a subtle unwinding of past events, the reader realizes that his wife Lisa's leaving him has set in motion his state of mental decay. One catastrophe after another forces Woo, deep in denial over the medical termination of his severely damaged child and unable to share in his wife's grief, to finally acknowledge his overwhelming anguish and start the mourning process.

Physical and mental abuse persists as one of Jen's themes in *Who's Irish?* "Chin," the sixth story, is another grim tale, this time of physical abuse that perhaps metaphorically epitomizes the immigrant family's frustration in their attempts to meld into

American culture. A Chinese American boy newly moved into a Westchester County suburb, who is "not like the others" and who eats special food, is battered by high school ruffians. He gets beat up for missing school, for talking back to his father, for getting poor grades, and for pilfering little gifts for his mother and sister. Interestingly, the tale's narrator, the secretly bright class underachiever, is one of the bullies who hounds him. Chin's agony is palpable. The child not only suffers physically at the hands of his schoolmates but also experiences a traumatic home life. At night, the narrator watches through his window to see son, sister, and mother abused at every turn by the tyrannical father. The reader wonders if it is for this reason that the family keeps their windows continually closed. The sense of futility is overwhelming by the story's conclusion, when the battered family returns home helpless, dragging a broken suitcase through the snow, to the hands of the persecutor they had earlier found the courage to leave. Perhaps the strongest indictment presented in this story revolves around the thought that while neighbors, close enough to touch each other, watch and record such circumstances, they remain frozen, wishing actually that they had kept their eyes on the television instead.

Sharply detailed and poignant, the third story, "The Water Faucet Vision," defines again the helplessness and alienation of the outsider striving to become acclimated to American life. In this story, readers encounter the Chang family debuted in Jen's *Mona in the Promised Land:* Callie, the narrator; Mona, her sister; Helen, the Chinese mother who attempts to assimilate into American culture; and Ralph, the resistant father. As an adult, Callie recalls how, as a fifth-grade Catholic school girl, she cherished three malachite beads—worry beads?—as her sole source of comfort after her mother somehow fell out the window of their second-floor apartment during the course of an argument with Callie's father. After losing these precious beads, young Callie convinces herself she is experiencing a miraculous vision, an experience to which every young Catholic girl aspires. Somehow, she postulates, turning on all the faucets in the house will result in the return of her sole comfort through the city water system.

Who's Irish? thematically demonstrates how the foreigner, the outsider, the outlander (or whatever the fashionable term is) attempts at any cost to fit in. "In the American Society" chronicles with great humor and pathos the disastrous attempts of the Chang family, this time as they attempt to gain admittance to the town country club—the ultimate American status symbol of acceptance. Things are going well financially for the family, now the proud owners of a pancake house, until the mother Helen gets the desire to move up socially. Father Ralph runs into trouble when he allows himself to be talked into hiring illegal Chinese aliens in a magnanimous gesture. When Chinese workers clash with the Latino chef, turmoil ensues. After they are turned down by the club, a friend invites the Changs to a disastrous high-society party where Ralph practically comes to blows with the drunken guest of honor. Callie and Mona are reduced to acting as servants. Clearly, East cannot meet West here.

Unlike her dark, traumatic tales of family abuse, Jen weaves through her lighter stories the thread of family renewal and solidarity. "Just Wait," the fifth story, set amid a baby shower, epitomizes family rejuvenation. Annie Wing's three brothers, studies in contrasts, renew and restore their familial relationship by coming together to share a gift for their sister, who is about to give birth. Billy, a woodsy, ice-fishing type, who reads Herodotus by lantern light; Mark, the money-making Mr. Real World; and Neddie, who lives in a mental hospital, find that despite their differences, they are united by blood and the promise of family continuity.

"House, House, Home," the final and longest story, fully one-third of the book, drags. It would have been better as two individual stories. Pammie is a free-spirited art student before she marries Sven, a much older, iconoclastic art history professor. Here Jen proposes the outcome of a relationship between what most would call an odd couple: Pammie, a timid "elective outsider," and Sven, whose looks and height, according to the author, always represent power in American society. Although they are determined to live life on the margins, once their children are born life changes drastically. Pammie finds herself rigidly entrenched in the bourgeoisie: meetings of the Parent-Teacher Association, soccer games, and school lunches. Sven, indifferent about money and possessions, whom Pammie unknowingly married during his midlife crisis, does not understand that although he has managed to amass half a million dollars, he needs to pay less attention to artful shadows and more attention to his stock portfolio. The atypical, architecturally unsound house they buy becomes a financial hindrance: It never becomes the home they anticipate. Ultimately, and not surprisingly, the couple's differences drive them apart. In time, they come to hate not only each other but also, interestingly, the negative things they find within themselves. Sven heads north, leaving Pammie, his third and, as he says, "easiest" wife and the two children, Phoebe and Adam, in order to live out the rest of his life in blissful indifference in the Maine woods. Pammie jumps from the cold, slim, Nordic Sven to a new relationship with Carver, a burly, warm, pineapple grower from Hawaii. Frankly, Jen's shorter tales are better crafted. Their brevity strengthens their overall intensity.

Although oftentimes filled with satirical humor, the stories in *Who's Irish?* brim with anguish and pathos. While she also represents the Asian American literary genre, standing alongside Amy Tan and Maxine Hong Kingston, her works encompass the complete immigrant experience. The stories in *Who's Irish?* further distinguish Jen as a principal chronicler of the immigrant in search of the American Dream.

M. Casey Diana

Sources for Further Study

Boston Magazine 91 (June, 1999): 145.
The New York Times Book Review 104 (June 27, 1999): 13.
Newsweek 133 (June 7, 1999): 75.
Publishers Weekly 246 (April 26, 1999): 52.

WHY THEY KILL
The Discoveries of a Maverick Criminologist

Author: Richard Rhodes (1937-)
Publisher: Alfred A. Knopf (New York). 371 pp. $26.95
Type of work: Sociology, current affairs, and biography

A Pulitzer Prize-winning author reviews the life and scholarship of Lonnie Athens, maverick criminologist and groundbreaking researcher into the dynamics of violent human behavior

In *Why They Kill*, Richard Rhodes has written a hybrid book that combines social science and biography. The book is made all the more profound in that it has autobiographical elements as well. Rhodes has previously authored sixteen books, including *The Making of the Atom Bomb* (1986), which won a Pulitzer Prize in nonfiction, a National Book Award, and a National Book Critics Circle Award. Rhodes also wrote *A Hole in the World: An American Boyhood* (1990), an autobiographical account of the child abuse he suffered at the hands of his stepmother. It was this personal experience that, in part, inspired Rhodes to take an interest in the life and work of "maverick criminologist" Lonnie Athens. More specifically, Rhodes puts much of his focus on the vital link between Athens's violence-soaked childhood and his groundbreaking work on the social-psychological dynamics and root causes of criminal violence. In doing so, Rhodes raises the reader's awareness that truly insightful social science sometimes comes from deep emotional concerns and personal experience rather than book learning and dispassionate number crunching. In addition to explaining Athens's research and theories in the light of his (Athens's) upbringing, Rhodes tests Athens's ideas by applying them to several notorious murder cases and using them to examine historical patterns of violence. He also looks at the phenomena of war and military training in the light of Athens's work. Rhodes concludes with a brief chapter suggesting some possible solutions to the problem of violence.

Lonnie Athens was born in 1949 in Richmond, Virginia, to Petro (Pete) and Irene Athens. The Athens family was lower middle class, blue collar, and, during one particularly harrowing stretch, borderline transient. They often made do in tough neighborhoods where males especially had to be handy with their fists—or worse. However, the main threat of violence to Lonnie came from his father. Pete Athens was a rugged man who never shrank from a fight outside the household and who, though he did not engage in spousal abuse, did use disproportionate and brutal physical force to discipline both Lonnie and his older brother Rico, born in 1945. Lonnie watched his brother take the brunt of the violence but often shared in the victimization. Lonnie was deeply affected by this violence. Both he and Rhodes believe that he would have replicated his father's violent pattern if not for the intervention of several softening forces: his grandfather on his mother's side, a good friend in school (and the friend's family), and some teachers and professors. In line with his own theory, as readers shall see, Lonnie was saved from playing out the legacy of violence received from his father. Instead, goaded by his deep personal concern and experience, and also by the inadequacies of the accepted scholarly wisdom, he applied his powers of intellect to the task of better understanding violence. More specifically, through a somewhat checkered but ultimately successful career in academia, he tried to come up with more detailed and precise answers to questions such as the following: What do violent people think during the time leading up to their violent behavior, while they are behaving violently, and afterward? How do some people become inclined toward violence while others avoid such an inclination? What can be done to reduce the volume of violent behavior in a society?

Lonnie Athens pursued answers to these questions through a relatively small number of in-depth interviews with prisoners incarcerated for serious violent crimes. This methodology presented a number of problems. Prison authorities were sometimes uncooperative. Prisoners were sometimes threatening or less than candid. Scholars scoffed at the qualitative rather than quantitative nature of the work—that is, they doubted the relevancy of work that did not aim primarily at statistical significance drawn from a large sample of subjects. Luckily, on the other hand, some prison authorities were highly cooperative. Many prisoners welcomed a chance for their true feelings to be heard, and some academics saw the unique significance of Athens's work. As such, Athens was able to plunge on, producing a number of seminal books and articles. (Unfortunately, Athens's first marriage does seem to have been a casualty of his often-rocky academic career.)

In *Violent Criminal Acts and Actors* (1980; published in 1997 as *Violent Criminal Acts and Actors Revisited*), Athens presents his findings based on fifty-eight in-depth interviews with convicted violent criminals. Athens argues that, based on his research, violence is based on a conscious, reconstructible thought process, or "plan." This contradicts previous research that has described most seriously violent acts as being relatively unreflective acts of impulse (the "I just snapped and the next thing I knew he was dead" explanation). Rhodes quotes long passages from Athens's book revealing, in sometimes gruesome detail, the deliberative processes preceding violent acts. If nothing else, Rhodes and Athens both provide chilling, close-up evidence of how violent criminals remember their crimes. More to the point for Athens as well as Rhodes, these deliberative processes appear to be present in every single case.

In *The Creation of Dangerous Violent Criminals* (1992), also based on in-depth interviews, Athens goes on to explore the process of what he calls "violentization," that is, the way in which people are habituated to serious violent behavior. Athens describes four stages of the violentization process: brutalization, belligerency, violent performance, and virulency. In the first, brutalization, a young person is compelled to submit to a violent authority figure, observes violent subjugation of close friends or family members, and is "coached" to use violence to settle disputes. Belligerency involves the heeding of one's coach(es), that is, the resolution to use violence. Violent performance is largely self-explanatory, with the additional definition that the violent experience is at least partly successful. Virulency transforms this early success into a way of life, or well-rooted pattern of behavior. For Athens, all four stages must be experienced for a person to have become violentized. Once a person has become violentized, it is not clear that the process is reversible. Therefore, if intervention is to take place, it must be during one of the early stages—the earlier the better. In Athens's own case, the process of violentization was ameliorated by nonviolent relatives. Then, too, teachers and a particularly close school mate intervened in such a way as to help young Lonnie escape full immersion in his violent environment. The result: formation of a man prone to ideas and scholarship rather than violence.

In two later articles, "The Self as a Soliloquy" (1994) and "Dramatic Self-Change" (1995), both published in the *Sociological Quarterly*, Athens builds his theories of violence to a general model of behavior. Consistent with the previous work, Athens describes the crucial importance to behavior of an inner dialogue with one's "phantom community." Athens goes into greater detail as to how this community (or inner voice) is formed and how it can be transformed, sometimes with relative rapidity. Athens's current work attempts to fully develop these insights.

Along with his exegesis of Athens's work, Rhodes presents chapters that apply Athens's theories to notorious violent criminals, examining the cases of Perry Miller, the actual trigger man described in Truman Capote's *In Cold Blood* (1966); notoriously violent boxer Mike Tyson; Alex Kelly, the "preppy rapist"; John F. Kennedy assassin Lee Harvey Oswald; and Cheryl Crane, Lana Turner's teenage daughter who stabbed her mother's boyfriend, Johnny Stompanato. In all these cases, Rhodes finds that Athens's theories are borne out in full. Rhodes then looks to periods of history in which violent personal behavior was far more common and accepted than it is today, again finding confirmation for Athens's theories of violence and violentization. Rhodes devotes his penultimate chapter to an exploration of how military recruits are, quite appropriately, violentized for the necessities of making war, but also how often this process fails to take hold—and, on the other hand, the difficulty with which the process is reversed in some cases.

The book concludes with an all-too-brief discussion of possible solutions to the problem of violence. As suggested above, Athens recommends early intervention. Where violentization has proceeded to completion, he recommends incapacitation (thus, according to Rhodes, his prescription is partly "liberal" and partly "conservative"). There is precious little discussion of the proper form(s) successful intervention might take, though Rhodes does make it clear that both he and Athens think that different variations of "spare the rod and spoil the child," especially where the use of force is not carefully limited, are likely to be self-defeating since they themselves tend to foster violence.

Given the detailed analysis of the previous chapters, the truncated nature of Rhodes's conclusion may well be criticized. Certainly, it would seem that the main use of Athens's work is the practical one of making society less violent. Yet Rhodes devotes few pages to the topic, and some of what he does say is highly unoriginal, such as teaching nonviolent norms in schools. It is clear from the earlier sections of the book that families and neighborhoods are the main loci of violentization. It may or may not be possible to intervene effectively at this level, but, at the very least, the dilemma (with regard to privacy) as well as the difficulties of intervening in families and neighborhoods should be discussed at greater length.

Why They Kill may well be criticized on other grounds as well. While the value of Athens's work is clearly demonstrated, Rhodes makes methodological claims that are very difficult to support. He argues that Athens's work eschews statistical correlations in favor of a universally valid model. While this does allow room for critics to search for other cases that would refute the model, the effort made by Rhodes to do so in this book is insufficiently thorough. There would seem to be crimes, such as workplace and school shootings, to which Athens's theory may well be less applicable. Moreover, it is impossible to get all violent perpetrators to describe their experiences. Some are unwilling or unable to account verbally for their actions. Some commit suicide at the scene of the crime, taking their motives and actual violent experience to the grave with them. When violent acts are recounted, even with great sincerity, it may be possible that some of the account is constructed from the present rather than the past. While none of these criticisms refutes the value of Athens's work, they do argue for a more realistic assessment of his methodology and findings. Similarly, Rhodes's application of Athens's work to the cause of clearer criminal culpability is overstated. While it may be true that pleas of diminished criminal responsibility are all too common and that such pleas are often shakily founded, Athens himself shows that violent criminals have been previously victimized by their environments. As such, his own theories are partly deterministic. This does not mean that criminal culpability is, in practical terms, untenable. It does mean that culpability is not an absolute. Athens's work does not change this somewhat paradoxical fact. Finally, Rhodes makes no real effort to locate Athens's findings within the full range of scholarly work on the topic of criminal violence. No doubt, Athens is a maverick. However, that does not necessarily mean that his work is totally out of sync with the totality of contemporary social science.

Despite these criticisms, *Why They Kill* is a very valuable book. For one thing, it provides a well-written account of cutting-edge social science. Even more valuable is the fact that this research is put into a human context. The reader is treated not just to revelations of social science, but also to processes of social science and, more specifically, the interaction between down-to-earth human concerns, which sometimes can be very personal, and the application of rigorous scholarly methods. As such, Richard Rhodes can be very proud of this book. He also can reasonably assume that he has made a significant contribution to making society less violent.

Ira Smolensky

Sources for Further Study

Booklist 96 (September 15, 1999): 203.
The New York Times, September 27, 1999, p. E8.
The New York Times Book Review 104 (September 19, 1999): 13.
Psychology Today 32 (November, 1999): 79.
Publishers Weekly 246 (August 16, 1999): 71.

WITNESS TO HOPE
The Biography of Pope John Paul II

Author: George Weigel (1951-   )
Publisher: Cliff Street Books (New York). 992 pp. $35.00
Type of work: Biography, religion, and history
Time: 1920-1999
Locale: Poland and Italy

This extremely well written and sympathetic biography of Pope John Paul II describes very well his formative years before the Nazi invasion of Poland in 1939, the horrors of the Nazi and communist occupations of Poland, and John Paul II's accomplishments as pope

Principal personages:
KAROL WOJTYŁA, who became Pope John Paul II in 1978
POPE JOHN PAUL I, who was pope from late August, 1978, to late September, 1978
POPE PAUL VI, who served as pope from 1963 to 1978 and named Karol Wojtyła a cardinal in 1967
POPE JOHN XXIII, who served as pope from 1958 to 1963 and called the Vatican II Council
POPE PIUS XII, who served as pope from 1939 to 1958 and named Karol Wojtyła a bishop in 1958

George Weigel studied at St. Mary's Seminary in Baltimore and at St. Michael's College in Toronto. He has published extensively on Catholicism and the collapse of communism in eastern Europe. He is a prominent Catholic theologian, and he presently serves as a senior fellow at the Ethics and Public Policy Center in Washington, D.C.

Weigel's admiration for the actions and moral teachings of Pope John Paul II, both before and after his election as pope in October, 1978, is obvious to readers, and he presents his analysis of Pope John Paul II's life and religious career clearly, so that readers can understand thoroughly the horrendous conditions in Poland during the Nazi and communist occupations, the important role played by Pope John Paul II in the collapse of communism in eastern and central Europe, and his long service as pope.

The pope himself agreed to be interviewed several times by Weigel for this biography. Weigel also conducted extensive research in Poland and Rome. Friends in Krakow shared with him their knowledge of Karol Wojtyła's work as a parish priest and university chaplain in Krakow after his ordination in 1946, his service as a professor of theology and philosophy at Lublin's Catholic University, his important role in presenting to Polish Catholics theological reasons for opposing communism, and his skill and courage in defending Polish Catholics against real threats by successive communist regimes both before and after his election as pope. Weigel knows well Karol Wojtyła's extensive writings in Polish on theology and philosophy and the numerous encyclicals and books written by Pope John Paul II on such diverse topics as morality, the essential beliefs of Catholicism, ecumenism, the equality and dignity of women, and human rights. *Witness to Hope*, completed in early 1999, should remain the standard biography of Pope John Paul II for years to come.

Pope John Paul II is a humble man who does not like to talk about himself, but Weigel has succeeded in learning many facts about his life and ecclesiastical career. Karol Wojtyła was born on May 18, 1920, to Karol and Emilia Wojtyła in Bielsko-Biala, Poland, where his father was serving as an officer in the Polish army. After his father's retirement from the Polish Army in 1927, the Wojtyłas moved to Wadowice. During his high school years, the younger Karol acted in numerous plays and learned to speak effectively. His parents were very religious and not at all anti-Semitic. During the Nazi occupation of his homeland, Karol Wojtyła worked as a day slave laborer in a chemical plant; starting in 1942, he attended, at night, a clandestine seminary in Krakow from which numerous priests and seminarians were arrested by the Gestapo and later killed in concentration camps. Karol Wojtyła was not detected and was ordained a priest on November 1, 1946, in Krakow.

Even before his election as pope in 1978, Karol Wojtyła was very well known throughout Poland as an effective writer and defender of the Catholic faith. His intellectual training was first-rate. He earned two doctorates. From November, 1946, until June, 1948, he studied at the Angelicum in Rome and wrote a dissertation in Latin on the Spanish mystic St. John of the Cross. While in Rome, he met leading theologians of that era, and after his return to Poland he recognized the need to obtain a doctorate in Poland so that he could teach at a Polish university. In 1954, he defended at Krakow's Jagiellonian University his dissertation on the phenomenologist Max Scheler. In this work, Karol Wojtyła tried to reconcile modern philosophical thought with traditional Catholic beliefs. He persuaded Polish Catholic intellectuals that Catholicism made much more sense than communism. He developed effective logical arguments to support and encourage a commitment to Catholic values and dogma.

In 1958, Pope Pius XII named Karol Wojtyła an auxiliary bishop in Krakow. This was Pius's last appointment of a bishop. Nine years later Pope Paul VI, who had gotten to know Bishop Wojtyła during the Vatican II Council, named him a cardinal. During the twenty years between his appointment as bishop and his election as pope, Karol Wojtyła wrote extensively on topics that later dominated his papacy. He explained clearly the inalienable rights of each individual, the importance of religious freedom and the need for Catholics to respect other faiths, the liberating value of sexual love within marriage, the dignity and equality of women, youth ministry, and the need for social reform to ensure that each person can reach his or her full potential. As both a bishop and a cardinal, he reached out to clergy and laity alike in order to encourage the spiritual development of Polish Catholics and to teach them how to resist communism.

The year 1978 has become known as the year of three popes, because there were three different popes within just over two months. Pope Paul VI died on August 6. Just nineteen days later the Cardinals elected Albino Luciani as his successor. He chose the name Pope John Paul II but died of a massive heart attack during the early hours of September 29. On October 16, Cardinal Wojtyła was elected by his fellow cardinals, and he also selected the name of Pope John Paul II, in memory of the recently deceased pope. He was the first Polish pope ever and the first non-Italian pope since the Dutch Pope Adrian VI, whose reign extended from 1522 to 1523.

This election provoked intense joy among Polish Catholics and angered Polish communist leaders and their Soviet boss, Leonid Brezhnev. These reactions were perfectly understandable because the new pope's fellow Polish Catholics knew that he had given them consistent support and moral guidance, which helped them to survive decades of communist oppression, and the communists correctly viewed him as a real threat to their maintaining their colonial rule in central and eastern Europe. Weigel describes quite well the powerful effect of Pope John Paul II's first papal visit to Poland, in June, 1979. On the very day of his return to his homeland, he spoke to the faithful of the need for spiritual renewal in a new Poland, so that totalitarian regimes could no longer violate basic human rights. He also denounced the Warsaw Pact, which permitted other communist countries to invade other Soviet colonies in order to prevent any movement toward democracy. During this visit, he also went to Auschwitz and asked people to pray for the souls of all the victims of the Holocaust. This represented an early effort during his papacy to establish better relations between Catholics and Jews and to help Catholics realize that anti-Semitism was not compatible with Catholicism. Just a few months after his visit to Poland, the Soviet communist leaders approved "a plan of action to work against the policies of the Vatican in relation to socialist states."

Weigel discusses very carefully the probable role played by communist secret agents in the unsuccessful assassination attempt by Mehmet Ali Agca on Pope John Paul II's life on May 13, 1981, in St. Peter's Square. Weigel concludes that that Mehmet Ali Agca could not have acted alone; he simply did not have the money to travel as extensively as he did just before the assassination attempt. Weigel believed that the only credible explanation is that Bulgarian secret agents, acting on orders from Moscow, paid Agca to kill Pope John Paul II. The Soviet communist leaders hoped that the death of John Paul II would so discourage Poles that they would simply surrender to the communist occupation of their country. Weigel admits that written documents about Soviet involvement in this assassination attempt have most probably been destroyed, but he believes that the Soviets were most certainly involved in this attempt to kill Pope John Paul II. In any case, this attempt on the life of a revered pope produced an effect exactly opposite from what the Soviets had expected. Not only Polish Catholics but also people throughout the Soviet empire in eastern and central Europe began to actively resist interference in their daily lives. This bungled assassination attempt in 1981 emboldened people to resist their communist oppressors and contributed to the implosion of Soviet power in the early 1990's.

Although General Wojciech Jaruzelski, the Soviet puppet leader in Poland, began a reign of terror and murdered numerous members of the Polish Catholic laity and clergy, including Pope John Paul II's close friend Father Jerzy Popieluszko, their efforts failed miserably. The grave of Father Popieluszko became a pilgrimage site for Polish Catholics, and the pope himself prayed before his friend's grave during his visit to Poland in 1987. The successes of the trade union called Solidarity, whose leader, Lech Wałęsa, later became president in democratic Poland, would not have happened without strong guidance from Pope John Paul II.

Weigel describes Pope John Paul II's extraordinary success in reaching young people throughout the world during his numerous papal visits to all the continents, except, of course, Antarctica. Weigel describes objectively the complex unity in Pope John Paul II's writings on Catholic theology. Since he is firmly opposed to all violations of women's rights, he was consistent in condemning affronts to women's spiritual and moral dignity through such diverse types of exploitation of women as rape, pornography, restrictions on women's civil rights and freedom of religion, and abortion. In his 1995 encyclical *Evangelicun Vitae (Gospel of Life)*, Pope John Paul II explained that the Catholic church was opposed to both abortion and euthanasia because it wanted to protect the sanctity of life from the moment of creation in the mother's womb, throughout this life, and into the next. In this same encyclical, he also expressed his disapproval of capital punishment because it grants to the state a power that belongs to God alone: the right to determine the moment of a person's death.

Weigel also draws our attention to the fact that, despite financial difficulties in the Vatican, Pope John Paul II authorized the expenditure of large amounts of money to build churches and seminaries, to reduce starvation, and to improve medical care in poor countries of Africa, the continent where the Catholic Church had the greatest number of conversions during his papacy. He even visited Sudan, where Catholics were severely persecuted and often martyred for practicing their religion.

Weigel describes very well both the unity and the evolution of Pope John Paul II's writings and speeches on the essential teachings of Catholicism. Karol Wojtyła's exposure to the rich complexity of modern philosophy and theology during his studies in Rome and Poland and his years of teaching at Lublin's Catholic University made him more persuasive in presenting Catholic beliefs both to Catholics and to people of other faiths, but his core beliefs never changed. They simply evolved as the world became more diverse and complex.

Edmund J. Campion

Sources for Further Study

Booklist 96 (September 1, 1999): 6.
National Catholic Reporter 36 (November 5, 1999): 37.
National Review 51 (October 11, 1999): 53.
The New York Times Book Review 104 (November 14, 1999): 16.
Publishers Weekly 246 (September 13, 1999): 76.

WOMAN
An Intimate Geography

Author: Natalie Angier (1958-)
Publisher: Houghton Mifflin (Boston). 348 pp. $25.00
Type of work: Science and women's issues
Time: The 1990's
Locale: Primarily the United States

A wide-ranging examination of the body structures and body systems that make a woman female and how these features affect female behavior

Natalie Angier is a Pulitzer Prize-winning science writer for *The New York Times*. She has won the Lewis Thomas Award as well as the Journalism Award of the American Association for the Advancement of Science. Because she writes for a lay audience, Angier tends to use colorful metaphors and analogies to aid in reader understanding, yet her work comes from her studies in numerous scientific fields including biology, evolutionary psychology, anthropology, sociology, history, and biochemistry. Among her other nonfiction books are *The Beauty of the Beastly: New Views of the Nature of Life* (1995) and *Natural Obsessions: The Search for the Oncogene* (1988), which was also published in 1999 as *Natural Obsessions: Striving to Unlock the Deepest Secrets of the Cancer Cell.*

In her preface to *Woman: An Intimate Geography*, Angier discusses the organization, the purpose, and the features of her book. While examining the anatomy of the female body, she offers theories about the function and purpose of each part of the body. Early chapters, which focus primarily on the specific parts of the body, are resplendent with facts, historical anecdotes, and theories about the purpose and function of the various elements. Angier begins her book with discussions of the smallest element, the egg, and eventually works her way to the vagina, the clitoris, the uterus, the breast, then back to the ovaries and the Fallopian tubes. Her later chapters focus more on systems and female behaviors. Throughout the book, Angier consistently calls into question the reader's preconceived notions about the nature of being female, tackling such issues as female aggression, menopause, and woman's supposed monogamous nature. Though she often wants readers to adopt some call for action, most of her suggestions are tempered by good sense and buttressed by scientific evidence.

Angier's factual and often provocative details permeate her book. She looks at the exact makeup of the human egg, for example, discussing at length the hormonal and proximal triggering factors that cause only one egg to break loose each month. Her attention to the minutiae of female biology—the bland gray colors of the ovaries, the turnipy flesh of a fibroid tumor, the precise duct work in a lactating woman's breasts—underscores the microscopic precision of her facts. Furthermore, Angier takes on often underdiscussed aspects of the human anatomy such as the clitoris, looking at both its function and its physical makeup. Twice, Angier discusses the surgeries she witnessed so she could see elements of the female body.

In later chapters, Angier moves into broader discussions about female systems, such as endocrinology, as well as female behaviors. The primary sources for her theories are case studies from various fields of science, though many of her more radical theories often have less support than one might like. Yet, Angier does not claim that all of her beliefs are founded in absolute truth. In fact, in her preface, she suggests that she "toss[es] out ideas and theories" concerning the origins and purposes of female anatomy, sometimes including them for their "contrariety, their power to buck the party line of woman's 'nature.'" To her credit, Angier never couches these "theories" in the language of fact.

Though most of the book discusses the biology of women, Angier does not ignore the feminist implications of what she discovers, and her attitude toward feminism informs the kinds of discoveries she brings to the surface and her applications of those discoveries. In her preface, Angier separates herself from two distinct brands of feminism. She consistently undermines the idea of female biology as unknowable and superior because of its inherent mystery, debunking Camille Paglia and others of her ilk. Angier suggests that women are knowable and capable of being studied, not unfathomable at all. At the same time, she resists feminists who believe in intellect over biology, the idea that women have to rise above their inherent natures to get what they want. Angier does not want women to deny their biology or accept mystification as an easy answer in discussing body systems. Rather, she wants to illuminate areas of mystery, show how the body does inform the mind, then step back and let the reader assess her findings. For example, when she discusses menstruation, she does not cloak the discussion in the joys of this bodily function. Rather, she explains in scientific detail the features and behaviors of the body's reproductive mechanisms and the precision of the instruments involved. When she concludes the chapter on this system, she expects her readers to value the explanation, not for how it revels in the actual process, but rather in how precise the female body can be. Furthermore, she indicates how women should make use of their menstrual cycles, and learn to respect this aspect of the body's precision.

Even when her proof runs thin, her suppositions are offered in good faith. She very rarely expects her readers to embrace only her views. Instead, she asks her readers to become informed. For example, in her two chapters on menopause, Angier centers her discussion on the ongoing debate concerning postmenopausal women and their use of hormone replacement therapy. Angier sees the origins of this argument in the ongoing debate about the nature of menopause.

In her discussion of the many views about the evolution of menopause, Angier tries to stay neutral. Some theories posit that women lose their capacity to bear children at age forty-five or fifty because, evolutionarily, women died at about that time. Women who accept this theory may see menopause as something unnaturally forced upon them by virtue of their now-longer life span. Angier believes these women may be more apt to agree to hormone replacement therapy. If, however, women view menopause as an evolutionary adaptation, a natural occurrence which all women have been selected to go through, then Angier suggests that the rationale for taking hormones changes. Though Angier presents sample evidence to support both suppositions, in all of her discussions she remains neutral. She neither supports nor disapproves of hormone replacement therapy. Rather, she believes that the medical profession needs to use more caution in prescribing every postmenopausal woman the therapy. Furthermore, she believes that every woman should not immediately dismiss the treatment. Women instead need to understand more about why their bodies go through this change, then weigh the health risks and benefits of taking hormones. In the end, Angier expects women to learn about the female body, as well as their particular female body, before making any decisions.

Angier typically tries to look at all sides of an argument, and she works hard at creating doubt in her reader's mind about any proscribed notions about women, including qualities of female behavior. She undercuts the idea that women are not aggressive, citing physical evidence that testosterone, androstenedione, and estrogen—all hormones found in women—can create aggressive tendencies. Yet she also suggests that women have been socialized to use most of their aggression in a passive way, typically against other women. Angier also looks at the roots of maternal love and how one can learn about romantic attachment by looking at the biological factors that help create love.

Angier devotes her last chapter to her most interesting and potentially radical theory—the supposition that women are not monogamous by nature. By the time she gets to this chapter, the reader knows that females can be very aggressive toward each other; at the same time, women have always depended upon each other. Using this information, Angier suggests that women have historically been promiscuous—thus explaining their hidden estrus and the placement of the clitoris and other body parts—but that men have had to "control" female sexuality by making a promiscuous woman seem an anomaly. As Angier puts it,

> On the one hand we are told that women have a lower sex drive than men do. On the other hand we are told that the madonna-whore dichotomy is a universal stereotype. . . . Women are said to have lower sex drives than men, yet they are universally punished if they display evidence to the contrary—if they disobey their "natural" inclination toward a stifled libido.

This fear of the libidinous woman, who might become impregnated by another man, causes men to "mate guard." Angier indicates, "Men are under selective pressure to make sure they're chosen or, barring that, to subvert female choice and coerce the female to mate against her will." Angier suggests that men have demanded the faithfulness of women to make sure they do not raise another man's child.

While Angier's larger argument about how men have socialized women from being naturally promiscuous to predictably monogamous often seems plausible, her points tend to become muddled with frequent asides. Yet she does present several side arguments that merit attention. One of the most interesting theories she calls into question concerns the test groups that evolutionary psychologists use to demonstrate their faith in the promiscuous male and the monogamous female—the homosexual male and female. Angier suggests that in no other case would evolutionary psychologists use these groups of people as prototypes of masculinity or femininity, yet when they cite promiscuity as a "male" habit, they look toward a test group of homosexual men. When they want to cite monogamy as a female trait, they look to homosexual women. Angier posits that it may be that the trait of polygamy in gay men actually comes from their "feminized" qualities, rather than their "maleness." Angier may not totally erase the idea of males being more promiscuous, but she certainly forces the reader to rethink the idea that gender controls one's sexual appetites.

Throughout *Woman: An Intimate Geography*, Angier works hard at mixing facts with opinions and theories, then carefully delineates which is which. While her purpose seems to be to enlighten a female (and male) audience about the female body and its systems and tendencies, she also calls for several feminist actions. She believes women need to be better educated about health issues such as hormone replacement therapy. She takes issue with stereotypical female cattiness, believing that women need to stop aggressively undermining one another and learn to develop a deeper sense of sorority, particularly in intergenerational friendships. She believes that women need to be physically stronger. Though she pays lip service to other feminist topics such as abortion, she does not spend much time with typical debate. Instead, she continually usurps conventional beliefs, challenging the reader to look carefully at various arguments and suppositions. Fortunately, even when Angier becomes a bit dogmatic about an issue, such as woman's need to stay physically strong, her remarks seem tempered by both practicality and her own vision for women. Rather than present her opinions as law, Angier gently compels her readers to consider her alternate scenarios as distinct possibilities.

Rebecca Hendrick Flannagan

Sources for Further Study

Booklist 95 (March 1, 1999): 1140.
Discover 20 (May, 1999): 96.
Entertainment Weekly, May 28, 1999, p. 138.
Library Journal 124 (February 1, 1999): 115.
Ms. Magazine 9 (April, 1999): 107.
Natural History 108 (July, 1999): 58.
The New York Times, April 8, 1999, p. B8.
The New York Times Book Review 104 (May 23, 1999): 10.
Publishers Weekly 246 (March 15, 1999): 38.

THE WOMAN WHO CUT OFF HER LEG AT THE MAIDSTONE CLUB AND OTHER STORIES

Author: Julia Slavin
Publisher: Henry Holt (New York). 194 pp. $22.00
Type of work: Short fiction

A collection of quirky short stories that detail the everyday and the fantastic, marking the debut of a rising young American writer

After living in New York for ten years and working as a television producer, Julia Slavin moved to the suburbs of Washington, D.C., in 1992 to begin her career as a short story writer. She published a number of stories in journals and magazines such as *Arkansas Review*, *Crescent Review*, and *Story* over the next few years, garnering a Pushcart Prize and winning the prestigious Frederick Exley fiction competition along the way. Her first book-length publication, a collection of short stories entitled *The Woman Who Cut Off Her Leg at the Maidstone Club and Other Stories*, immediately met with very favorable reviews. Critics and readers alike found Slavin's first book an impressive debut. A *Washington Post* reviewer called Slavin "a major discovery," while *Booklist* labeled the work "a must read collection."

The Woman Who Cut Off Her Leg at the Maidstone Club and Other Stories is a collection of twelve stories. They are all slightly surreal and always quirky. Slavin sets most of her stories in the mundane, sometimes stuffy world of suburbia. Her characters are generally thirtysomethings trying to accommodate their ideas about love and relationships to the pressures of everyday life. In spite of this, the stories are highly imaginative flights of fancy. Slavin's straightforward prose contrasts deliciously with the outrageousness of her story.

To consider these stories only as offbeat, humorous fantasies, however, short-changes both the reader and the stories. Readers who are willing to look beneath the hip exterior will find that the internal workings of the stories serve to explore some very real and very deeply felt fears. In many ways, the predominant images in the stories reveal deeper psychological issues, in much the same way that dream images can be used in psychotherapy.

In the opening story, "Swallowed Whole," a suburban housewife named Sally admits to having a crush on her lawn boy, Chris. Within a few paragraphs, the two kiss, and the narrator swallows Chris whole. Sally and Chris carry on a strange affair, with Chris residing in her belly, until Sally awakens one day to bloody sheets and the sound of Chris mowing the lawn outside. While the story obviously and humorously turns on the double meaning of "swallowing" a man, the darker subtext of pregnancy and miscarriage perks along below the surface. The movement Sally feels in her abdomen, her vomiting, her fantasies, and the final bloody sheets all point to the ambivalence of pregnancy and the sorrow of miscarriage.

Slavin further taps into the anxieties of childbirth and child rearing in the next story in the collection, "Babyproofing." In this story, a young couple with one baby put themselves into the hands of Mitzy Baker, the president and CEO of Baby Safe, Inc., to babyproof their home. Sarah, the wife, is beset with fears of all the possible catastrophes that could take their child from them. By the time Mitzy Baker is finished with the home, however, all of the couple's belongings have been replaced with foam padding and all the trees have been cut down in the yard. Even Walter, the husband, has been banished from the home as a safety hazard for the duration of the "remodeling." At the story's close, Walter forces his way back into the house, which has been utterly transformed. Yet the family is not unhappy; as Walter says,

> The three of us sit on the cushy floor, covered with Mitzy Baker's foam padding. . . . Caroline can drag herself up on her toys and fall and not feel a thing. . . . Tomorrow we can wake up and relax, finally. Tonight we can sleep without dreaming.

In this story, Slavin taps into a parent's deepest fear, that her child will somehow be injured or taken away through some carelessness on her part. What parents have not considered extravagant and excessive ways of keeping their children from harm? Slavin's talent is that she is able to treat this fear sympathetically while carrying it to its absurd extreme.

The third story in the collection, "Dentaphilia," is about a woman, Helen, who begins growing teeth all over her body. The narrator of the story loves Helen, and finds her beautiful in spite of the odd dentition. The name Helen, of course, often carries with it the allusion to Helen of Troy, mythologically the most beautiful woman of the ancient world. Slavin's Helen finds herself completely covered with teeth, from her forehead to her toes. She enters into an odd relationship with a dentist, who cleans and fills her teeth with gold fillings. When all of the teeth begin to fall out, the narrator is relieved, although he loves her regardless. The respite is brief, however; it soon becomes clear that the first round were merely deciduous teeth. Helen's wisdom teeth come in "down there," as she tells the narrator. By the end of the story, Helen is completely calcified. She dies on the beach, the narrator sitting next to her. Again, Slavin taps into a cultural fear embodied by the motif of the *vagina dentata*. The notion of a vagina fully equipped with teeth occurs in mythology and folklore across the world. Psychologists suggest that the theme surfaces to render symbolically the fear of castration and the dangers of sexual intercourse. "Dentophilia" pushes the notion of the *vagina dentata* to its most extreme expression, revealing in the process another deeply rooted fear.

"Lives of the Invertebrates" features another creature with a bony exoskeleton, an eight-pound lobster named Max. That is, the lobster is named Max until the narrator discovers that Max is a female lobster. He then renames her Gina. The narrator is fixated on the lobster, whom he rescues from a seafood stand in an airport. Gina, it seems, is also fixated on the narrator. When the narrator demonstrates an attraction for a Katherine Crisp, an Associate Keeper of Invertebrates, Gina retaliates by biting her on the lip. Throughout the story, the narrator develops a close bond with the lobster, obviously identifying with it. He figures that they are both about the same age. Moreover, the narrator, with his constant thoughts of sex, is metaphorically "horny" while Gina is literally so. Indeed, in spite of Gina's sex change, there is something grotesquely phallic about the lobster. Although classified as an invertebrate, a lobster is hard and stiff. Likewise, the human penis is without a bony structure, yet it becomes hard and stiff in preparation for the sex act. Further, when the narrator takes the lobster into a store, a female clerk is startled: "Oh." She laughed, embarrassed. "I've just never seen one so big." Such a remark can just as easily be applied to a phallus as to a lobster. Even the final attack on Katherine has sexual overtones: "Gina, who'd been slack in my hands, suddenly arched the front section of her body back. . . . she lunged toward Katherine, scissoring through her upper lip with her cutter claw . . . ." This description sounds startlingly close to rape. Once again, Slavin calls attention to a psychological fixation by using an unlikely image.

Perhaps ironically, one of the loveliest stories in the collection is also the least bizarre. In "Pudding," Slavin treats issues that beset American families daily, using as her central image a bowl of spilled pudding that hardens into something symbolic on the kitchen floor. The story begins with the narrator making a bowl of chocolate pudding from scratch for her family. They, however, seem not to appreciate her effort; her son comments on the "scum on top," her daughter asks for Pepperidge Farm cookies instead, and her husband says that he has never liked any kind of pudding. The scene degenerates into an argument, and the narrator spills the pudding, which "hits the floor with a slap." Neither the narrator nor her husband will clean it up, and, over time, the pudding hardens into a permanent fixture on the kitchen floor, a concrete reminder of the family's ongoing problems. Phin, the son, catches gonorrhea from his girlfriend and engages in ongoing battles with his sister Miranda. Miranda pierces her lip and "loathes herself." Anastasia, the three-year-old, just wants everyone to get along; she does not want to take sides with any member of the family against another. Her mother worries that her speech is retarded. The narrator and her husband communicate poorly, if at all, the troubles of their daily lives crowding out their relationship to each other. The pudding on the floor continues to be an issue, and each child reacts to it: Anastasia walks through it, Phin puts out a cigarette in it (although he denies this), and Miranda wants to clean it up. Throughout, the narrator refuses to have it touched. Finally, however, she begins to reestablish contact with each of her children, providing for them the nurturing and care that they need. Indeed, it was her desire to nurture her family that led to the creation of the pudding in the first place. As the family reengages after an emergency trip to the hospital, the narrator reaches a compromise with her husband: They will clean up the pudding together. They discover that it is an easier job than they imagined it would be. As the story closes with the couple standing alone together in their sparkling kitchen, the narrator recalls her first date with her husband. There is a sense that the two are about to recapture some of that early romance in their maturing relationship.

Additional stories in the collection concern a woman whose lover is literally falling apart and losing pieces of his body; a woman who is intimately connected to the oak tree outside her window; a pair of stepsiblings who find comfort in each other's arms; a man who works as a short-order cook and falls in love with one of his customers;

and a woman who cuts off her leg while at an exclusive club because she has been dumped by a man below her in social class. What all the stories share, in spite of their often grotesque or bizarre subject matter, is a concern with the issues that loom large in contemporary life. How does one find love? How does one nurture and protect one's family? How can one talk to, listen to, and understand another human being? How can one not be alone in a world that so often is cruel? These are stories that deserve to be read, and to be reread, for their humorous and fantastic use of language, for the vividness of their images, and for the currents that swirl along just below the surface.

Diane Andrews Henningfeld

Sources for Further Study

Booklist 95 (June 1, 1999): 1794.
Library Journal 124 (April 15, 1999): 147.
New York 32 (July 12, 1999): 81.
The New York Times Book Review 104 (August 15, 1999): 8.
Publishers Weekly 246 (May 17, 1999): 53.
Time 154 (August 2, 1999): 91.

THE WONDERS OF THE INVISIBLE WORLD
Stories

Author: David Gates (1947-)
Publisher: Alfred A. Knopf (New York). 258 pp. $23.00
Type of work: Short fiction
Time: The 1990's
Locale: Connecticut, New Hampshire, Vermont, and New York State

In his first collection of short stories, Gates explores the demons that possess overeducated baby boomers

Principal characters:
BILLY, a young gay man who assumes the care of his sister's son after she becomes institutionalized for drug addiction
PAULA WILSON-STURDIVANT, a wife who gets drunk while four months pregnant
LEN, an older divorced man whose daughter gets into a car accident
FINN, a film professor who discovers that his gay live-in lover has starred in a pornographic film
FAYE, a former New Yorker going insane in the country
RICK, a wronged husband married to Cindy
HOLLY, an often-stoned wife in the suburbs
LEW, a retired research chemist recovering from a stroke

David Gates established himself as a first-rate novelist with the publication of *Jernigan* (1991). A highly entertaining but bleak first-person narrative, *Jernigan* depicts an unrepentant alcoholic who makes all the wrong choices and drifts from the periphery of respectable middle-class life. Both aware and unaware of the devastating consequences of his actions, he poisons his relations with his wife until she suicidally crashes her car, and he shoots himself in the hand just to see what it is like. After he loses his job, his life unravels with a mixture of bravado and irony that is exhilaratingly foolhardy, if only because he defines himself by his lack of remorse.

After producing this initial tour de force, Gates wrote another well-received and modestly successful novel, *Preston Falls* (1998), which chronicled a man's rejection of his family and career in New York until he disappears altogether. Ultimately about the mystery of motivation, *Preston Falls* alarms the reader because Doug and Jean Willis are both highly intelligent, culturally savvy people who are, however, unable to rise above the escalating crises of their daily lives. Doug wants to escape his conformist job for a youthful, redneck, swaggering lifestyle, but all he attains is a fearful retreat to a small hotel not far from his wife's home. Throughout both novels, Gates shows us that only a few decisions separate people from throwing away their lives. The novel format suits Gates's abilities because its relentlessness is, in part, the point of the narrative and the dramatic equivalent of the free fall into the abyss.

In his collection of short stories, *The Wonders of the Invisible World*, Gates adheres to many of the same themes and situations as in his novels, but he is also looking to expand on his repertoire. All of the characters live within driving distance of New York

City, but in this collection Gates includes some retired characters, more female narrators, and several gay men in the mix. Whereas his novels relied on cumulative impact, these short stories sometimes have to compress complex issues, such as race relations and AIDS, into a small space, with mixed results. Petty demons possess most of the characters. Blessed with good liberal arts educations and often top-notch jobs, they are still subject to perversely willful behavior. Gates foreshadows this theme in his epigraph from Mark 5:8-9, wherein the "unclean spirit" or devil speaks: "My name is Legion: for we are many." The title of the collection refers to a Cotton Mather book about devils in America. Gates need not refer to any specific demon in his stories; his character's actions speak for themselves.

Much of the time, characters are often critically self-aware of how others may view them. Gates shows how their intellects turn on themselves in a kind of mental twist that often ironically anticipates some nastiness in others that may be justified or just imagined. In the title story of the collection, the unnamed assistant dean of a university narrates his tale, fully anticipating any possible critical take on what he has to say. If he conjures an image of a subway sound like a phoebe's call, he is quick to point out the "cheap irony" of "juxtaposing urban and pastoral" themes. When his story begins to revolve around his twin anxieties over the possible pregnancy of his married girlfriend and his lost clarinet, he quickly deconstructs his hidden agenda in italics: "*Wants to abandon his responsibilities as a man.*" When his girlfriend mentions Cotton Mather's *The Wonders of the Invisible World* (1693), however, he does not see the connection between the demons of the underworld and his relentlessly calculating self-consciousness, but he does struggle for a cold enough ending that ultimately emphasizes his indifference to the unborn child. His lost clarinet ultimately matters more than the loss of his mistress. In this same way, his tastes hold predominance over his relations with other people. Therefore, a homeless woman becomes "another disagreeable feature of the mise-en-scène."

Gates once tried and failed to write a dissertation on Samuel Beckett, and sometimes he shares Beckett's gallows humor in the face of negation. His characters seem more comfortable hating each other than in experiencing pleasure. "The Crazy Thought" chronicles Faye's descent into insanity in the country, as her husband adopts all of the trappings of the redneck lifestyle, including a truck, a shotgun, and a drawl, while still "[knowing] perfectly well who Huysmans was." When her sister and husband come to visit, Faye betrays her delusional jealousy with her caustic comments. Even though she is surrounded by idyllic nature, Faye feels imprisoned by the lack of New York City culture, claiming that "New York's the only place a nature lover should really live. Put up your Ansel Adams calendar, and you're in business." Her poisonous irony soon drives off her sister, and she sits stranded at the end of the story, trying not to think of shooting herself with her husband's newly purchased shotgun. She imagines "[s]trange and terrible powers" that would bring back the former husband whom she loved and restore to her life some measure of satisfaction, but she proves an impotent witch, powerless before the objects around her and her "crazy" thoughts.

Given Gates's bent toward depicting evil behavior, he has to guard against sounding moralistic, because many of his more politically correct characters do that for him. Sometimes the lesser stories like "Beating" read like extended rants on homelessness and race relations without enough plot to justify them. "Vigil" carefully depicts an older divorced man's perspective on his daughter's comatose state following a car accident and the way the separated strands of the family must come together as a result. The climax of the story combines the young woman's awakening with the general realization that she was returning from an adulterous liaison in a hotel when she was hit by another driver. The reader is left wondering about the connection between her adultery and her mother's similar relationship that led to her divorce. Was her accident a kind of judgment for her transgressions? Did she deserve it? Gates hints at that possibility.

Because his characters take so little pleasure in life, the reader wonders about Gates's aesthetics. What kind of joy does he find in creation? While other writers play with words and images, Gates's brand of dirty realism surgically examines the source of his characters' malaise. Perhaps his vision is too ironic to depict unmediated pleasure. In "A Wronged Husband," Gates returns to the happily perverse morality of *Jernigan* in the figure of a wife, Cindy, who gleefully fools around on her husband. The story begins with the husband, Rick, avoiding his job, spilling his gin on the floor, and having his car impounded in New York City. Rick does admit to having an affair, so his wife cheerfully lies to him about her sister dying in a car crash as an excuse to spend the weekend with another man. When he learns of her lie, she treats it ironically, jokingly confessing to having affairs with all of his friends, and slaps his face, causing his glasses to fly across the room. Like Jernigan, she remains unrepentant. When she leaves, she says "presto: wifey's just an unpleasant memory" and claims that this is what he wanted all along. Gates never tries to explain or rationalize her behavior. She remains pleasantly and inexplicably defiant to the end.

Gates's best stories often concern aging. While his men in their midlife crises look to country roughneck culture away from the hypercivilized city to affirm their masculinity, other characters face retirement either with open rebellion or with graceful resignation. The divorced man in "Vigil" embodies the latter. He lives a quiet life as a machinist, too busy working and raising his daughter to let old age bother him. In contrast, the best story of the collection, "Saturn," concerns Van, a retiree fully in revolt against his age. After tending to his wheelchair-bound wife, the victim of a stroke, until her death, he comes to visit Holly, the story's narrator, and her husband Seth in their large Connecticut home. Holly has been simultaneously having an affair and reading Gustave Flaubert's *Madame Bovary* (1857) to gain some perspective. Seth keeps smoking marijuana as his final revolt against middle-class conformity, thus leading to the rising marijuana-related paranoia felt throughout the story's scenes. Van acts chummy, stares at Holly carnally, and departs in her Saturn to get drunk in the afternoon, driving drunk and without her permission. He jokes about aging, mentioning Alzheimer's disease repeatedly, and generally acts like a man in second childhood. By the story's end, Van serves as a catalyst for Holly's flight from her home, but her adulterous lover cannot save her from losing all control. Stoned, she collides into another car at a rest stop on the highway.

By the end of the collection, Gates does begin to sketch some new directions for his fiction, even as many of his characters box themselves in. One gay character, Billy, finds himself adopting his drug-addicted sister's son, thereby anchoring him to a family relationship he is not expecting. In "The Mail Lady," a retired chemist, Lew, labors to express himself after a stroke. With its severe disjunction between a meditative Christian interior monologue and Lew's blurred, incomprehensible speech with others, this last story resembles both James Joyce's *Dubliners* (1914), with its emphasis on paralysis, and Flannery O'Connor's short fiction, with its search for meaning in the decrepitude of age. Eventually, Lew has to confront his bigotry against homosexuals when the lesbian "mail lady" comes to save his stranded car. Gates's characters do contain hints of grace, if only because they remain conscious of their transgressions.

With this first collection of short stories, Gates cements his reputation as a chronicler of middle-class baby-boomer angst. In the tradition of author John Cheever, Gates writes of characters within commuting distance of New York but otherwise adrift between jobs, spouses, and the reasons to pursue them. In an interview for *Publishers Weekly*, Gates described how his career hit bottom in the 1980's shortly before his divorce: "No job, no prospects, no direction." He went on to regain his footing as a staff writer for *Newsweek*, but his artistic path might have begun with that moment of complete loss. In his unflinching way, Gates likes to strip the comforts away from his characters to see what good remains, if any. As one of his characters thinks: "Surely there must be some good somewhere in the world that wouldn't exist if not for you."

Roy C. Flannagan

Sources for Further Study

Library Journal 124 (June 1, 1999): 182.
New York 32 (July 12, 1999): 51.
The New York Times Book Review 104 (July 18, 1999): 11.
Publishers Weekly 246 (May 3, 1999): 65.

WORDS AND RULES
The Ingredients of Language

Author: Steven Pinker (1954-   )
Publisher: Basic Books (New York) 348 pp. $26.00
Type of work: Language

Pinker, a professor of psychology at the Massachusetts Institute of Technology (MIT) and author of the 1997 best-seller How the Mind Works, *explores the mysteries of language*

One of the great mysteries of the human mind is how language is acquired. In the first years of life, children quickly become fluent in their native tongue, learning the rules of language quite naturally. Just how is it that children can master the complexities of language, in spite of all of its quirks and irregularities?

Some linguists, such as Noam Chomsky, have argued that human speech is the result of hidden rules of language that are "hard wired" somewhere in the brain. Many computer scientists, following the ideas of the seventeenth century British philosopher John Locke, believe that the mind is a *tabula rasa*, or blank slate, at birth, and children learn language by picking up raw data from the outside world and then forming associations between words and objects.

Pinker argues that the human brain utilizes both kinds of thought. Words are memorized links between a sound and a meaning. The word "dog," for example, does not look, walk, or bark like a dog, but once one connects the sound with the idea, one has formed an association. Humans also combine words into larger words and into sentences, based on a set of rules. Hence, the two ingredients of language, according to Pinker, are words and rules. Languages are composed of a list of memorized words, each an arbitrary pairing between a sound and a meaning, and a set of productive rules that assemble words into combinations. As children's vocabulary begins to grow, they learn to generate ever more complex sentences based on the rules of language. Pinker believes that such rules appear to be innate; it is part of what he calls "mental machinery." As new verbs come into the language, people use these rules to determine their forms with the various tenses.

The evolution of language can best be seen through the application of regular and irregular verbs. Looking back at the English language through the centuries, Pinker believes that it has not evolved haphazardly but according to a set of rules that determine future verb forms. He argues that irregular verbs are the result of words becoming increasingly distorted over time, until eventually the rule governing their use becomes lost. This is especially true of words that have fallen into disuse—words such as "smote," "slew," and "forsook" that are so infrequently used by English speakers that they will most likely disappear.

The words and rules theory neatly explains how one acquires fluency in a language and learns to predict past-tense forms of a verb, but it does not explain the overwhelming presence of irregular verbs. Irregular verbs such as "go" and "went" and "be" and "was" do not conform to any established pattern or rules of language but must be memorized by rote, as anyone who tries to learn a foreign soon learns. The apparent failure of cognitive scientists to discover a consistent rule to explain the presence of irregular verbs has wide-ranging implications in explaining how words are used in conversation and in reading, how new words are created, how children learn their mother tongue, how language is organized in the brain, and whether the languages of the world conform to a universal design. It appears that the centuries-old debate between rationalism and empiricism—whether human knowledge is innate or obtained only through experiences with the surrounding world—has taken on a new relevance. According to Pinker, while the rules of language appear to be innate, irregular verbs must rely upon mental recall. For example, a person learning the English language could not deduce the past tense of "go" as "went"; such irregularities must be committed to memory. The English language has 180 such irregular verb forms, which simply must be memorized. With regular verbs, humans seem to apply the rules instinctively. Therefore, a child encountering an unfamiliar word, such as "wug," will give the past tense as "wugged." It appears, Pinker concludes, that two parts of the mind and two different types of thinking are utilized in the use of language. He believes that this complex interplay between words and rules and regular and irregular verb forms are a basic characteristic of all language and possibly of all human thought.

Such discoveries help to explain and predict the future course of a language as new words and colloquialisms are introduced. How, Pinker asks, does the human mind handle new inflected and derived words such as "mosh" or "bork"? Does it rely on an enormous dictionary that lists all the common forms of every word? Does it function like a computer spell-checker and rely on a minimal dictionary and a set of rules, carving unfamiliar words into prefixes, stems, and suffixes? According to the words and rules theory, the mind has rules for regular forms and relies on a pattern-associating memory for the irregular forms. Experiments reveal that for irregular verb-forms, subjects appeared to be "blocking" the rule-making part of language and instead relied upon their memory of similar words to come up with a proper past-tense form. All of this seems to strengthen Pinker's contention that the use of language involves at least two different types of cognition.

The words and rules theory can be most easily seen at work with children. As all parents have observed, very young children often misuse irregular word forms, such as when they say "mouses" instead of "mice." However, such errors are not simply cute missteps in a child's developing speech proficiency: Pinker believes that they are windows into the workings of language and the human mind. Children's speech errors are more than simply cute. They may, Pinker claims, help humans untangle one of the thickest knots in science: nature and nurture. When a child says "bleeded" and "singed," the fingerprints of learning are all over the sentence. Every bit of every word had to be learned, and the very existence of the error demonstrates that the child still has not mastered the irregular forms.

The true test of Pinker's ideas is to see if the theory of words and rules holds true for languages other than English. When studying the instance of irregular verbs, no language confounds students more than German. The German language contains far more irregular verbs than does English, though German verb inflections basically work the same way. However, English and German are closely related. Would the theory hold as one examines those languages with non-Indo-European or non-Germanic origins? Examining French, Dutch, Hungarian, Hebrew, and Chinese, Pinker concludes that although there are many complications and counterexamples, and admitting that it would be presumptuous to assert that a simple words and rules theory could encompass all the world's diverse languages, the same basic rules of language construction apply. The most extreme example, and one about as far from the English language as possible, is the language spoken in New Guinea. Separated from the rest of civilization by a vast ocean for thousands of years, New Guineans' eight hundred or so dialects are totally unrelated to any other world language. Surprisingly, many of the same rules of gender and verb use in their ancient language can be seen. These deep parallels of language, so different in sounds and symbols on the surface and yet so similar in their underlying structure, may point to, Pinker claims, a "psychic unity" of humankind.

Language is a product of human cognition, yet precious little is known about the inner workings of the brain. Indeed, as Pinker describes it, the human brain is like the "black box" problem engineering students are often presented with to deduce the design of a circuit inside a sealed box by measuring the inputs and outputs coming from the box. Powerful new tools, such as magnetic resonance imaging (MRI), have given scientists incredible insight into the workings of the brain but have not revealed those areas inside the brain where words and rules of language might be stored. Far more complex than the hard drive on a computer, the physiology of the brain reveals an elaborate system of billions of neurons linked together in an intricate structure that is still not well understood.

One way to obtain a glimpse of the inner workings of the brain from the outside is to study human subjects with brain damage from tumors, infections, malnutrition, blocked or burst arteries, falls, bullets, car accidents, and strokes. In many cases the injury manifests itself in an inability to properly use language. Because their ability to process information from the outside world has been impaired, patients may have difficulty associating words with objects or forming words into sentences, or they may be unable to retrieve and recognize words. Pinker notes that when a patient with a brain injury can no longer do something, it is tempting to conclude that the damaged part of the brain must be the neural center responsible for the impaired task. However, this theory does not necessarily hold true when it comes to the loss of language skills in brain-injured patients, although the research does seem to indicate that the ability to form and use regular and irregular verb forms depends upon different sets of areas of the brain.

Neurodegenerative diseases such as Alzheimer's, Parkinson's, and Huntington's diseases also reveal clues to the brain's ability to generate language. One common symptom of such diseases as they progress is the loss of memory for words and a difficulty in understanding sentences. The errors by such patients in applying the rules of grammar, combined with their declining memory, further suggests that the ability to detect changes in tense, gender, and word structure depend upon different systems within the brain.

Perhaps, as Pinker suggests, further research into the brain's remarkable ability to create and utilize language will finally be completely revealed by genetics. New techniques in genetic research are beginning to identity certain genes that may be tied to language and thought. Studies on a remarkable group of people with a genetic defect known as specific language impairment (SLI) has led to the discovery of a specific genetic region linked to this language disorder by tracing inheritance patterns of afflicted families. This discovery suggests that the loss of certain genes can interfere with the development of the grammatical circuitry in the brain.

This book makes it quite obvious that Pinker is fascinated by language and how it works, but it is even more obvious that his true intent is to use language as a tool for further investigating the workings of the human mind. Language, he believes, can provide deep insight into the mysteries of cognition, because it is the link to one another and to the surrounding world.

Pinker has a gift for making such a complex subject interesting, lighthearted, and fun. Although the first few chapters, which delve deeply into the mechanics of word construction, may intimidate some readers, those who stay for the rest of the journey will be rewarded in the end. His discussions of common dinner-table grammar disputes, such as why the Canadian hockey team is called the Toronto Maple "Leafs" instead of the Maple "Leaves," and the inclusion of several humorous syndicated cartoons taken from newspapers and magazines, serve to enliven the discussion. This book is must reading for all serious grammarians and for anyone fascinated by the workings of language.

Raymond Frey

Sources for Further Study

The Christian Science Monitor, October 28, 1999, p. 18.
The New York Times, September 22, 1999, p. G14.
Publishers Weekly 246 (September 6, 1999): 91.
Science News 156 (November 13, 1999): 306.

YEARS OF RENEWAL

Author: Henry A. Kissinger (1923-)
Publisher: Simon & Schuster (New York). Illustrated. 1151 pp. $35.00
Type of work: Memoirs
Time: 1969-1977
Locale: The world

The Nobel Prize-winning American diplomat tells of his years working on foreign policy in the service of Presidents Richard Nixon and Gerald Ford and of how he helped to safeguard American interests in a dangerous world

Principal personages:

HENRY A. KISSINGER, national security adviser from 1969 to 1975 and secretary of state from 1973 to 1977; his third volume of memoirs focuses on his work in the trying times after Nixon's resignation, when America faces numerous global challenges

RICHARD M. NIXON, president of the United States from 1969 to 1974, who brought Kissinger to Washington and made him instrumental for executing America's foreign policy; Kissinger's importance increases when the Watergate scandal leads to Nixon's resignation

GERALD R. FORD, president of the United States from 1974 to 1977; Kissinger admires him for trying to heal American society and conduct a sensible foreign policy

RONALD REAGAN, California governor who loses to Ford in the Republican primary elections of 1976 but who later becomes president of the United States; Kissinger claims that Reagan shares his goal of standing up to communism but differs over tactics

MAO ZEDONG, chair of the Chinese Communist Party and president of the People's Republic of China from 1949 until 1976; Kissinger admires his lack of sentimentality in foreign policy issues and his skill as a negotiator

LEONID I. BREZHNEV, general secretary of the Communist Party of the Soviet Union from 1966 to 1982; disliked by Kissinger as a difficult negotiator, he presides over a period of gradual relaxation of Cold War tensions known as détente, a policy distrusted by Kissinger's critics

ANWAR EL-SADAT, the president of Egypt from 1970 to 1981 who begins serious peace negotiations with Israel, with encouragement from Kissinger

YITZHAK RABIN, prime minister of Israel from 1974 to 1977 who signs an important agreement with Egypt

Henry Kissinger's monumental *Years of Renewal* begins at one of the most dramatic points in American domestic history, when President Richard Nixon is forced to resign on August 9, 1974, in the aftermath of the Watergate scandal. With the exception of the brief first part, Kissinger's book gives an extremely detailed account of his service to Nixon's chosen successor, President Gerald Ford. Moving through the many foreign crises and challenges America had to face from 1974 to 1977, Kissinger offers a fascinating insider's account on how Ford, he, and their team sought to execute foreign policy in a difficult time for America.

Kissinger organizes his memoirs in ten parts which, in generally chronological order, deal with the crises, catastrophes, and challenges of the years from 1974 to 1977, including a first part reflecting on the Nixon administration from 1969 to 1974. Thus, his readers get an exclusive view of dramatic historic events ranging in scope from the avoidance of a Greek-Turkish war over Cyprus to intense superpower negotiations with the former Soviet Union and the People's Republic of China in the penultimate decade of the Cold War.

As Kissinger describes his encounters with Leonid Brezhnev and Mao Zedong, his book illuminates how relationships between nations are shaped by the people operating at the highest level of government. *Years of Renewal* also offers a welcome reminder of how tense the competition between American and Soviet interests had been before the rise of Mikhail Gorbachev and how much, all over the world, people and politicians were concerned about the threat of nuclear war.

Kissinger's famous "shuttle diplomacy" in the Middle East, as he tries to mediate between Israel and its Arab neighbors in the aftermath of the 1973 Yom Kippur War, shows how persistently Kissinger strove to calm this global hot spot. Working closely with Egyptian president Anwar el-Sadat and the Israeli prime minister Yitzhak Rabin, Kissinger shows how the second Sinai agreement is finally reached. Tragically, both of Kissinger's negotiation partners, Sadat and Rabin, would later be assassinated by fanatics.

The catastrophic fall of Cambodia and South Vietnam in the early spring of 1975 occupies a central spot in Kissinger's memoirs. This tragic event is followed by a reflection on his attempts to reunify America's Western European allies and to come up with a successful political response to the world energy crisis of the mid-1970's, which threatens to ruin Western industrial productivity. Emboldened by their perception of American weakness in the wake of the fall of Saigon, the Soviet Union begins to interfere in the civil war in Angola following this country's release from Portuguese colonial rule in 1975. Here, *Years of Renewal* lucidly shows how skillfully Kissinger has to maneuver between Soviet expansionism, congressional disapproval of an active American intervention, and the troubling existence of white minority governments in the former Rhodesia and apartheid-era South Africa.

Given all these crises and challenges to America's global interests, however, the title of Kissinger's book seems oddly inappropriate. In the wake of Watergate, most political analysts and historians agree, American power did not yet see a sense of renewal. Instead, there was a precarious decline illustrated most dramatically by the communist victories in Cambodia, Vietnam, and Laos in April, 1975, American economic recession in response to the oil crisis triggered by the Organization of Petroleum Exporting Countries (OPEC), and Soviet and Cuban intervention in Angola. At home, there was still a sense of economic despair, moral decline, disillusionment with politics, and a climbing crime rate perhaps best illustrated by Martin Scorsese's famous film masterpiece *Taxi Driver* (1977).

As if to justify his choice of his title, Kissinger stresses the point that President Ford managed to restore a minimum of prestige and respect to the institution of the presidency. It is imaginable that without Kissinger's able diplomatic activities, things could have become far worse for America than what happened historically. It would appear more adequate, however, to speak of a period of recovery, as America recuperates from the damages Nixon's Watergate scandal had wrought on the national psyche.

Kissinger had worked very closely with Nixon, first as his National Security Adviser and, beginning in 1973, also as secretary of state. Kissinger's first two books of memoirs, *White House Years* (1979) and *Years of Upheaval* (1982), deal at length with his work in the first and then in the truncated second term of Nixon's presidency. In *Years of Renewal*, Kissinger generously describes Nixon as "the perhaps most complex President of the twentieth century," who possessed conflicting character traits that made it very difficult to know him as a person.

After Nixon, Kissinger praises Gerald Ford for his dedication to healing the great rifts which had opened up in America's political landscape. *Years of Renewal* is unanimous in its praise for Ford, who is described as a man of character who "had courage and leadership ability" and did the best he could to preserve American interests and American honor in a hostile, turbulent period.

Kissinger's claim of a straight trajectory from Ford's foreign policy to the collapse of the Soviet Union and the fall of the Berlin Wall appears somewhat stretched, and it has met with rejection from quite a few critics of his book. In the field of foreign policy, things certainly first worsened during the Iranian hostage crisis and Soviet expansionism in Africa and Central America before taking a turn for the better. Some critics would argue that a genuine renewal of American confidence did not take place until the Reagan presidency was under way and Mikhail Gorbachev decided on his own to release Eastern Europe from its Soviet grip and to establish a cordial relationship with Reagan's successor, George Bush.

Throughout his tenure in office, critics on the Left and the Right have charged that Kissinger preferred order and a stable world to the point of being too reluctant to engage communist regimes aggressively, either on issues of human rights or on allegedly disadvantageous arms treaties. Kissinger emphatically denies that charge. "But the Germany of my youth had a great deal of order and very little justice; it was not the sort of place likely to inspire devotion to order in the abstract," is his final assessment. Since his Jewish family escaped from the Nazis in 1933 when Adolf Hitler came to power, Kissinger's personal recollection represents a powerful rebuttal. In the light of his background, it is also interesting to read that because of his German accent, Kissinger's voice was not broadcast on television or radio until 1972.

Years of Renewal is at its fascinating best when it reveals how American foreign policy was shaped both on the level of long-range strategies and in reaction to crises that threatened to spin out of control. Kissinger is also passionate in his defense of Ford's foreign policy, which sought to hold the Soviet Union at bay while negotiating with its leaders to lessen lingering Cold War tensions.

Persistently, *Years of Renewal* stresses that in the mid-1970's, overt confrontation of the Soviet Union would not have been politically feasible. It is Kissinger's firm conviction that trying to negotiate a limit on nuclear arms and dealing with the Soviet Union as a lasting player in world politics was the only realistic course of action in the 1970's.

Another strong conviction expressed by Kissinger in this book of memoirs is the belief that congressional micromanagement of foreign policy issues, which he sees as beginning in the post-Watergate atmosphere, has been truly harmful to America's interests. Kissinger blames Congress for sabotaging many of his political maneuvers.

The fall of Cambodia and Vietnam was one of the most painful defeats of American foreign policy, and *Years of Renewal* powerfully evokes the atmosphere of darkness and despair enshrouding these events. In 1973, Kissinger and his North Vietnamese diplomatic counterpart Le Duc Tho (who declined the award) received the Nobel Peace Price for negotiating the Paris Peace Agreement to end American military involvement in the Vietnam War. It was thus especially painful for Kissinger to witness, in early 1975, the de facto violation of the Paris agreement to the point of becoming moot when North Vietnamese tanks rolled through the gates of the presidential palace in Saigon on April 30, 1975, ending the war with a complete communist victory.

Kissinger betrays a certain sense of wishful thinking when he writes that in January, 1975, when North Vietnam launched an offensive in South Vietnam, American military aid of at least three hundred million dollars, which Congress refused to authorize, could have saved the situation. "The survival of Vietnam now depended on our ability to obtain the supplemental appropriation" of this amount, *Years of Renewal* states. Yet the problems of South Vietnam, and Cambodia, at this point, were too immense to have been solved merely by an American cash infusion to buy ammunition and weapons.

In the end, it appears that Kissinger realizes that the granting of this aid, which Congress denied, would have only enabled America to believe it had really done all it could to help, and that it would not have changed the outcome on the ground. Yet it is harrowing to read how mean-spiritedly some politicians behaved in their desire to forget and abandon America's allies, to the point of not wanting to spend money on the Indochinese refugees fleeing the communist forces.

For a reader interested in a fascinating account by one of the era's principal players on the stage of world politics, *Years of Renewal* offers an exciting reward. In its many pages are dramatic stories of world leaders trying to outfox each other, moments of great pain, and occasions of triumph when the worst had been avoided. Kissinger's informative and detailed descriptions bring back to life years that were certainly traumatic for the United States. That Ford and Kissinger were dedicated to give their best to protect and safeguard American interests worldwide is one of the key insights to emerge from the final volume of this Nobel Prize-winning American statesman.

R. C. Lutz

Sources for Further Study

Booklist 95 (March 1, 1999): 1100.
Foreign Affairs 78 (May, 1999): 123.
The New York Times Book Review 104 (March 21, 1999): 6.
Newsweek 133 (March 29, 1999): 42.
Publishers Weekly 246 (February 15, 1999): 95.
Time 153 (March 15, 1999): 59.

MAGILL'S
LITERARY ANNUAL

2000

BIOGRAPHICAL WORKS BY SUBJECT

1977-2000

BIOGRAPHICAL WORKS BY SUBJECT

CATEGORY INDEX

1977-2000

BIOGRAPHY. *See also* LITERARY BIOGRAPHY

CURRENT AFFAIRS and SOCIAL ISSUES

ETHICS and LAW

FICTION

CATEGORY INDEX

CATEGORY INDEX

CATEGORY INDEX

LITERARY CRITICISM, HISTORY, and THEORY

CATEGORY INDEX

POETRY and DRAMA

CATEGORY INDEX

CATEGORY INDEX

PSYCHOLOGY

RELIGION. *See* PHILOSOPHY and RELIGION

SCIENCE, HISTORY OF SCIENCE, and TECHNOLOGY

SOCIAL ISSUES. *See* CURRENT AFFAIRS and SOCIAL ISSUES

SOCIOLOGY, ARCHAEOLOGY, and ANTHROPOLOGY

TITLE INDEX

1977-2000

TITLE INDEX

AUTHOR INDEX

1977-2000

AUTHOR INDEX

AUTHOR INDEX

AUTHOR INDEX